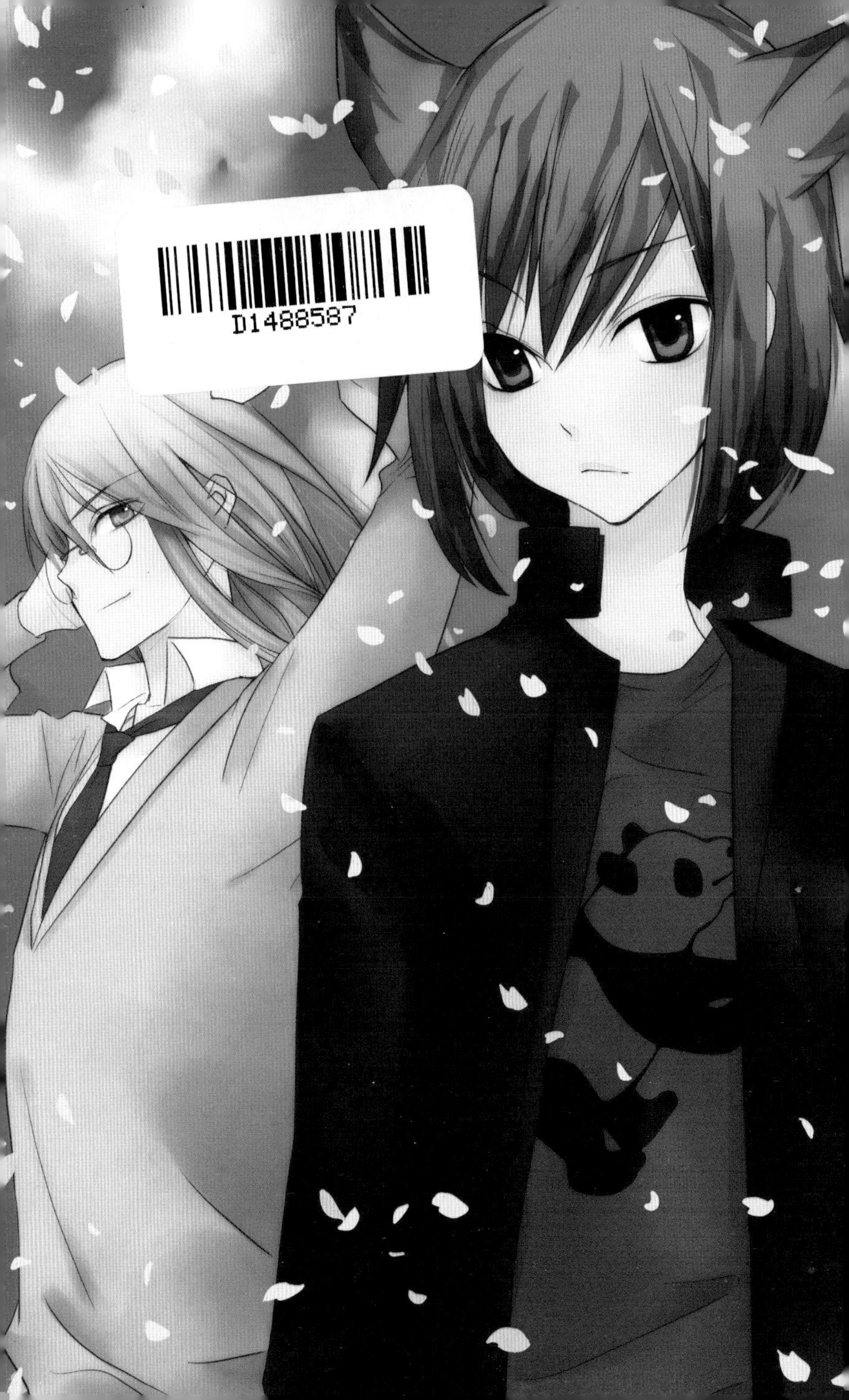

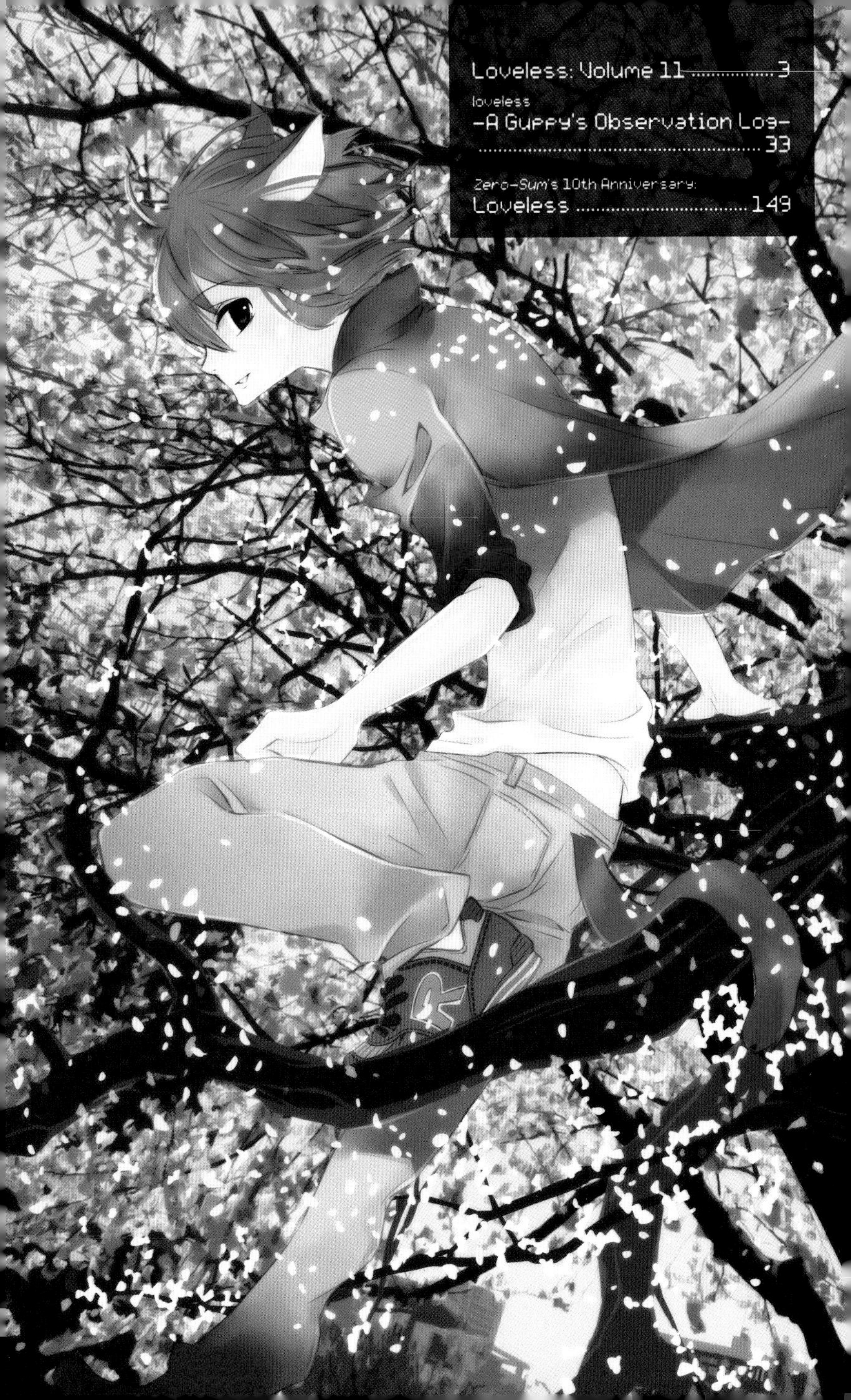

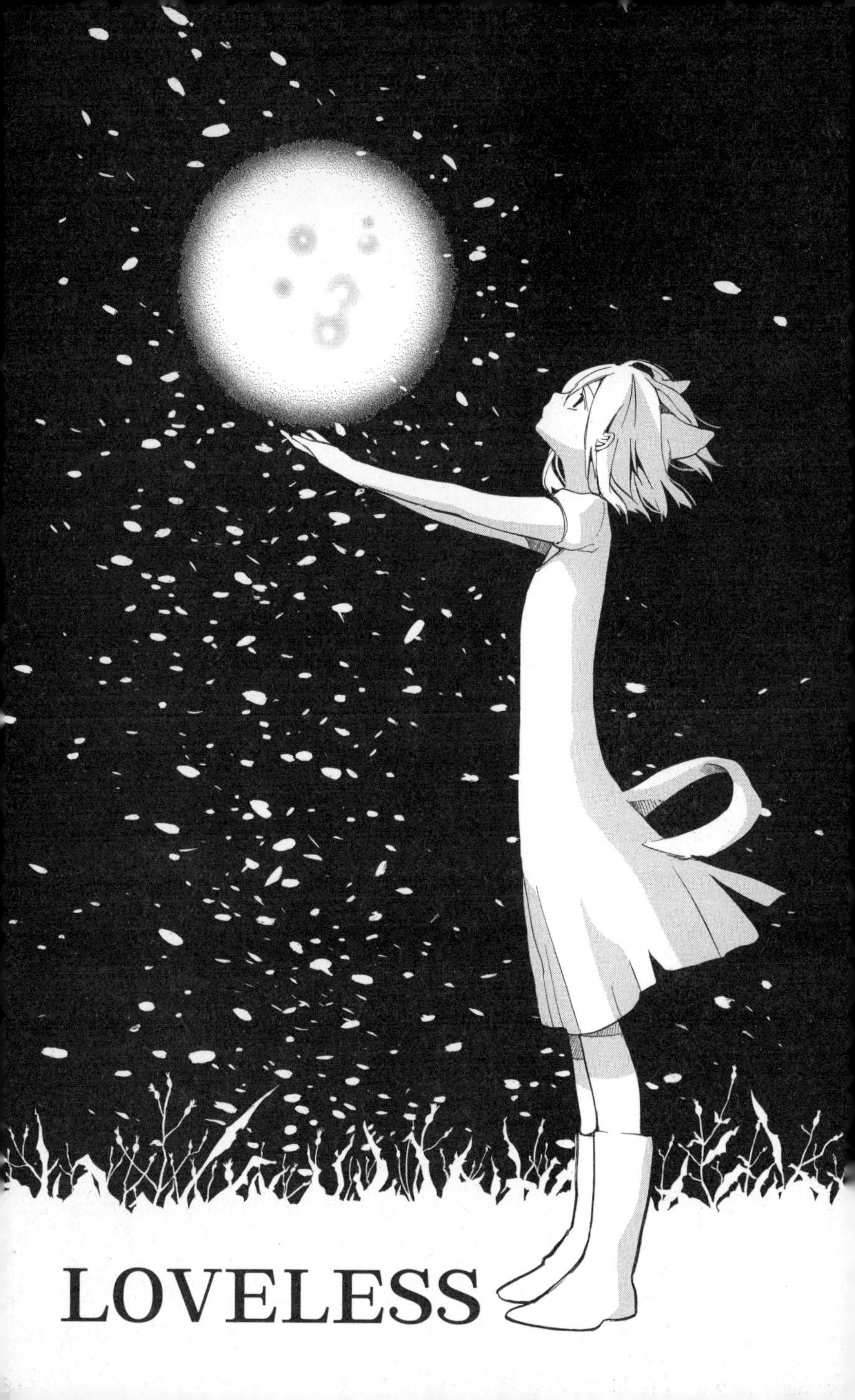
LOVELESS

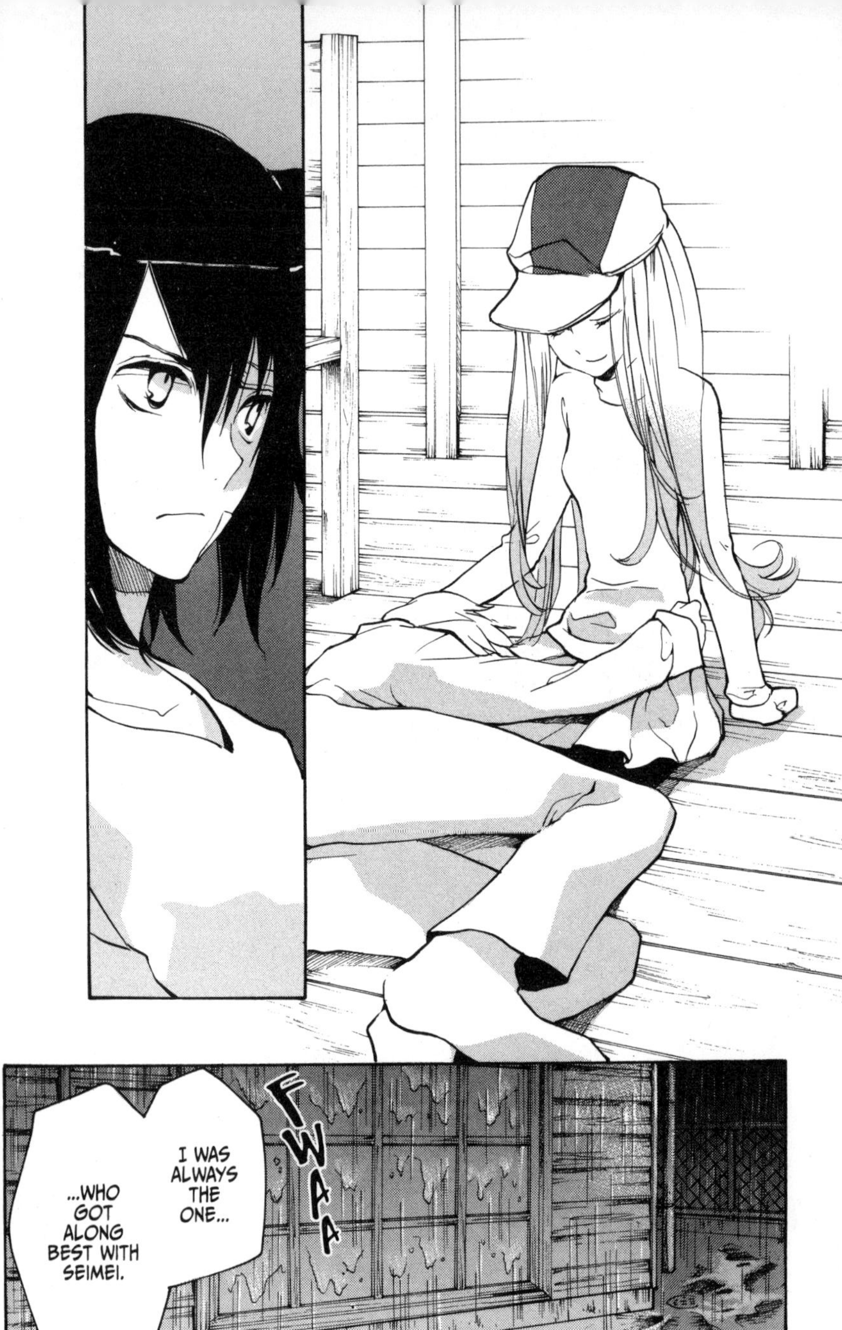
FWAA
I WAS ALWAYS THE ONE...
...WHO GOT ALONG BEST WITH SEIMEI.

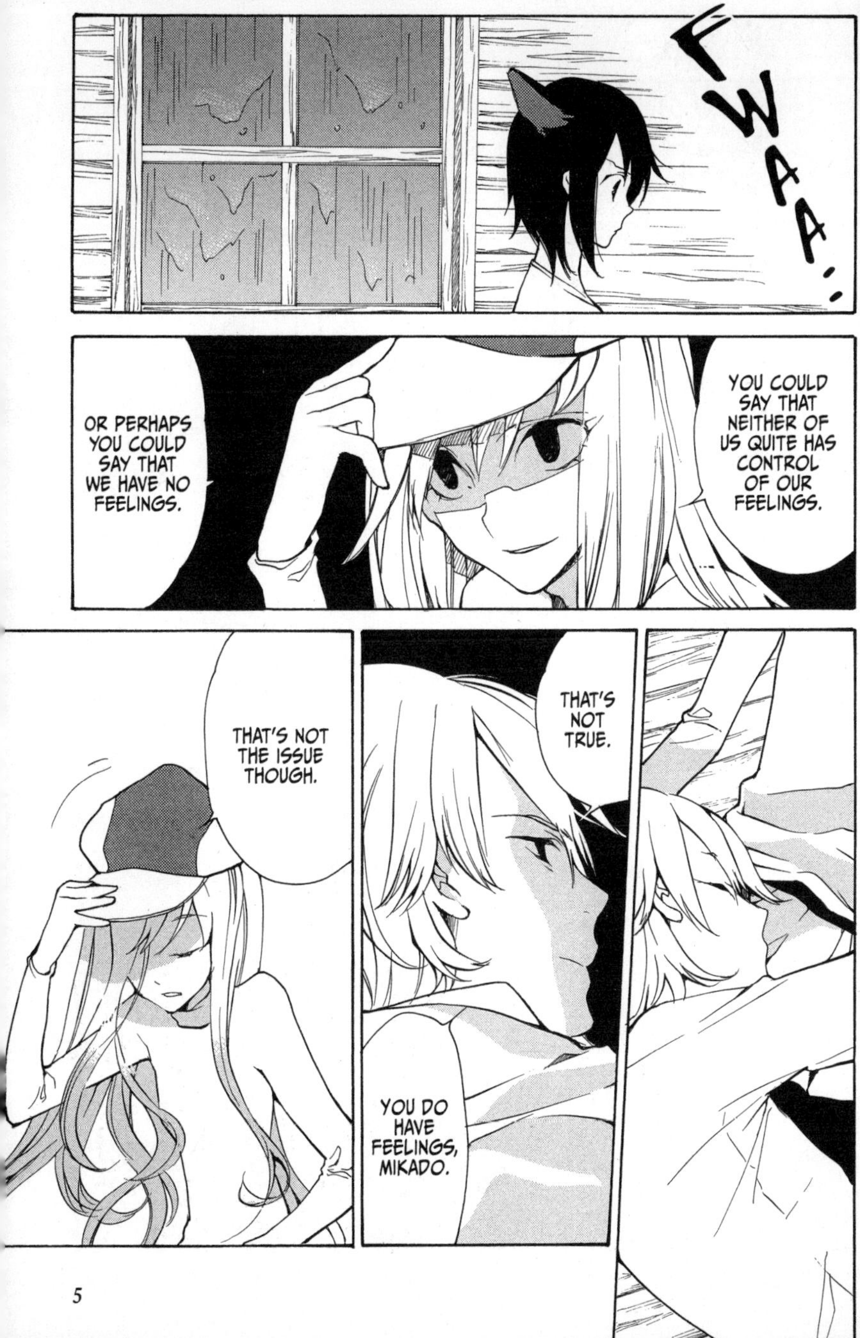
FWAA..
YOU COULD SAY THAT NEITHER OF US QUITE HAS CONTROL OF OUR FEELINGS.
OR PERHAPS YOU COULD SAY THAT WE HAVE NO FEELINGS.
THAT'S NOT TRUE.
YOU DO HAVE FEELINGS, MIKADO.
THAT'S NOT THE ISSUE THOUGH.

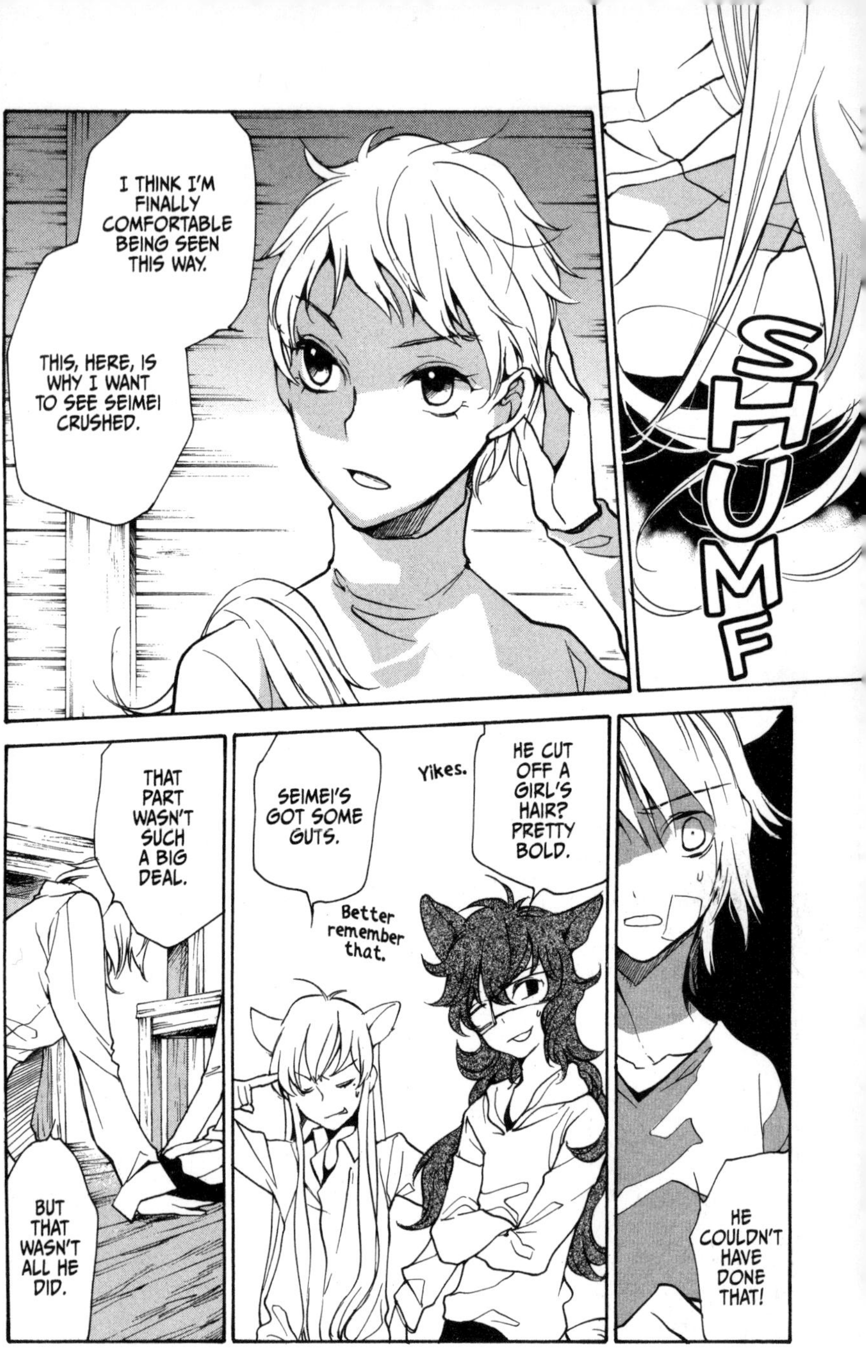
SHUMF
I THINK I'M FINALLY COMFORTABLE BEING SEEN THIS WAY.
THIS, HERE, IS WHY I WANT TO SEE SEIMEI CRUSHED.
HE COULDN'T HAVE DONE THAT!
HE CUT OFF A GIRL'S HAIR? PRETTY BOLD.
Yikes.
SEIMEI'S GOT SOME GUTS.
Better remember that.
THAT PART WASN'T SUCH A BIG DEAL.
BUT THAT WASN'T ALL HE DID.

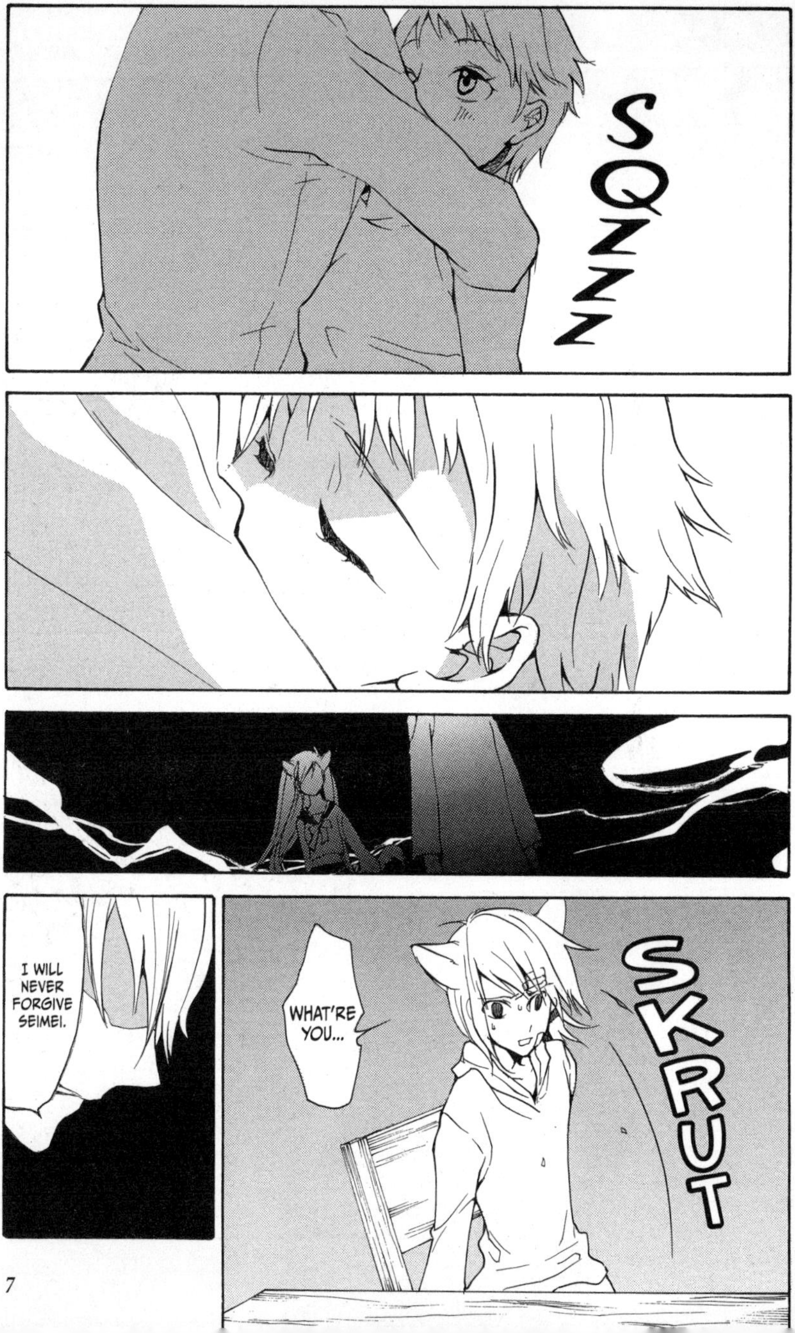
SQZZZ
SKRUT
WHAT'RE YOU...
I WILL NEVER FORGIVE SEIMEI.

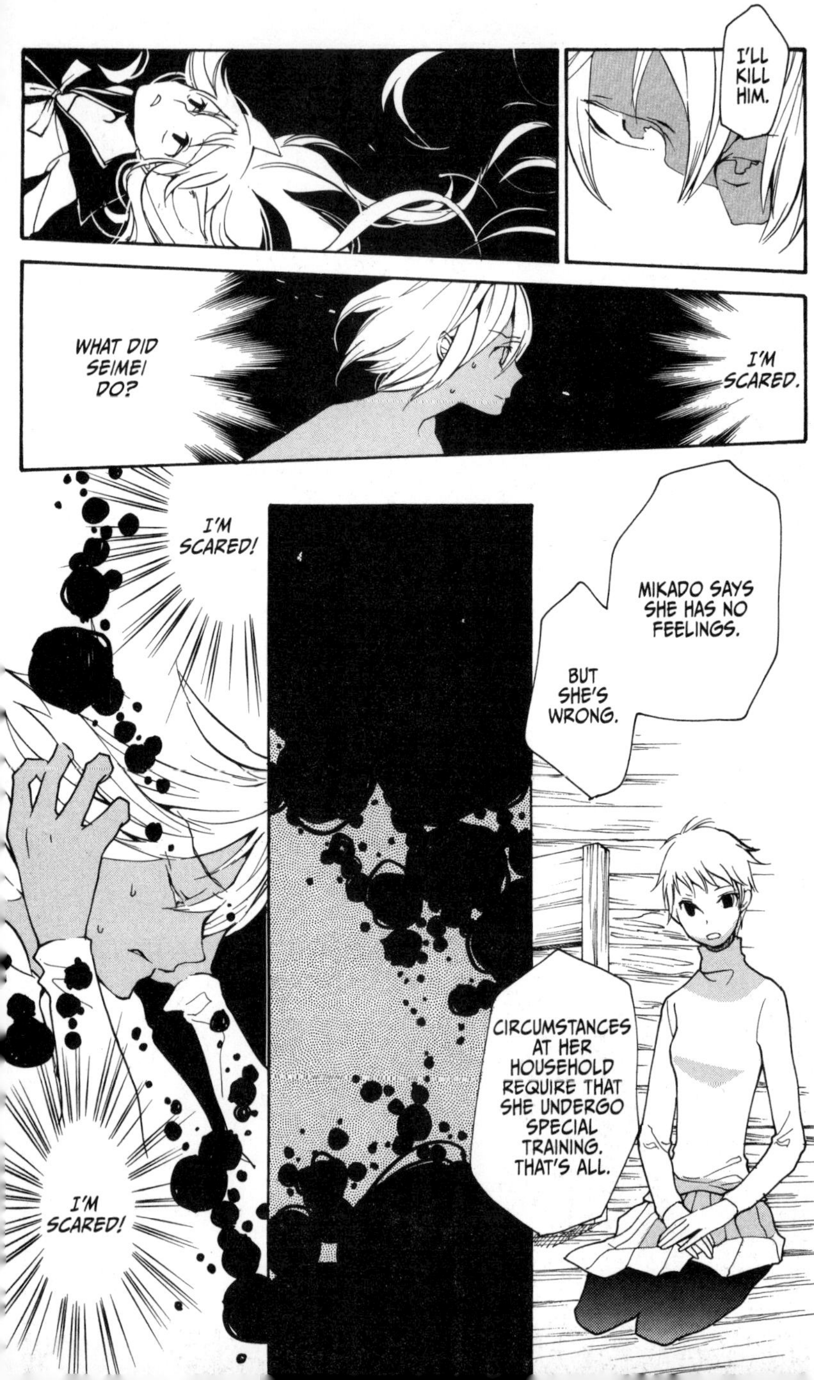
I'LL KILL HIM.
I'M SCARED.
WHAT DID SEIMEI DO?
MIKADO SAYS SHE HAS NO FEELINGS.
BUT SHE'S WRONG.
CIRCUMSTANCES AT HER HOUSEHOLD REQUIRE THAT SHE UNDERGO SPECIAL TRAINING. THAT'S ALL.
I'M SCARED!
I'M SCARED!

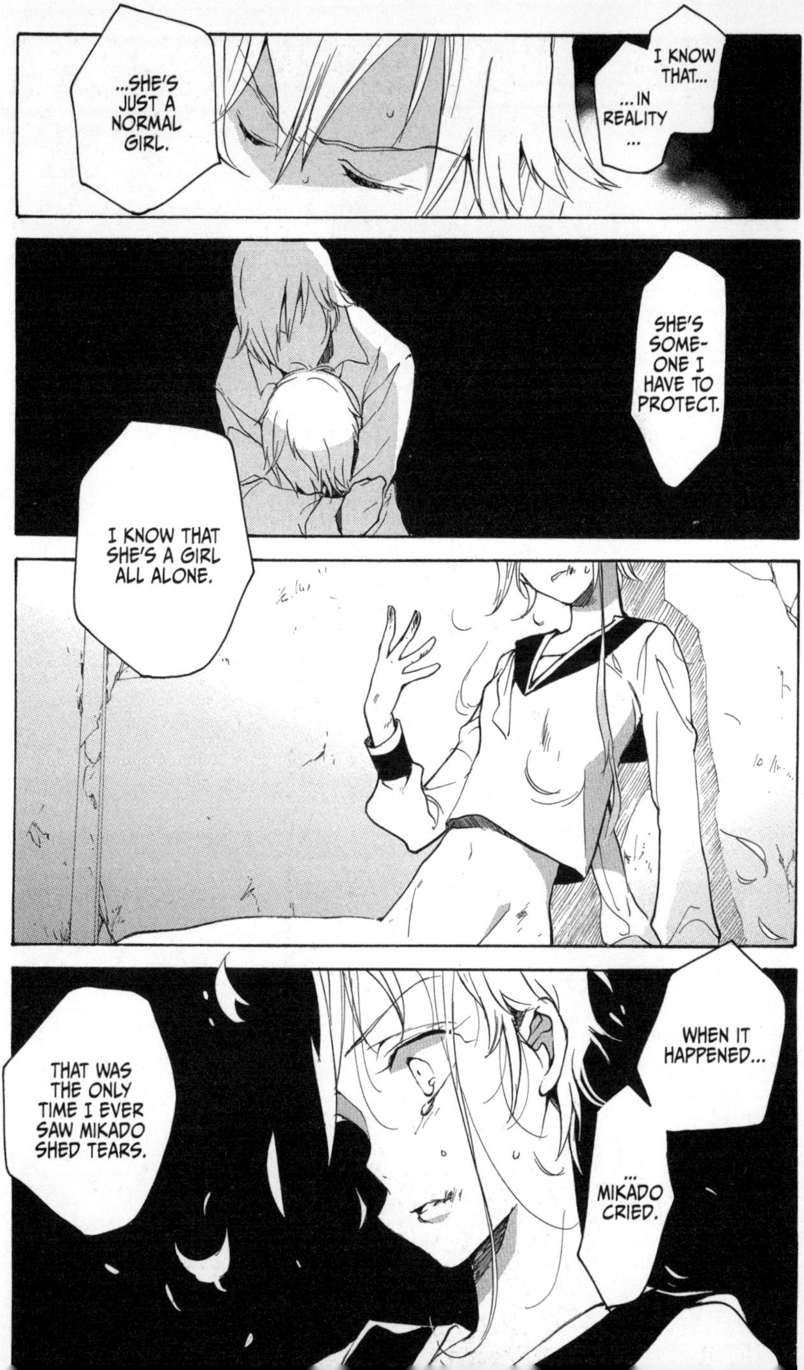
I KNOW THAT...
...IN REALITY ...
...SHE'S JUST A NORMAL GIRL.
SHE'S SOME-ONE I HAVE TO PROTECT.
I KNOW THAT SHE'S A GIRL ALL ALONE.
WHEN IT HAPPENED...
...MIKADO CRIED.
THAT WAS THE ONLY TIME I EVER SAW MIKADO SHED TEARS.

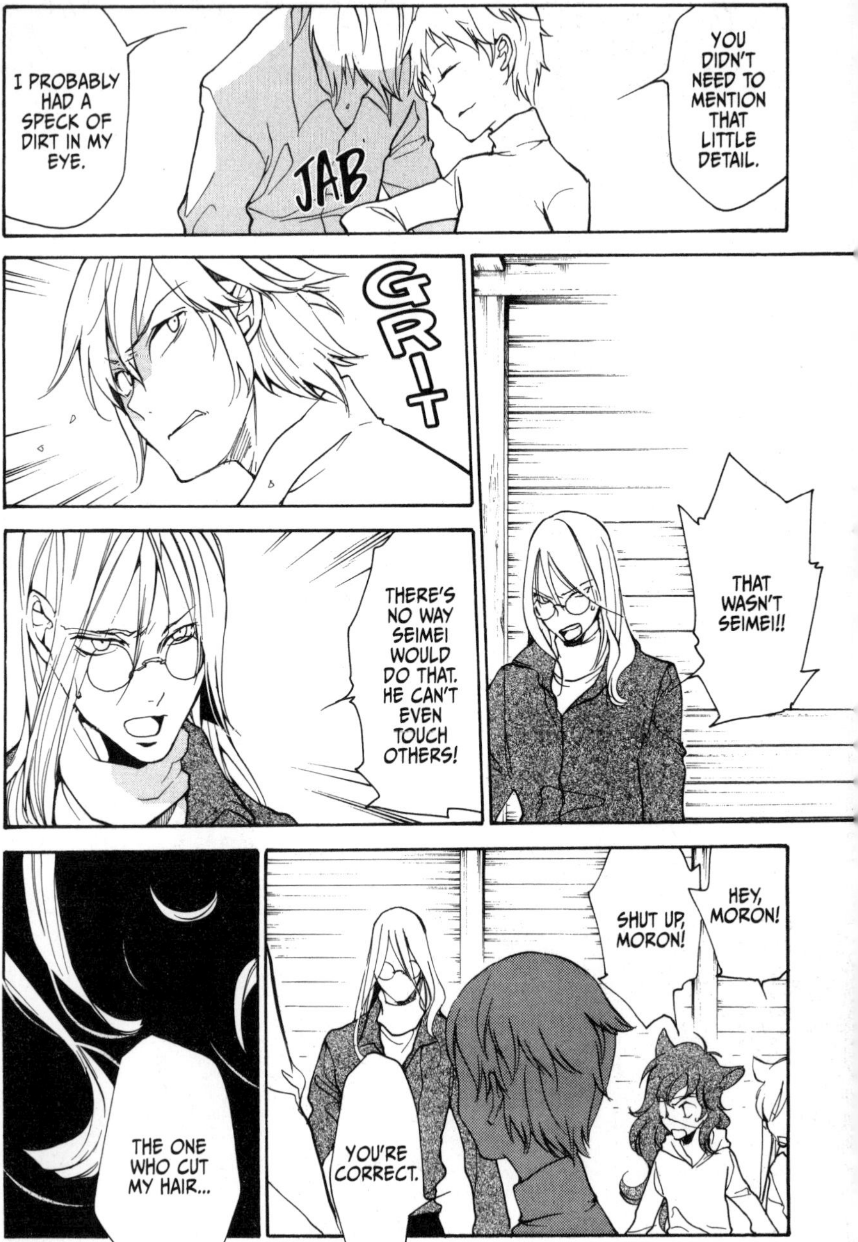
YOU DIDN'T NEED TO MENTION THAT LITTLE DETAIL.
JAB
I PROBABLY HAD A SPECK OF DIRT IN MY EYE.
THAT WASN'T SEIMEI!!
GRIT
THERE'S NO WAY SEIMEI WOULD DO THAT. HE CAN'T EVEN TOUCH OTHERS!
HEY, MORON!
SHUT UP, MORON!
YOU'RE CORRECT.
THE ONE WHO CUT MY HAIR...

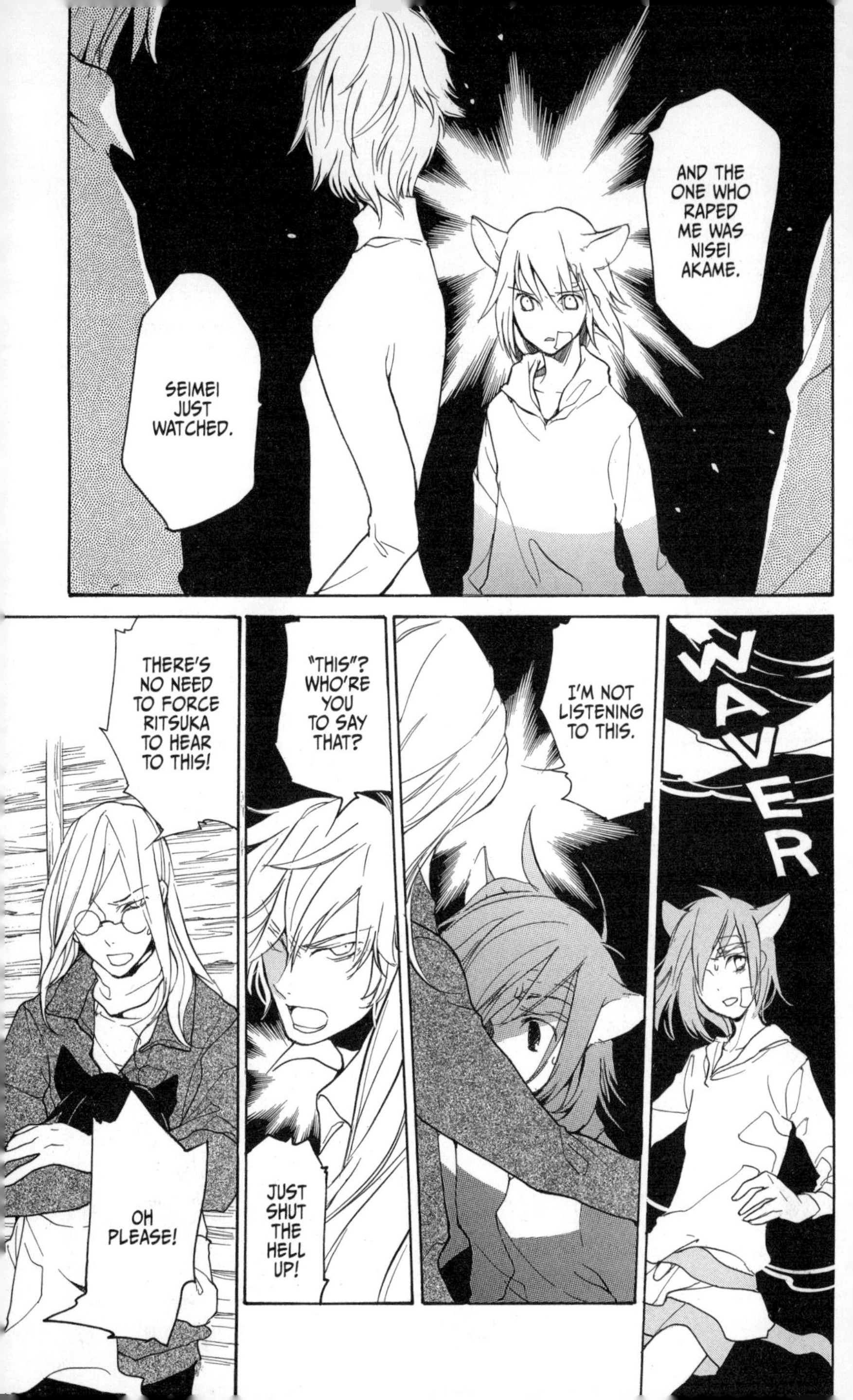
AND THE ONE WHO RAPED ME WAS NISEI AKAME.
SEIMEI JUST WATCHED.
WAVER
I'M NOT LISTENING TO THIS.
"THIS"? WHO'RE YOU TO SAY THAT?
JUST SHUT THE HELL UP!
THERE'S NO NEED TO FORCE RITSUKA TO HEAR TO THIS!
OH PLEASE!

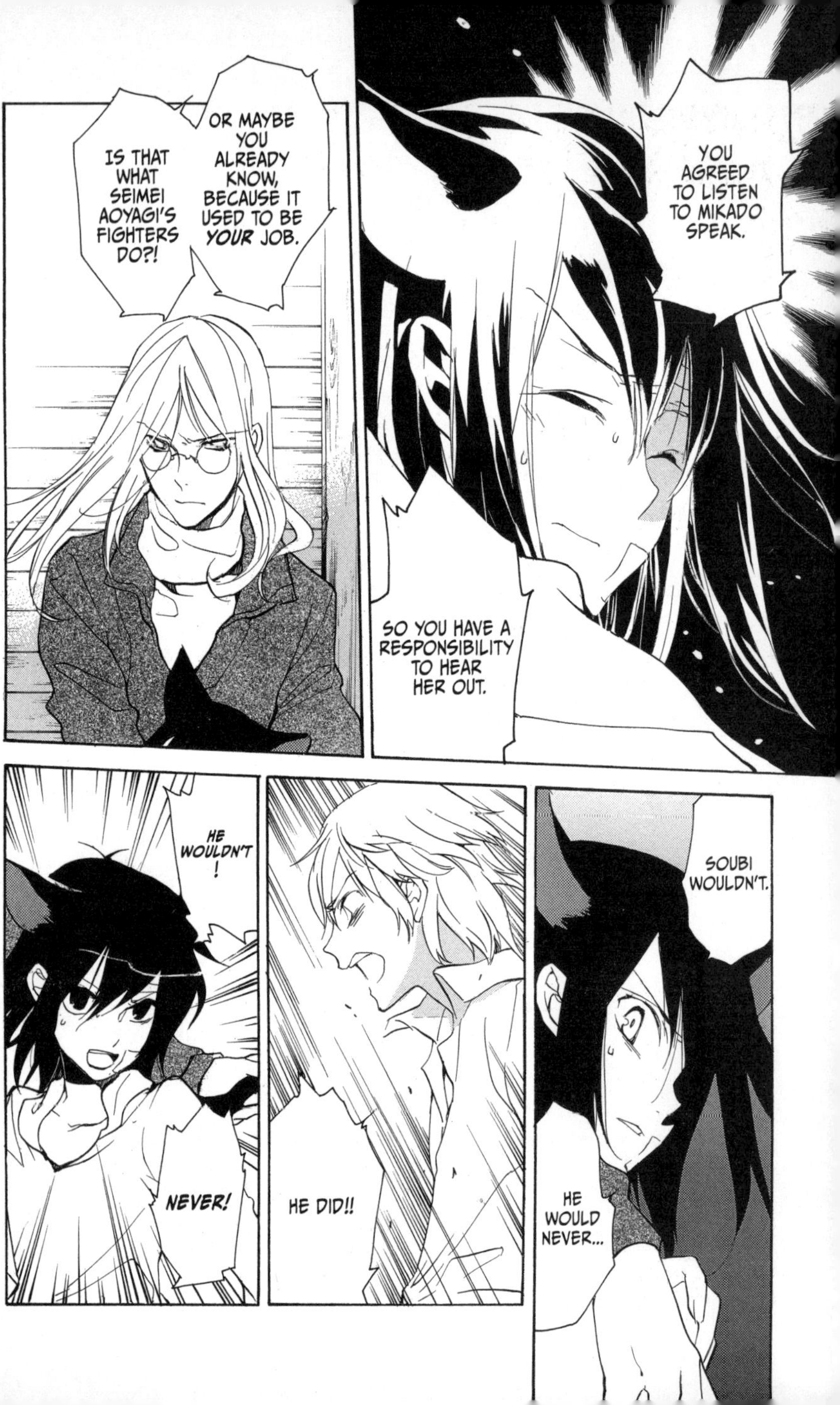
YOU AGREED TO LISTEN TO MIKADO SPEAK.
SO YOU HAVE A RESPONSIBILITY TO HEAR HER OUT.
OR MAYBE YOU ALREADY KNOW, BECAUSE IT USED TO BE *YOUR* JOB.
IS THAT WHAT SEIMEI AOYAGI'S FIGHTERS DO?!
SOUBI WOULDN'T.
HE WOULD NEVER...
HE DID!!
HE WOULDN'T!
*NEVER!*

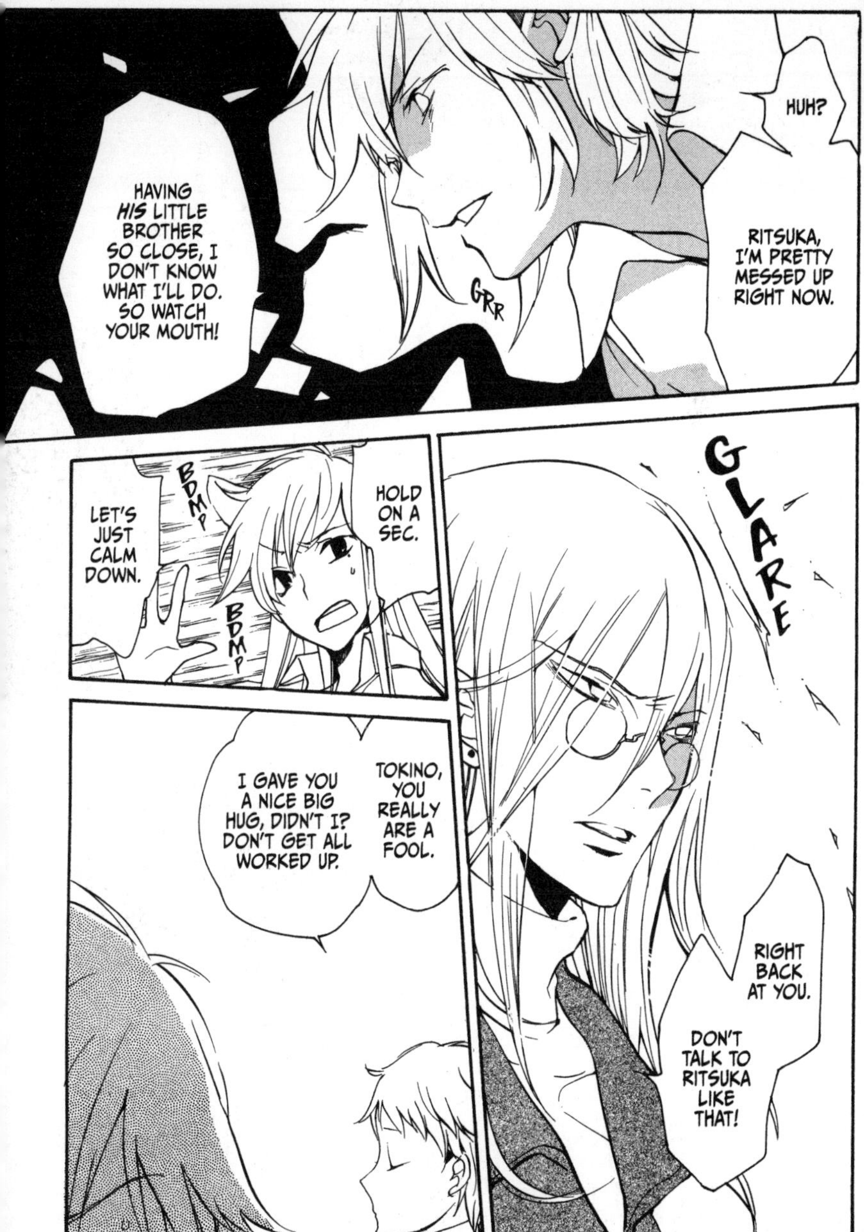
HUH?
RITSUKA, I'M PRETTY MESSED UP RIGHT NOW.
HAVING HIS LITTLE BROTHER SO CLOSE, I DON'T KNOW WHAT I'LL DO. SO WATCH YOUR MOUTH!
GRR
GLARE
RIGHT BACK AT YOU.
DON'T TALK TO RITSUKA LIKE THAT!
HOLD ON A SEC.
BDMP
BDMP
LET'S JUST CALM DOWN.
TOKINO, YOU REALLY ARE A FOOL.
I GAVE YOU A NICE BIG HUG, DIDN'T I? DON'T GET ALL WORKED UP.

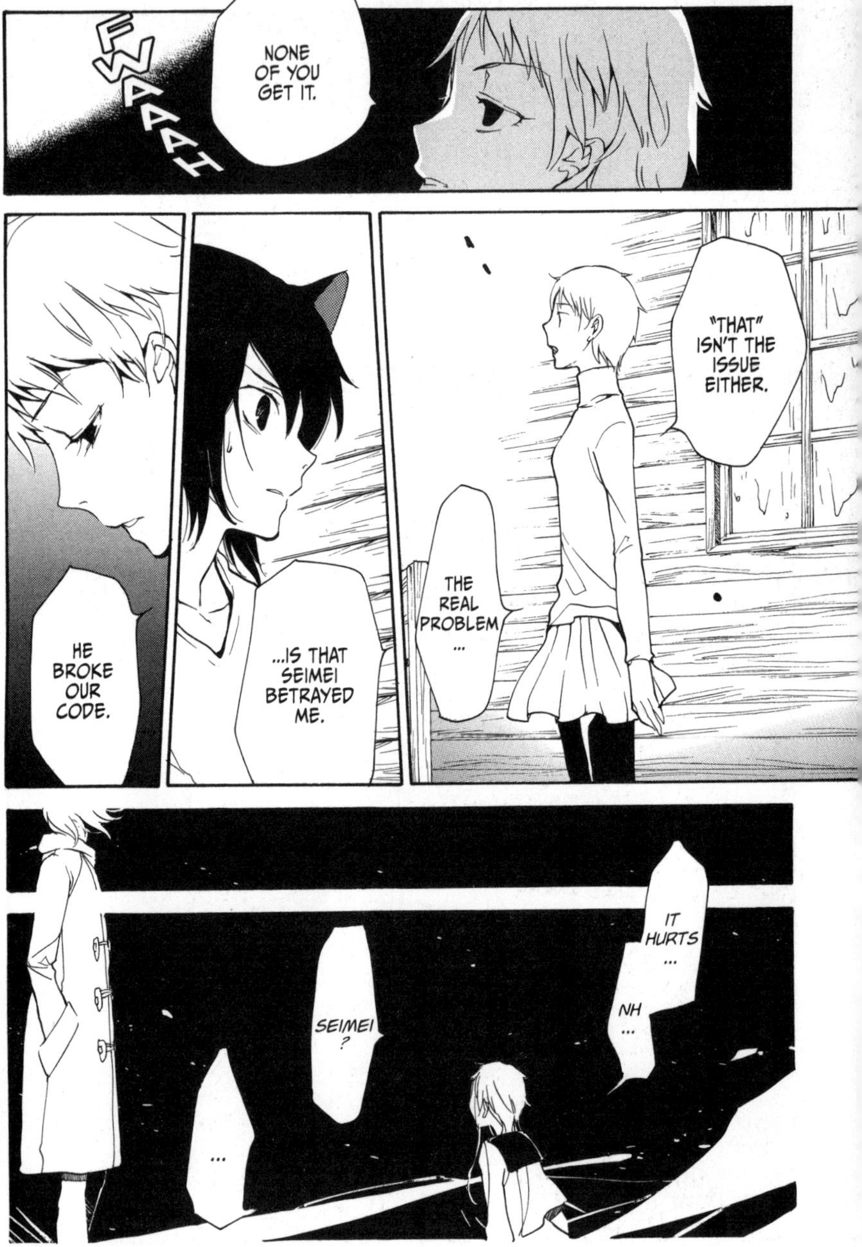
NONE OF YOU GET IT.
FWAAAH
"THAT" ISN'T THE ISSUE EITHER.
THE REAL PROBLEM...
...IS THAT SEIMEI BETRAYED ME.
HE BROKE OUR CODE.
IT HURTS...
NH...
SEIMEI?
...

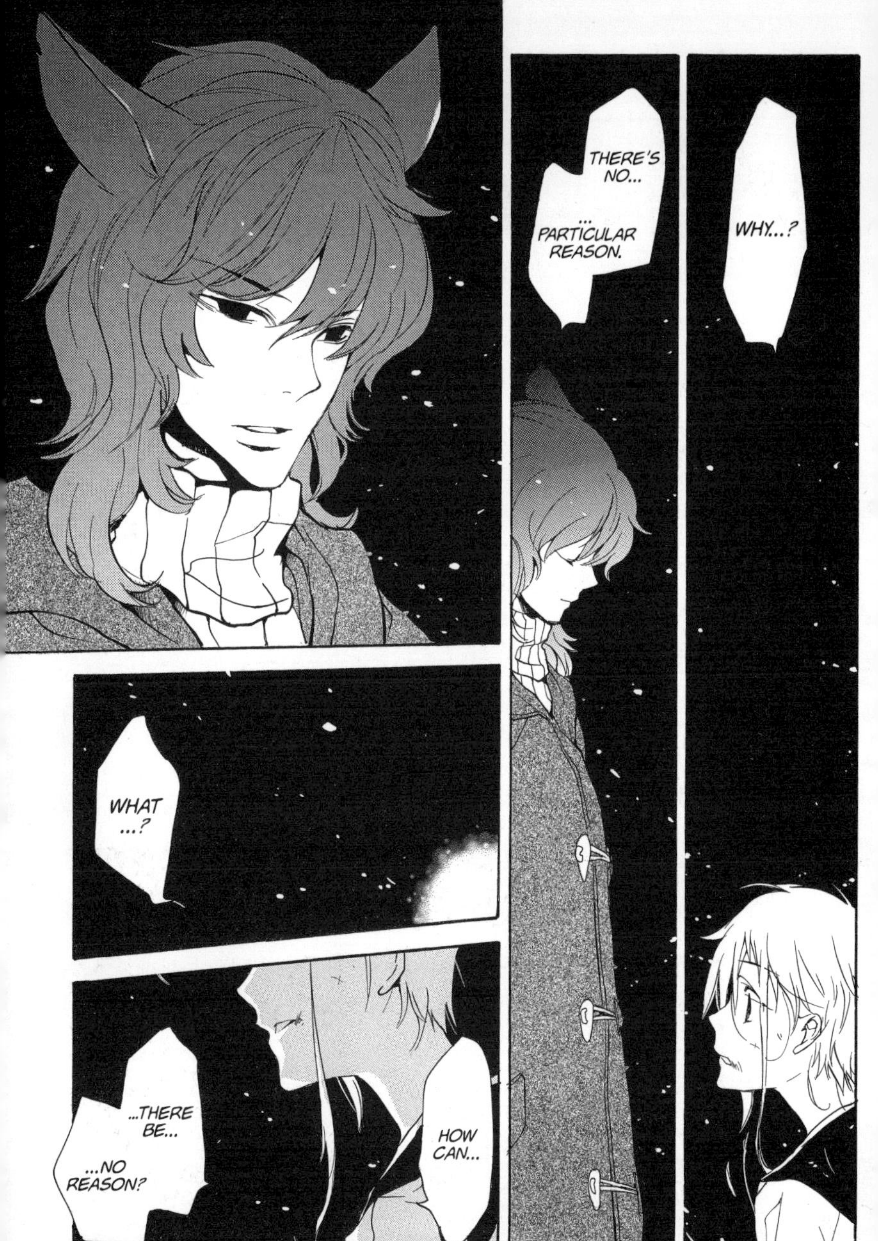
WHY...?
THERE'S NO... ... PARTICULAR REASON.
WHAT ...?
HOW CAN...
...THERE BE... ...NO REASON?

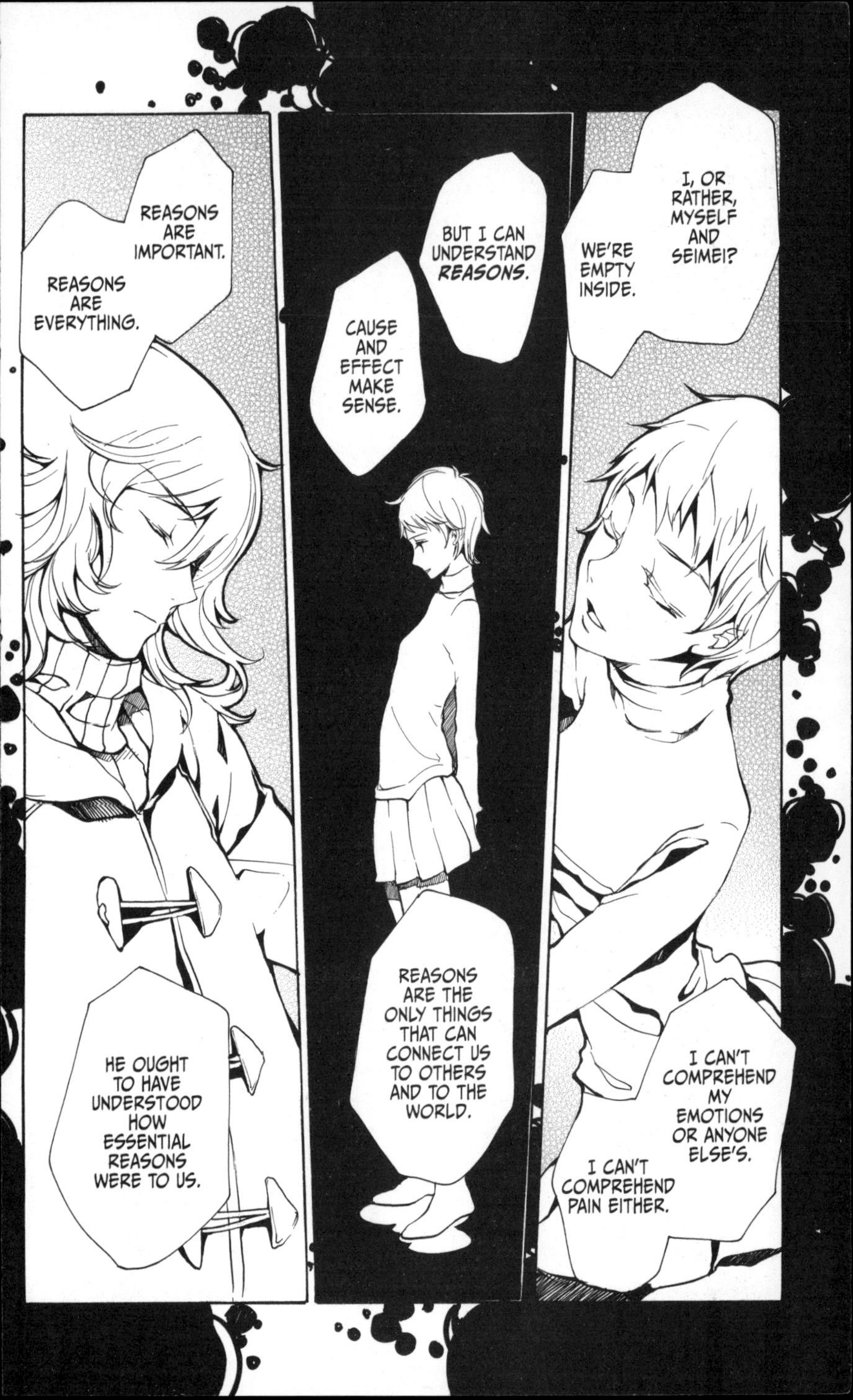
I, OR RATHER, MYSELF AND SEIMEI?
WE'RE EMPTY INSIDE.
I CAN'T COMPREHEND MY EMOTIONS OR ANYONE ELSE'S.
I CAN'T COMPREHEND PAIN EITHER.
BUT I CAN UNDERSTAND *REASONS.*
CAUSE AND EFFECT MAKE SENSE.
REASONS ARE THE ONLY THINGS THAT CAN CONNECT US TO OTHERS AND TO THE WORLD.
REASONS ARE IMPORTANT.
REASONS ARE EVERYTHING.
HE OUGHT TO HAVE UNDERSTOOD HOW ESSENTIAL REASONS WERE TO US.

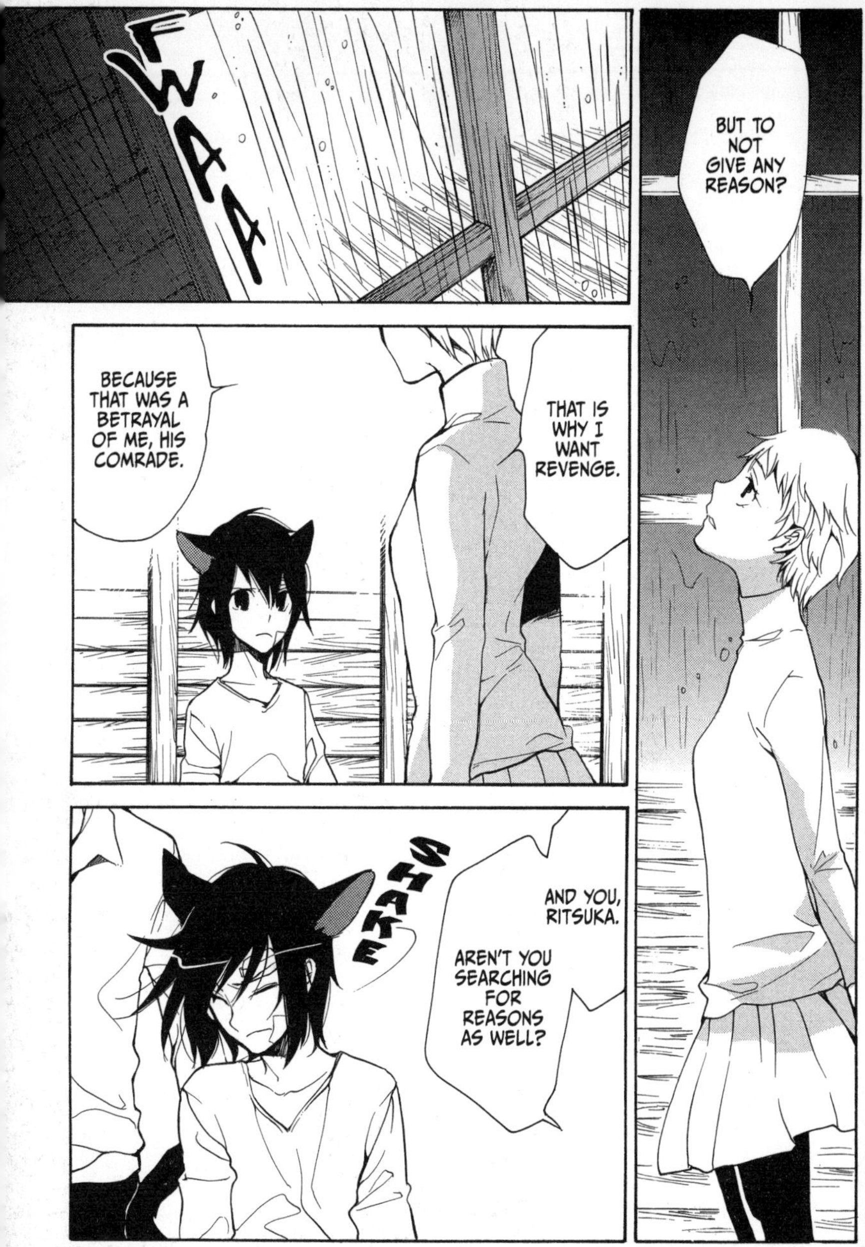
BUT TO NOT GIVE ANY REASON?
FWAA
THAT IS WHY I WANT REVENGE.
BECAUSE THAT WAS A BETRAYAL OF ME, HIS COMRADE.
AND YOU, RITSUKA.
AREN'T YOU SEARCHING FOR REASONS AS WELL?
SHAKE

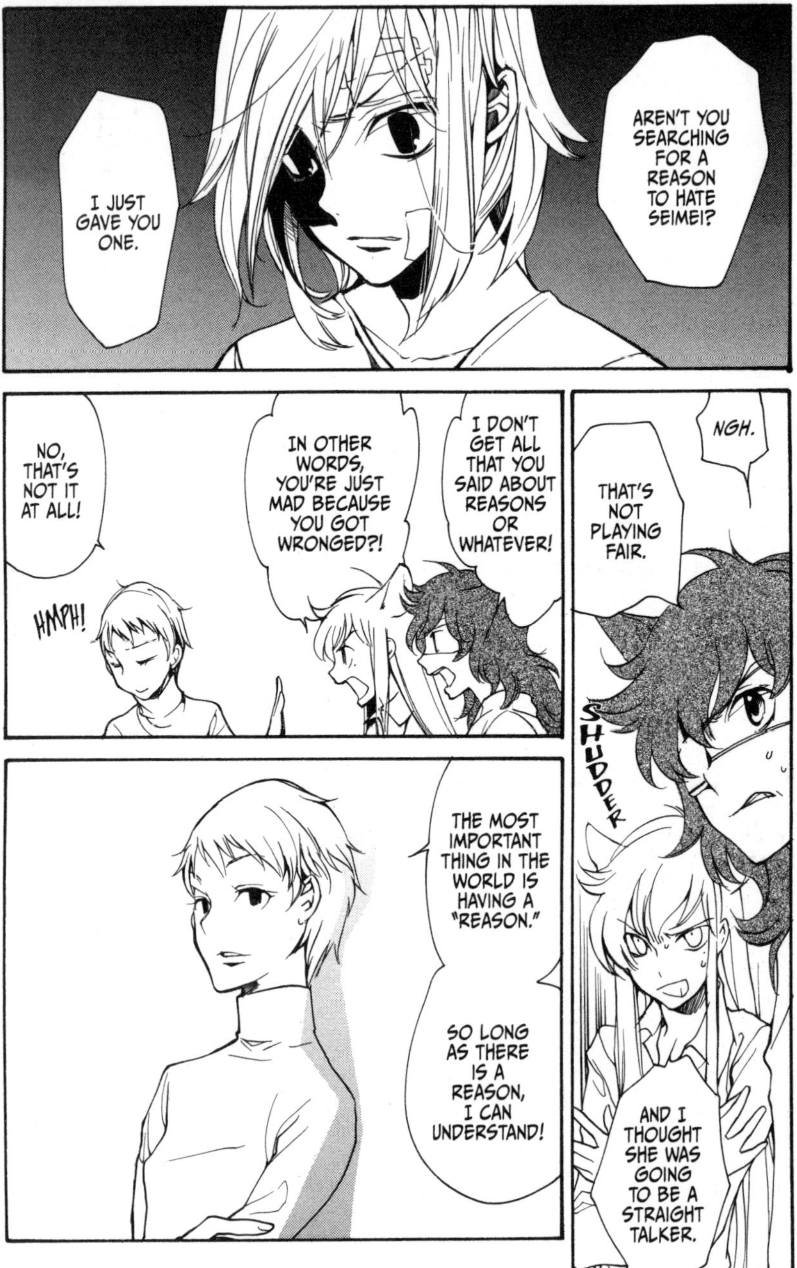
AREN'T YOU SEARCHING FOR A REASON TO HATE SEIMEI?
I JUST GAVE YOU ONE.
NGH.
THAT'S NOT PLAYING FAIR.
SHUDDER
AND I THOUGHT SHE WAS GOING TO BE A STRAIGHT TALKER.
I DON'T GET ALL THAT YOU SAID ABOUT REASONS OR WHATEVER!
IN OTHER WORDS, YOU'RE JUST MAD BECAUSE YOU GOT WRONGED?!
NO, THAT'S NOT IT AT ALL!
HMPH!
THE MOST IMPORTANT THING IN THE WORLD IS HAVING A "REASON."
SO LONG AS THERE IS A REASON, I CAN UNDERSTAND!

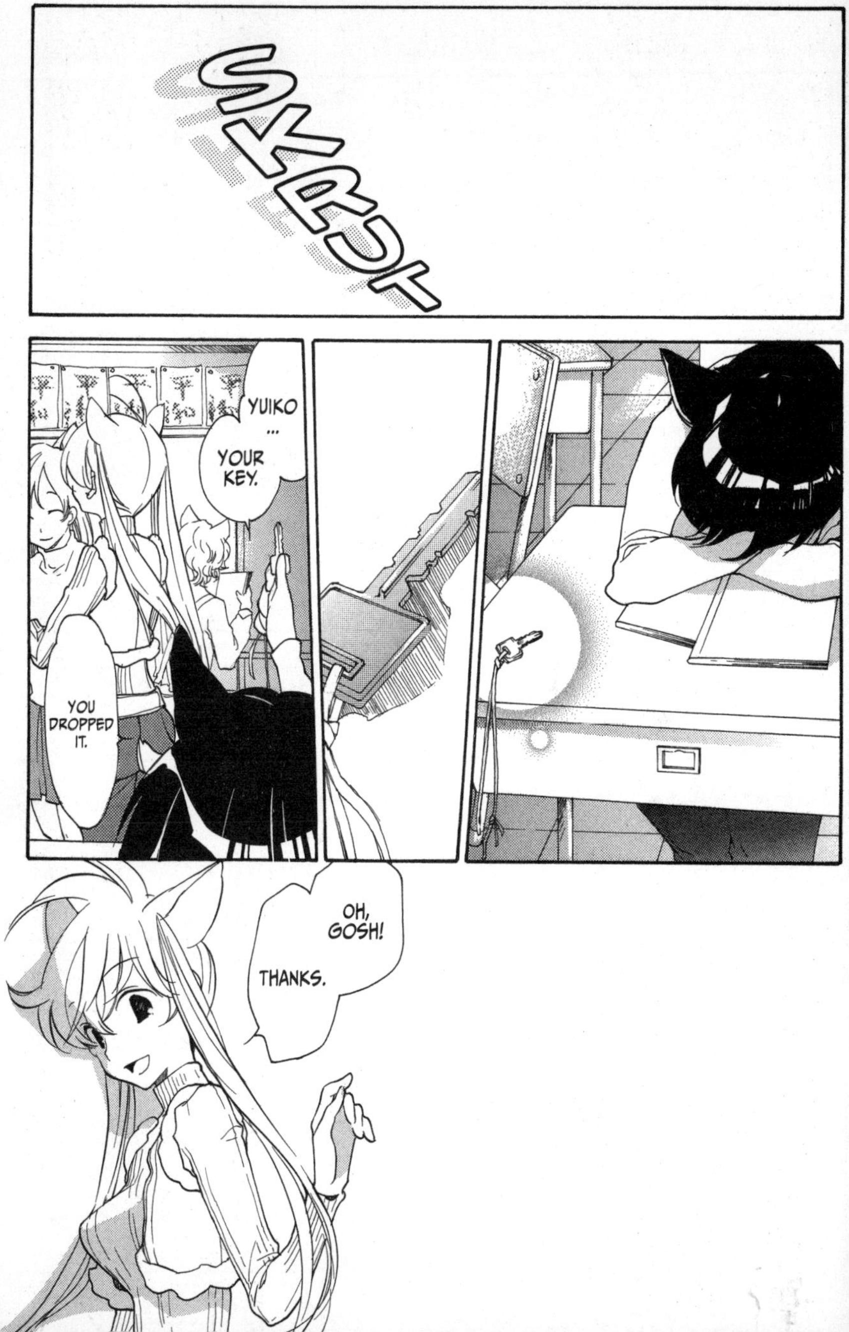
SKRUT
YUIKO ... YOUR KEY.
YOU DROPPED IT.
OH, GOSH!
THANKS.

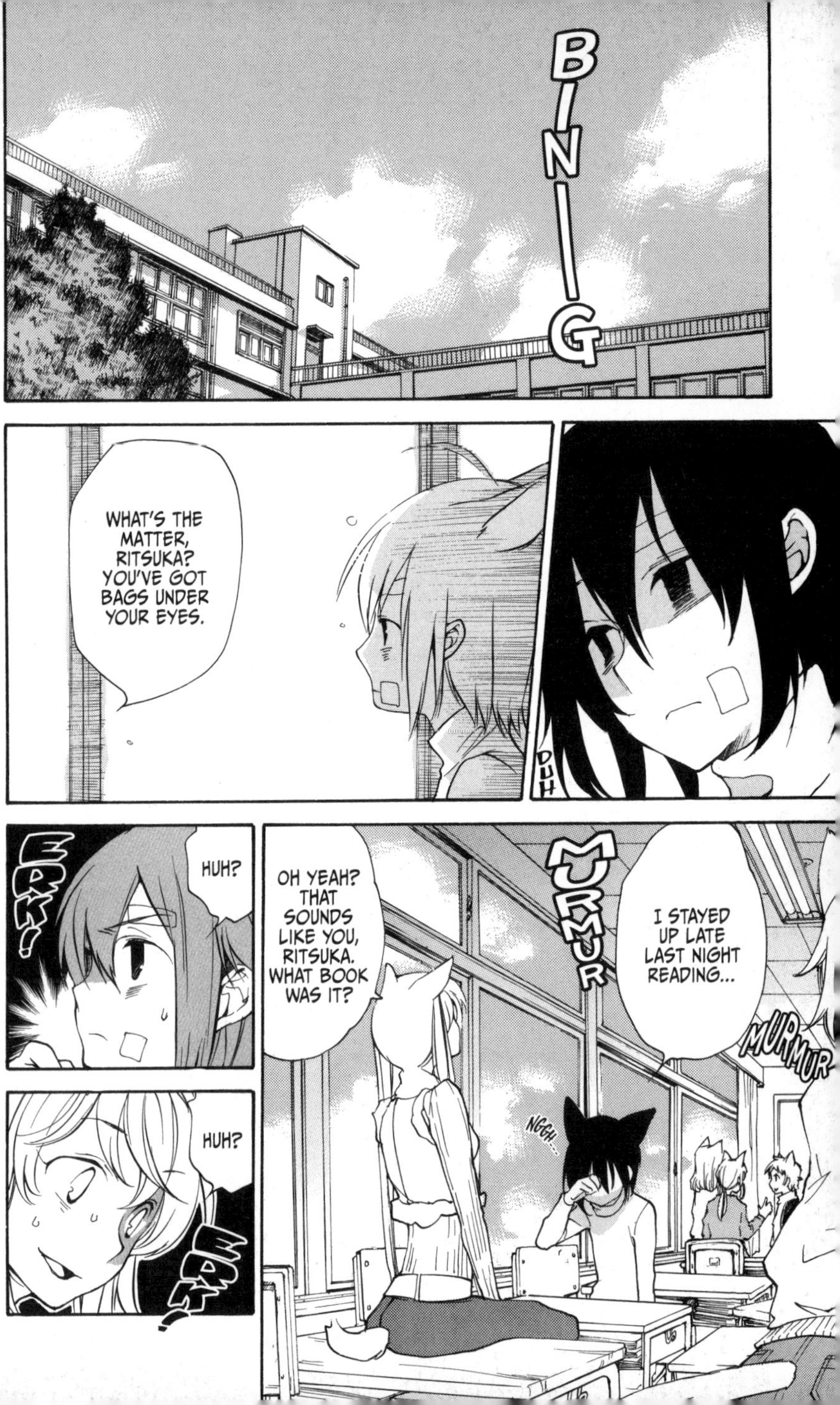
BINIG
DUH
WHAT'S THE MATTER, RITSUKA? YOU'VE GOT BAGS UNDER YOUR EYES.
I STAYED UP LATE LAST NIGHT READING...
MURMUR
MURMUR
OH YEAH? THAT SOUNDS LIKE YOU, RITSUKA. WHAT BOOK WAS IT?
NGGH...
HUH?
ERK!
HUH?
ERK!

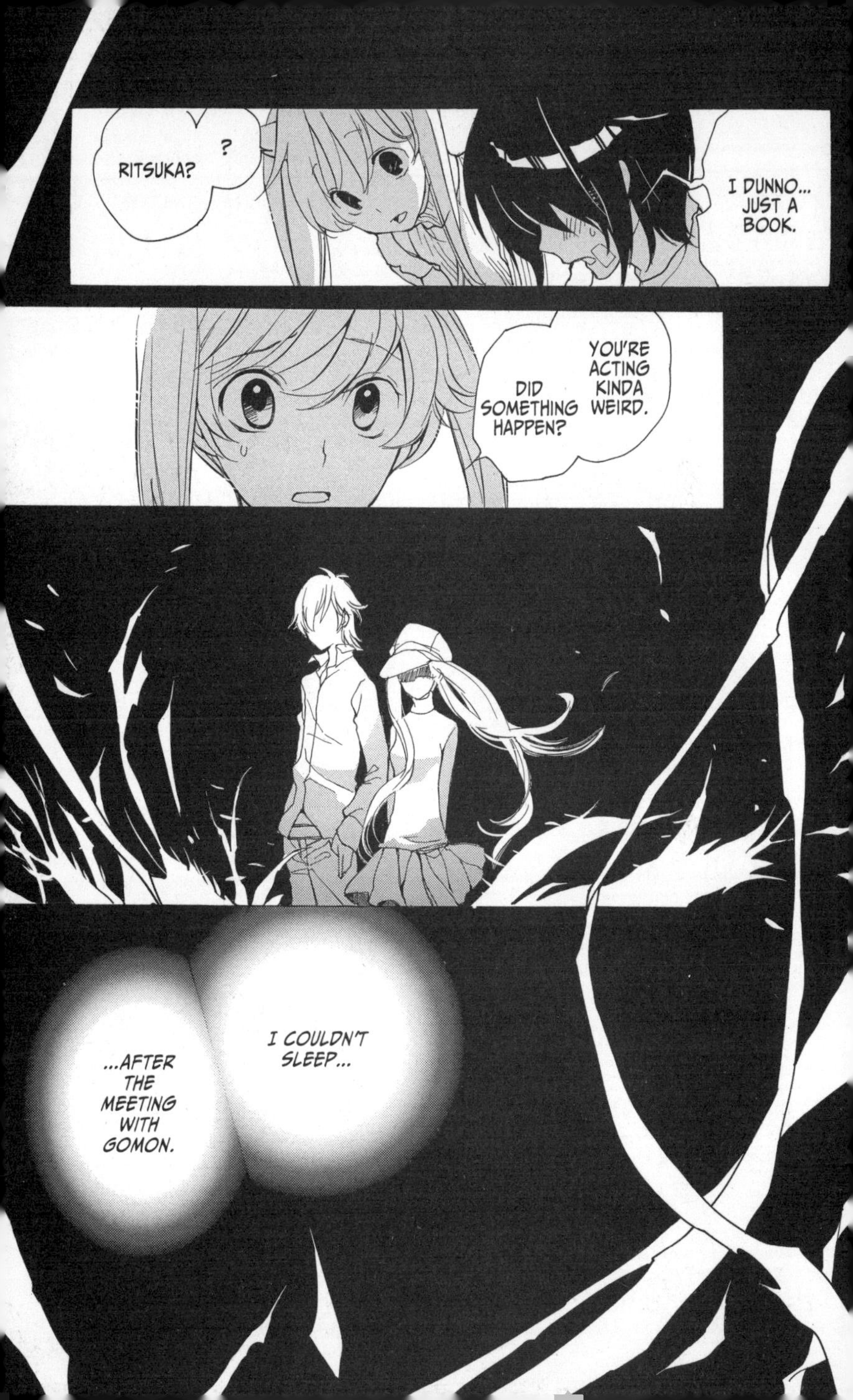
I DUNNO... JUST A BOOK.
?
RITSUKA?
YOU'RE ACTING KINDA WEIRD.
DID SOMETHING HAPPEN?
I COULDN'T SLEEP...
...AFTER THE MEETING WITH GOMON.

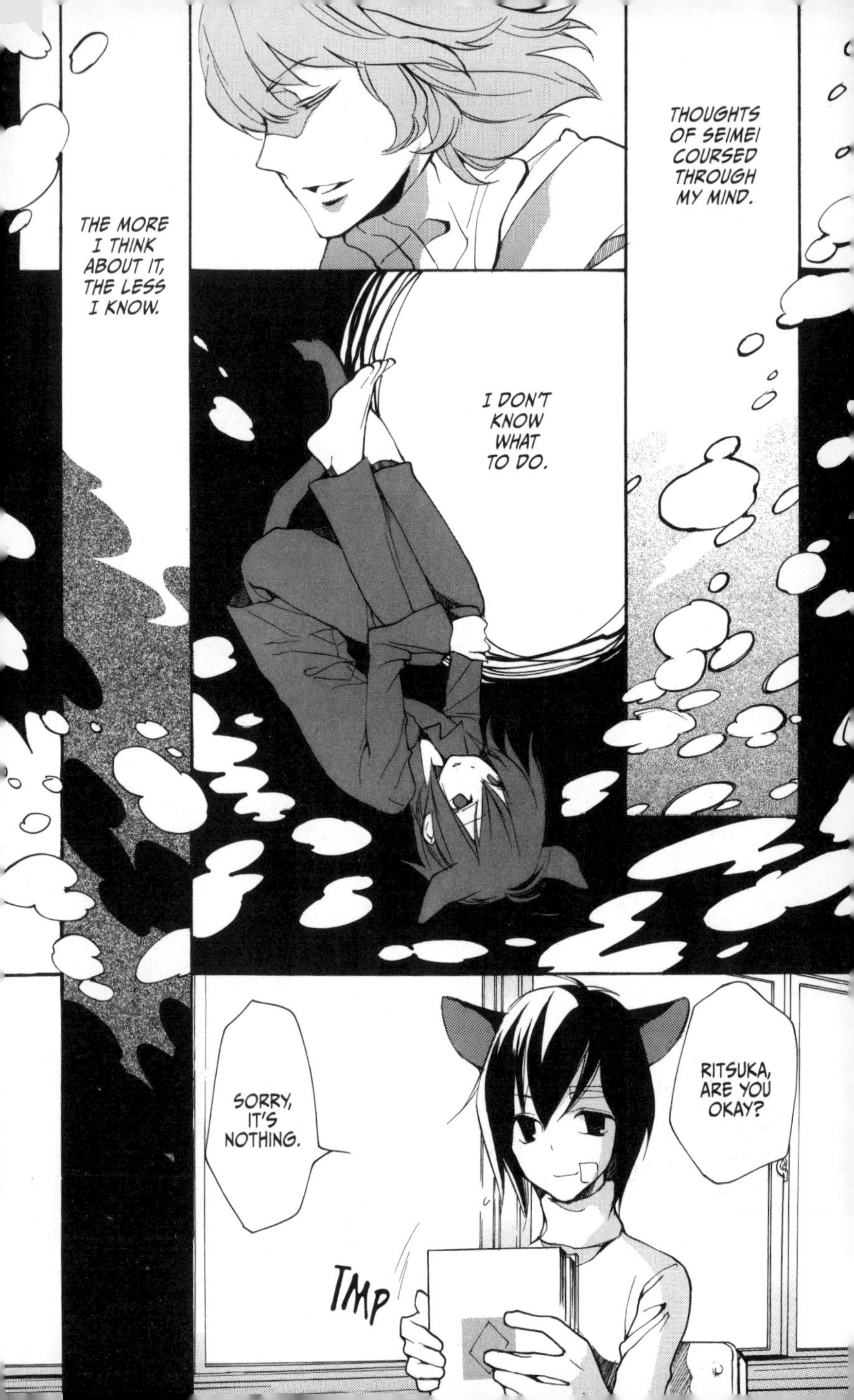
THOUGHTS OF SEIMEI COURSED THROUGH MY MIND.
THE MORE I THINK ABOUT IT, THE LESS I KNOW.
I DON'T KNOW WHAT TO DO.
RITSUKA, ARE YOU OKAY?
SORRY, IT'S NOTHING.
TMP

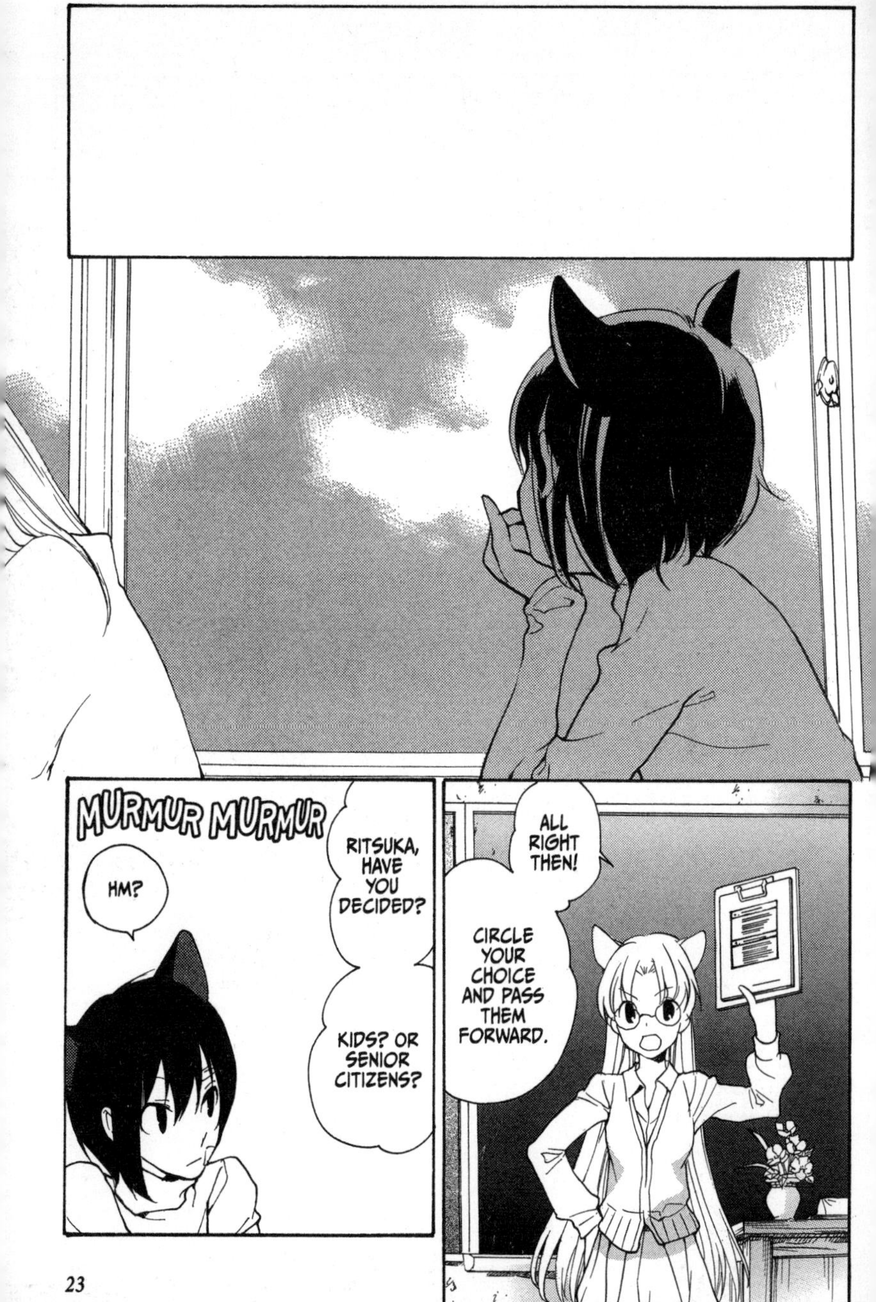
ALL RIGHT THEN!
CIRCLE YOUR CHOICE AND PASS THEM FORWARD.
RITSUKA, HAVE YOU DECIDED?
MURMUR MURMUR
KIDS? OR SENIOR CITIZENS?
HM?

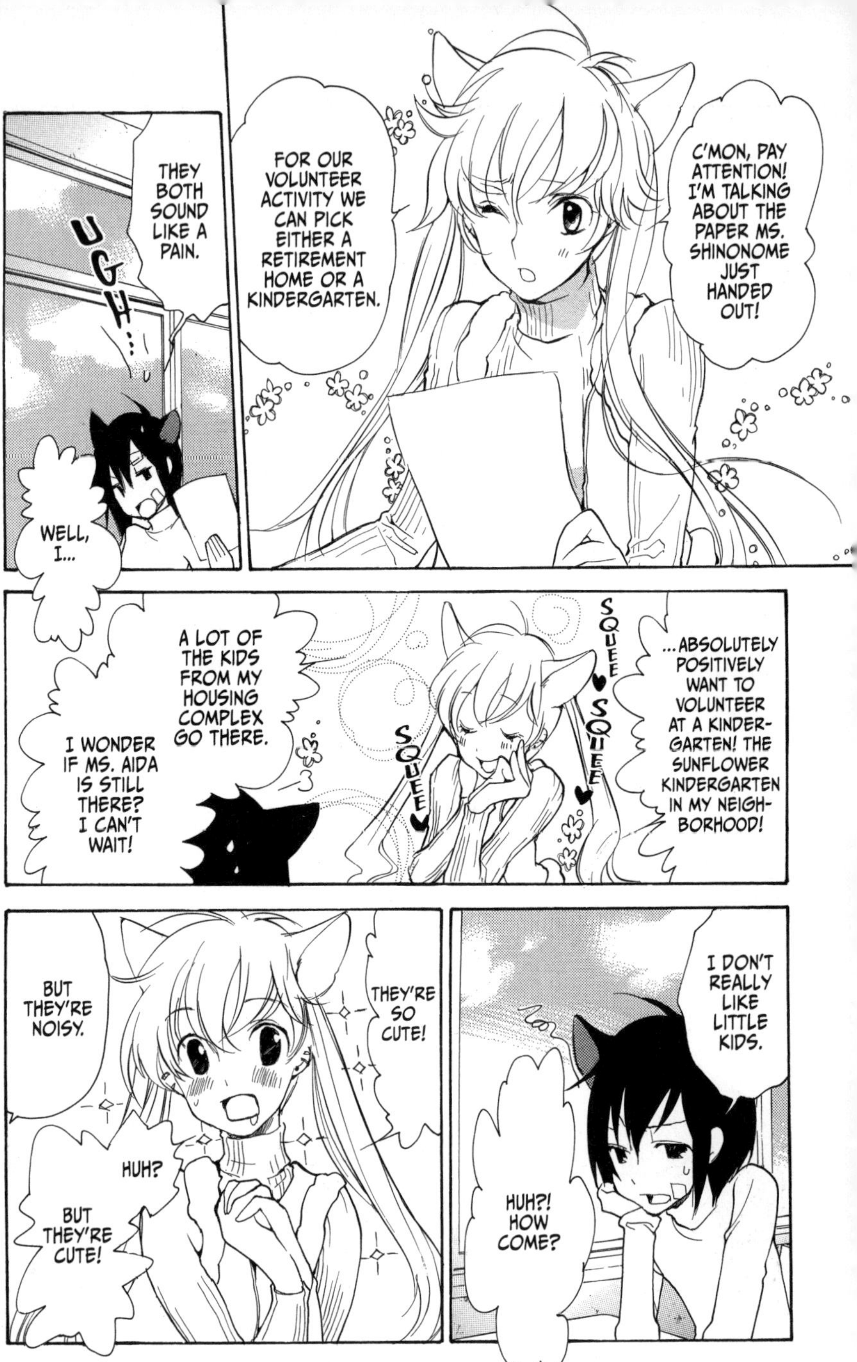
C'MON, PAY ATTENTION! I'M TALKING ABOUT THE PAPER MS. SHINONOME JUST HANDED OUT!
FOR OUR VOLUNTEER ACTIVITY WE CAN PICK EITHER A RETIREMENT HOME OR A KINDERGARTEN.
THEY BOTH SOUND LIKE A PAIN.
UGH...
WELL, I...
...ABSOLUTELY POSITIVELY WANT TO VOLUNTEER AT A KINDER-GARTEN! THE SUNFLOWER KINDERGARTEN IN MY NEIGH-BORHOOD!
SQUEE
SQUEE
SQUEE
A LOT OF THE KIDS FROM MY HOUSING COMPLEX GO THERE.
I WONDER IF MS. AIDA IS STILL THERE? I CAN'T WAIT!
I DON'T REALLY LIKE LITTLE KIDS.
HUH?! HOW COME?
THEY'RE SO CUTE!
BUT THEY'RE NOISY.
HUH?
BUT THEY'RE CUTE!

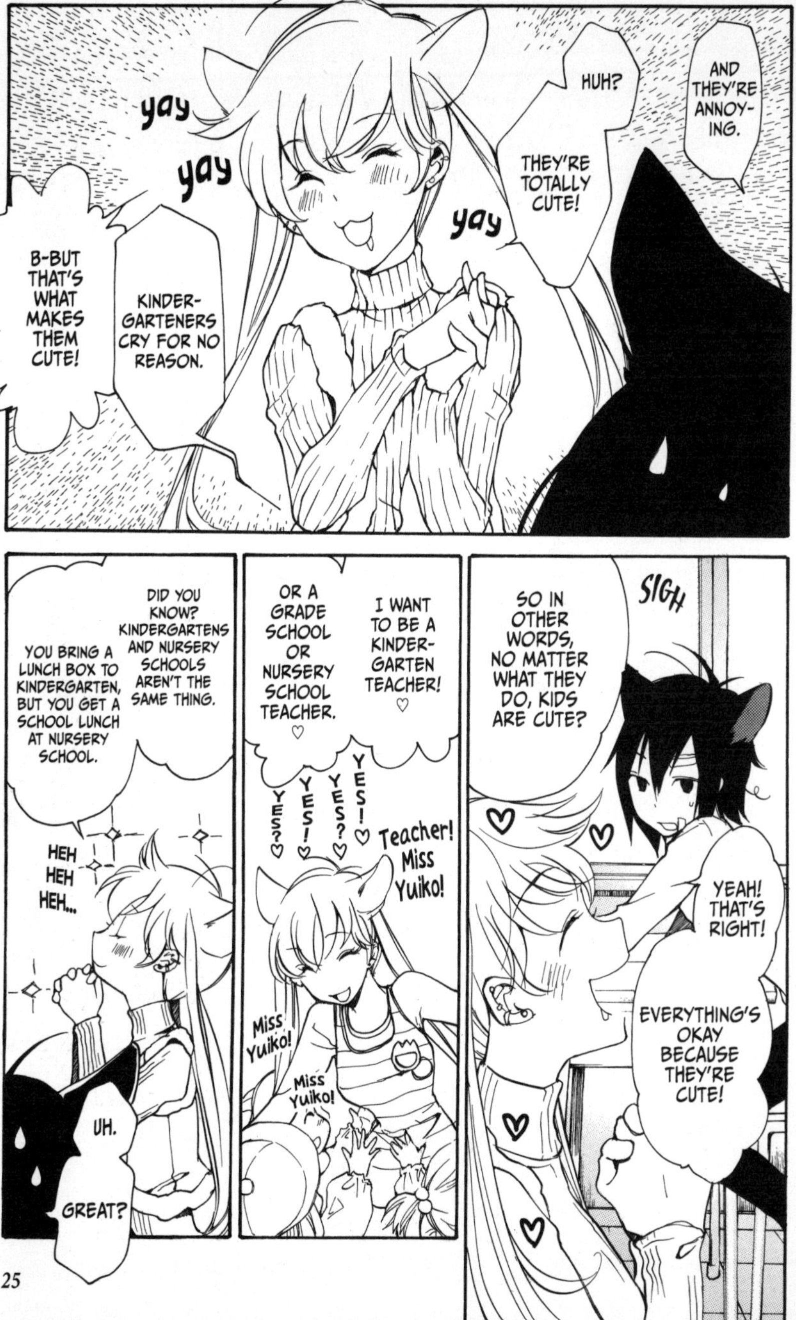
AND THEY'RE ANNOYING.
HUH?
THEY'RE TOTALLY CUTE!
yay
yay
yay
KINDERGARTENERS CRY FOR NO REASON.
B-BUT THAT'S WHAT MAKES THEM CUTE!
SIGH
SO IN OTHER WORDS, NO MATTER WHAT THEY DO, KIDS ARE CUTE?
YEAH! THAT'S RIGHT!
EVERYTHING'S OKAY BECAUSE THEY'RE CUTE!
I WANT TO BE A KINDERGARTEN TEACHER! ♡
OR A GRADE SCHOOL OR NURSERY SCHOOL TEACHER. ♡
YES! ♡
YES? ♡
YES! ♡
YES? ♡
Teacher! Miss Yuiko!
Miss Yuiko!
Miss Yuiko!
DID YOU KNOW? KINDERGARTENS AND NURSERY SCHOOLS AREN'T THE SAME THING.
YOU BRING A LUNCH BOX TO KINDERGARTEN, BUT YOU GET A SCHOOL LUNCH AT NURSERY SCHOOL.
HEH HEH HEH...
UH.
GREAT?

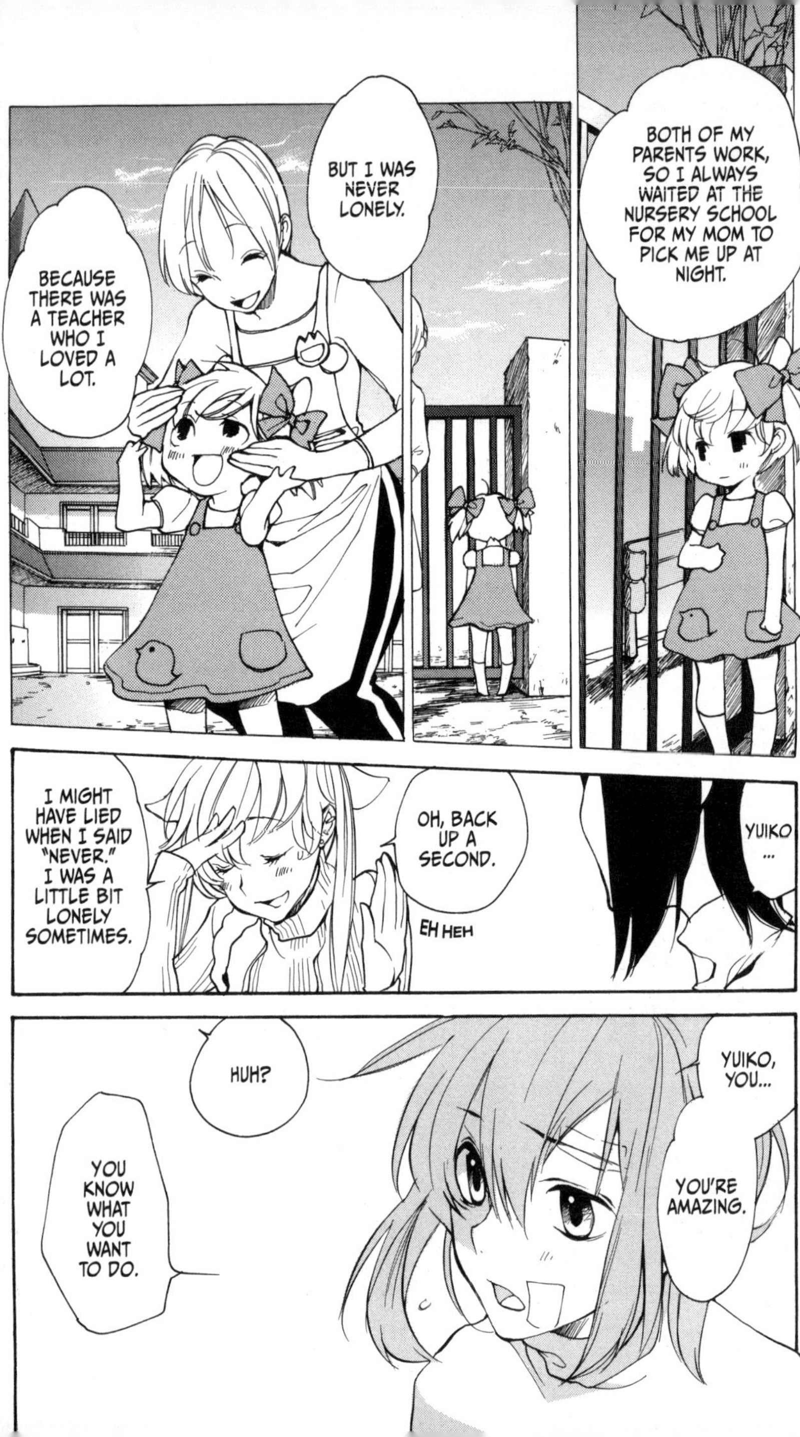
BOTH OF MY PARENTS WORK, SO I ALWAYS WAITED AT THE NURSERY SCHOOL FOR MY MOM TO PICK ME UP AT NIGHT.
BUT I WAS NEVER LONELY.
BECAUSE THERE WAS A TEACHER WHO I LOVED A LOT.
YUIKO ...
OH, BACK UP A SECOND.
EH HEH
I MIGHT HAVE LIED WHEN I SAID "NEVER." I WAS A LITTLE BIT LONELY SOMETIMES.
YUIKO, YOU...
YOU'RE AMAZING.
HUH?
YOU KNOW WHAT YOU WANT TO DO.

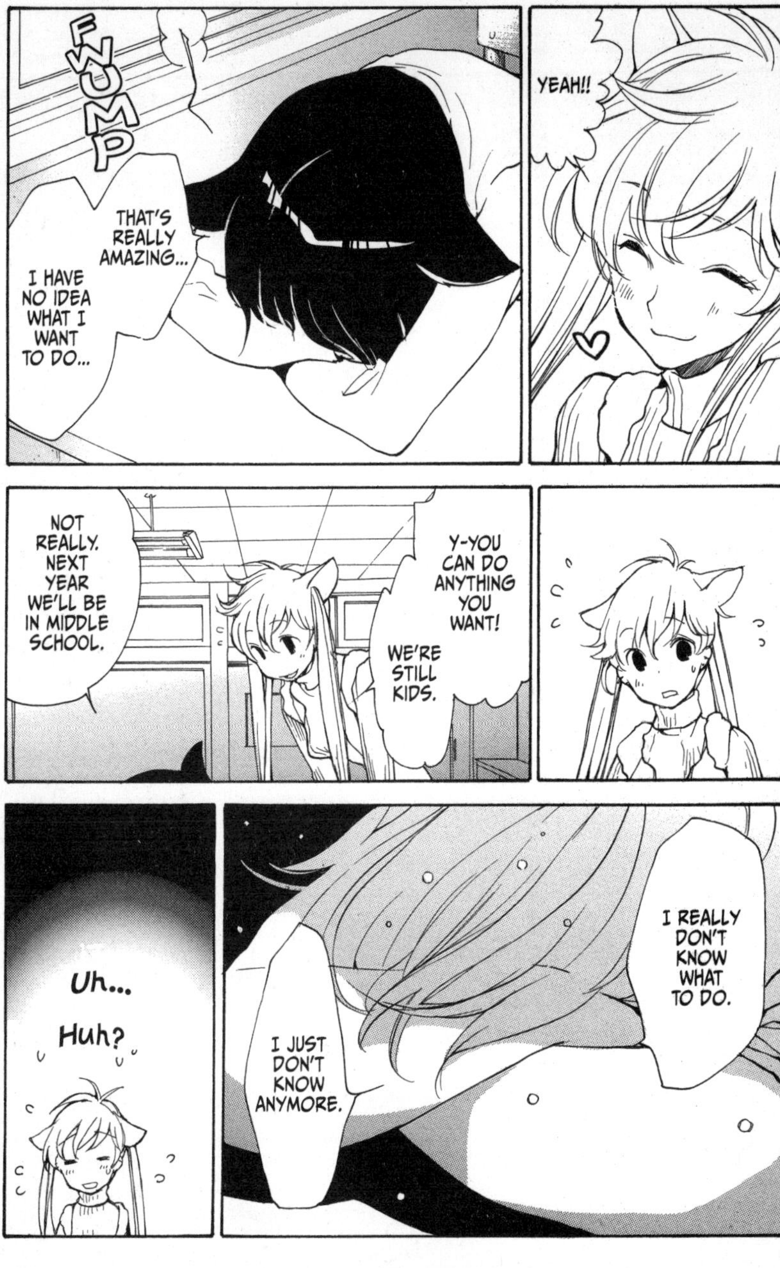
YEAH!!
FWUMP
THAT'S REALLY AMAZING...
I HAVE NO IDEA WHAT I WANT TO DO...
Y-YOU CAN DO ANYTHING YOU WANT!
WE'RE STILL KIDS.
NOT REALLY. NEXT YEAR WE'LL BE IN MIDDLE SCHOOL.
I REALLY DON'T KNOW WHAT TO DO.
I JUST DON'T KNOW ANYMORE.
Uh...
Huh?

RIT-SUKA...

I DON'T KNOW ANY-MORE...

Whoo...

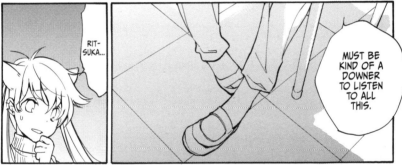

RIT-SUKA...

MUST BE KIND OF A DOWNER TO LISTEN TO ALL THIS.

...

...

...

SORRY.

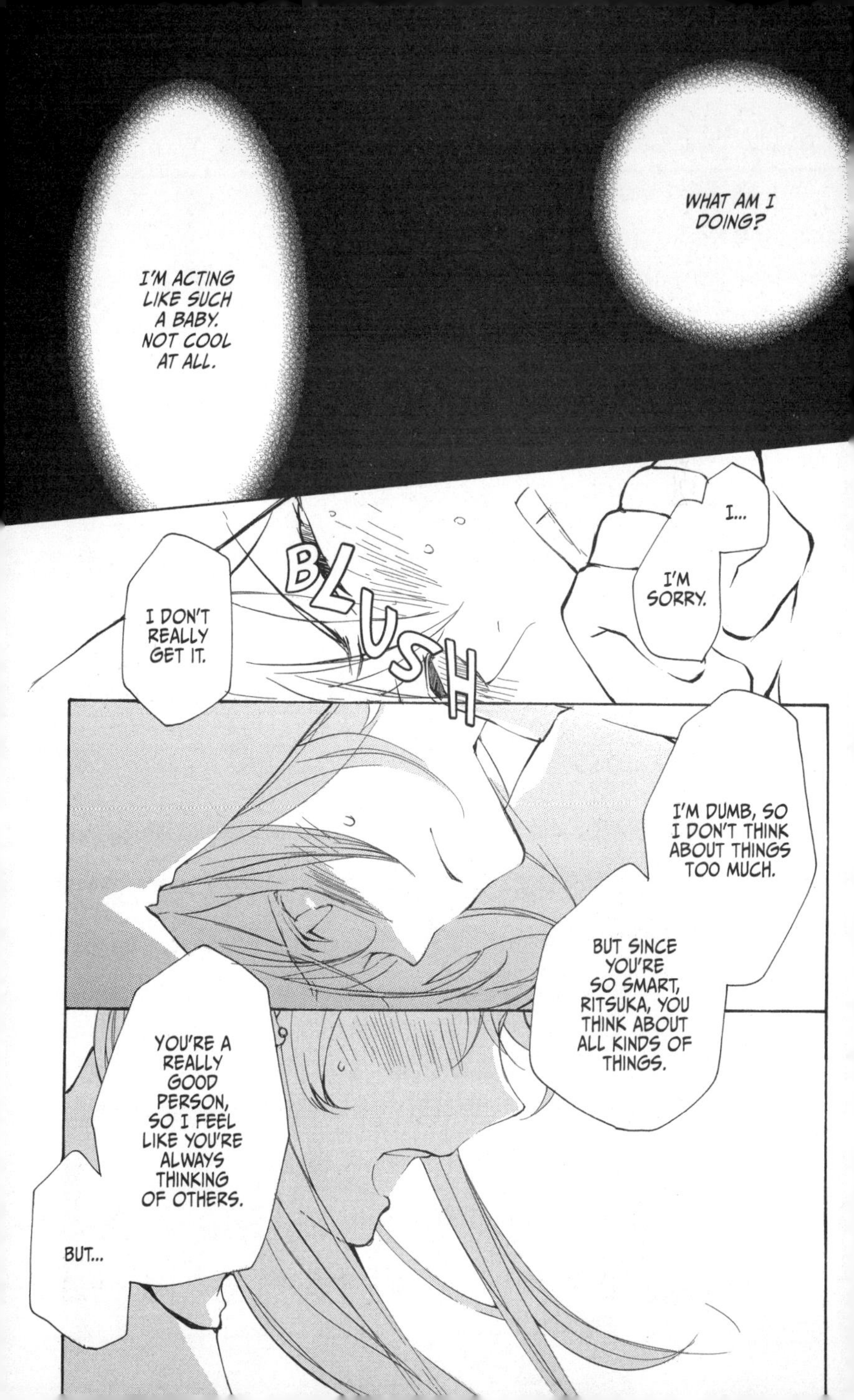
WHAT AM I DOING?
I'M ACTING LIKE SUCH A BABY. NOT COOL AT ALL.
I...
I'M SORRY.
BLUSH
I DON'T REALLY GET IT.
I'M DUMB, SO I DON'T THINK ABOUT THINGS TOO MUCH.
BUT SINCE YOU'RE SO SMART, RITSUKA, YOU THINK ABOUT ALL KINDS OF THINGS.
YOU'RE A REALLY GOOD PERSON, SO I FEEL LIKE YOU'RE ALWAYS THINKING OF OTHERS.
BUT...

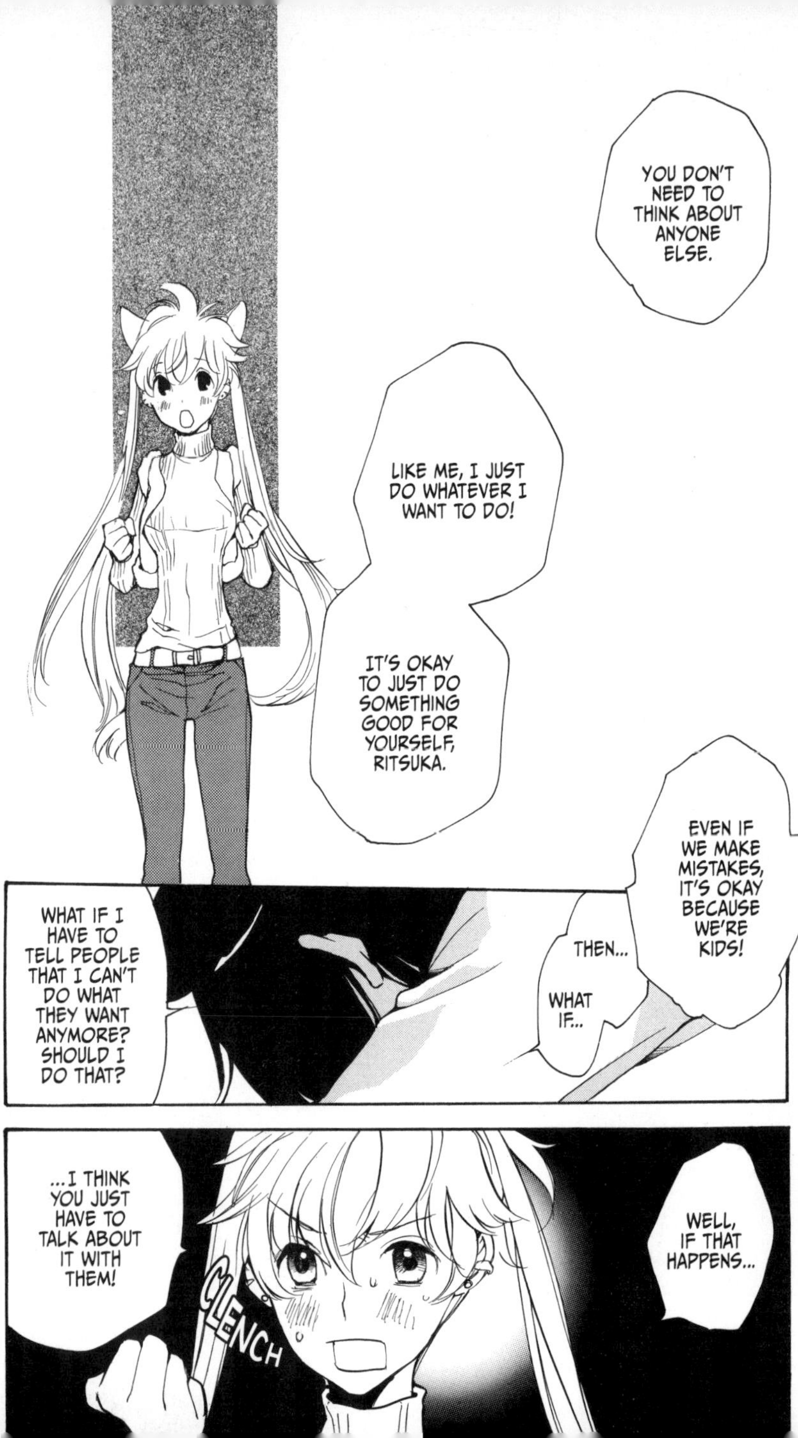
YOU DON'T NEED TO THINK ABOUT ANYONE ELSE.
LIKE ME, I JUST DO WHATEVER I WANT TO DO!
IT'S OKAY TO JUST DO SOMETHING GOOD FOR YOURSELF, RITSUKA.
EVEN IF WE MAKE MISTAKES, IT'S OKAY BECAUSE WE'RE KIDS!
THEN...
WHAT IF...
WHAT IF I HAVE TO TELL PEOPLE THAT I CAN'T DO WHAT THEY WANT ANYMORE? SHOULD I DO THAT?
WELL, IF THAT HAPPENS...
CLENCH
...I THINK YOU JUST HAVE TO TALK ABOUT IT WITH THEM!

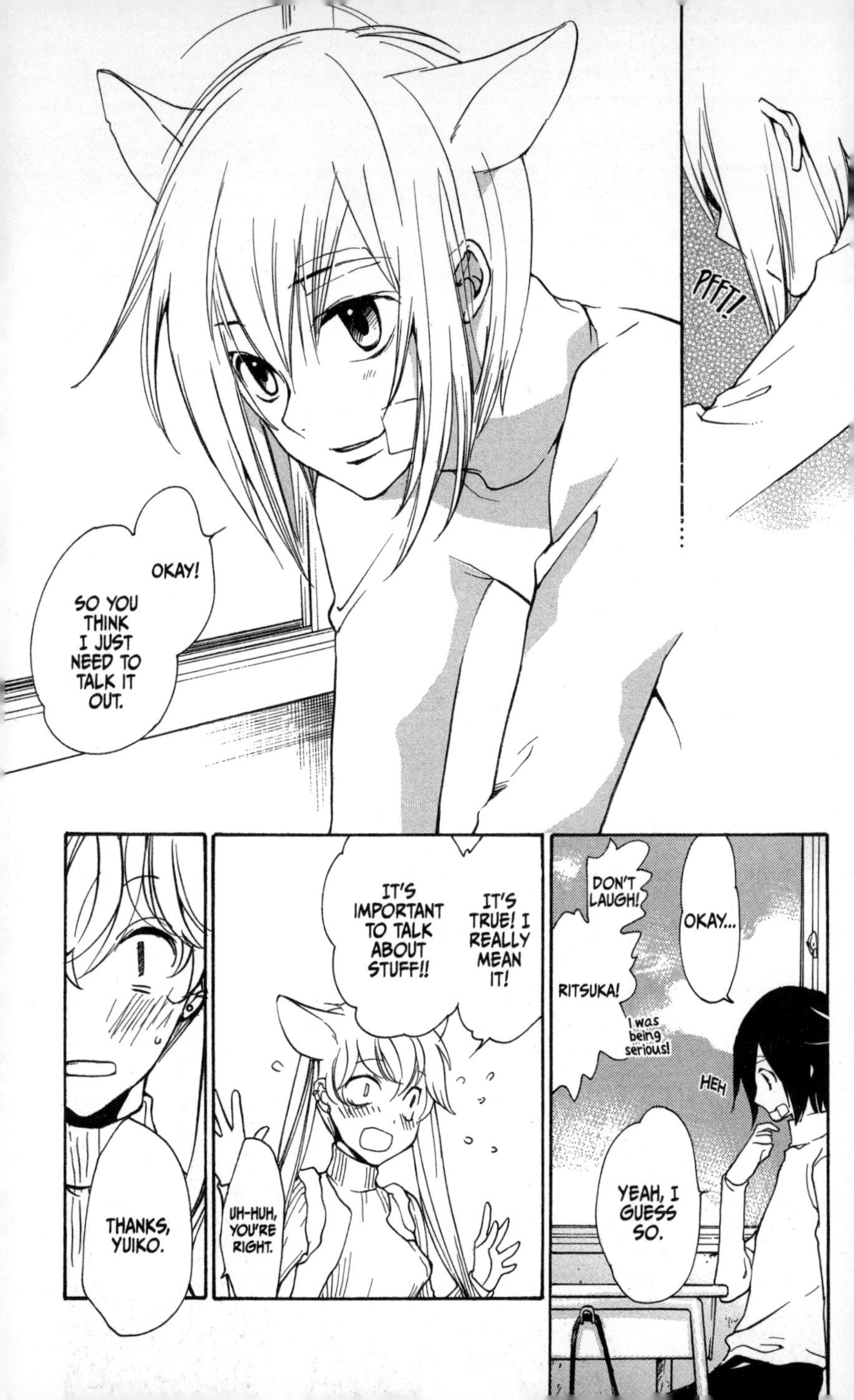
PFFT!
OKAY!
SO YOU THINK I JUST NEED TO TALK IT OUT.
OKAY...
DON'T LAUGH!
RITSUKA!
I was being serious!
HEH
YEAH, I GUESS SO.
IT'S TRUE! I REALLY MEAN IT!
IT'S IMPORTANT TO TALK ABOUT STUFF!!
UH-HUH, YOU'RE RIGHT.
THANKS, YUIKO.

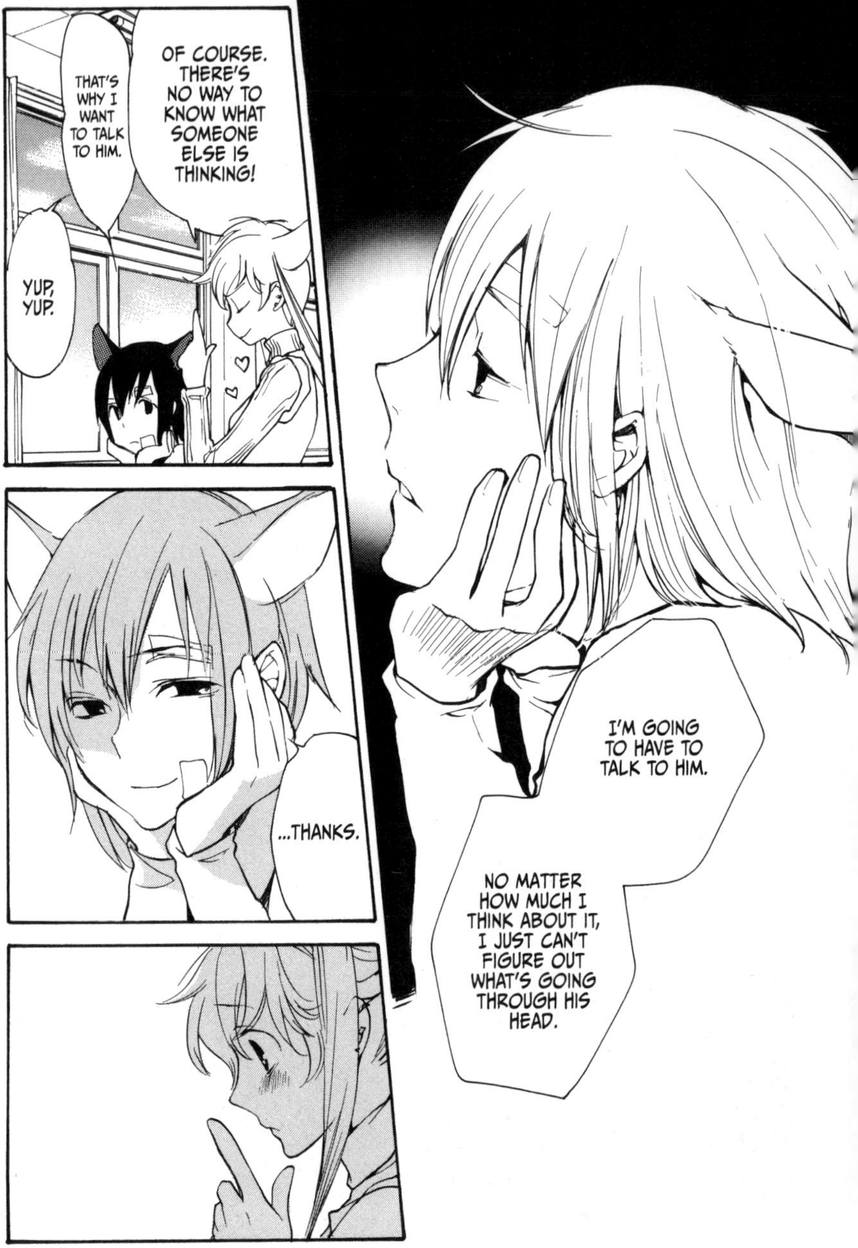
I'M GOING TO HAVE TO TALK TO HIM.
NO MATTER HOW MUCH I THINK ABOUT IT, I JUST CAN'T FIGURE OUT WHAT'S GOING THROUGH HIS HEAD.
OF COURSE. THERE'S NO WAY TO KNOW WHAT SOMEONE ELSE IS THINKING!
THAT'S WHY I WANT TO TALK TO HIM.
YUP, YUP.
...THANKS.

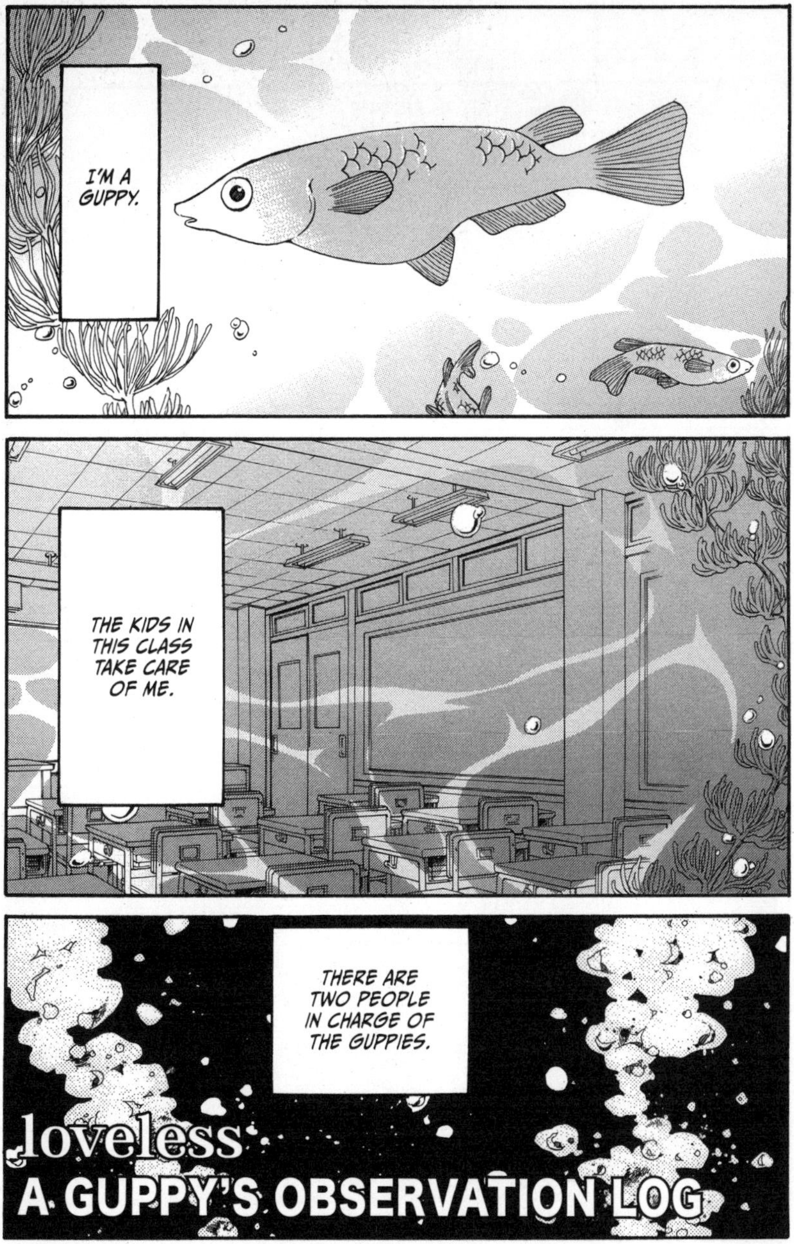
I'M A GUPPY.
THE KIDS IN THIS CLASS TAKE CARE OF ME.
THERE ARE TWO PEOPLE IN CHARGE OF THE GUPPIES.
loveless
A GUPPY'S OBSERVATION LOG

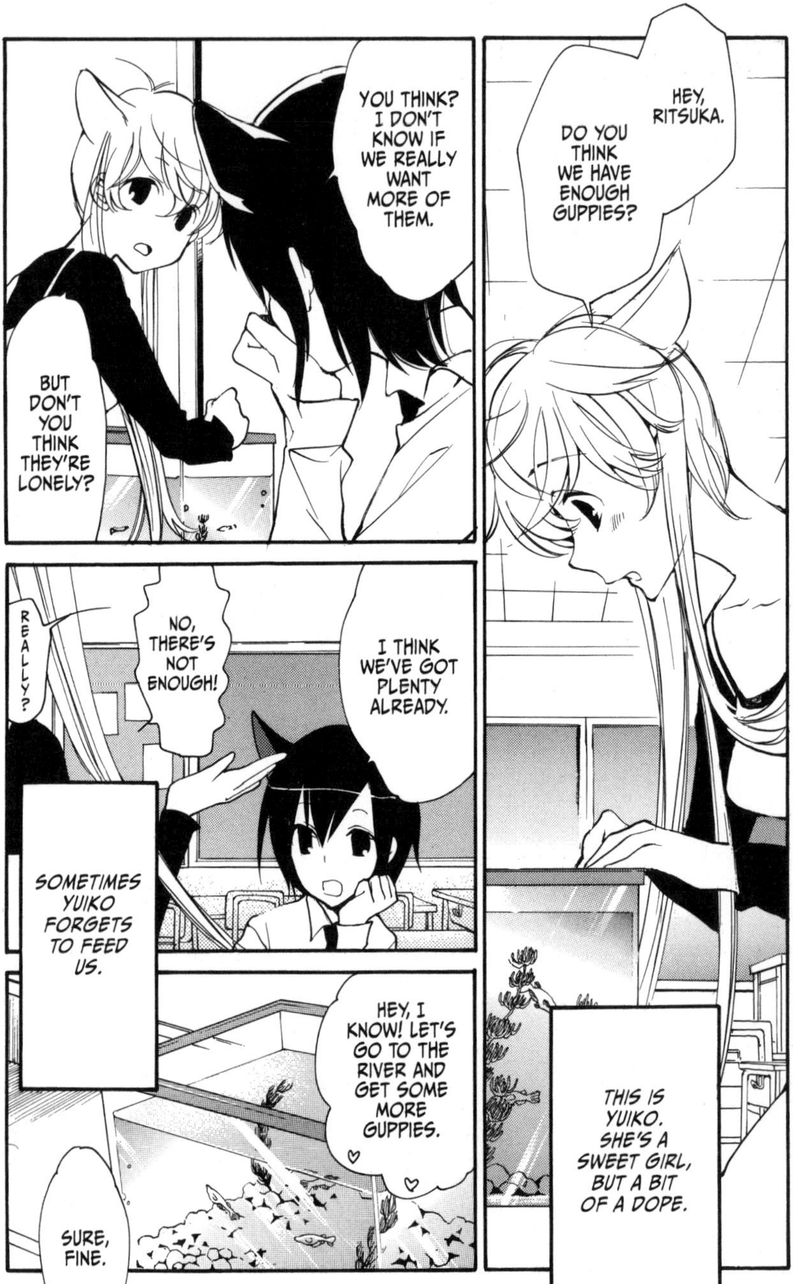
HEY, RITSUKA.
DO YOU THINK WE HAVE ENOUGH GUPPIES?
THIS IS YUIKO. SHE'S A SWEET GIRL, BUT A BIT OF A DOPE.
YOU THINK? I DON'T KNOW IF WE REALLY WANT MORE OF THEM.
BUT DON'T YOU THINK THEY'RE LONELY?
I THINK WE'VE GOT PLENTY ALREADY.
NO, THERE'S NOT ENOUGH!
REALLY?
SOMETIMES YUIKO FORGETS TO FEED US.
HEY, I KNOW! LET'S GO TO THE RIVER AND GET SOME MORE GUPPIES.
SURE, FINE.

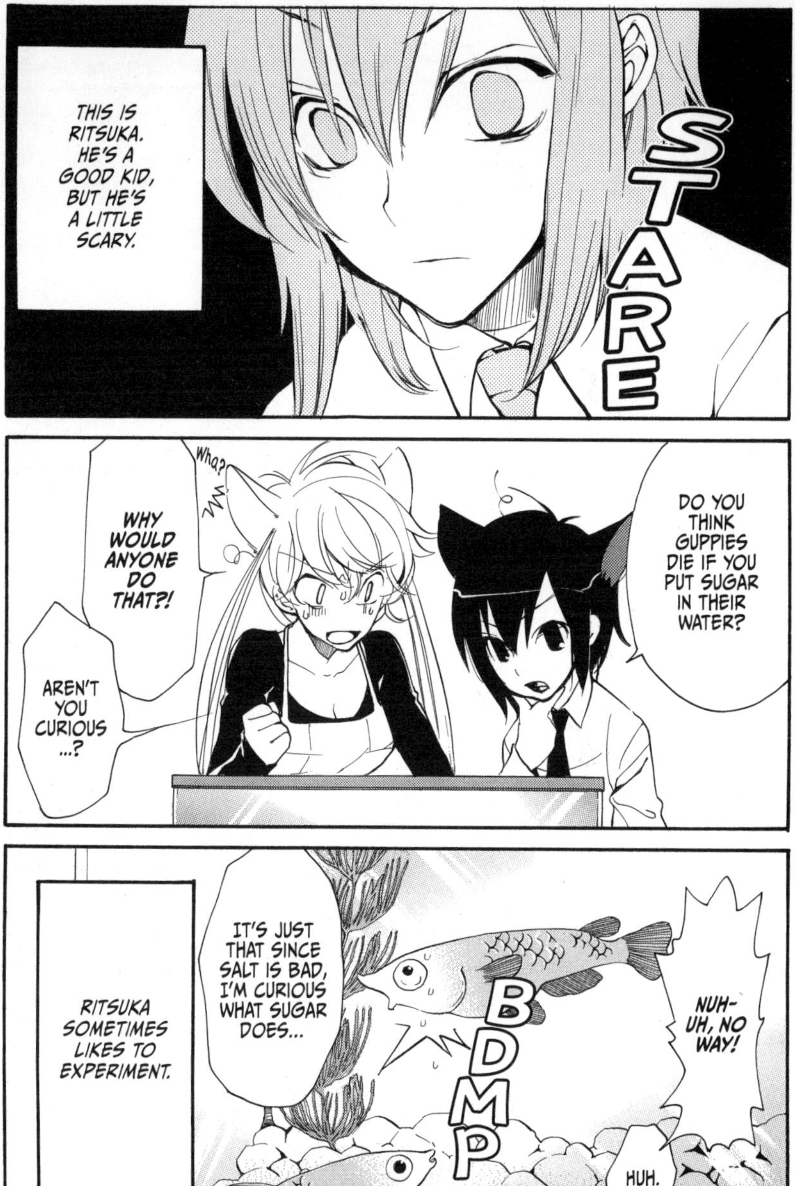
STARE
THIS IS RITSUKA. HE'S A GOOD KID, BUT HE'S A LITTLE SCARY.
DO YOU THINK GUPPIES DIE IF YOU PUT SUGAR IN THEIR WATER?
Wha?
WHY WOULD ANYONE DO THAT?!
AREN'T YOU CURIOUS ...?
NUH-UH, NO WAY!
IT'S JUST THAT SINCE SALT IS BAD, I'M CURIOUS WHAT SUGAR DOES...
BDMP
HUH.
RITSUKA SOMETIMES LIKES TO EXPERIMENT.

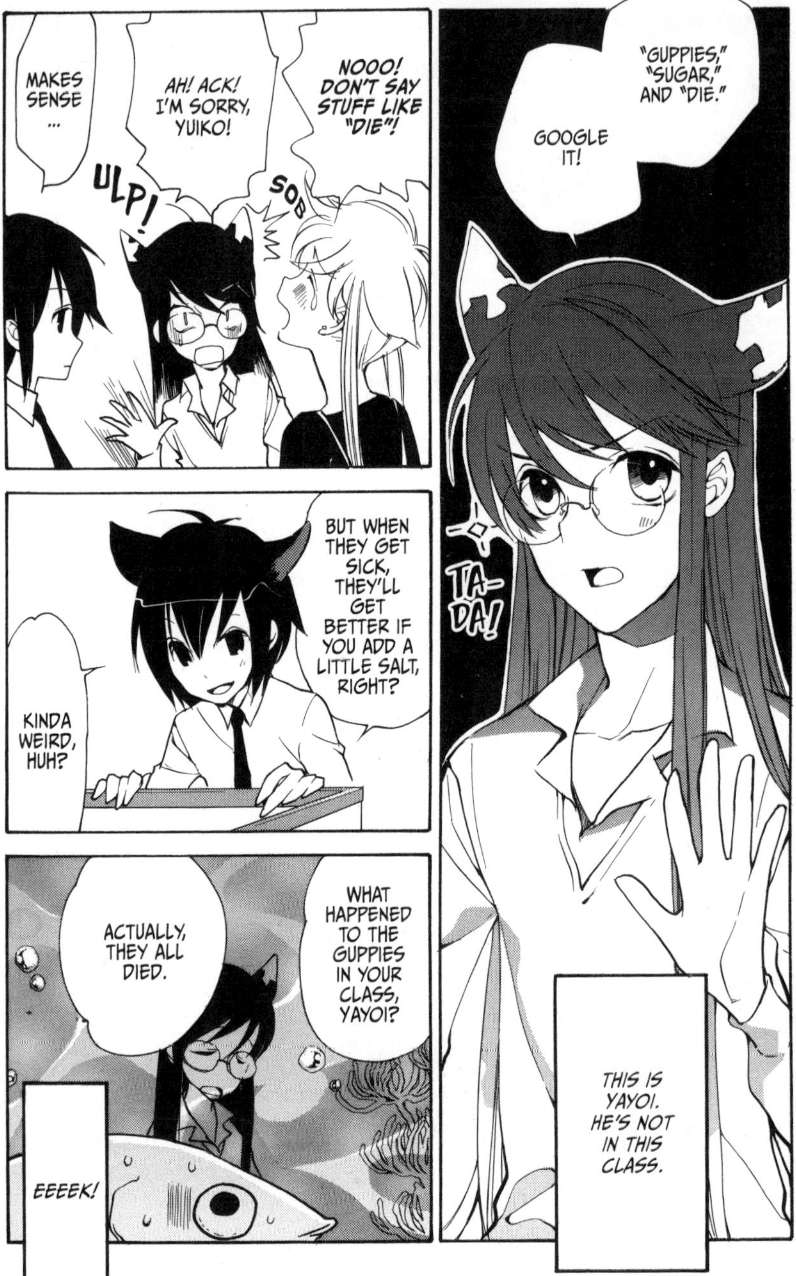
"GUPPIES," "SUGAR," AND "DIE."
GOOGLE IT!
TA-DA!
THIS IS YAYOI. HE'S NOT IN THIS CLASS.
NOOO! DON'T SAY STUFF LIKE "DIE"!
SOB
AH! ACK! I'M SORRY, YUIKO!
ULP!
MAKES SENSE ...
BUT WHEN THEY GET SICK, THEY'LL GET BETTER IF YOU ADD A LITTLE SALT, RIGHT?
KINDA WEIRD, HUH?
WHAT HAPPENED TO THE GUPPIES IN YOUR CLASS, YAYOI?
ACTUALLY, THEY ALL DIED.
EEEEK!

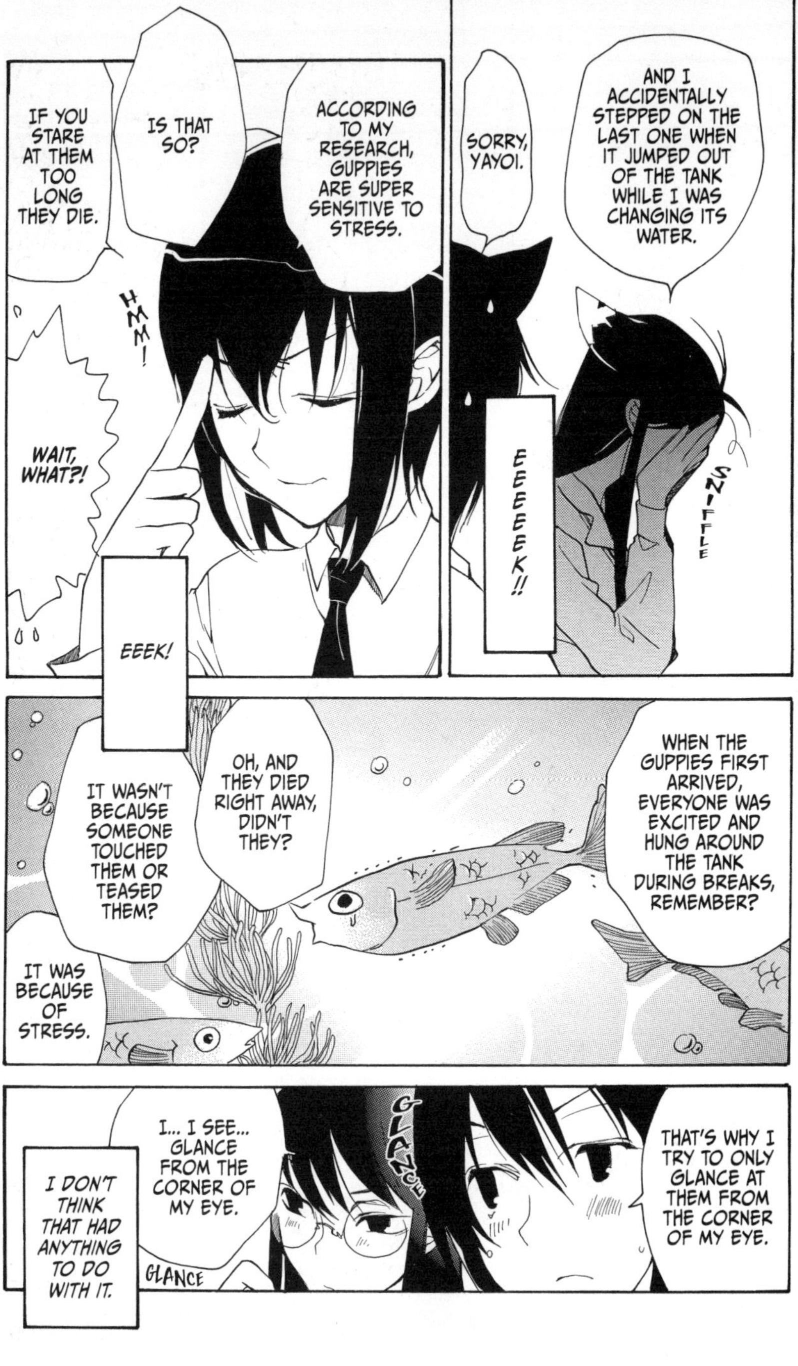
AND I ACCIDENTALLY STEPPED ON THE LAST ONE WHEN IT JUMPED OUT OF THE TANK WHILE I WAS CHANGING ITS WATER.
SORRY, YAYOI.
EEEEEEK!!
SNIFFLE
ACCORDING TO MY RESEARCH, GUPPIES ARE SUPER SENSITIVE TO STRESS.
IS THAT SO?
IF YOU STARE AT THEM TOO LONG THEY DIE.
HMM!
WAIT, WHAT?!
EEEK!
WHEN THE GUPPIES FIRST ARRIVED, EVERYONE WAS EXCITED AND HUNG AROUND THE TANK DURING BREAKS, REMEMBER?
OH, AND THEY DIED RIGHT AWAY, DIDN'T THEY?
IT WASN'T BECAUSE SOMEONE TOUCHED THEM OR TEASED THEM?
IT WAS BECAUSE OF STRESS.
THAT'S WHY I TRY TO ONLY GLANCE AT THEM FROM THE CORNER OF MY EYE.
GLANCE
I... I SEE... GLANCE FROM THE CORNER OF MY EYE.
GLANCE
I DON'T THINK THAT HAD ANYTHING TO DO WITH IT.

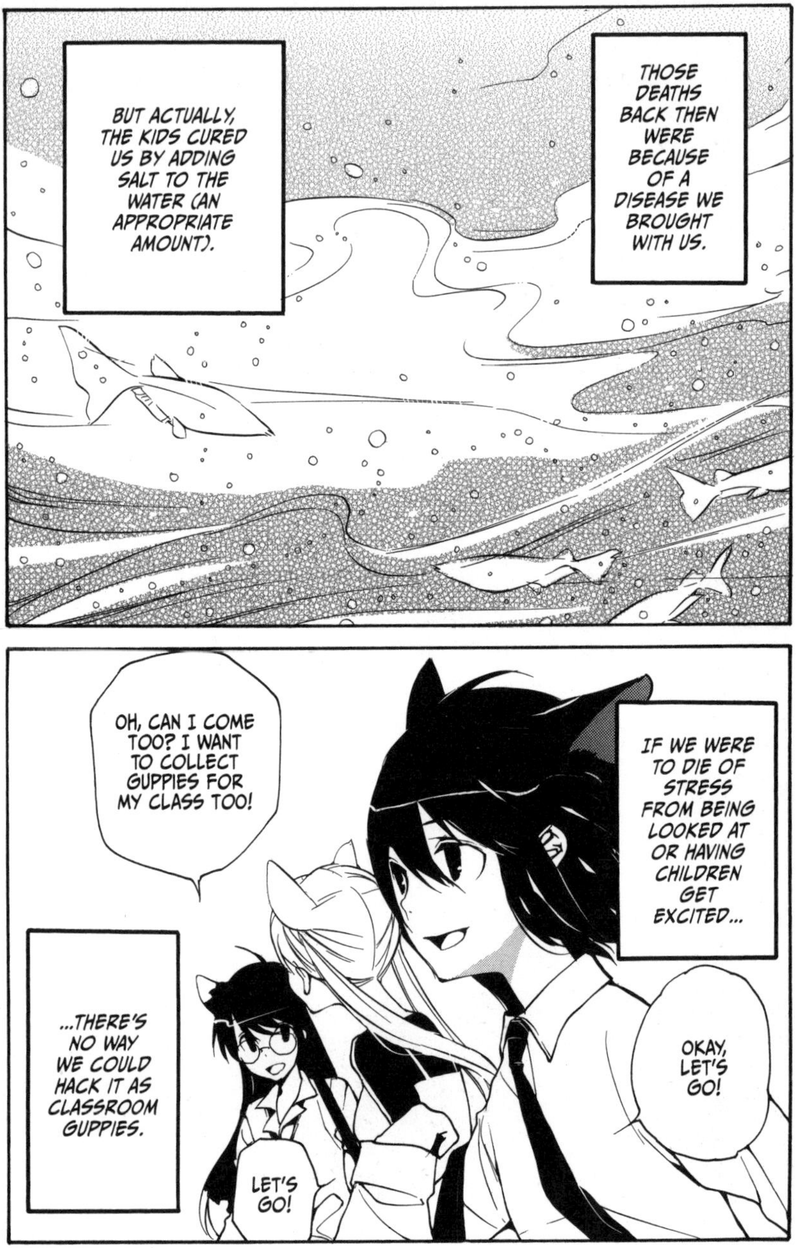
THOSE DEATHS BACK THEN WERE BECAUSE OF A DISEASE WE BROUGHT WITH US.
BUT ACTUALLY, THE KIDS CURED US BY ADDING SALT TO THE WATER (AN APPROPRIATE AMOUNT).
IF WE WERE TO DIE OF STRESS FROM BEING LOOKED AT OR HAVING CHILDREN GET EXCITED...
OH, CAN I COME TOO? I WANT TO COLLECT GUPPIES FOR MY CLASS TOO!
OKAY, LET'S GO!
...THERE'S NO WAY WE COULD HACK IT AS CLASSROOM GUPPIES.
LET'S GO!

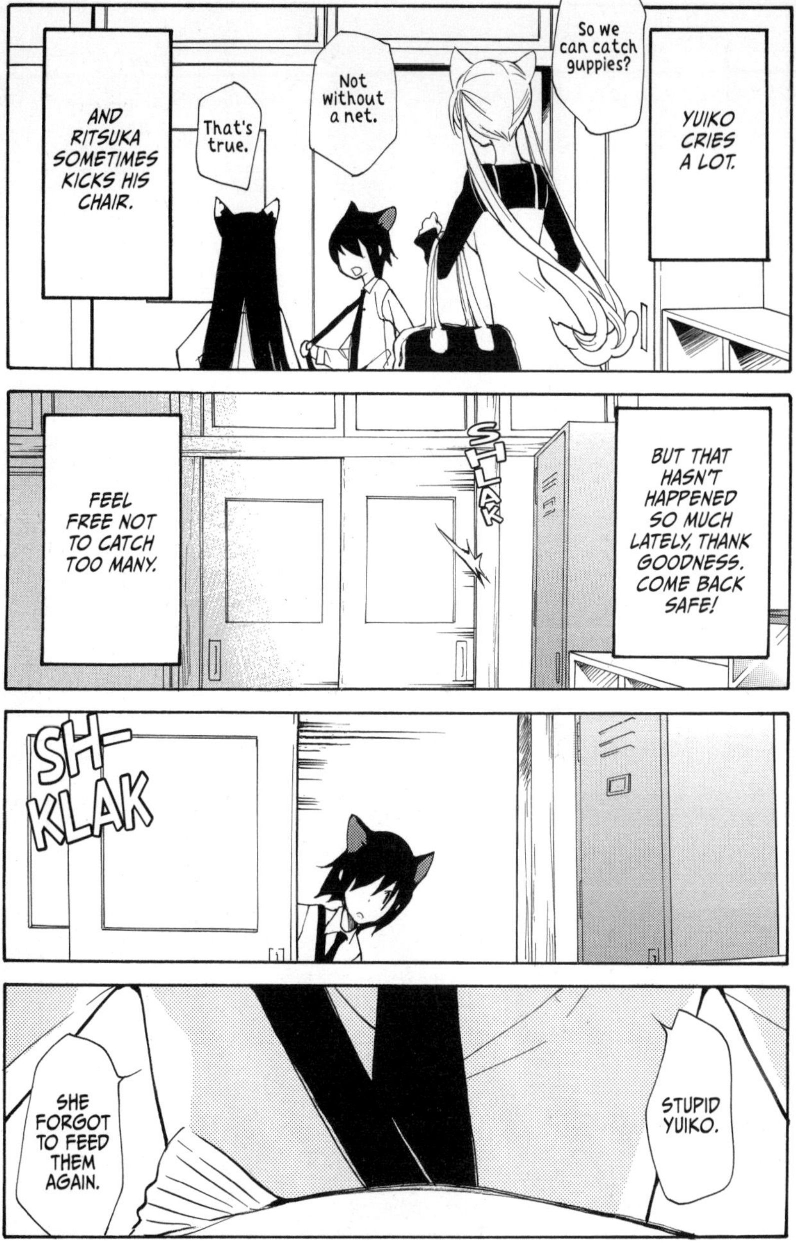
YUIKO CRIES A LOT.
So we can catch guppies?
Not without a net.
That's true.
AND RITSUKA SOMETIMES KICKS HIS CHAIR.
BUT THAT HASN'T HAPPENED SO MUCH LATELY, THANK GOODNESS. COME BACK SAFE!
SHLAK
FEEL FREE NOT TO CATCH TOO MANY.
SH-KLAK
STUPID YUIKO.
SHE FORGOT TO FEED THEM AGAIN.

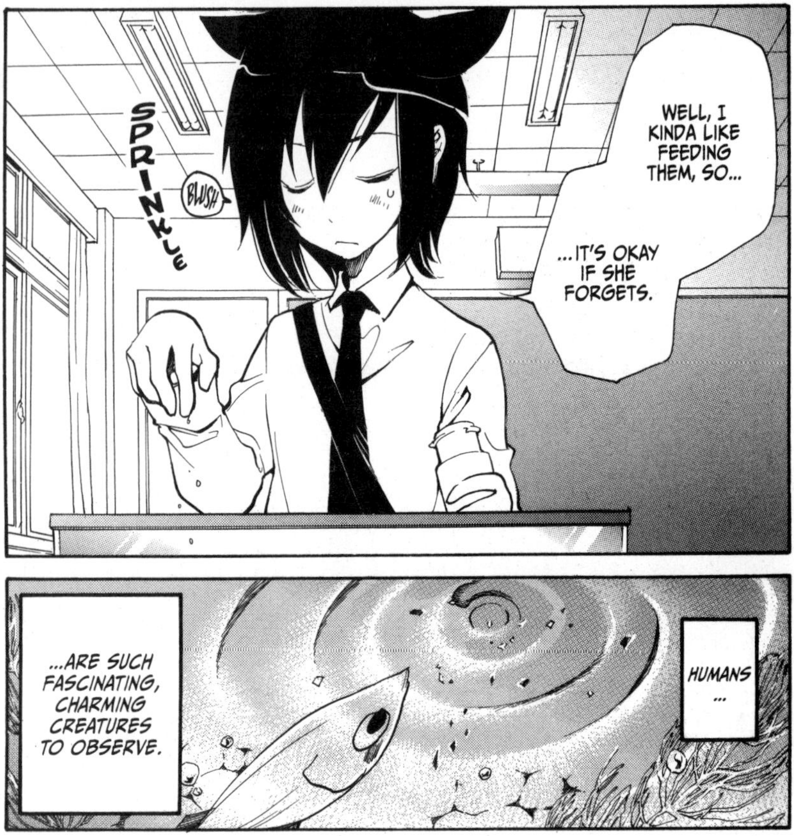
WELL, I KINDA LIKE FEEDING THEM, SO...
...IT'S OKAY IF SHE FORGETS.
BLUSH
SPRINKLE
HUMANS...
...ARE SUCH FASCINATING, CHARMING CREATURES TO OBSERVE.

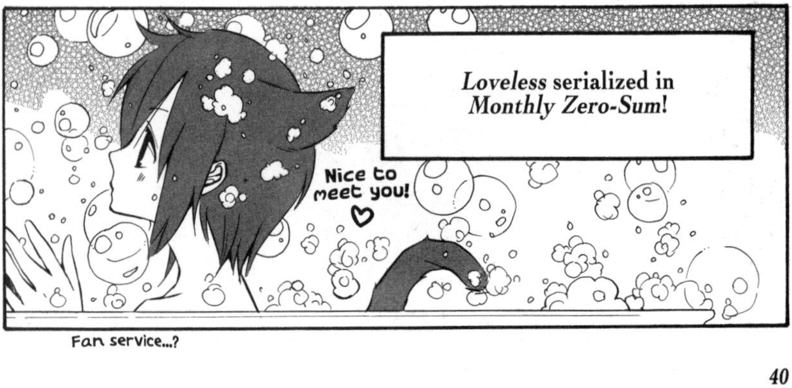
Loveless serialized in Monthly Zero-Sum!
Nice to meet you!

Fan service...?

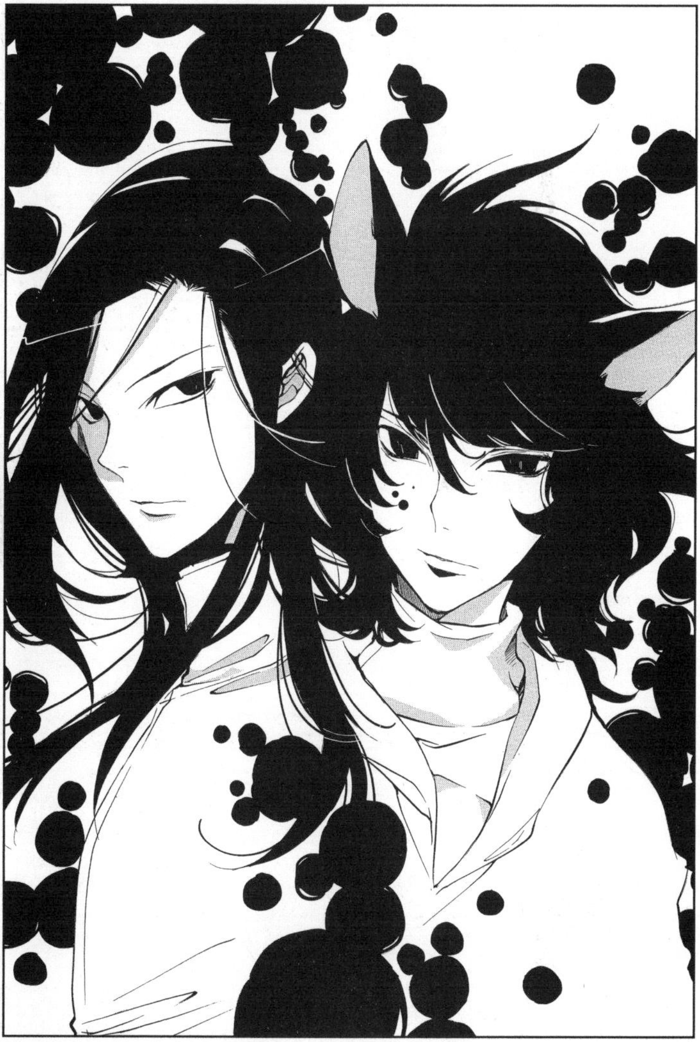

LOVELESS

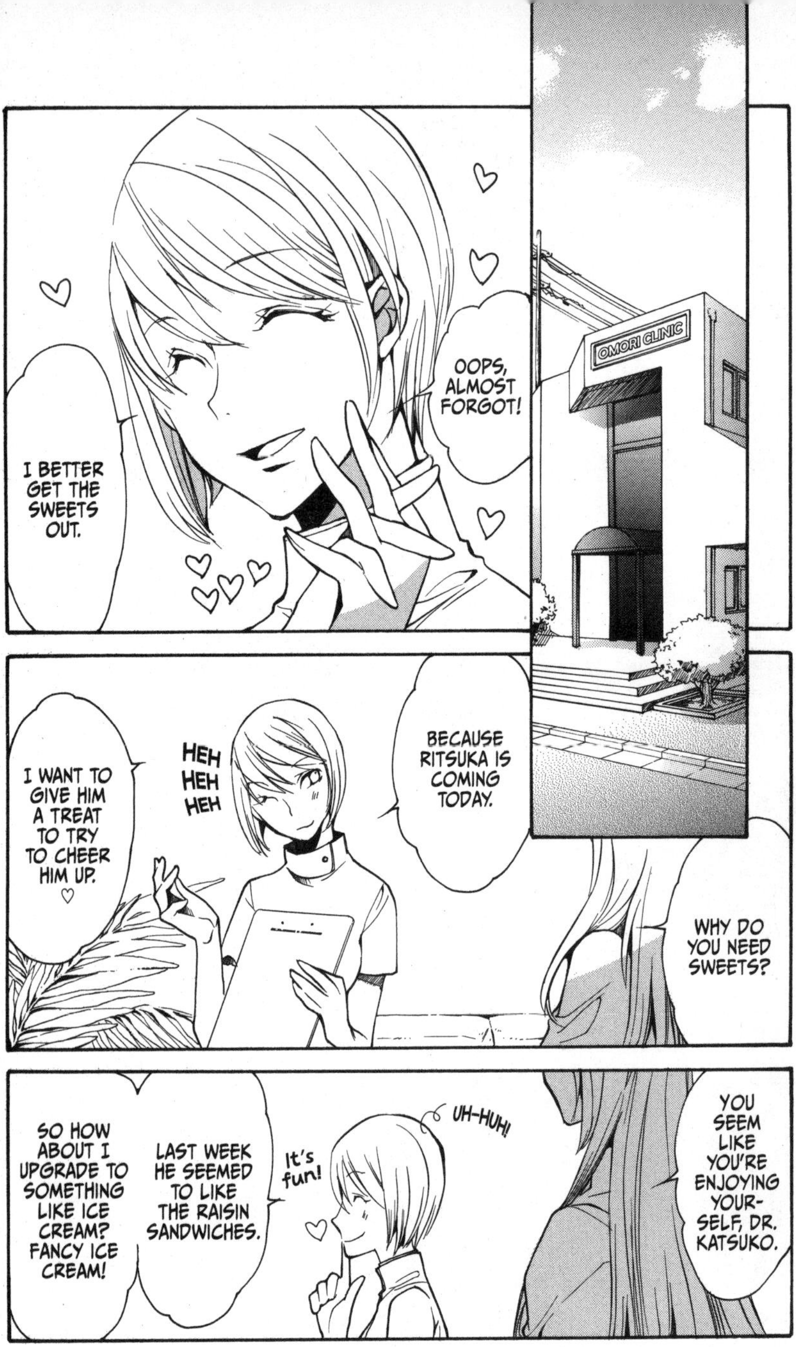
OMORI CLINIC
OOPS, ALMOST FORGOT!
I BETTER GET THE SWEETS OUT.
WHY DO YOU NEED SWEETS?
BECAUSE RITSUKA IS COMING TODAY.
HEH HEH HEH
I WANT TO GIVE HIM A TREAT TO TRY TO CHEER HIM UP. ♡
YOU SEEM LIKE YOU'RE ENJOYING YOURSELF, DR. KATSUKO.
UH-HUH!
It's fun!
LAST WEEK HE SEEMED TO LIKE THE RAISIN SANDWICHES.
SO HOW ABOUT I UPGRADE TO SOMETHING LIKE ICE CREAM? FANCY ICE CREAM!

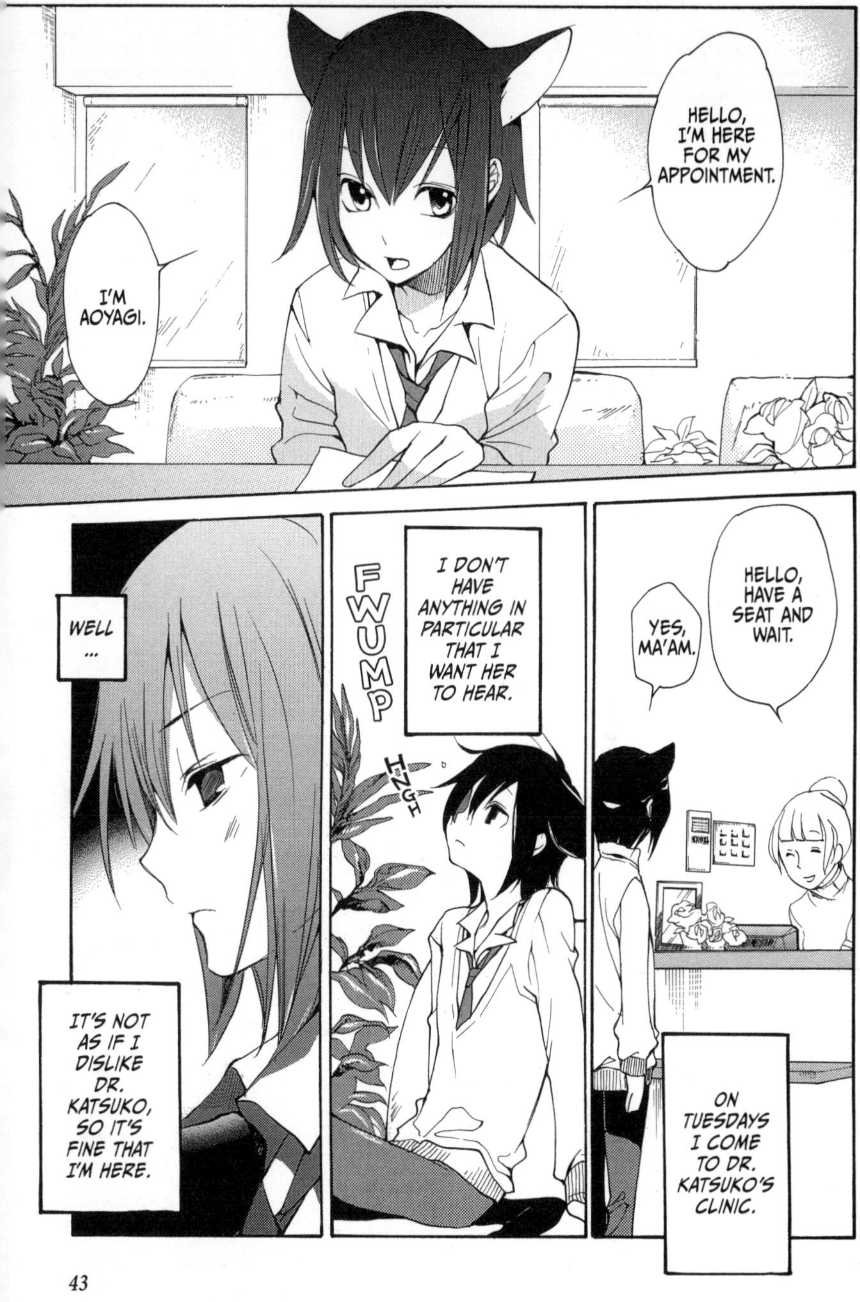
HELLO, I'M HERE FOR MY APPOINTMENT.
I'M AOYAGI.
HELLO, HAVE A SEAT AND WAIT.
YES, MA'AM.
ON TUESDAYS I COME TO DR. KATSUKO'S CLINIC.
I DON'T HAVE ANYTHING IN PARTICULAR THAT I WANT HER TO HEAR.
FWUMP
HNGH
WELL ...
IT'S NOT AS IF I DISLIKE DR. KATSUKO, SO IT'S FINE THAT I'M HERE.

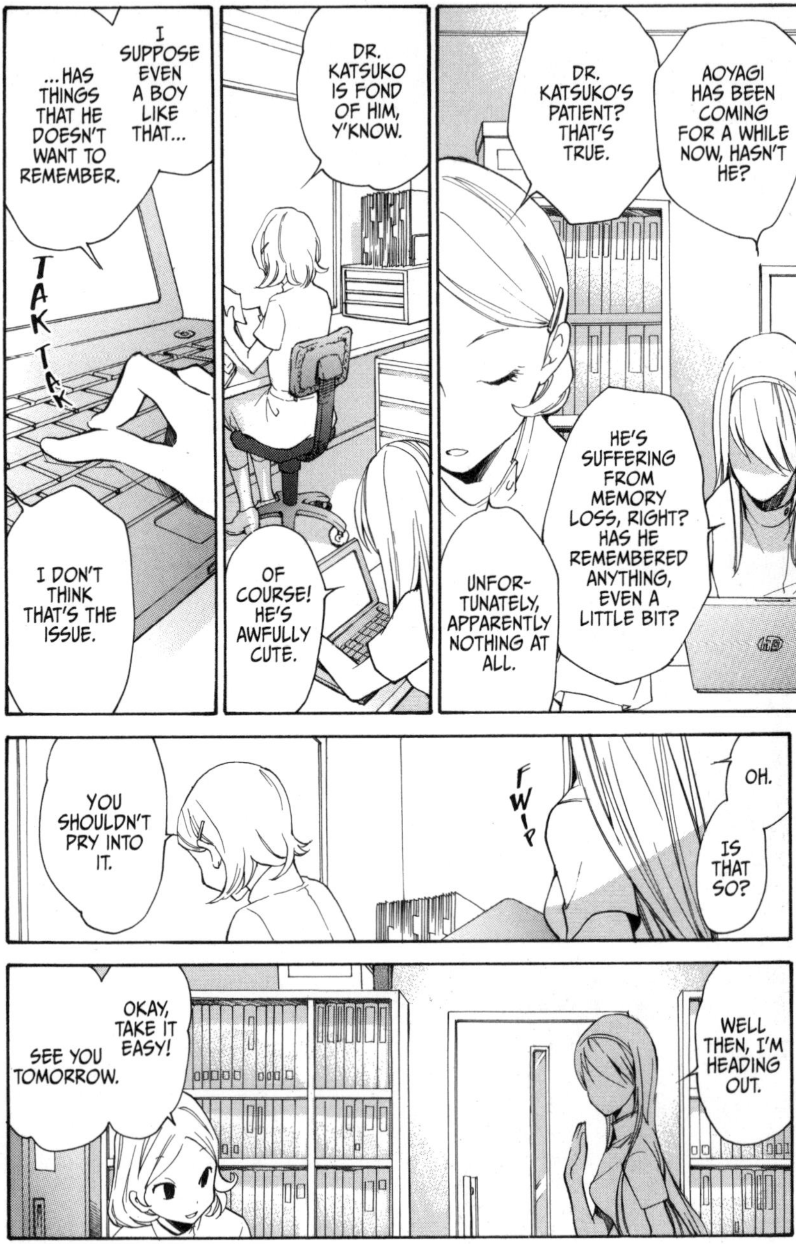
AOYAGI HAS BEEN COMING FOR A WHILE NOW, HASN'T HE?
DR. KATSUKO'S PATIENT? THAT'S TRUE.
HE'S SUFFERING FROM MEMORY LOSS, RIGHT? HAS HE REMEMBERED ANYTHING, EVEN A LITTLE BIT?
UNFOR-TUNATELY, APPARENTLY NOTHING AT ALL.
DR. KATSUKO IS FOND OF HIM, Y'KNOW.
OF COURSE! HE'S AWFULLY CUTE.
I SUPPOSE EVEN A BOY LIKE THAT...
...HAS THINGS THAT HE DOESN'T WANT TO REMEMBER.
TAK TAK
I DON'T THINK THAT'S THE ISSUE.
OH.
IS THAT SO?
FWIP
YOU SHOULDN'T PRY INTO IT.
WELL THEN, I'M HEADING OUT.
OKAY, TAKE IT EASY!
SEE YOU TOMORROW.

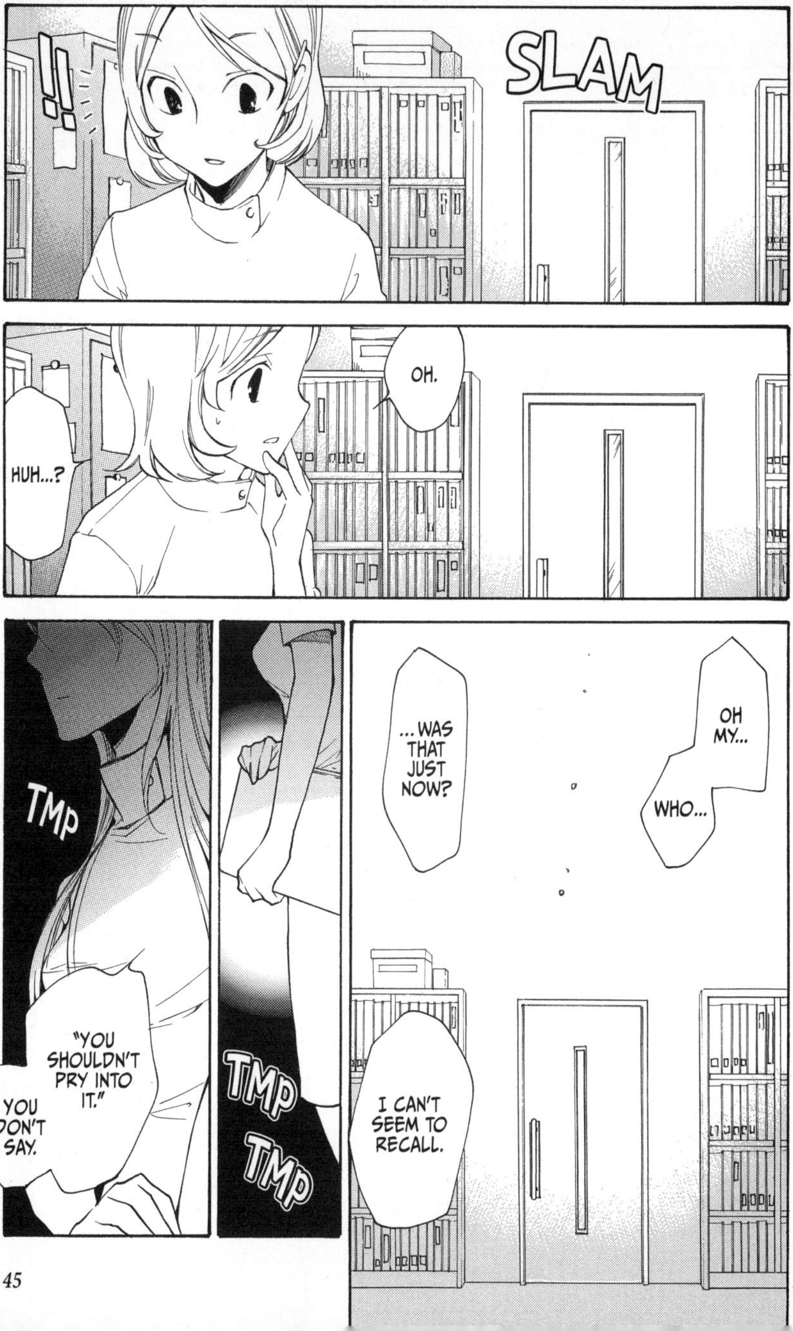
SLAM
!!
OH.
HUH...?
OH MY...
WHO...
...WAS THAT JUST NOW?
I CAN'T SEEM TO RECALL.
TMP
TMP
TMP
"YOU SHOULDN'T PRY INTO IT."
YOU DON'T SAY.

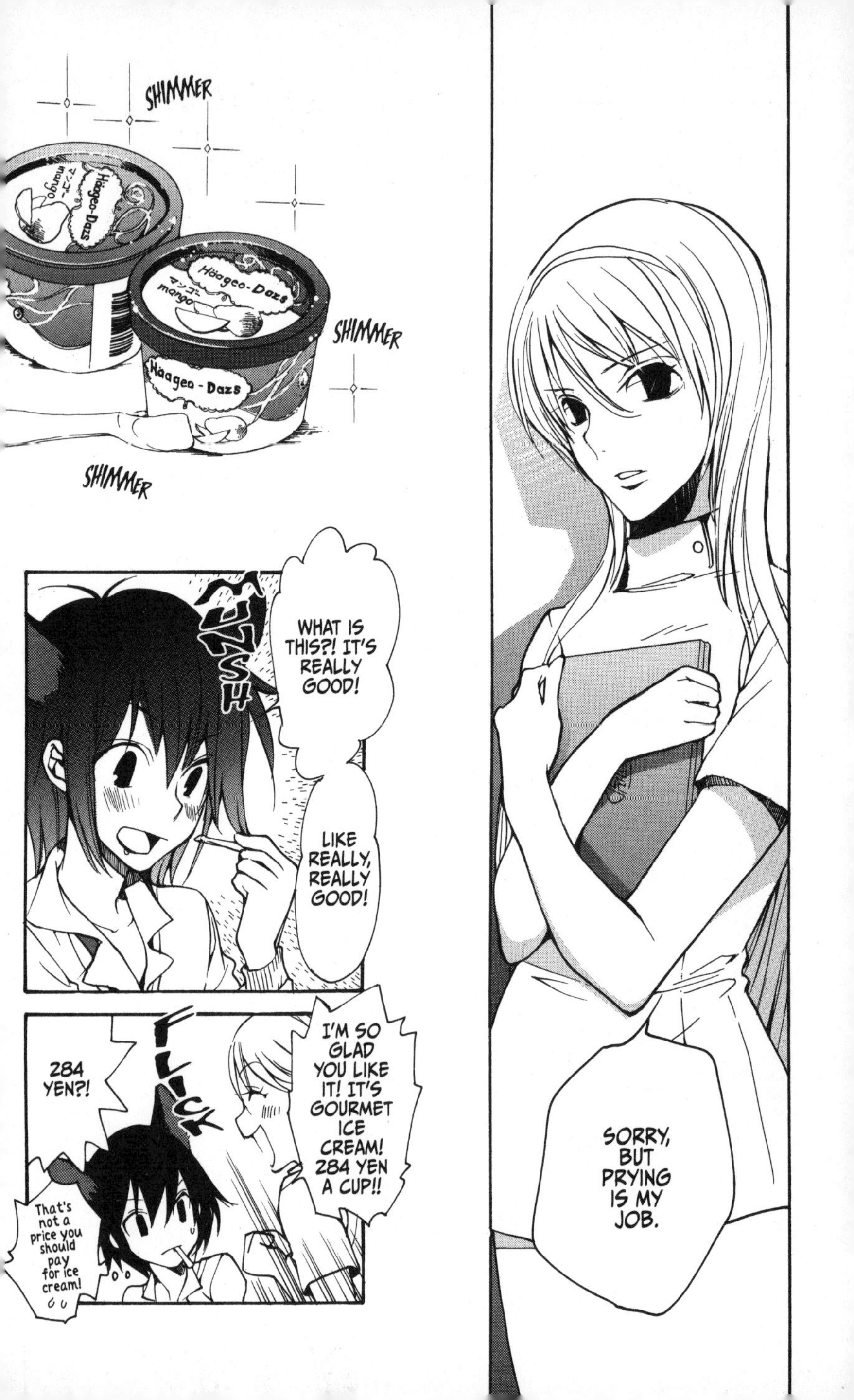

SORRY, BUT PRYING IS MY JOB.
SHIMMER
Häagen-Dazs
mango
SHIMMER
SHIMMER
WHAT IS THIS?! IT'S REALLY GOOD!
LIKE REALLY, REALLY GOOD!
I'M SO GLAD YOU LIKE IT! IT'S GOURMET ICE CREAM! 284 YEN A CUP!!
284 YEN?!
FLICK
That's not a price you should pay for ice cream!

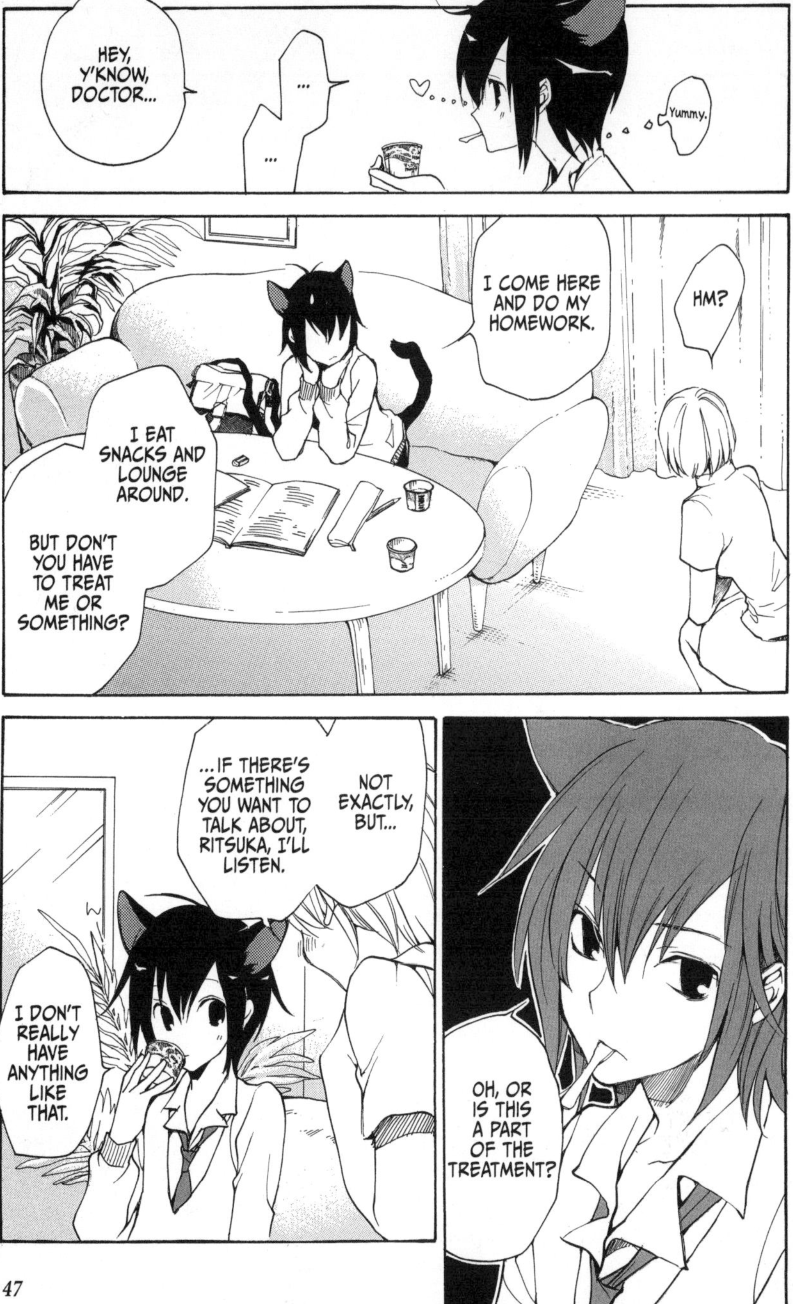
Yummy.
...
...
HEY, Y'KNOW, DOCTOR...
HM?
I COME HERE AND DO MY HOMEWORK.
I EAT SNACKS AND LOUNGE AROUND.
BUT DON'T YOU HAVE TO TREAT ME OR SOMETHING?
OH, OR IS THIS A PART OF THE TREATMENT?
NOT EXACTLY, BUT...
...IF THERE'S SOMETHING YOU WANT TO TALK ABOUT, RITSUKA, I'LL LISTEN.
I DON'T REALLY HAVE ANYTHING LIKE THAT.

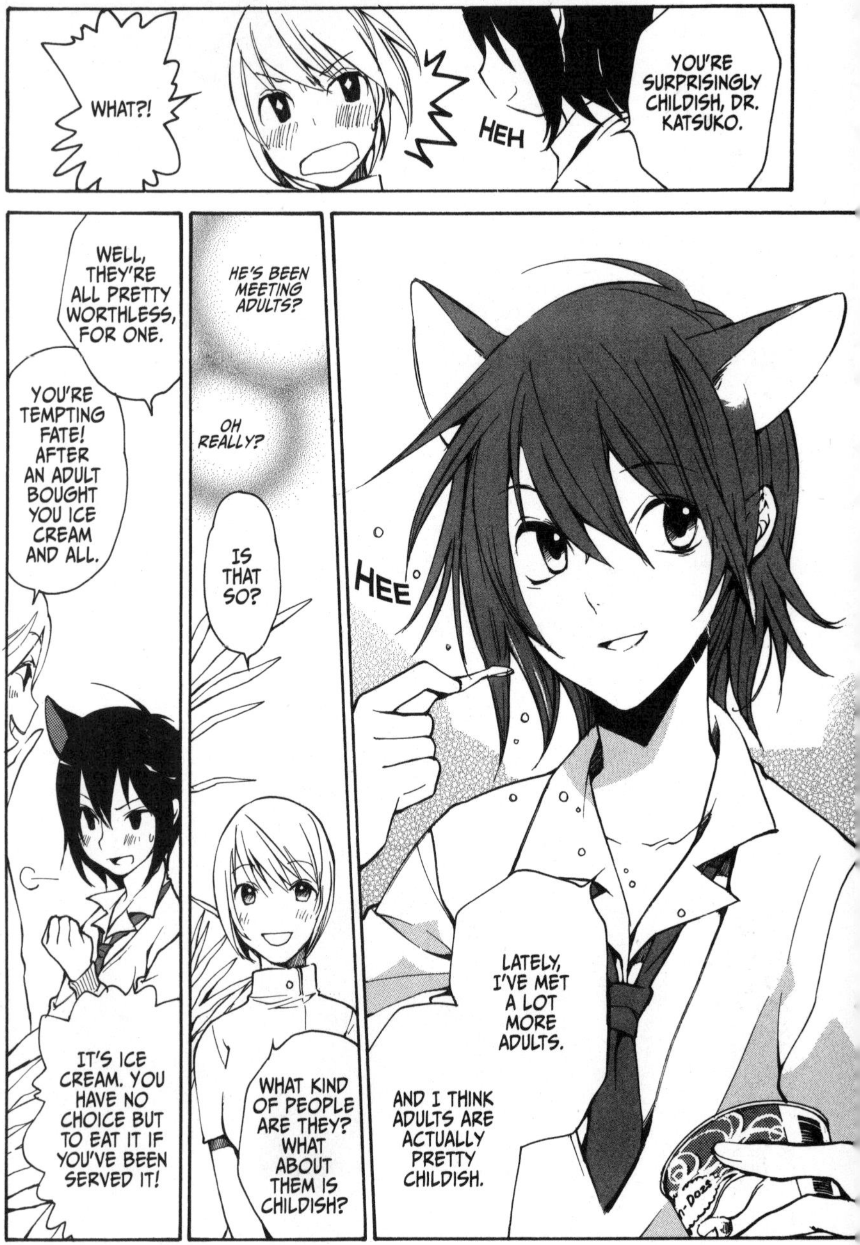
YOU'RE SURPRISINGLY CHILDISH, DR. KATSUKO.
HEH
WHAT?!
HEE
LATELY, I'VE MET A LOT MORE ADULTS.
AND I THINK ADULTS ARE ACTUALLY PRETTY CHILDISH.
HE'S BEEN MEETING ADULTS?
OH REALLY?
IS THAT SO?
WHAT KIND OF PEOPLE ARE THEY? WHAT ABOUT THEM IS CHILDISH?
WELL, THEY'RE ALL PRETTY WORTHLESS, FOR ONE.
YOU'RE TEMPTING FATE! AFTER AN ADULT BOUGHT YOU ICE CREAM AND ALL.
IT'S ICE CREAM. YOU HAVE NO CHOICE BUT TO EAT IT IF YOU'VE BEEN SERVED IT!

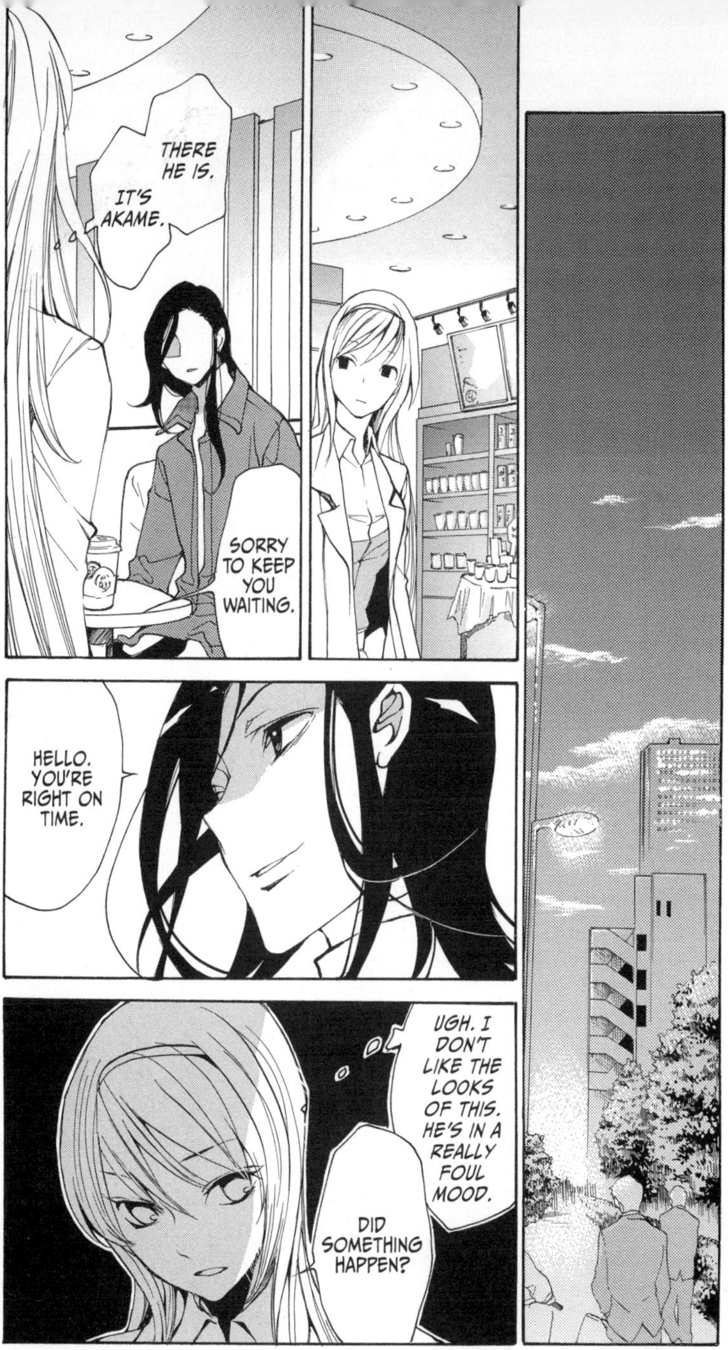
THERE HE IS.
IT'S AKAME.
SORRY TO KEEP YOU WAITING.
HELLO. YOU'RE RIGHT ON TIME.
UGH. I DON'T LIKE THE LOOKS OF THIS. HE'S IN A REALLY FOUL MOOD.
DID SOMETHING HAPPEN?

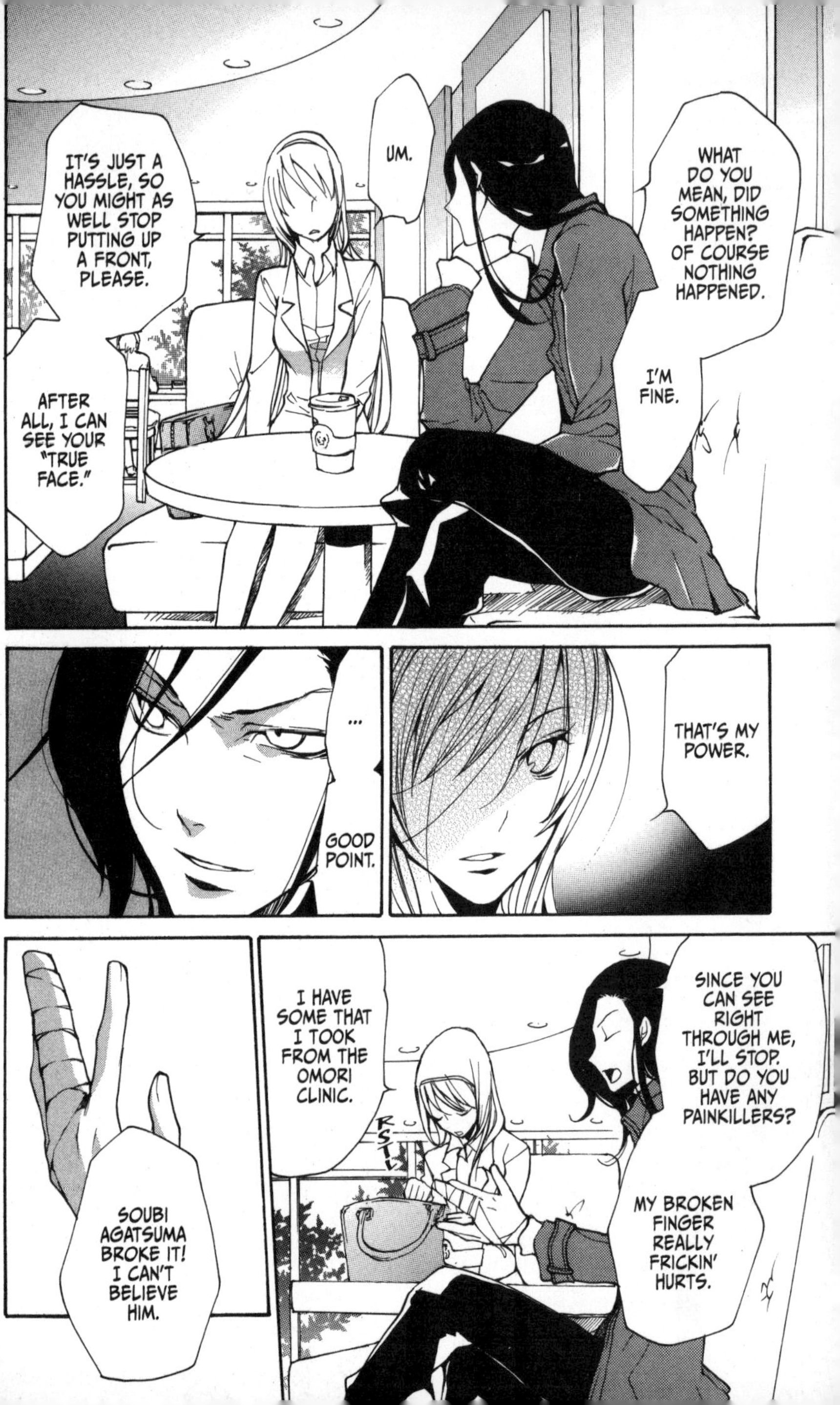
WHAT DO YOU MEAN, DID SOMETHING HAPPEN? OF COURSE NOTHING HAPPENED.
I'M FINE.
UM.
IT'S JUST A HASSLE, SO YOU MIGHT AS WELL STOP PUTTING UP A FRONT, PLEASE.
AFTER ALL, I CAN SEE YOUR "TRUE FACE."
THAT'S MY POWER.
...
GOOD POINT.
SINCE YOU CAN SEE RIGHT THROUGH ME, I'LL STOP. BUT DO YOU HAVE ANY PAINKILLERS?
MY BROKEN FINGER REALLY FRICKIN' HURTS.
I HAVE SOME THAT I TOOK FROM THE OMORI CLINIC.
RSTL
SOUBI AGATSUMA BROKE IT! I CAN'T BELIEVE HIM.

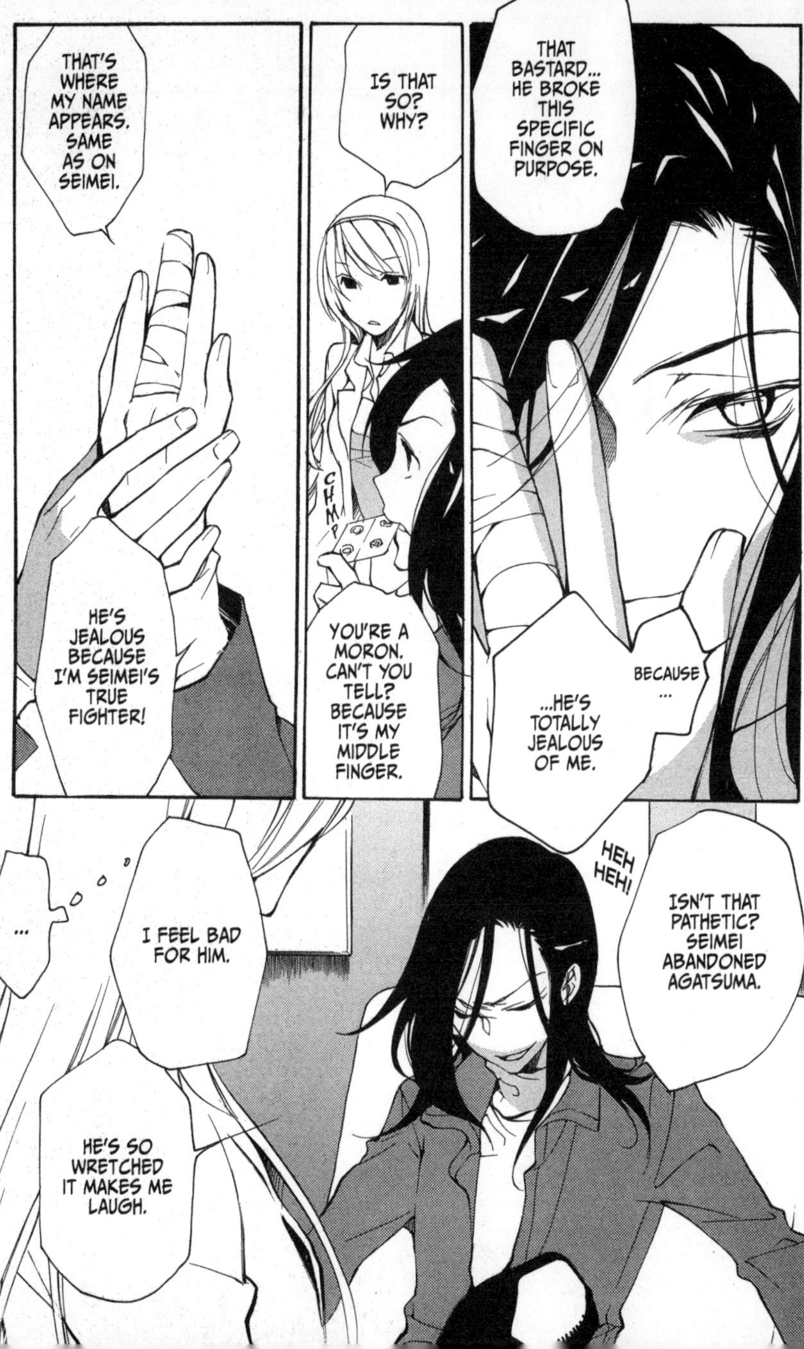
THAT BASTARD... HE BROKE THIS SPECIFIC FINGER ON PURPOSE.
BECAUSE ...
...HE'S TOTALLY JEALOUS OF ME.
IS THAT SO? WHY?
CHMP
YOU'RE A MORON. CAN'T YOU TELL? BECAUSE IT'S MY MIDDLE FINGER.
THAT'S WHERE MY NAME APPEARS. SAME AS ON SEIMEI.
HE'S JEALOUS BECAUSE I'M SEIMEI'S TRUE FIGHTER!
HEH HEH!
ISN'T THAT PATHETIC? SEIMEI ABANDONED AGATSUMA.
I FEEL BAD FOR HIM.
...
HE'S SO WRETCHED IT MAKES ME LAUGH.

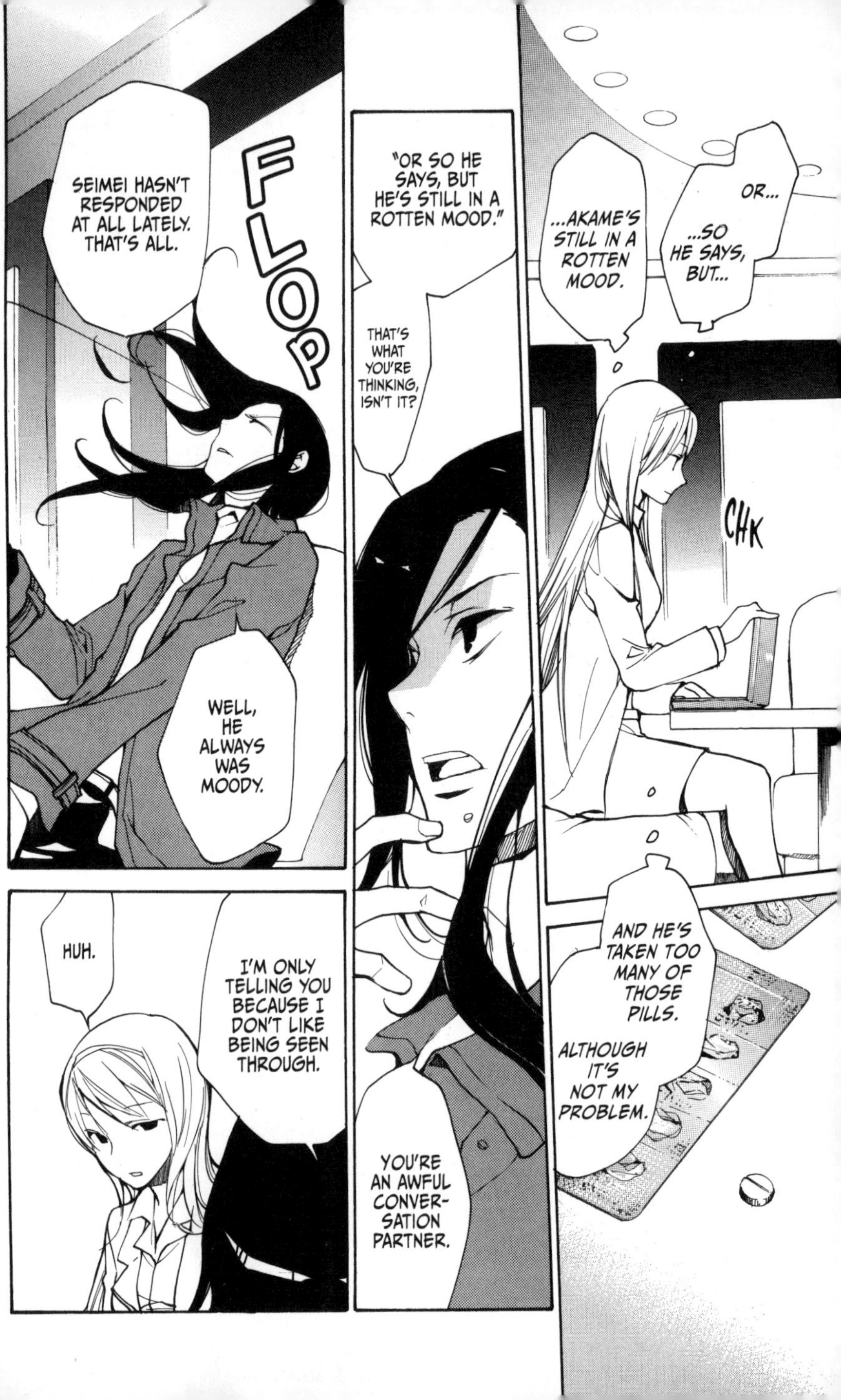
OR... ...SO HE SAYS, BUT...
...AKAME'S STILL IN A ROTTEN MOOD.
CHK
AND HE'S TAKEN TOO MANY OF THOSE PILLS.
ALTHOUGH IT'S NOT MY PROBLEM.
"OR SO HE SAYS, BUT HE'S STILL IN A ROTTEN MOOD."
THAT'S WHAT YOU'RE THINKING, ISN'T IT?
YOU'RE AN AWFUL CONVER-SATION PARTNER.
SEIMEI HASN'T RESPONDED AT ALL LATELY. THAT'S ALL.
FLOP
WELL, HE ALWAYS WAS MOODY.
I'M ONLY TELLING YOU BECAUSE I DON'T LIKE BEING SEEN THROUGH.
HUH.

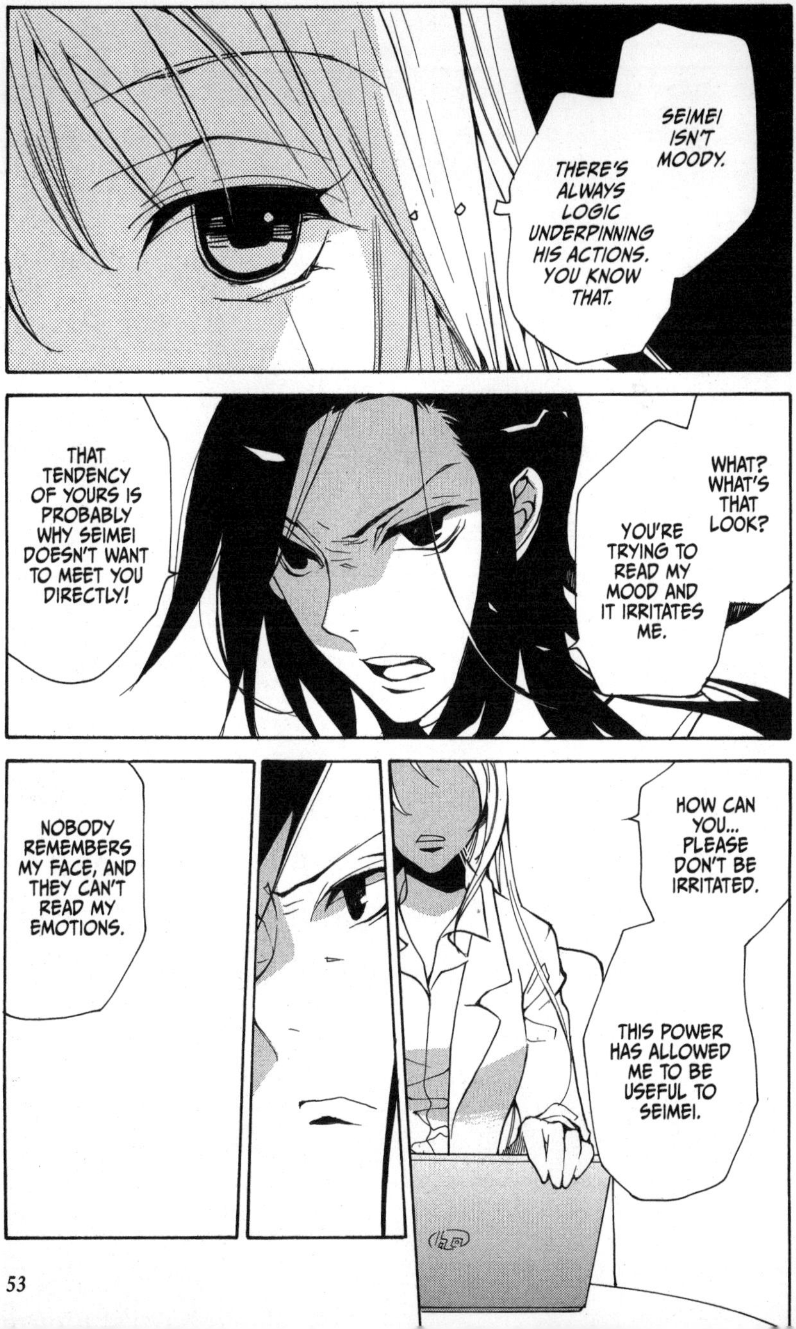
SEIMEI ISN'T MOODY.
THERE'S ALWAYS LOGIC UNDERPINNING HIS ACTIONS. YOU KNOW THAT.
WHAT? WHAT'S THAT LOOK?
YOU'RE TRYING TO READ MY MOOD AND IT IRRITATES ME.
THAT TENDENCY OF YOURS IS PROBABLY WHY SEIMEI DOESN'T WANT TO MEET YOU DIRECTLY!
HOW CAN YOU... PLEASE DON'T BE IRRITATED.
THIS POWER HAS ALLOWED ME TO BE USEFUL TO SEIMEI.
NOBODY REMEMBERS MY FACE, AND THEY CAN'T READ MY EMOTIONS.

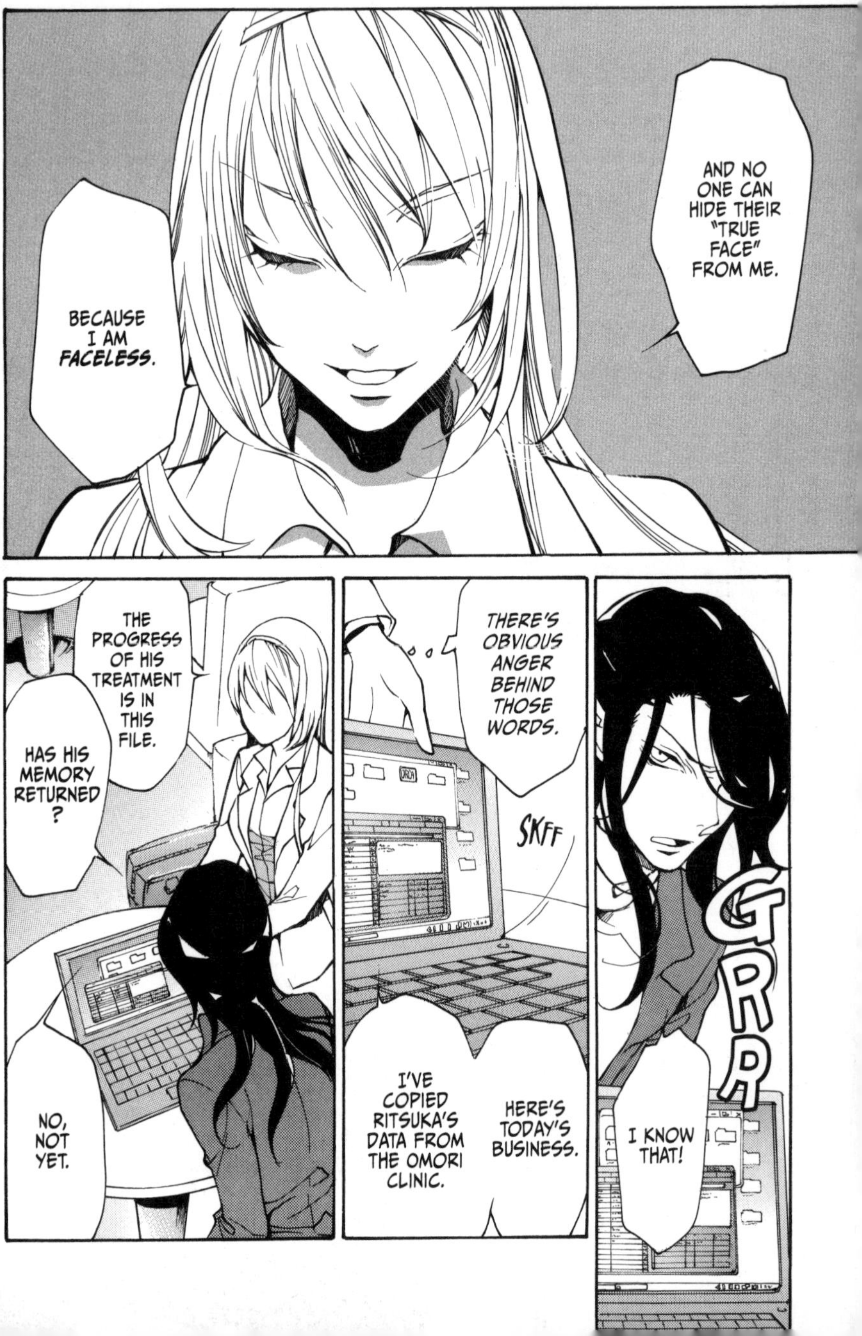
AND NO ONE CAN HIDE THEIR "TRUE FACE" FROM ME.
BECAUSE I AM *FACELESS*.
GRR
I KNOW THAT!
THERE'S OBVIOUS ANGER BEHIND THOSE WORDS.
SKFF
HERE'S TODAY'S BUSINESS.
I'VE COPIED RITSUKA'S DATA FROM THE OMORI CLINIC.
THE PROGRESS OF HIS TREATMENT IS IN THIS FILE.
HAS HIS MEMORY RETURNED?
NO, NOT YET.

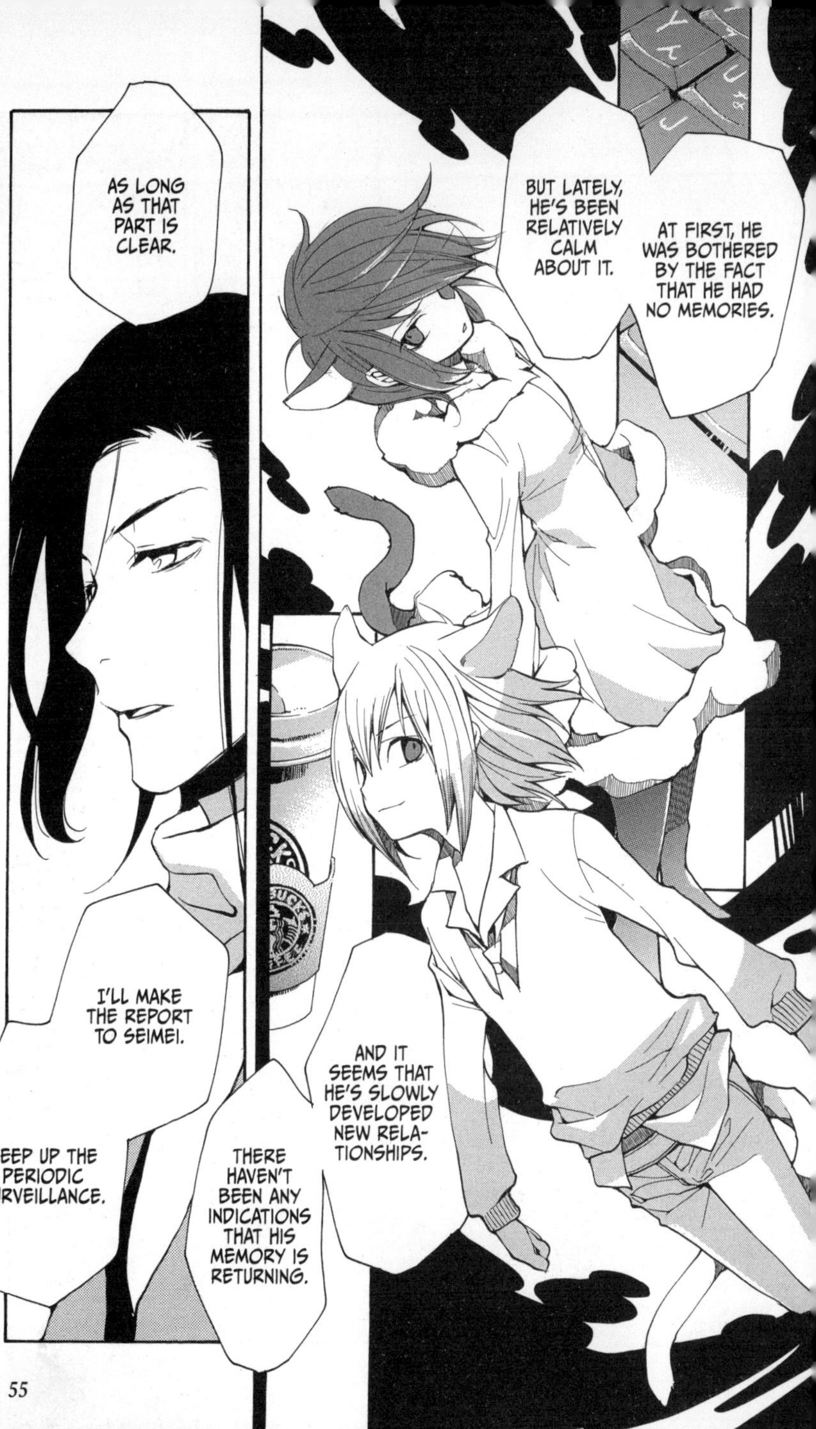
AT FIRST, HE WAS BOTHERED BY THE FACT THAT HE HAD NO MEMORIES.
BUT LATELY, HE'S BEEN RELATIVELY CALM ABOUT IT.
AND IT SEEMS THAT HE'S SLOWLY DEVELOPED NEW RELA-TIONSHIPS.
THERE HAVEN'T BEEN ANY INDICATIONS THAT HIS MEMORY IS RETURNING.
AS LONG AS THAT PART IS CLEAR.
I'LL MAKE THE REPORT TO SEIMEI.
KEEP UP THE PERIODIC SURVEILLANCE.

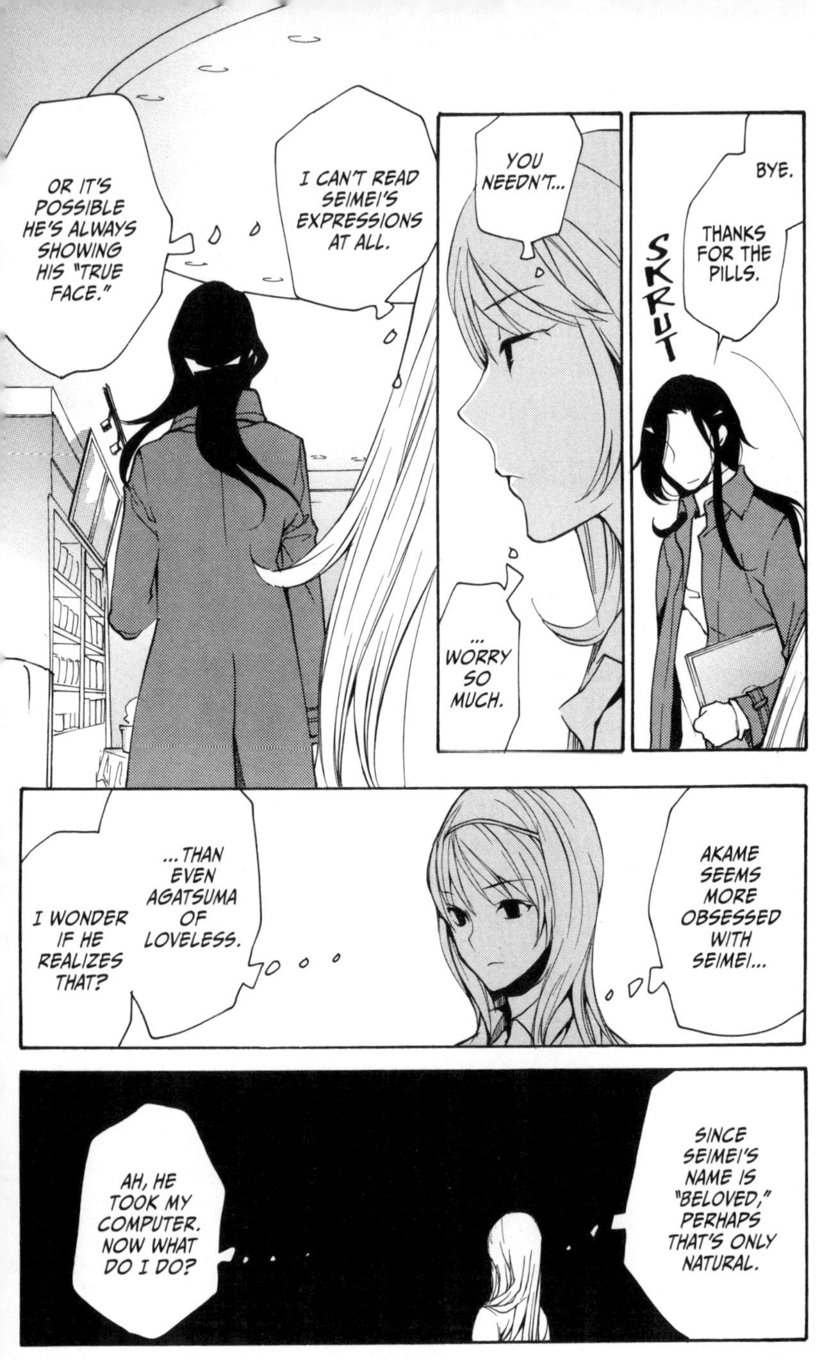

BYE.
THANKS FOR THE PILLS.
SKRUT
YOU NEEDN'T...
...WORRY SO MUCH.
I CAN'T READ SEIMEI'S EXPRESSIONS AT ALL.
OR IT'S POSSIBLE HE'S ALWAYS SHOWING HIS "TRUE FACE."
AKAME SEEMS MORE OBSESSED WITH SEIMEI...
...THAN EVEN AGATSUMA OF LOVELESS.
I WONDER IF HE REALIZES THAT?
SINCE SEIMEI'S NAME IS "BELOVED," PERHAPS THAT'S ONLY NATURAL.
AH, HE TOOK MY COMPUTER. NOW WHAT DO I DO?

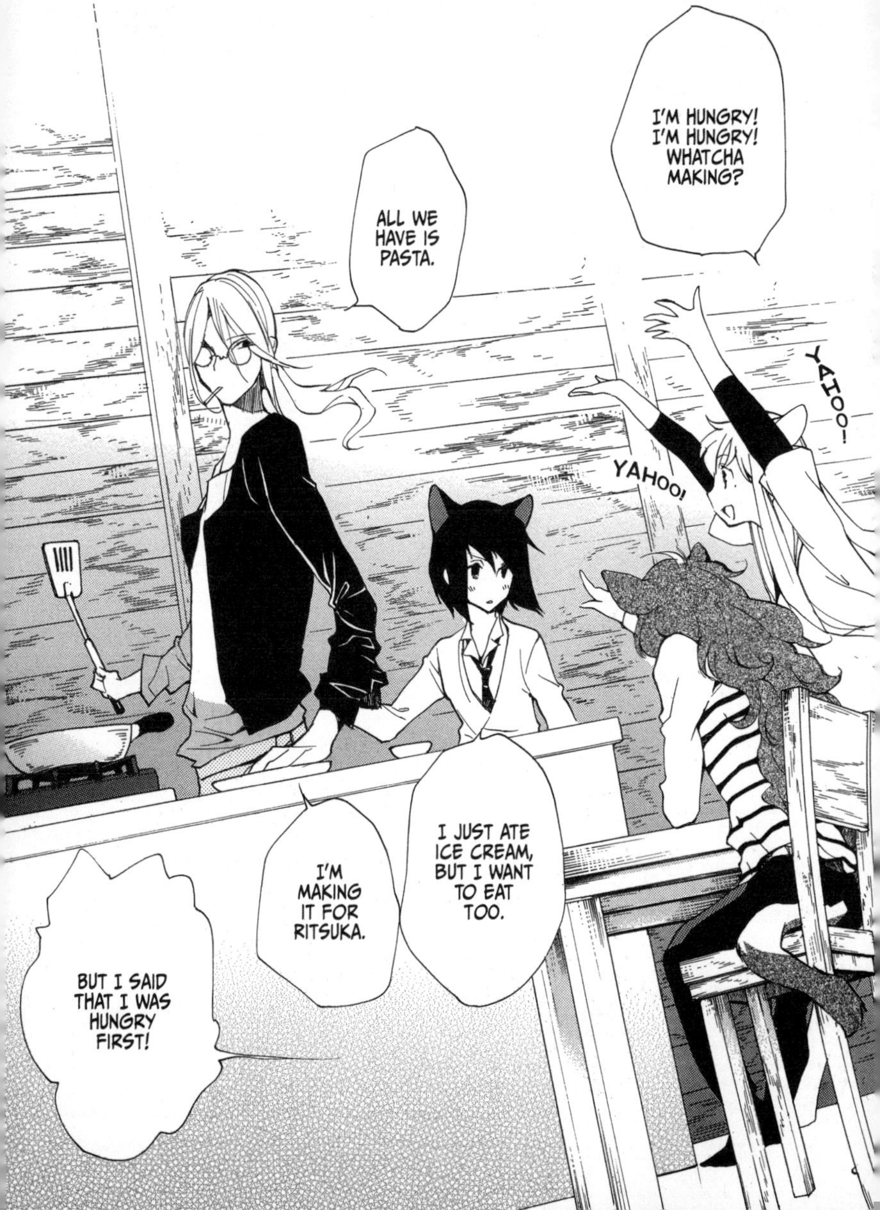

I'M HUNGRY! I'M HUNGRY! WHATCHA MAKING?
YAHOO!
YAHOO!
ALL WE HAVE IS PASTA.
I JUST ATE ICE CREAM, BUT I WANT TO EAT TOO.
I'M MAKING IT FOR RITSUKA.
BUT I SAID THAT I WAS HUNGRY FIRST!

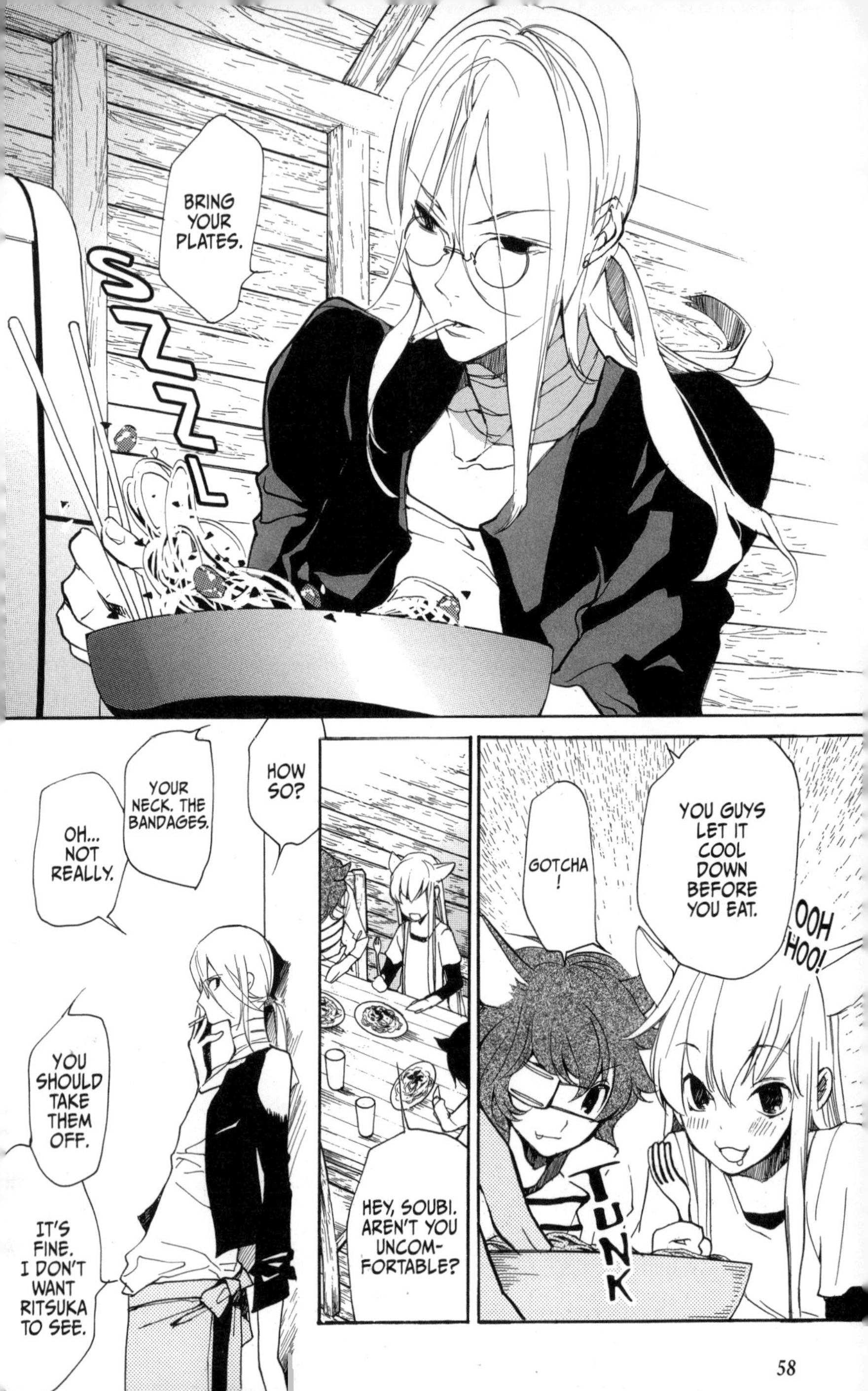
BRING YOUR PLATES.
SZZL
YOU GUYS LET IT COOL DOWN BEFORE YOU EAT.
OOH HOO!
GOTCHA!
TUNK
HEY, SOUBI. AREN'T YOU UNCOM-FORTABLE?
HOW SO?
YOUR NECK. THE BANDAGES.
OH... NOT REALLY.
YOU SHOULD TAKE THEM OFF.
IT'S FINE. I DON'T WANT RITSUKA TO SEE.

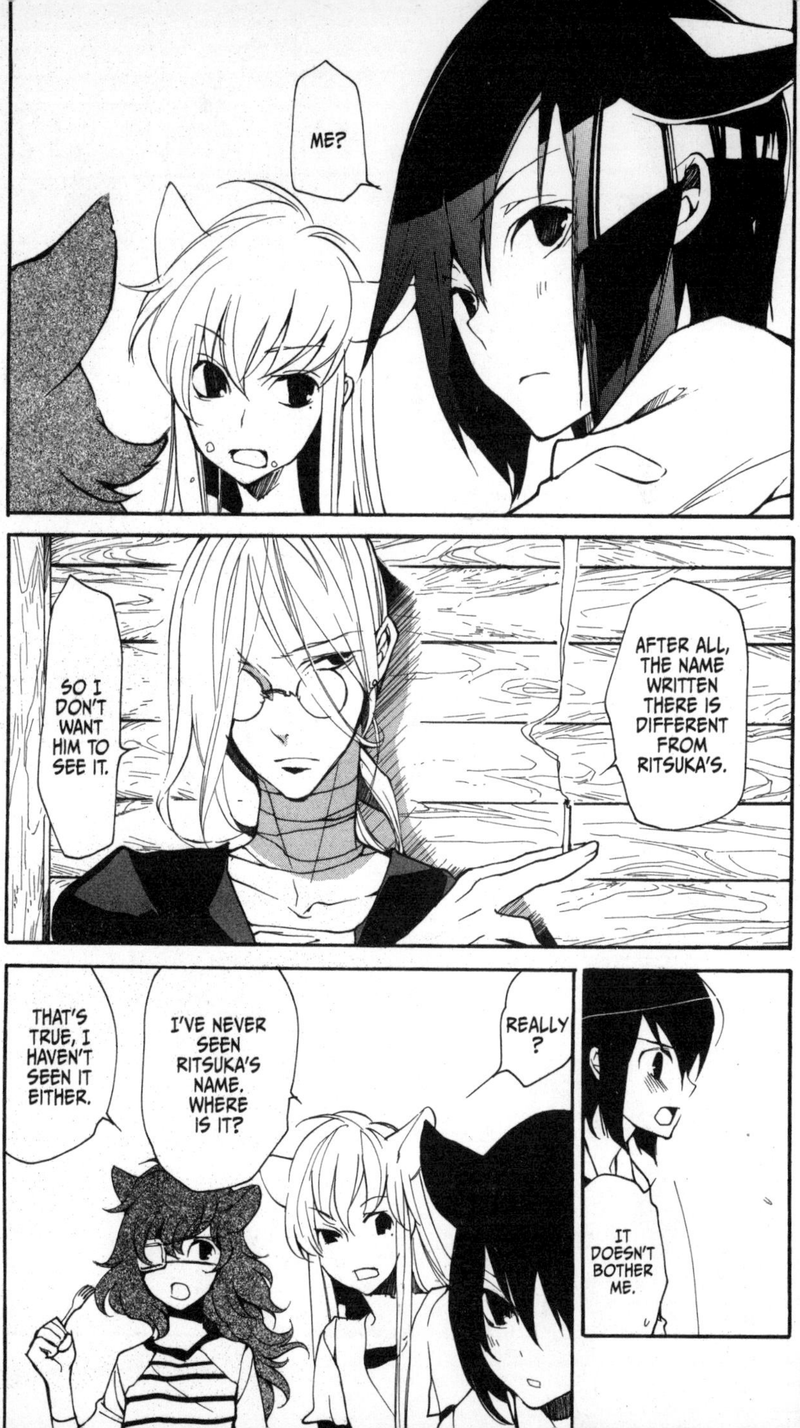
ME?
AFTER ALL, THE NAME WRITTEN THERE IS DIFFERENT FROM RITSUKA'S.
SO I DON'T WANT HIM TO SEE IT.
IT DOESN'T BOTHER ME.
REALLY?
I'VE NEVER SEEN RITSUKA'S NAME. WHERE IS IT?
THAT'S TRUE, I HAVEN'T SEEN IT EITHER.

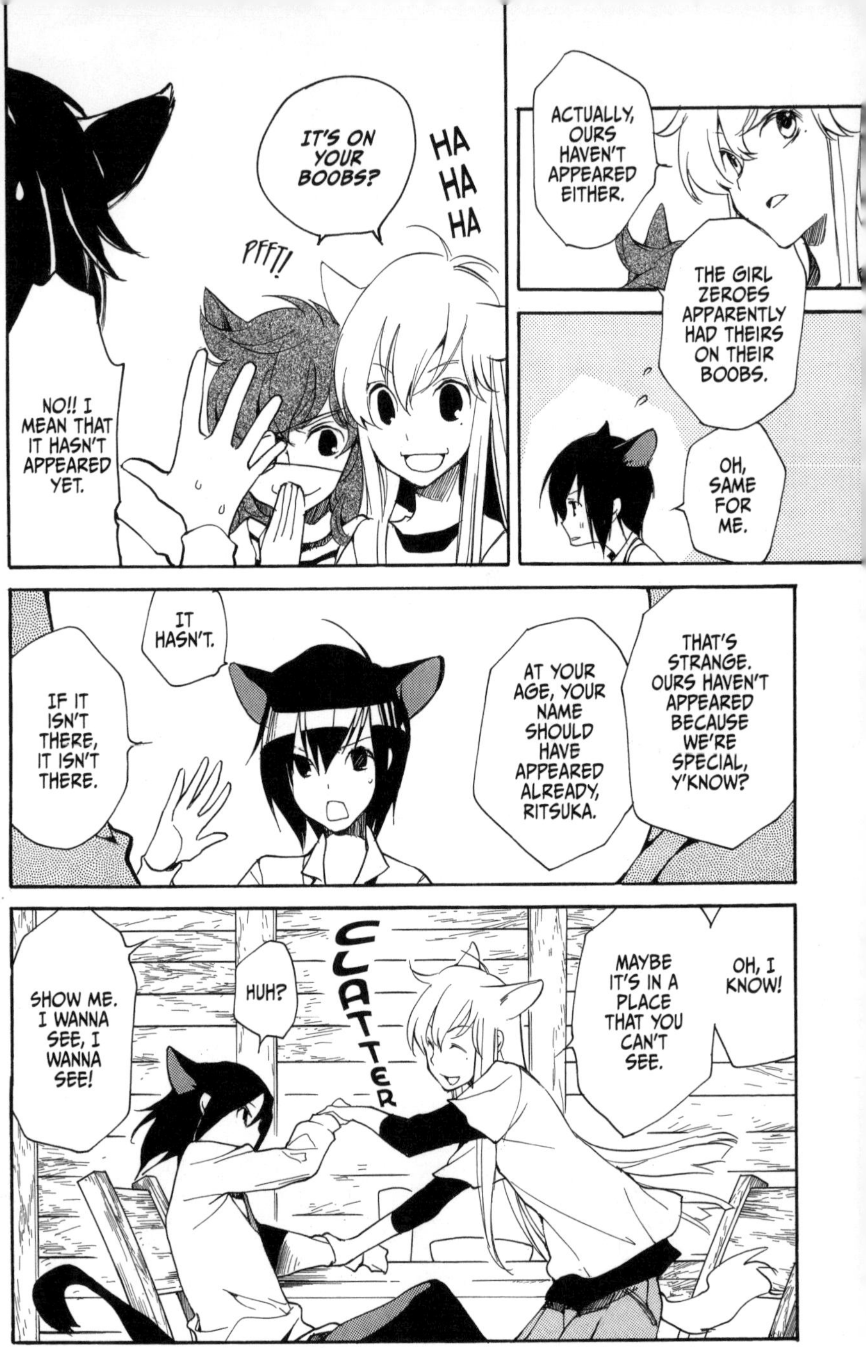
ACTUALLY, OURS HAVEN'T APPEARED EITHER.
THE GIRL ZEROES APPARENTLY HAD THEIRS ON THEIR BOOBS.
OH, SAME FOR ME.
IT'S ON YOUR BOOBS?
HA HA HA
PFFT!
NO!! I MEAN THAT IT HASN'T APPEARED YET.
THAT'S STRANGE. OURS HAVEN'T APPEARED BECAUSE WE'RE SPECIAL, Y'KNOW?
AT YOUR AGE, YOUR NAME SHOULD HAVE APPEARED ALREADY, RITSUKA.
IT HASN'T.
IF IT ISN'T THERE, IT ISN'T THERE.
OH, I KNOW!
MAYBE IT'S IN A PLACE THAT YOU CAN'T SEE.
CLATTER
HUH?
SHOW ME. I WANNA SEE, I WANNA SEE!

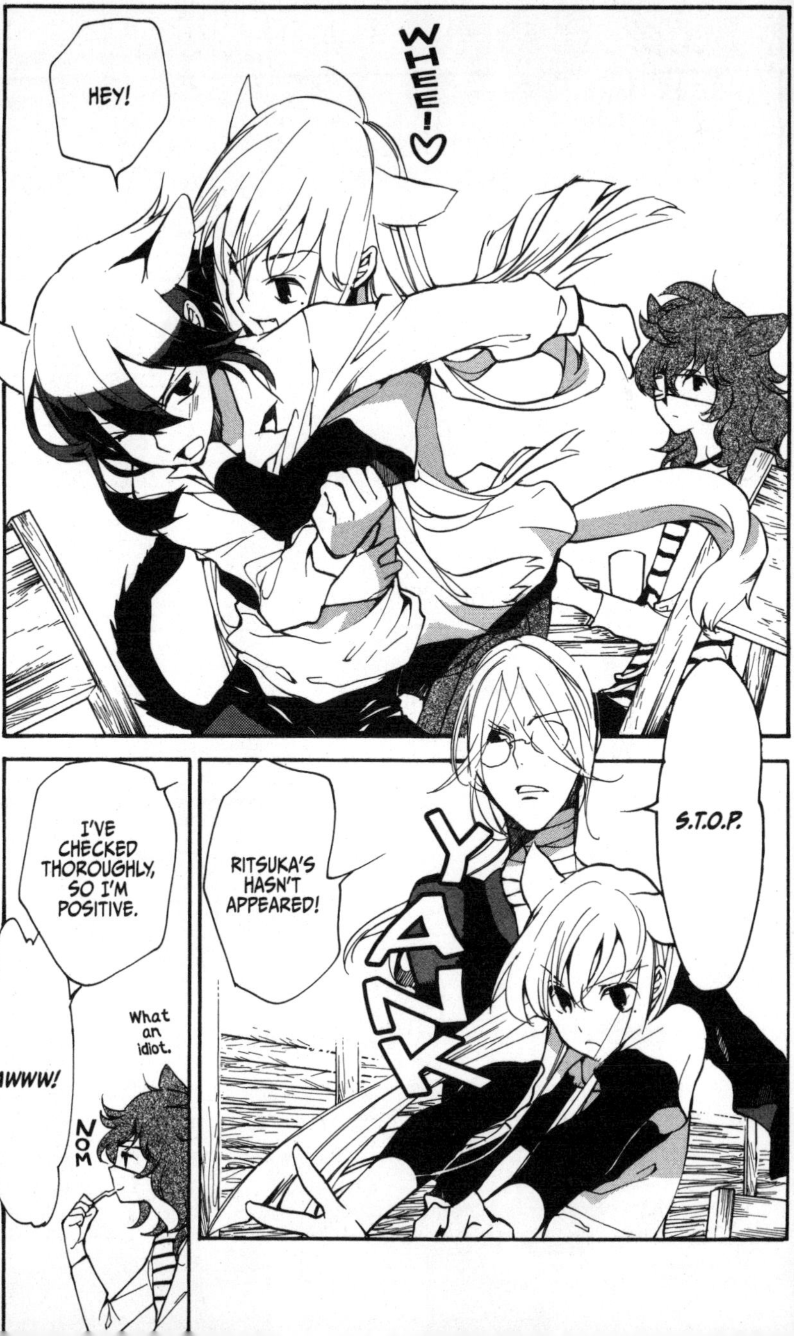
WHEE!♥
HEY!
S.T.O.P.
YANK
RITSUKA'S HASN'T APPEARED!
I'VE CHECKED THOROUGHLY, SO I'M POSITIVE.
That's no fun.
What an idiot.
AWWW!
NOM

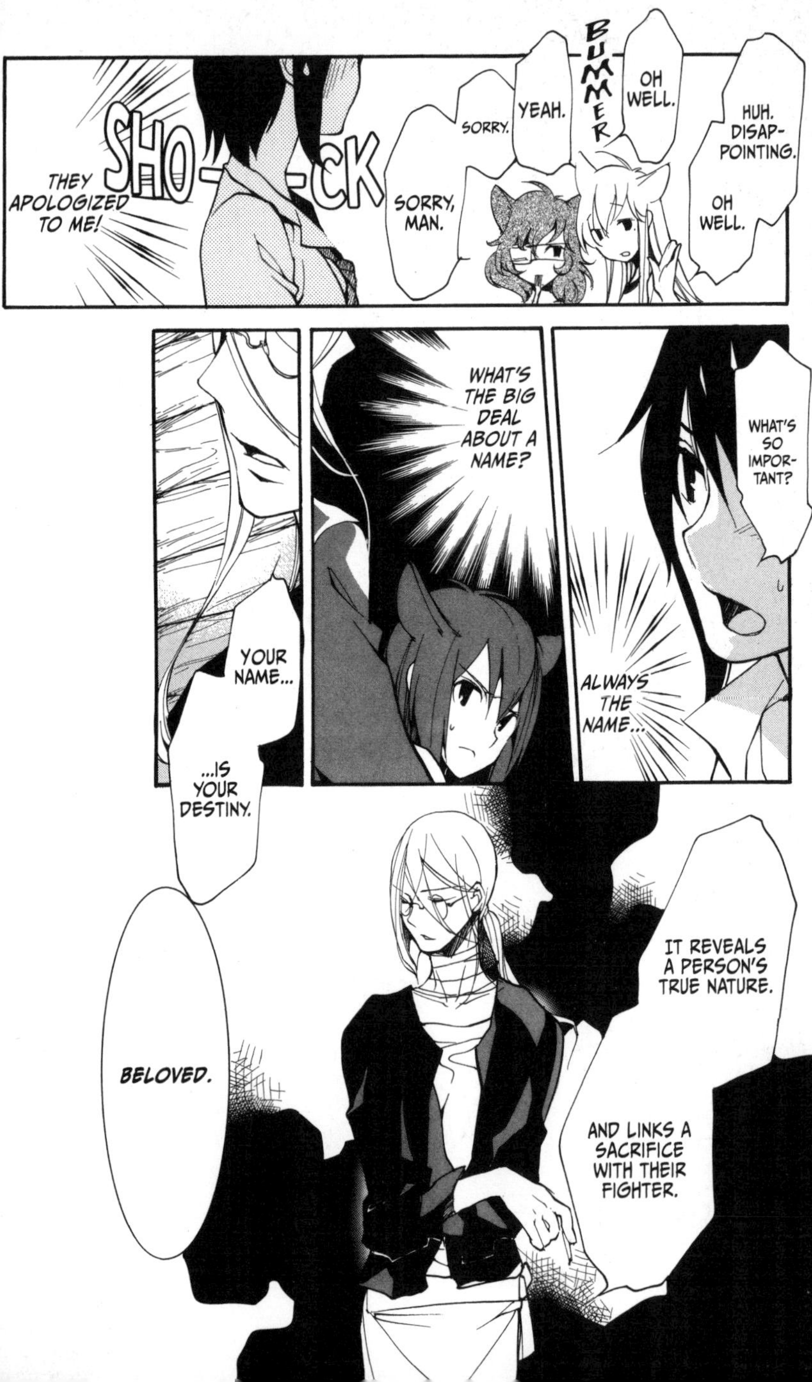
HUH. DISAP-POINTING.
OH WELL.
OH WELL.
BUMMER
YEAH.
SORRY.
SORRY, MAN.
SHO--CK
THEY APOLOGIZED TO ME!
WHAT'S SO IMPOR-TANT?
ALWAYS THE NAME...
WHAT'S THE BIG DEAL ABOUT A NAME?
YOUR NAME...
...IS YOUR DESTINY.
IT REVEALS A PERSON'S TRUE NATURE.
AND LINKS A SACRIFICE WITH THEIR FIGHTER.
BELOVED.

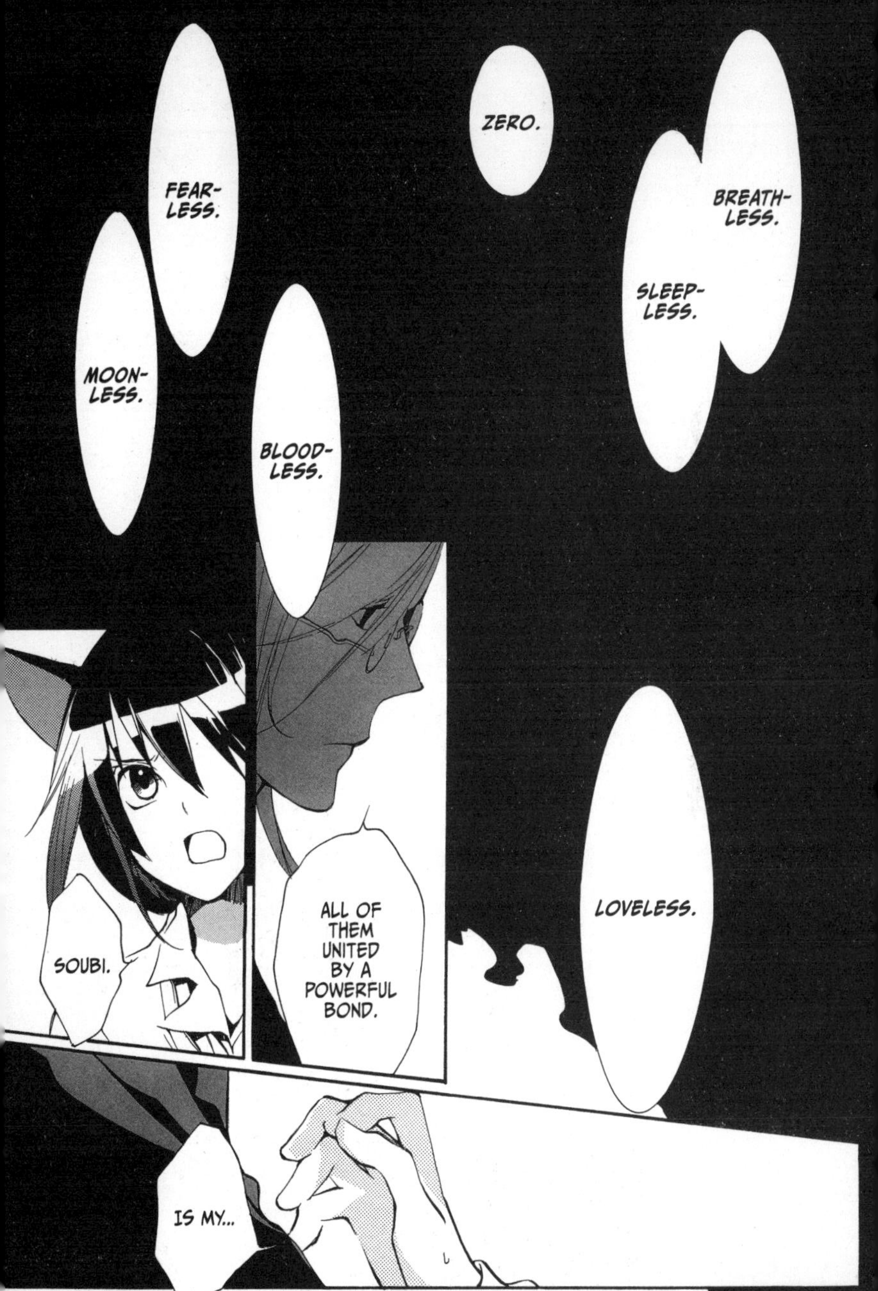
BREATH-LESS.
SLEEP-LESS.
ZERO.
FEAR-LESS.
BLOOD-LESS.
MOON-LESS.
LOVELESS.
ALL OF THEM UNITED BY A POWERFUL BOND.
SOUBI.
IS MY...

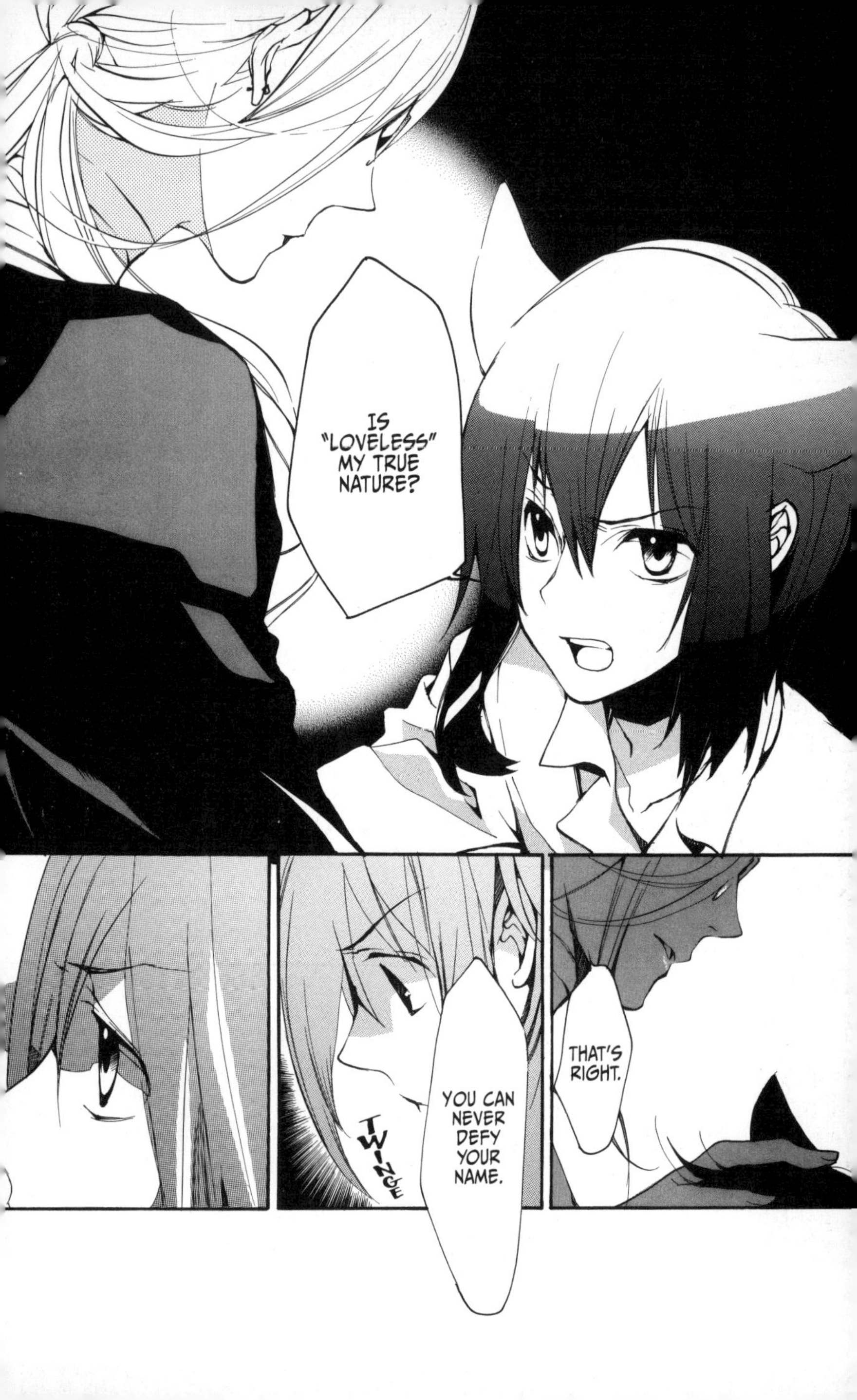
IS "LOVELESS" MY TRUE NATURE?
THAT'S RIGHT.
YOU CAN NEVER DEFY YOUR NAME.
TWINGE

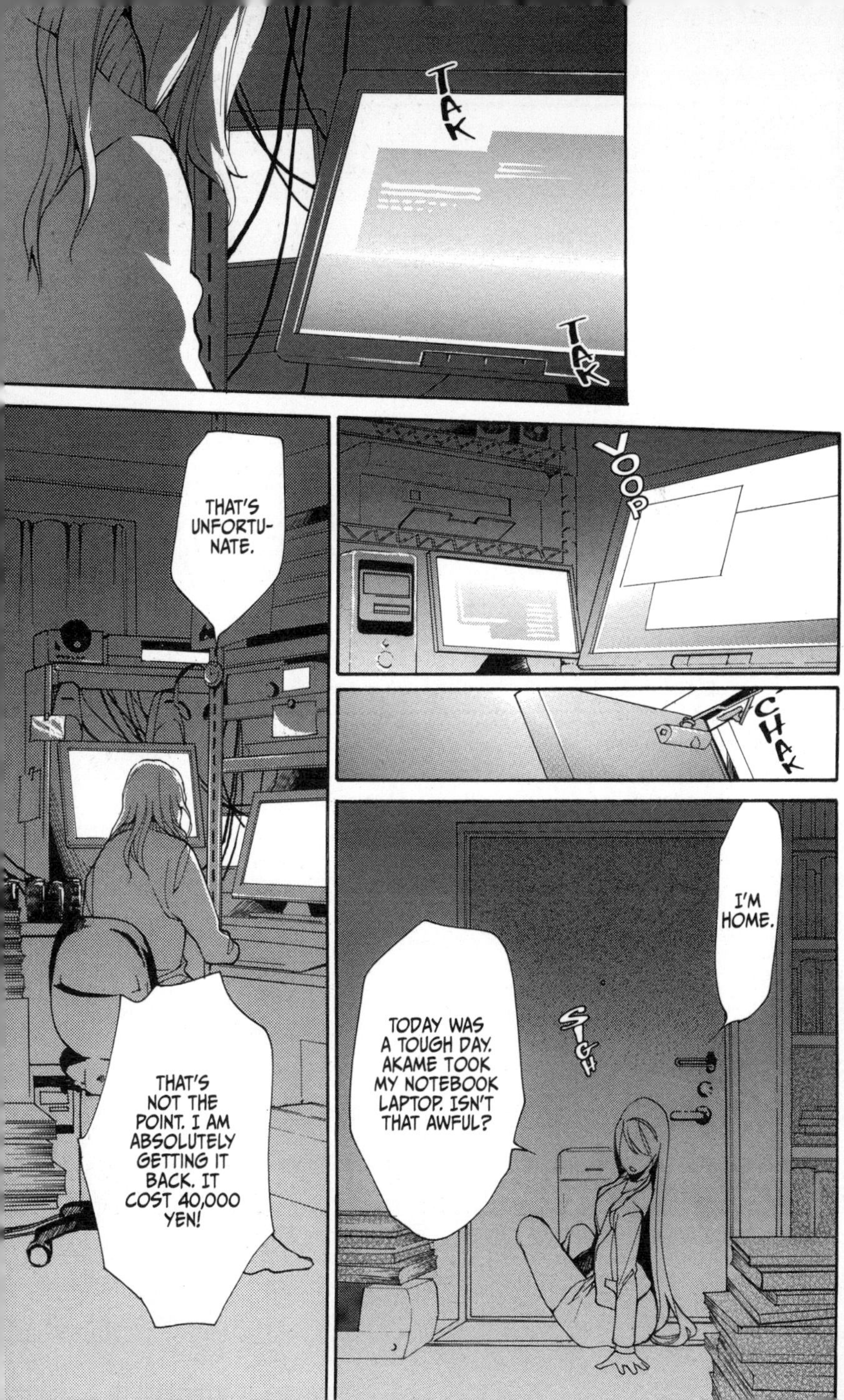
TAK
TAK
VOOP
CHAK
I'M HOME.
TODAY WAS A TOUGH DAY. AKAME TOOK MY NOTEBOOK LAPTOP. ISN'T THAT AWFUL?
SIGH
THAT'S UNFORTU-NATE.
THAT'S NOT THE POINT. I AM ABSOLUTELY GETTING IT BACK. IT COST 40,000 YEN!

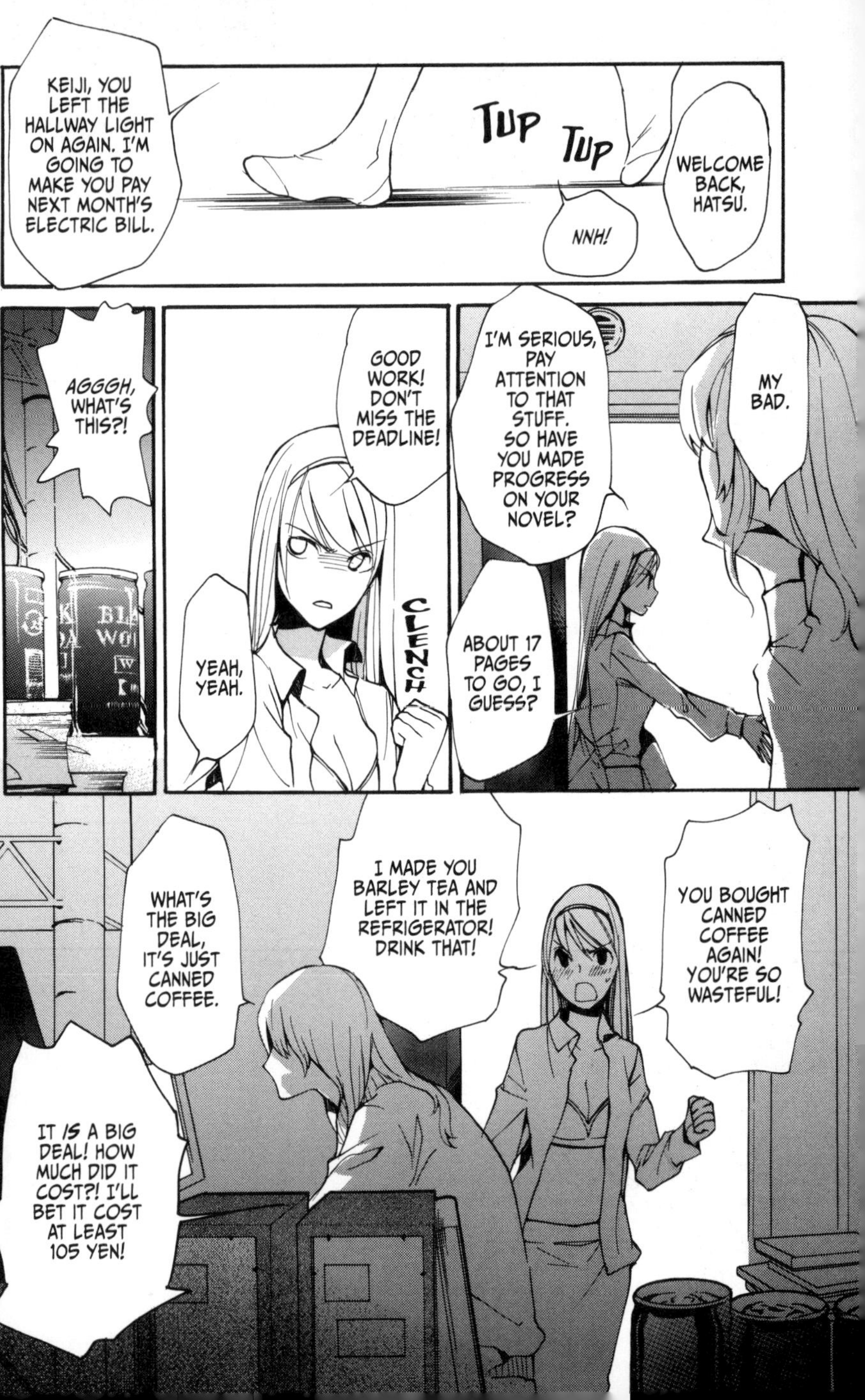
WELCOME BACK, HATSU.
TUP TUP
NNH!
KEIJI, YOU LEFT THE HALLWAY LIGHT ON AGAIN. I'M GOING TO MAKE YOU PAY NEXT MONTH'S ELECTRIC BILL.
MY BAD.
I'M SERIOUS, PAY ATTENTION TO THAT STUFF. SO HAVE YOU MADE PROGRESS ON YOUR NOVEL?
ABOUT 17 PAGES TO GO, I GUESS?
GOOD WORK! DON'T MISS THE DEADLINE!
CLENCH
YEAH, YEAH.
AGGGH, WHAT'S THIS?!
YOU BOUGHT CANNED COFFEE AGAIN! YOU'RE SO WASTEFUL!
I MADE YOU BARLEY TEA AND LEFT IT IN THE REFRIGERATOR! DRINK THAT!
WHAT'S THE BIG DEAL, IT'S JUST CANNED COFFEE.
IT IS A BIG DEAL! HOW MUCH DID IT COST?! I'LL BET IT COST AT LEAST 105 YEN!

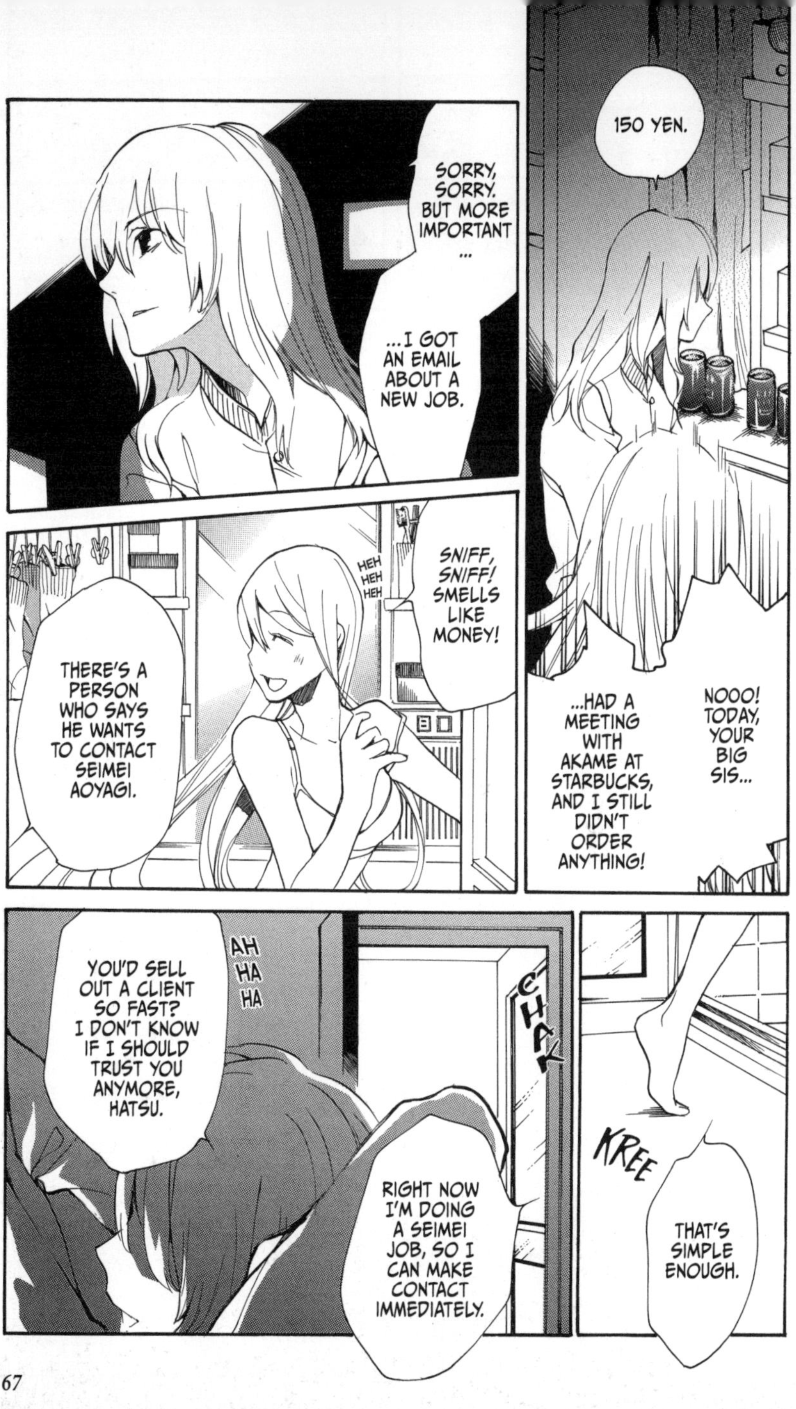
150 YEN.
NOOO! TODAY, YOUR BIG SIS...
...HAD A MEETING WITH AKAME AT STARBUCKS, AND I STILL DIDN'T ORDER ANYTHING!
SORRY, SORRY. BUT MORE IMPORTANT...
...I GOT AN EMAIL ABOUT A NEW JOB.
SNIFF, SNIFF! SMELLS LIKE MONEY!
HEH HEH HEH
THERE'S A PERSON WHO SAYS HE WANTS TO CONTACT SEIMEI AOYAGI.
KREE
THAT'S SIMPLE ENOUGH.
CHAK
RIGHT NOW I'M DOING A SEIMEI JOB, SO I CAN MAKE CONTACT IMMEDIATELY.
AH HA HA
YOU'D SELL OUT A CLIENT SO FAST? I DON'T KNOW IF I SHOULD TRUST YOU ANYMORE, HATSU.

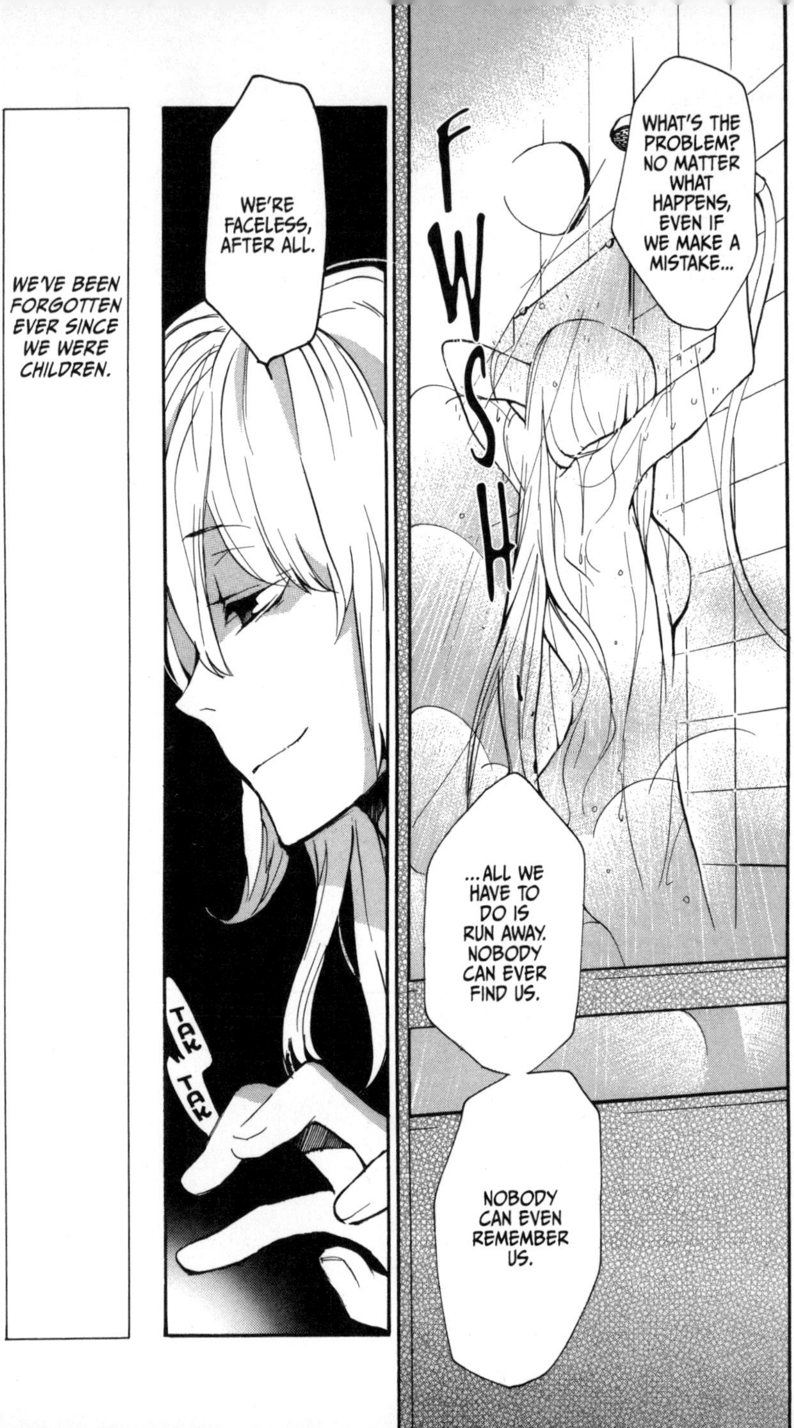
WHAT'S THE PROBLEM? NO MATTER WHAT HAPPENS, EVEN IF WE MAKE A MISTAKE...
FWSH
...ALL WE HAVE TO DO IS RUN AWAY. NOBODY CAN EVER FIND US.
NOBODY CAN EVEN REMEMBER US.
WE'RE FACELESS, AFTER ALL.
TAK TAK
WE'VE BEEN FORGOTTEN EVER SINCE WE WERE CHILDREN.

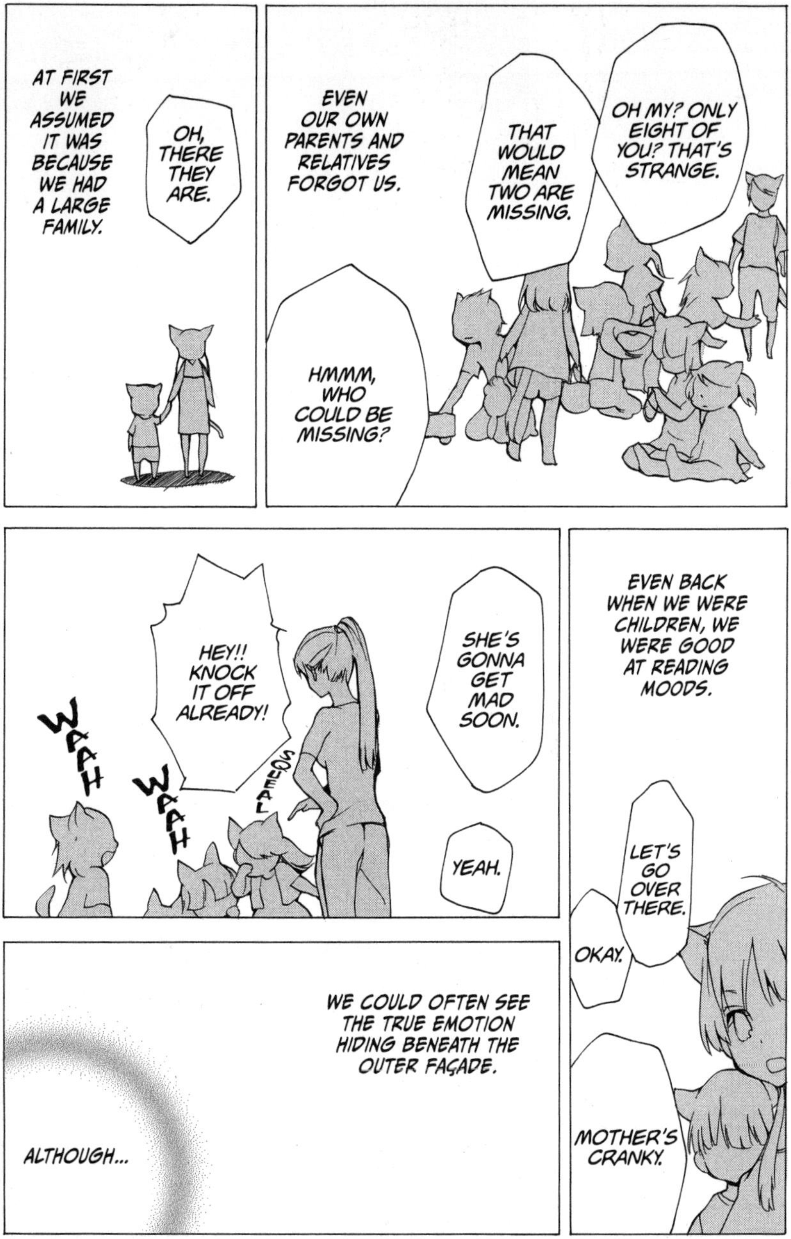
OH MY? ONLY EIGHT OF YOU? THAT'S STRANGE.
THAT WOULD MEAN TWO ARE MISSING.
EVEN OUR OWN PARENTS AND RELATIVES FORGOT US.
HMMM, WHO COULD BE MISSING?
OH, THERE THEY ARE.
AT FIRST WE ASSUMED IT WAS BECAUSE WE HAD A LARGE FAMILY.
EVEN BACK WHEN WE WERE CHILDREN, WE WERE GOOD AT READING MOODS.
LET'S GO OVER THERE.
OKAY.
MOTHER'S CRANKY.
SHE'S GONNA GET MAD SOON.
YEAH.
HEY!! KNOCK IT OFF ALREADY!
SQUEAL
WAAH
WAAH
WE COULD OFTEN SEE THE TRUE EMOTION HIDING BENEATH THE OUTER FAÇADE.
ALTHOUGH...

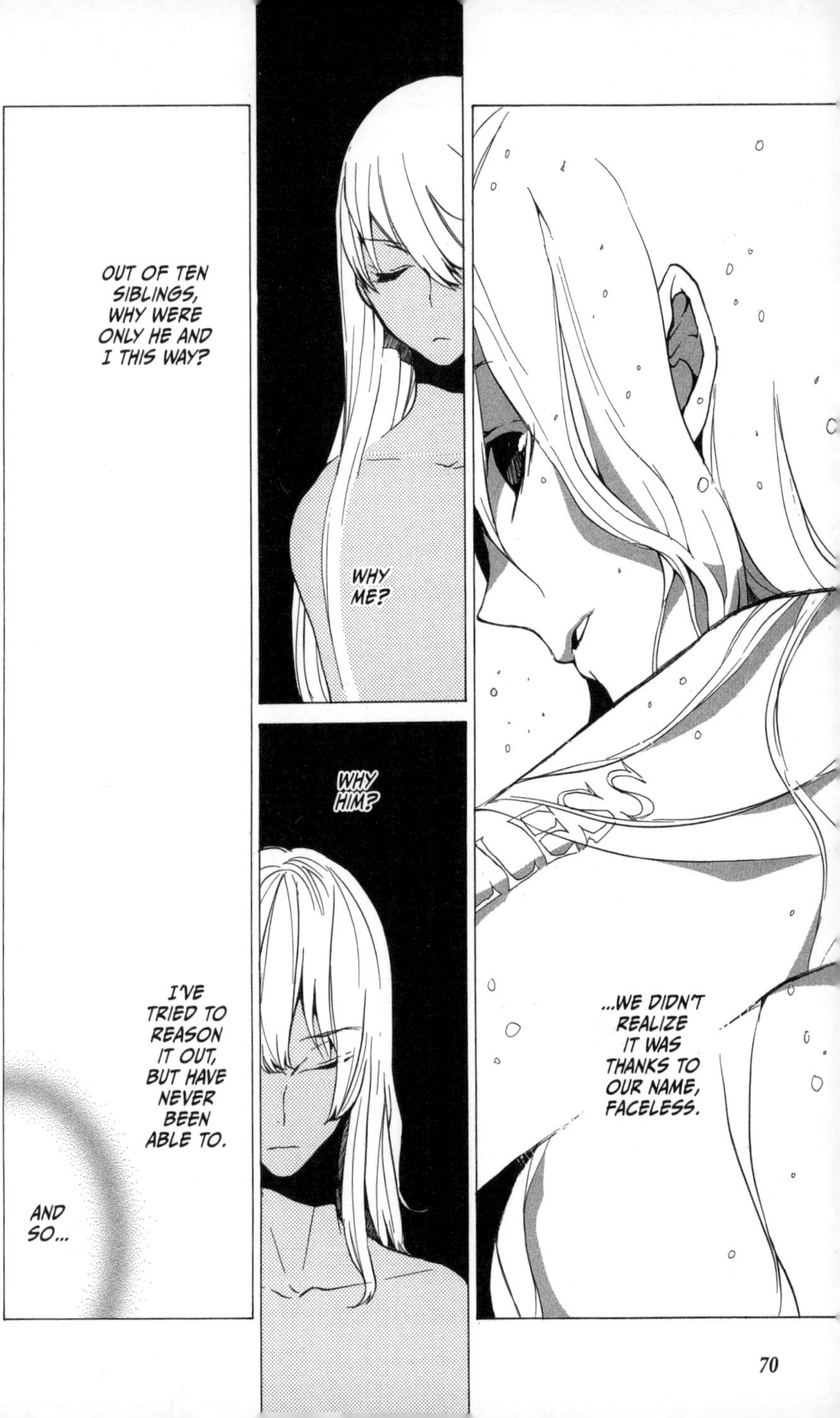
...WE DIDN'T REALIZE IT WAS THANKS TO OUR NAME, FACELESS.
WHY ME?
WHY HIM?
OUT OF TEN SIBLINGS, WHY WERE ONLY HE AND I THIS WAY?
I'VE TRIED TO REASON IT OUT, BUT HAVE NEVER BEEN ABLE TO.
AND SO...

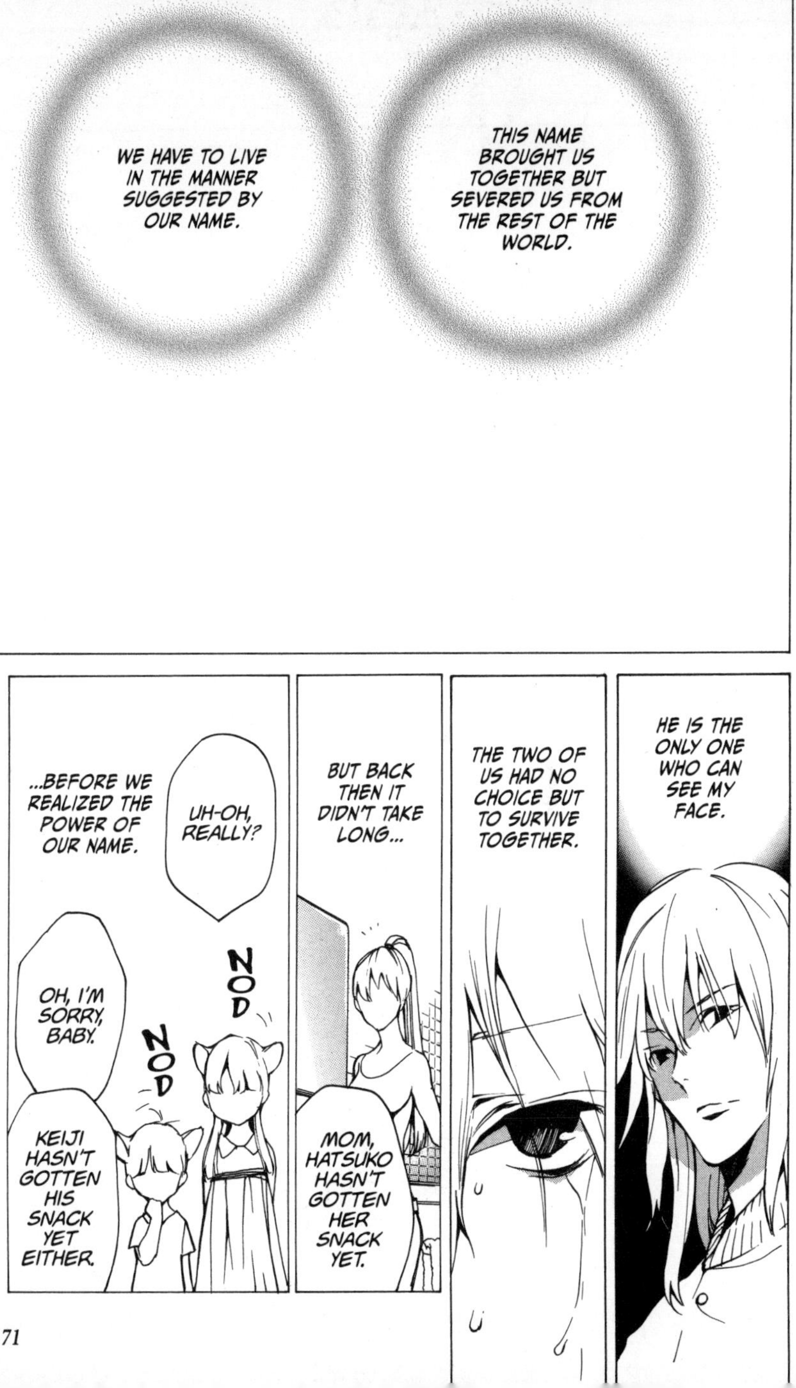
THIS NAME BROUGHT US TOGETHER BUT SEVERED US FROM THE REST OF THE WORLD.
WE HAVE TO LIVE IN THE MANNER SUGGESTED BY OUR NAME.
HE IS THE ONLY ONE WHO CAN SEE MY FACE.
THE TWO OF US HAD NO CHOICE BUT TO SURVIVE TOGETHER.
BUT BACK THEN IT DIDN'T TAKE LONG...
MOM, HATSUKO HASN'T GOTTEN HER SNACK YET.
...BEFORE WE REALIZED THE POWER OF OUR NAME.
UH-OH, REALLY?
NOD
NOD
OH, I'M SORRY, BABY.
KEIJI HASN'T GOTTEN HIS SNACK YET EITHER.

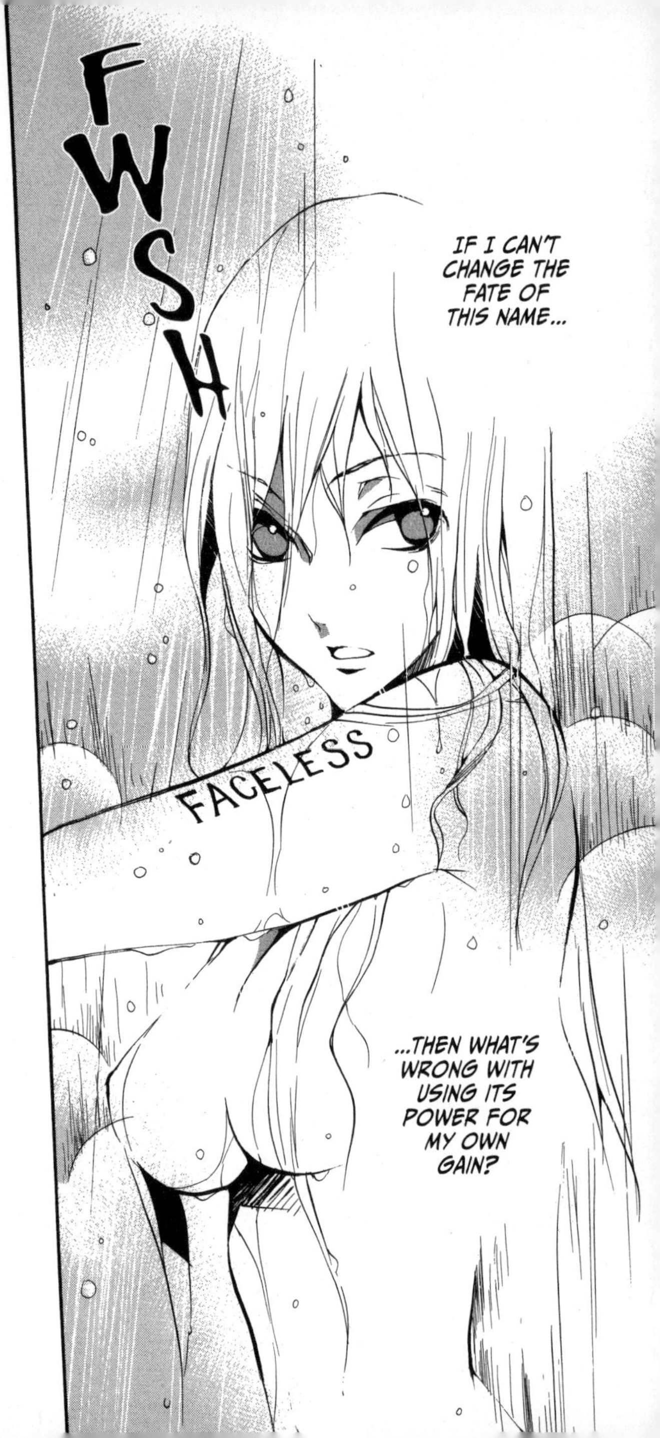
IF I CAN'T CHANGE THE FATE OF THIS NAME...
FWSH
FACELESS
...THEN WHAT'S WRONG WITH USING ITS POWER FOR MY OWN GAIN?

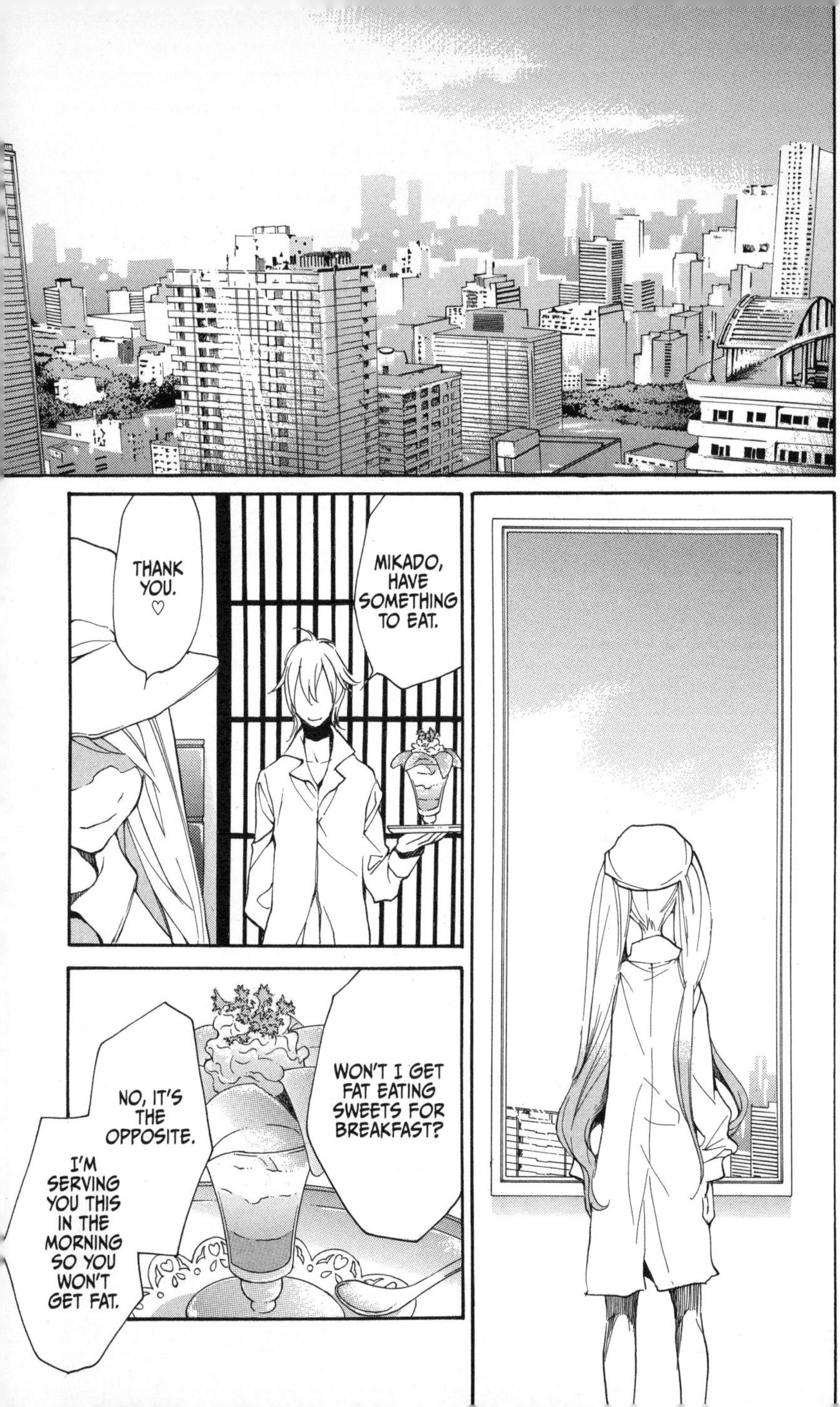
MIKADO, HAVE SOMETHING TO EAT.
THANK YOU. ♡
WON'T I GET FAT EATING SWEETS FOR BREAKFAST?
NO, IT'S THE OPPOSITE.
I'M SERVING YOU THIS IN THE MORNING SO YOU WON'T GET FAT.

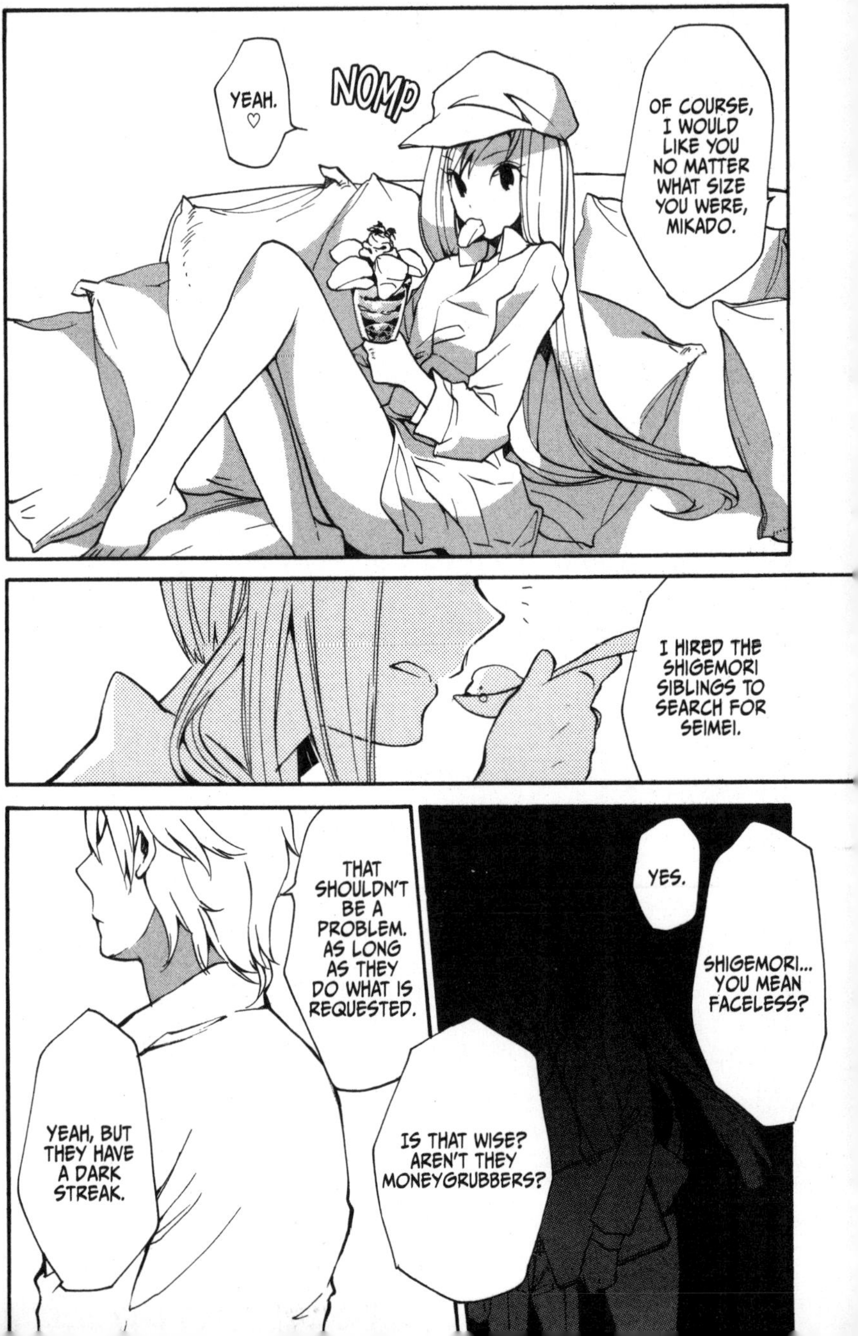

OF COURSE, I WOULD LIKE YOU NO MATTER WHAT SIZE YOU WERE, MIKADO.
NOMP
YEAH. ♡
I HIRED THE SHIGEMORI SIBLINGS TO SEARCH FOR SEIMEI.
SHIGEMORI... YOU MEAN FACELESS?
YES.
IS THAT WISE? AREN'T THEY MONEYGRUBBERS?
THAT SHOULDN'T BE A PROBLEM. AS LONG AS THEY DO WHAT IS REQUESTED.
YEAH, BUT THEY HAVE A DARK STREAK.

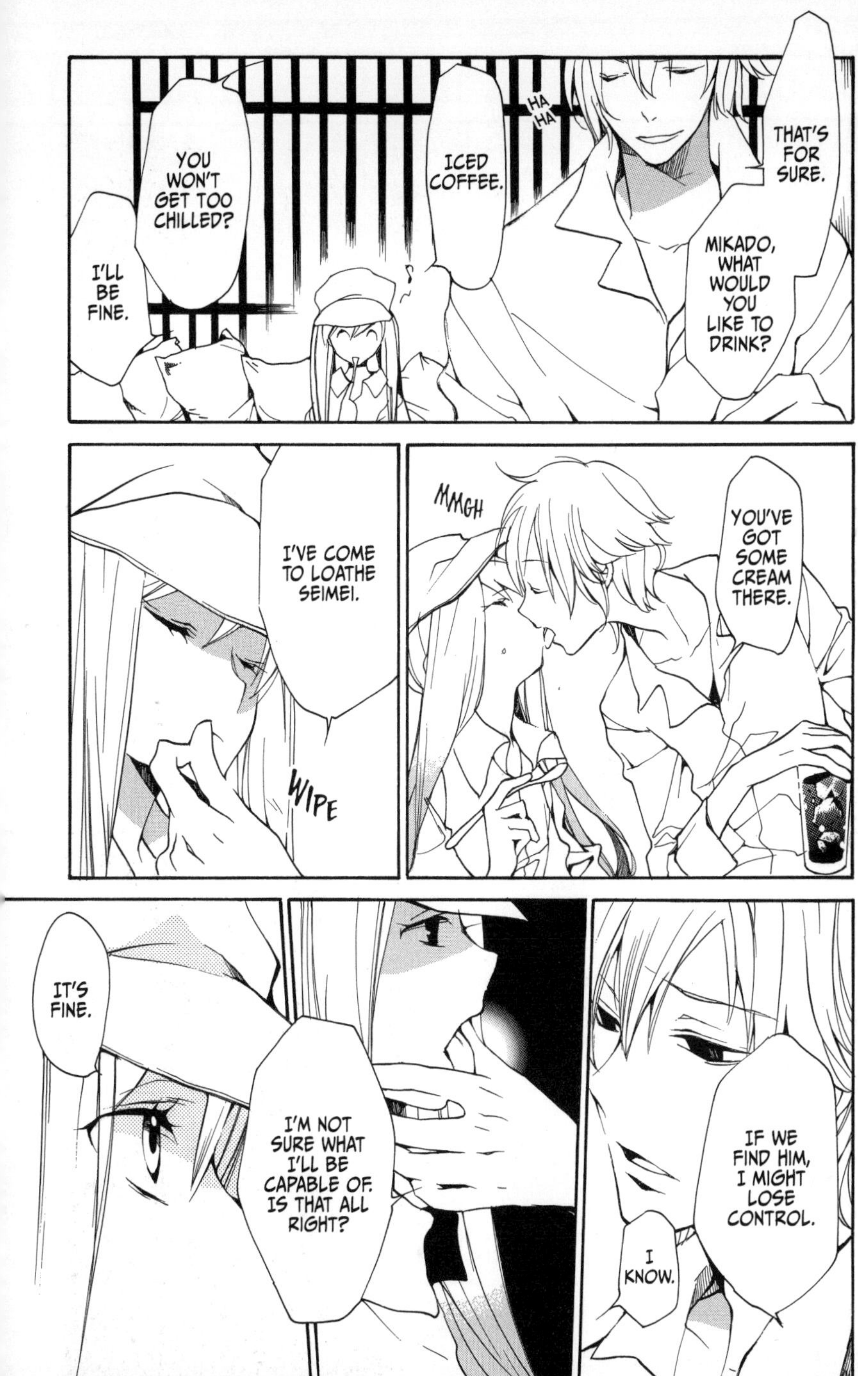

THAT'S FOR SURE.
MIKADO, WHAT WOULD YOU LIKE TO DRINK?
HA HA
ICED COFFEE.
YOU WON'T GET TOO CHILLED?
I'LL BE FINE.
YOU'VE GOT SOME CREAM THERE.
MMGH
I'VE COME TO LOATHE SEIMEI.
WIPE
IF WE FIND HIM, I MIGHT LOSE CONTROL.
I KNOW.
I'M NOT SURE WHAT I'LL BE CAPABLE OF. IS THAT ALL RIGHT?
IT'S FINE.

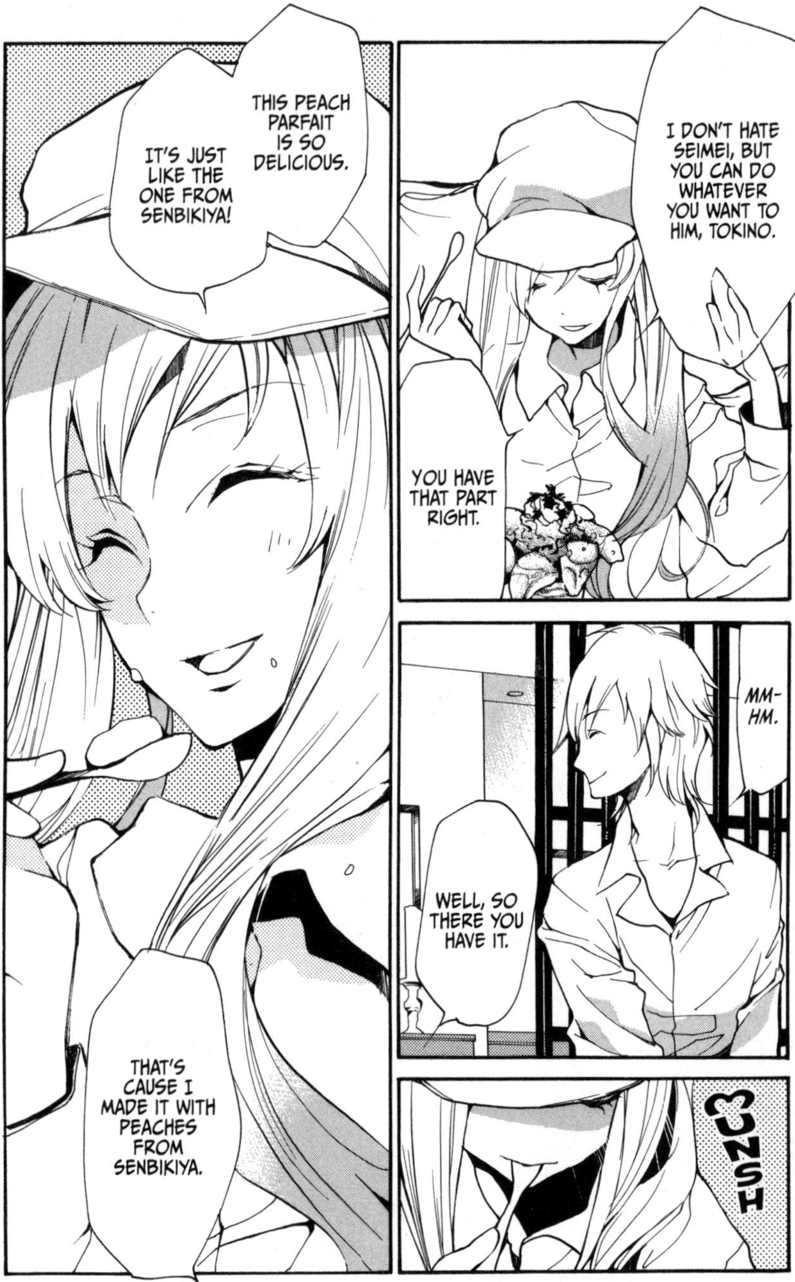
I DON'T HATE SEIMEI, BUT YOU CAN DO WHATEVER YOU WANT TO HIM, TOKINO.
YOU HAVE THAT PART RIGHT.
MM-HM.
WELL, SO THERE YOU HAVE IT.
MUNSH
THIS PEACH PARFAIT IS SO DELICIOUS.
IT'S JUST LIKE THE ONE FROM SENBIKIYA!
THAT'S CAUSE I MADE IT WITH PEACHES FROM SENBIKIYA.

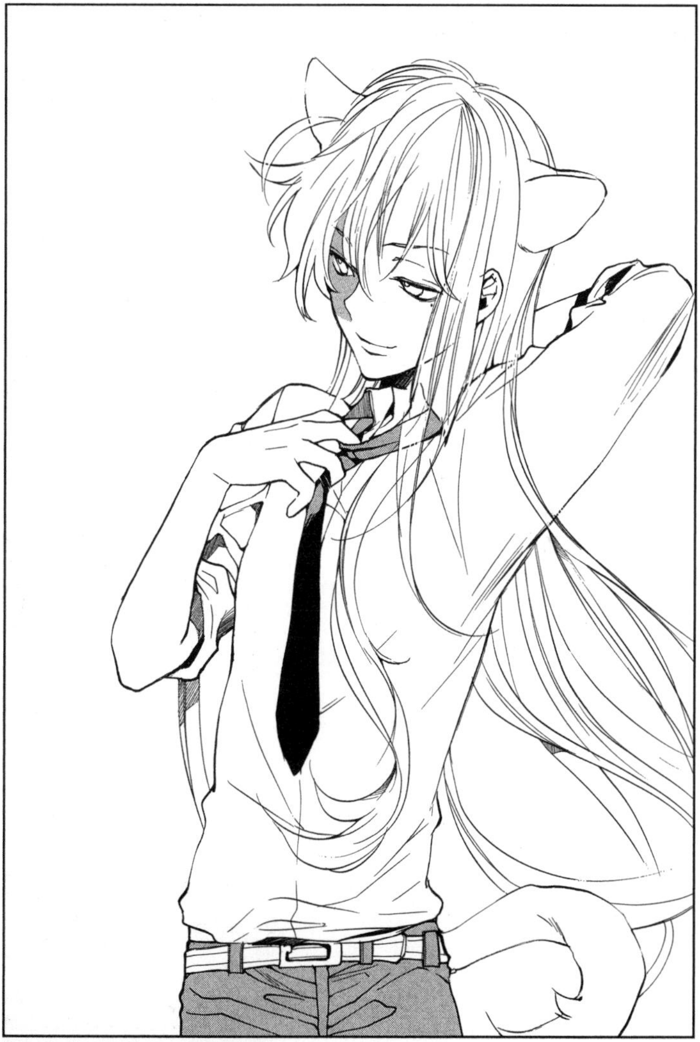

LOVELESS

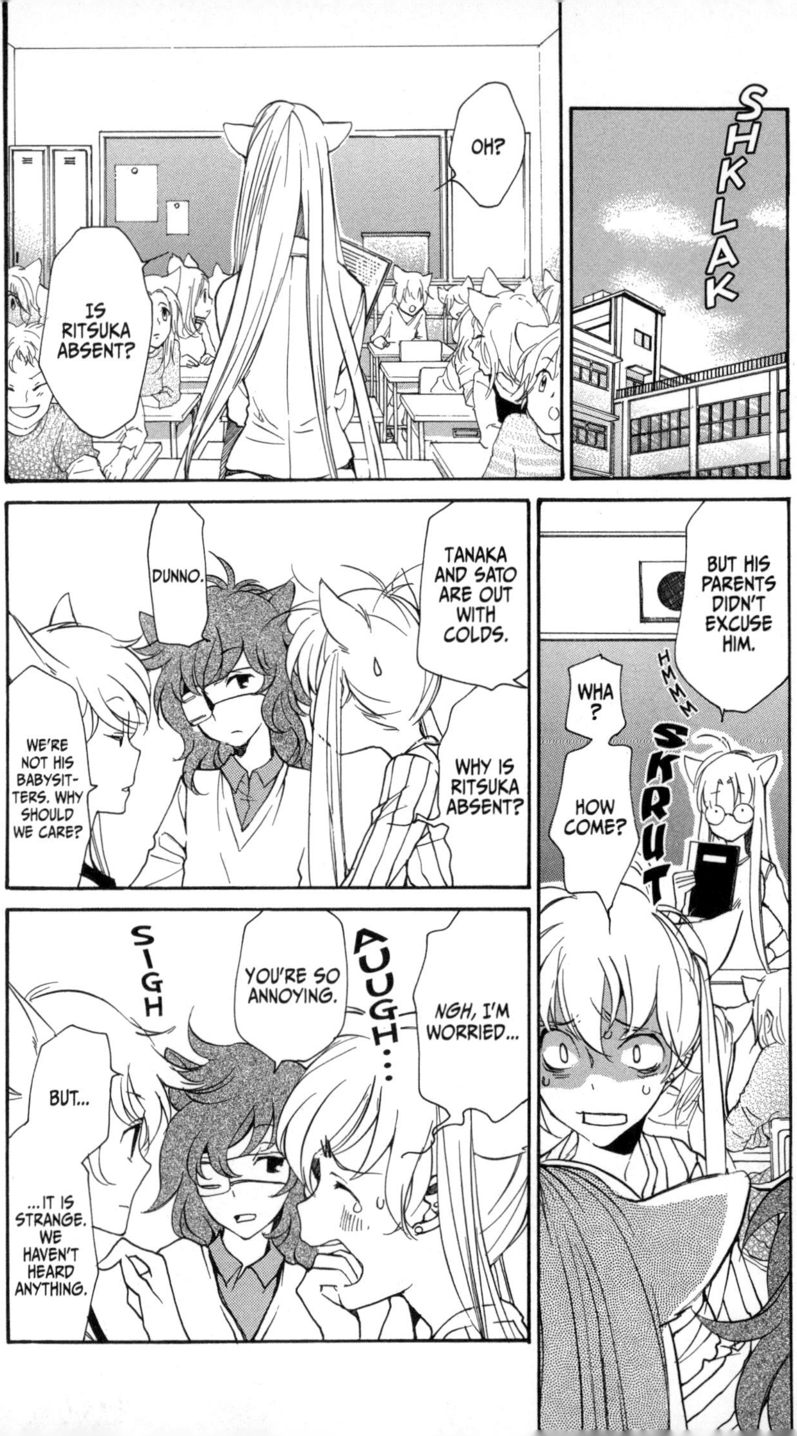
SHKLAK
OH?
IS RITSUKA ABSENT?
BUT HIS PARENTS DIDN'T EXCUSE HIM.
HMMM
SKRUT
WHA?
HOW COME?
TANAKA AND SATO ARE OUT WITH COLDS.
DUNNO.
WHY IS RITSUKA ABSENT?
WE'RE NOT HIS BABYSIT-TERS. WHY SHOULD WE CARE?
NGH, I'M WORRIED...
AUUGH...
YOU'RE SO ANNOYING.
SIGH
BUT...
...IT IS STRANGE. WE HAVEN'T HEARD ANYTHING.

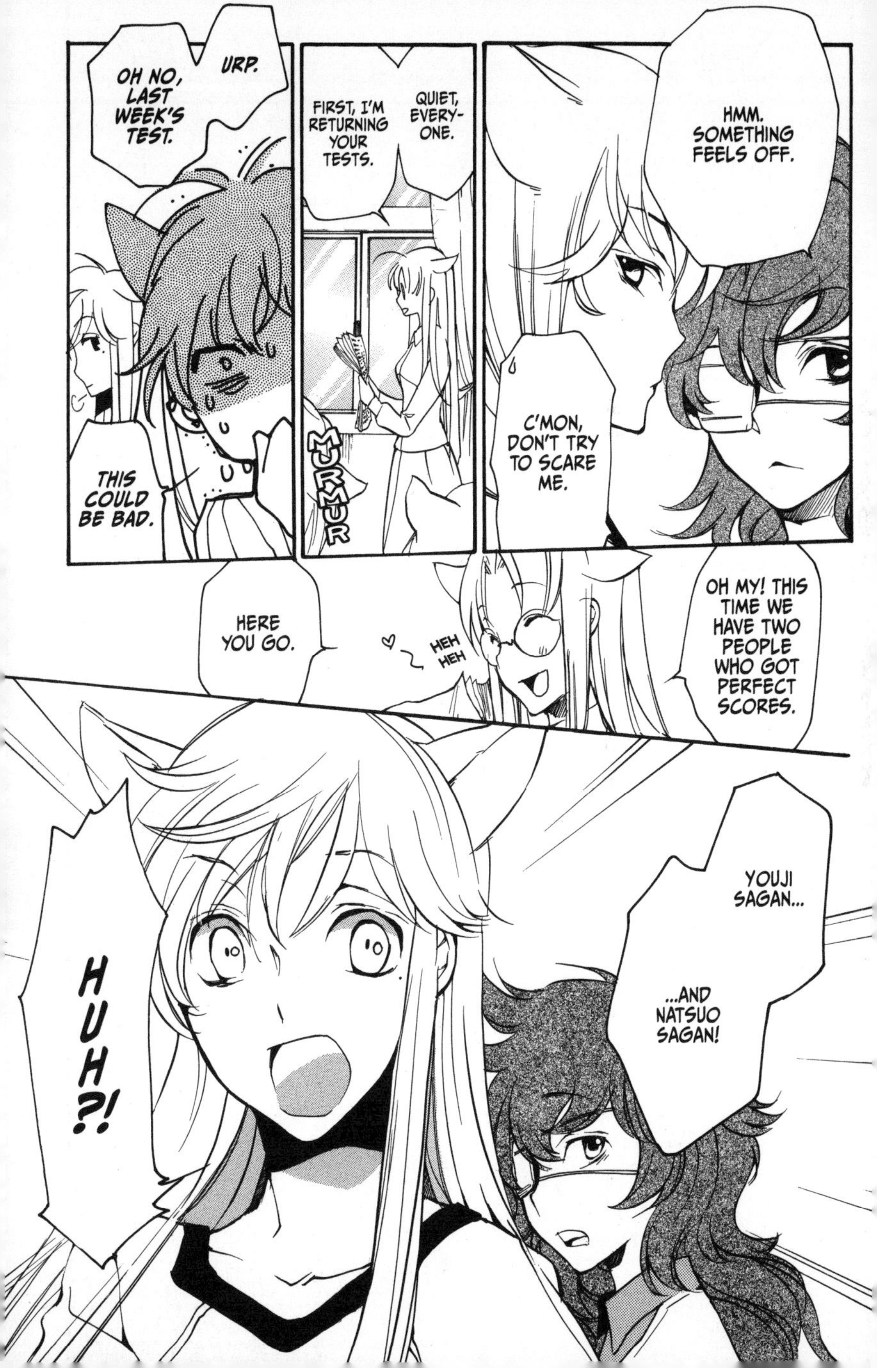
HMM. SOMETHING FEELS OFF.
C'MON, DON'T TRY TO SCARE ME.
QUIET, EVERYONE.
FIRST, I'M RETURNING YOUR TESTS.
MURMUR
URP.
OH NO, LAST WEEK'S TEST.
THIS COULD BE BAD.
OH MY! THIS TIME WE HAVE TWO PEOPLE WHO GOT PERFECT SCORES.
HEH HEH
HERE YOU GO.
YOUJI SAGAN...
...AND NATSUO SAGAN!
HUH?!

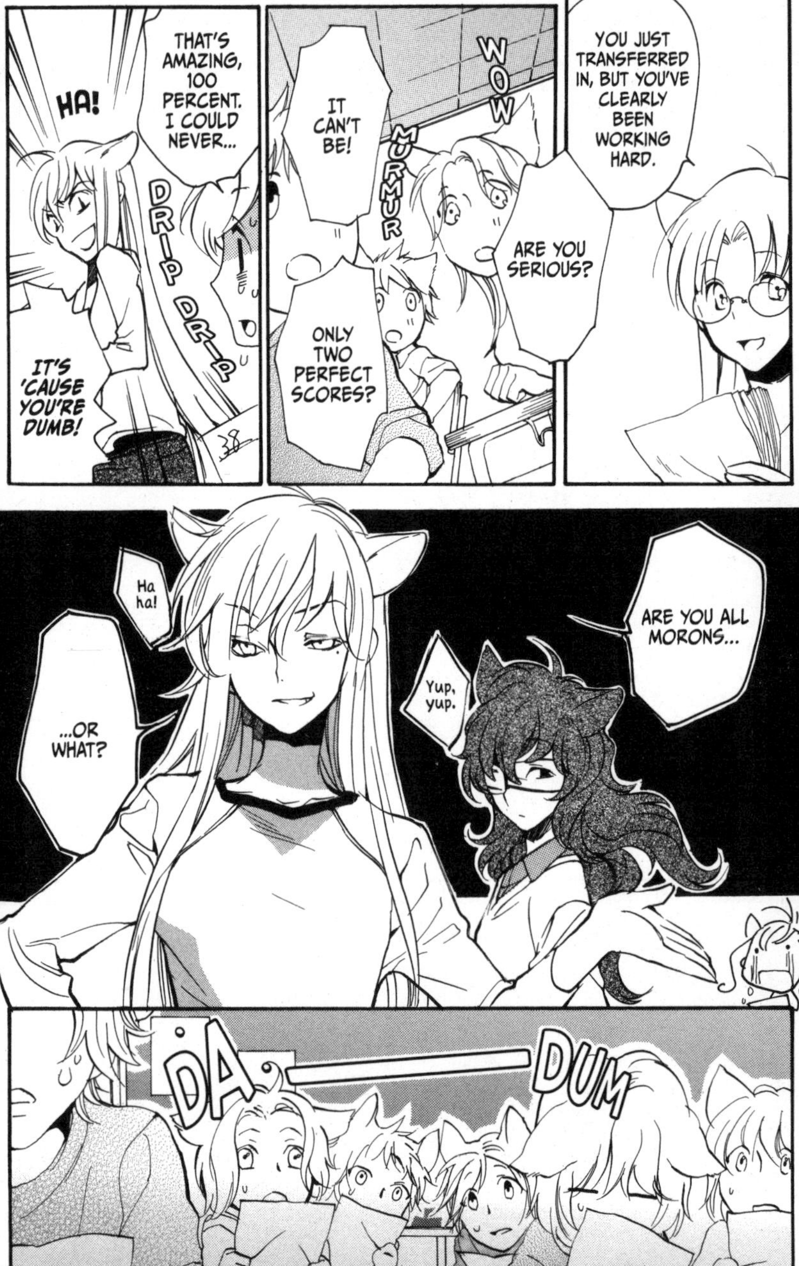
YOU JUST TRANSFERRED IN, BUT YOU'VE CLEARLY BEEN WORKING HARD.
WOW
IT CAN'T BE!
MURMUR
ARE YOU SERIOUS?
ONLY TWO PERFECT SCORES?
THAT'S AMAZING, 100 PERCENT. I COULD NEVER...
HA!
DRIP DRIP
IT'S 'CAUSE YOU'RE DUMB!
ARE YOU ALL MORONS...
Yup, yup.
Ha ha!
...OR WHAT?
DA——DUM

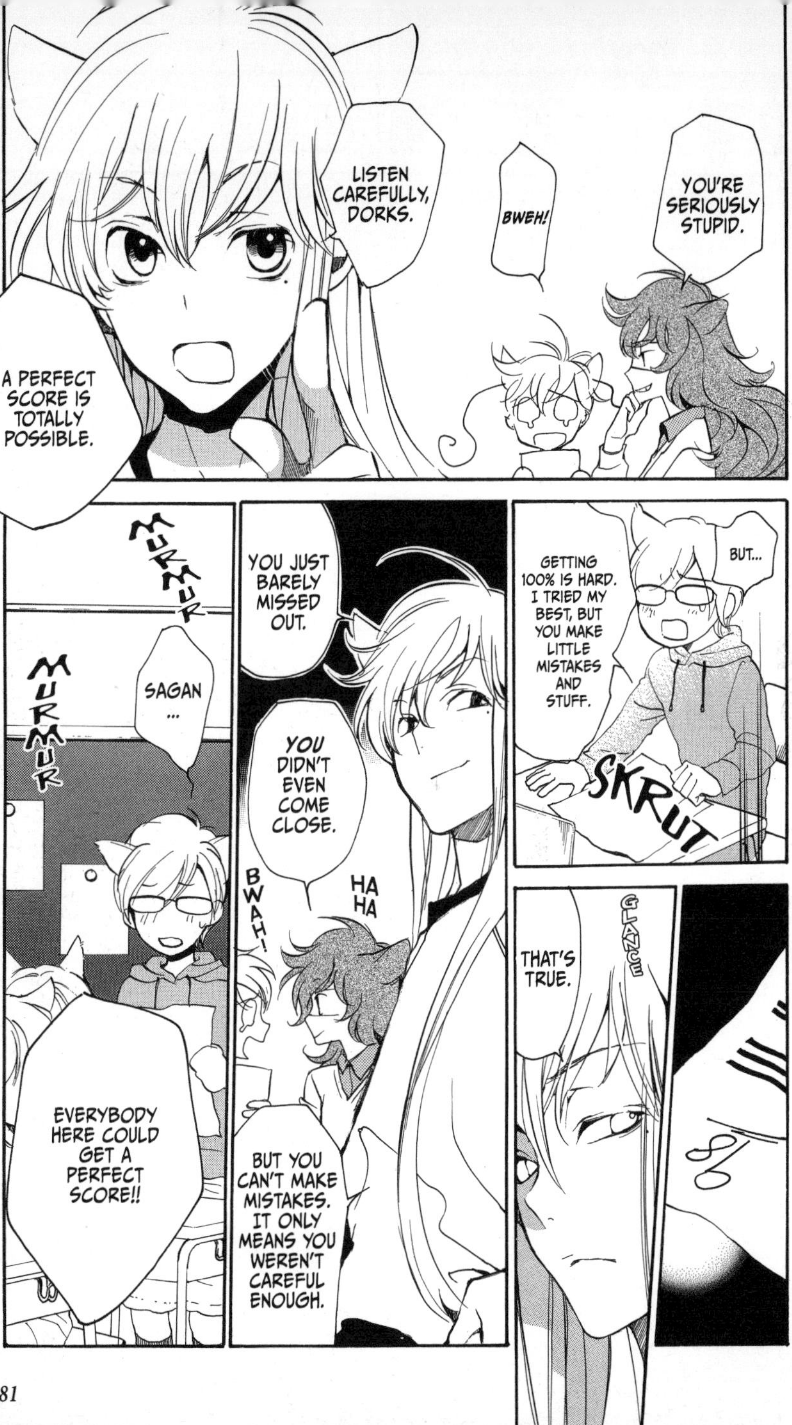
YOU'RE SERIOUSLY STUPID.
BWEH!
LISTEN CAREFULLY, DORKS.
A PERFECT SCORE IS TOTALLY POSSIBLE.
BUT...
GETTING 100% IS HARD. I TRIED MY BEST, BUT YOU MAKE LITTLE MISTAKES AND STUFF.
SKRUT
GLANCE
THAT'S TRUE.
YOU JUST BARELY MISSED OUT.
YOU DIDN'T EVEN COME CLOSE.
HA HA
BWAH!
BUT YOU CAN'T MAKE MISTAKES. IT ONLY MEANS YOU WEREN'T CAREFUL ENOUGH.
MURMUR
MURMUR
SAGAN...
EVERYBODY HERE COULD GET A PERFECT SCORE!!

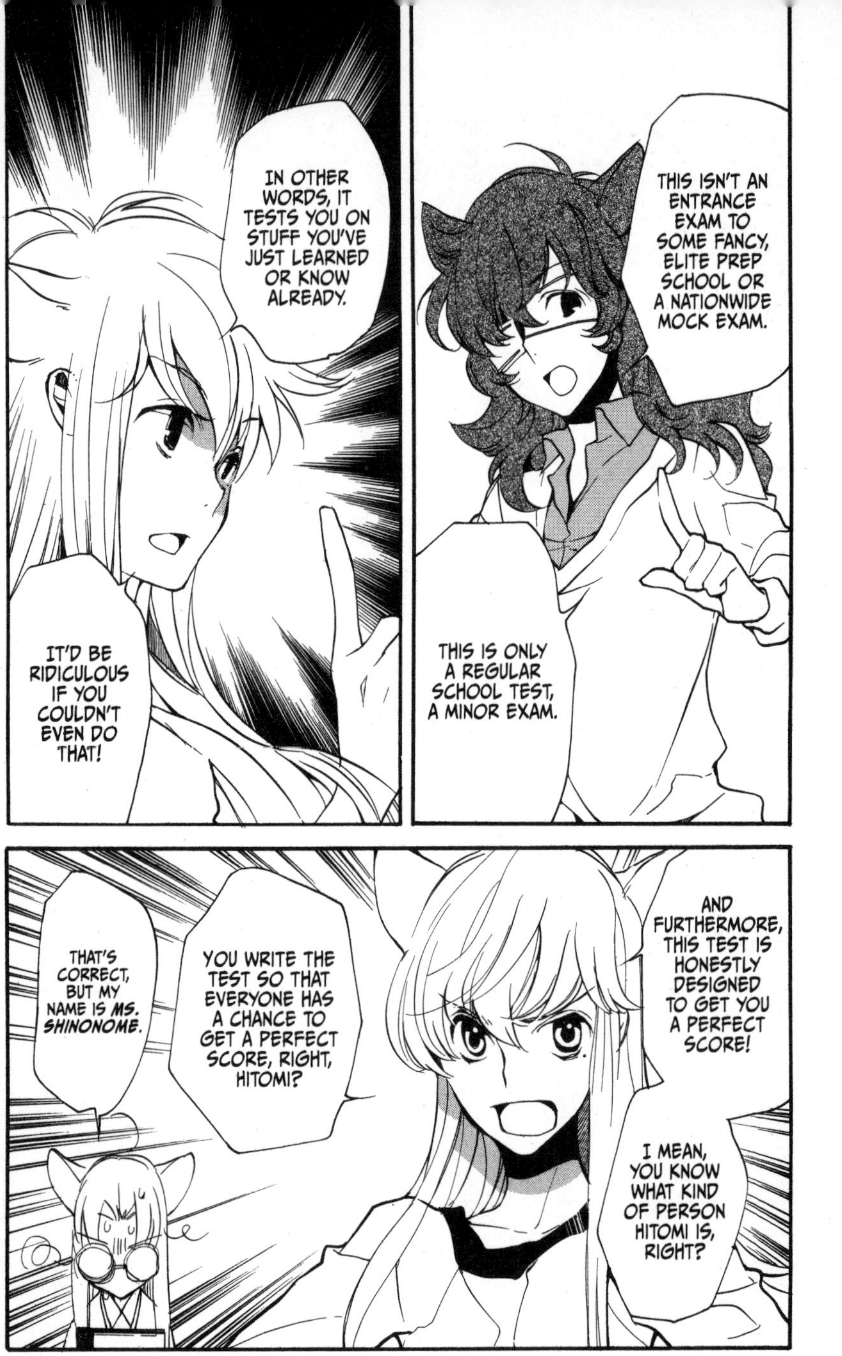
THIS ISN'T AN ENTRANCE EXAM TO SOME FANCY, ELITE PREP SCHOOL OR A NATIONWIDE MOCK EXAM.
THIS IS ONLY A REGULAR SCHOOL TEST, A MINOR EXAM.
IN OTHER WORDS, IT TESTS YOU ON STUFF YOU'VE JUST LEARNED OR KNOW ALREADY.
IT'D BE RIDICULOUS IF YOU COULDN'T EVEN DO THAT!
AND FURTHERMORE, THIS TEST IS HONESTLY DESIGNED TO GET YOU A PERFECT SCORE!
I MEAN, YOU KNOW WHAT KIND OF PERSON HITOMI IS, RIGHT?
YOU WRITE THE TEST SO THAT EVERYONE HAS A CHANCE TO GET A PERFECT SCORE, RIGHT, HITOMI?
THAT'S CORRECT, BUT MY NAME IS ***MS. SHINONOME***.

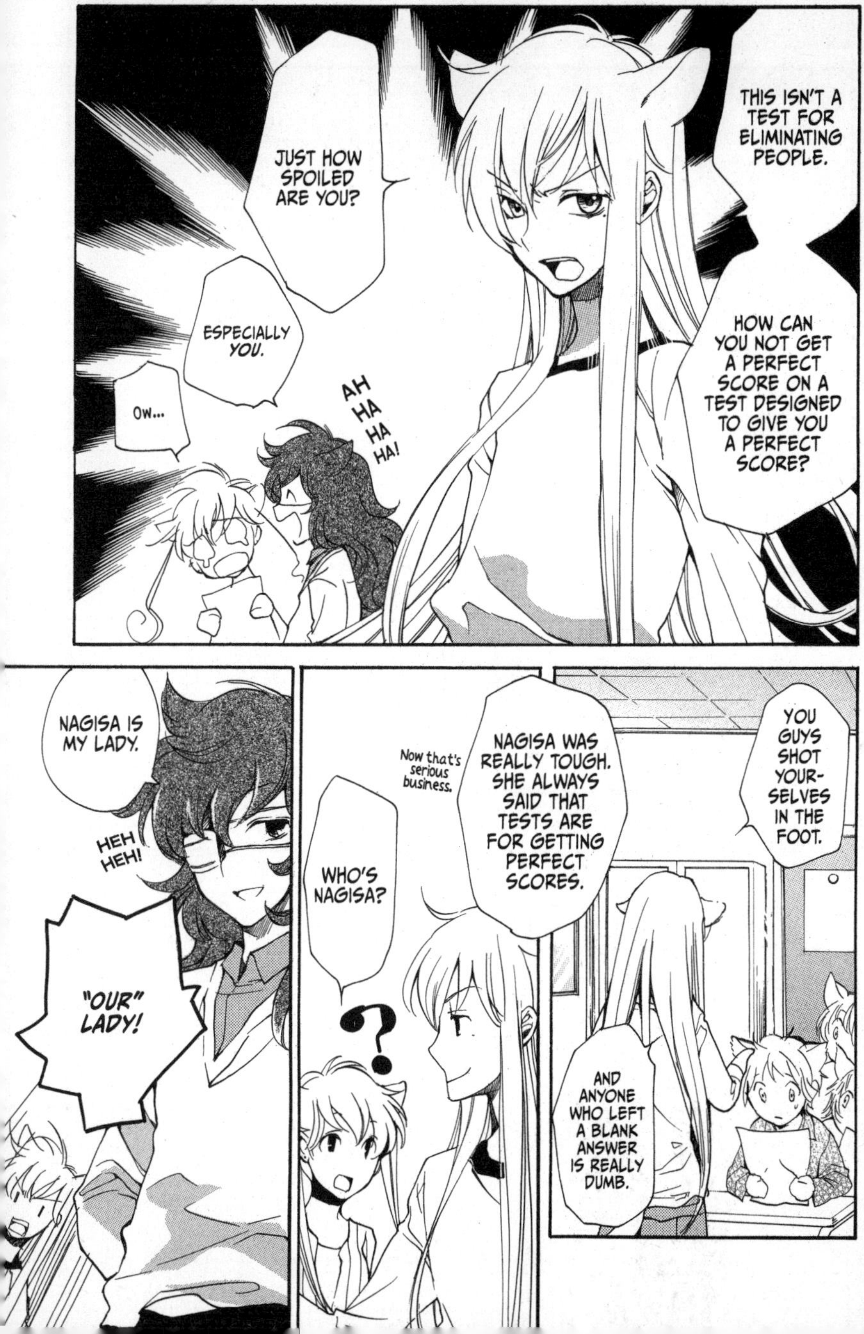
THIS ISN'T A TEST FOR ELIMINATING PEOPLE.
HOW CAN YOU NOT GET A PERFECT SCORE ON A TEST DESIGNED TO GIVE YOU A PERFECT SCORE?
JUST HOW SPOILED ARE YOU?
ESPECIALLY *YOU.*
AH HA HA HA!
OW...
YOU GUYS SHOT YOUR-SELVES IN THE FOOT.
AND ANYONE WHO LEFT A BLANK ANSWER IS REALLY DUMB.
NAGISA WAS REALLY TOUGH. SHE ALWAYS SAID THAT TESTS ARE FOR GETTING PERFECT SCORES.
Now that's serious business.
WHO'S NAGISA?
?
NAGISA IS MY LADY.
HEH HEH!
"OUR" LADY!

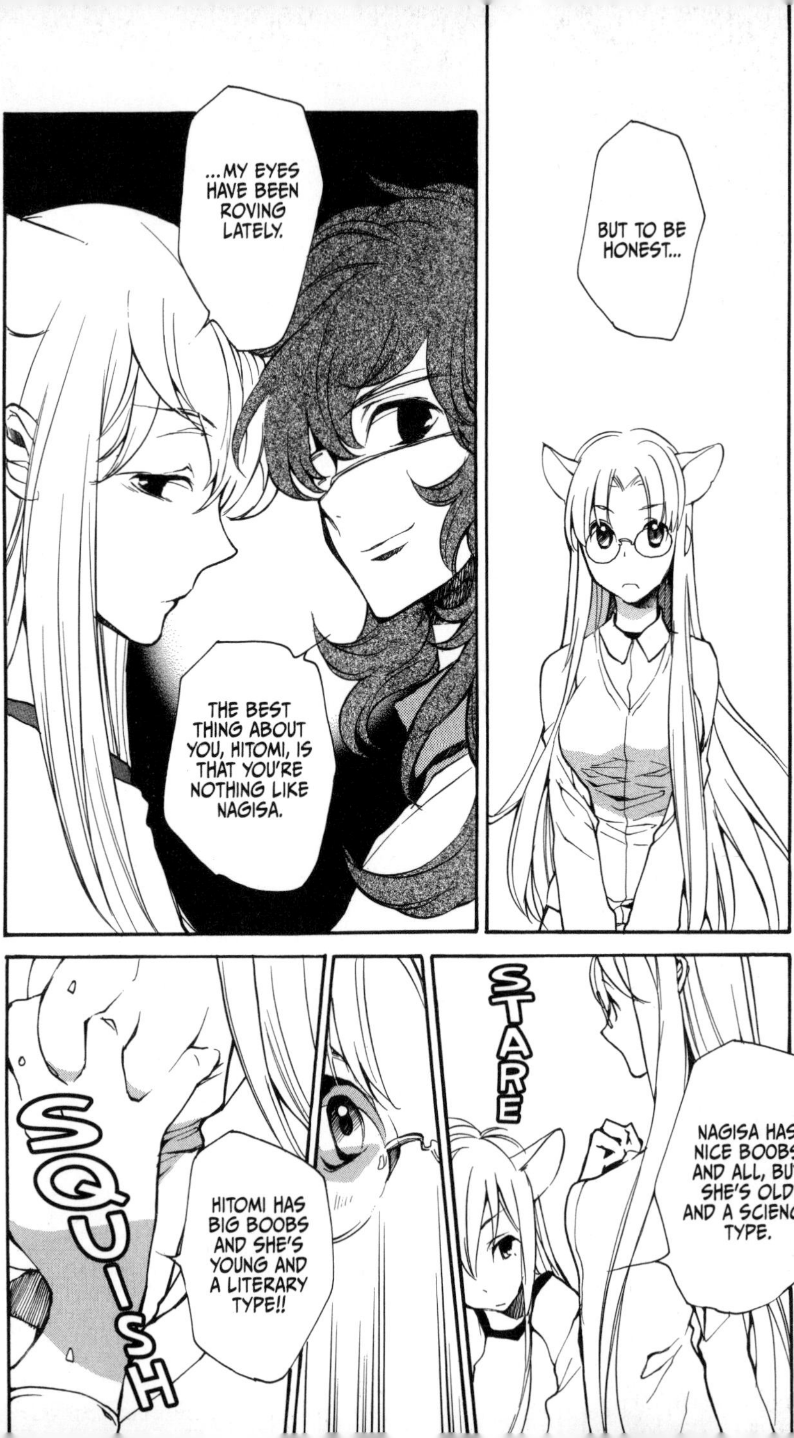
BUT TO BE HONEST...
...MY EYES HAVE BEEN ROVING LATELY.
THE BEST THING ABOUT YOU, HITOMI, IS THAT YOU'RE NOTHING LIKE NAGISA.
NAGISA HAS NICE BOOBS AND ALL, BUT SHE'S OLD AND A SCIENCE TYPE.
STARE
HITOMI HAS BIG BOOBS AND SHE'S YOUNG AND A LITERARY TYPE!!
SQUISH

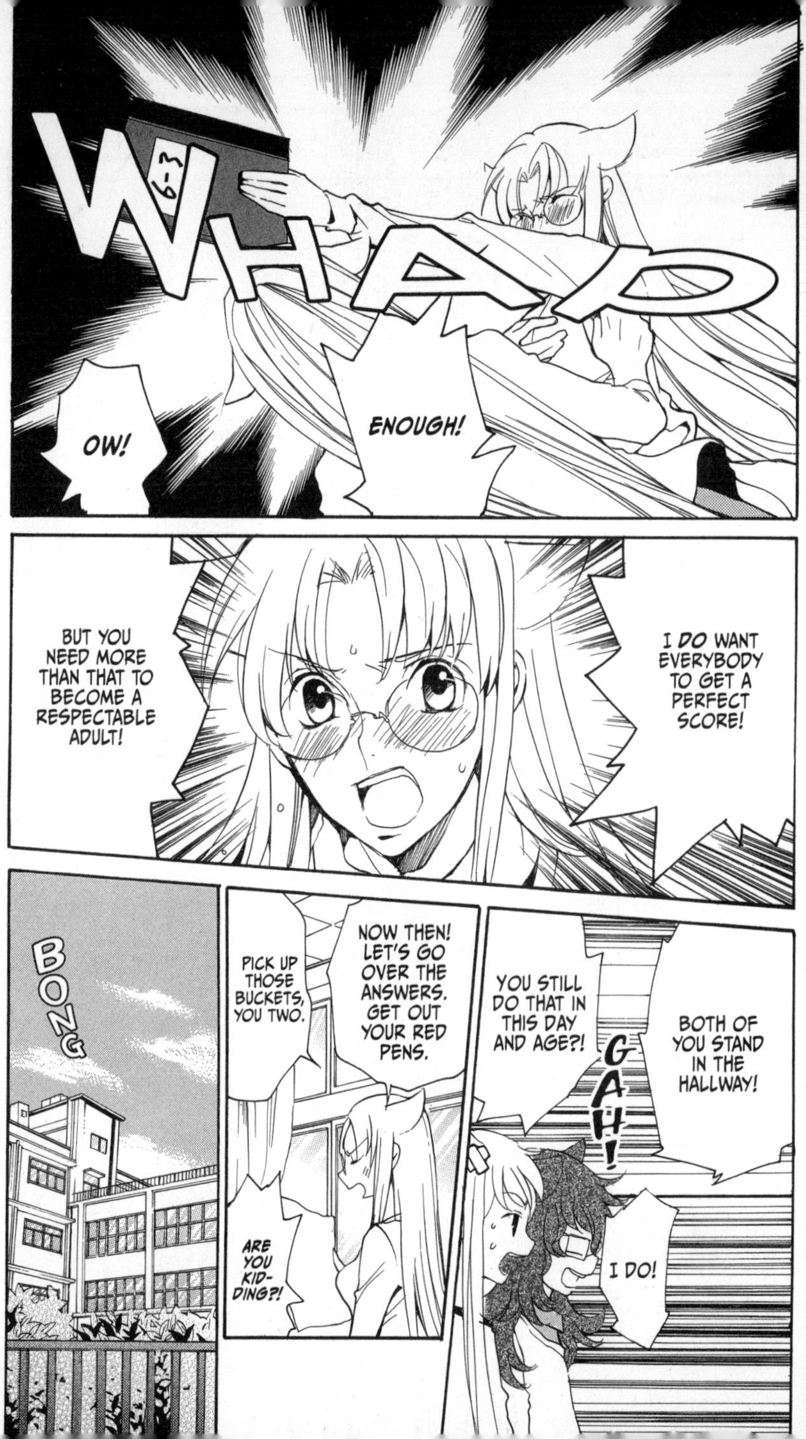
WHAP
ENOUGH!
OW!
I DO WANT EVERYBODY TO GET A PERFECT SCORE!
BUT YOU NEED MORE THAN THAT TO BECOME A RESPECTABLE ADULT!
BOTH OF YOU STAND IN THE HALLWAY!
GAH!
YOU STILL DO THAT IN THIS DAY AND AGE?!
I DO!
NOW THEN! LET'S GO OVER THE ANSWERS. GET OUT YOUR RED PENS.
PICK UP THOSE BUCKETS, YOU TWO.
ARE YOU KID-DING?!
BONG

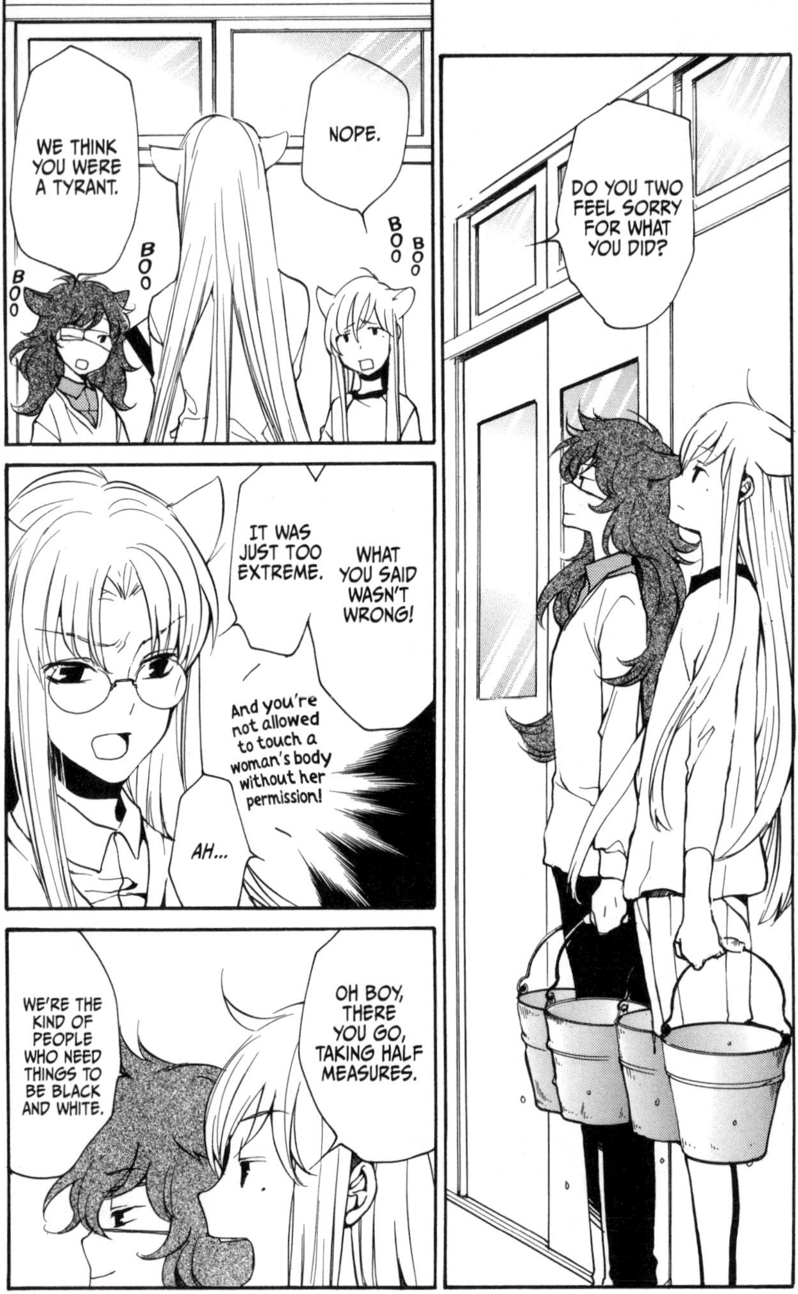
DO YOU TWO FEEL SORRY FOR WHAT YOU DID?
NOPE.
BOO BOO
BOO BOO
WE THINK YOU WERE A TYRANT.
BOO
WHAT YOU SAID WASN'T WRONG!
IT WAS JUST TOO EXTREME.
And you're not allowed to touch a woman's body without her permission!
AH...
OH BOY, THERE YOU GO, TAKING HALF MEASURES.
WE'RE THE KIND OF PEOPLE WHO NEED THINGS TO BE BLACK AND WHITE.

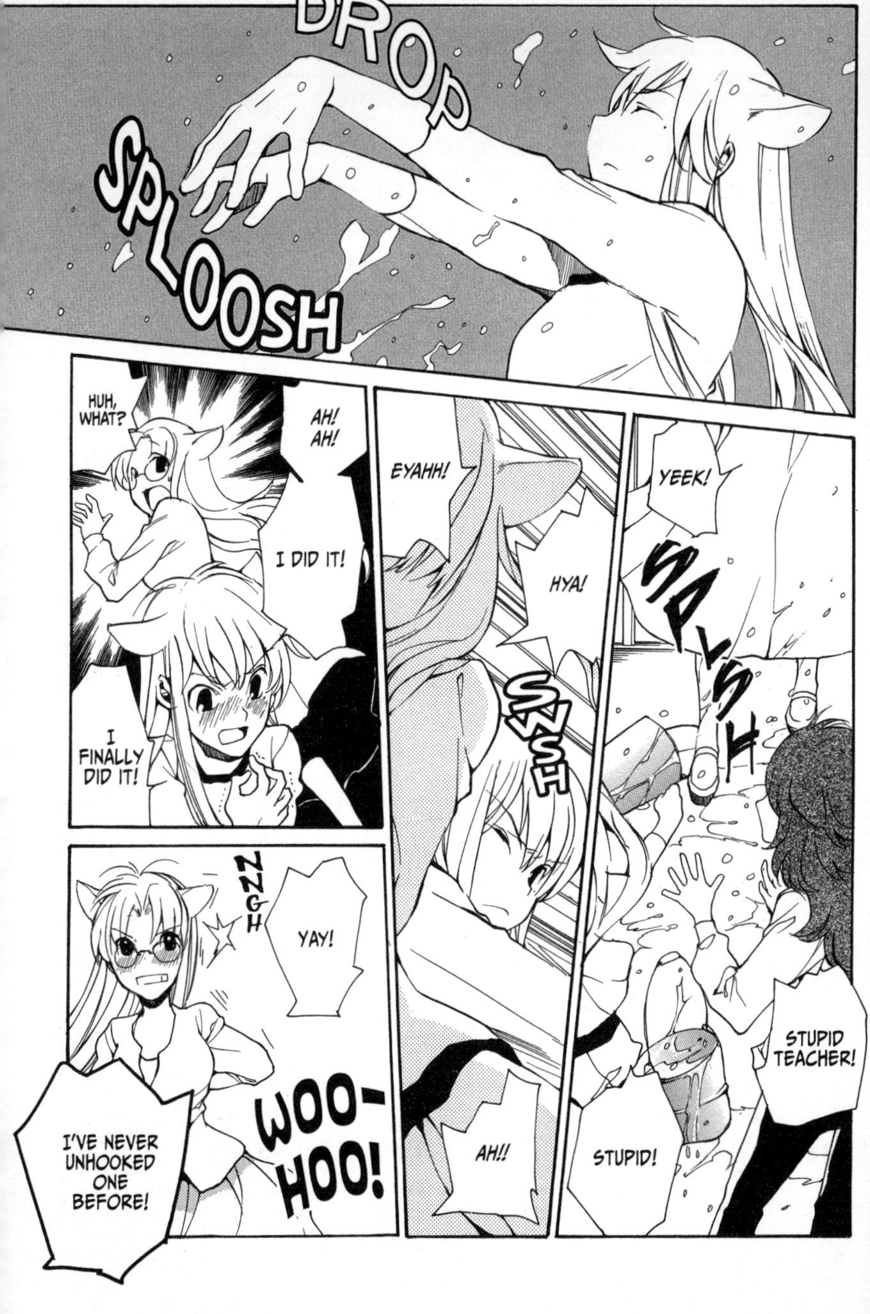
DROP
SPLOOSH
YEEK!
SPLASH
STUPID TEACHER!
STUPID!
EYAHH!
HYA!
SWSH
AH!!
AH! AH!
HUH, WHAT?
I DID IT!
I FINALLY DID IT!
NNGH
YAY!
WOO-HOO!
I'VE NEVER UNHOOKED ONE BEFORE!

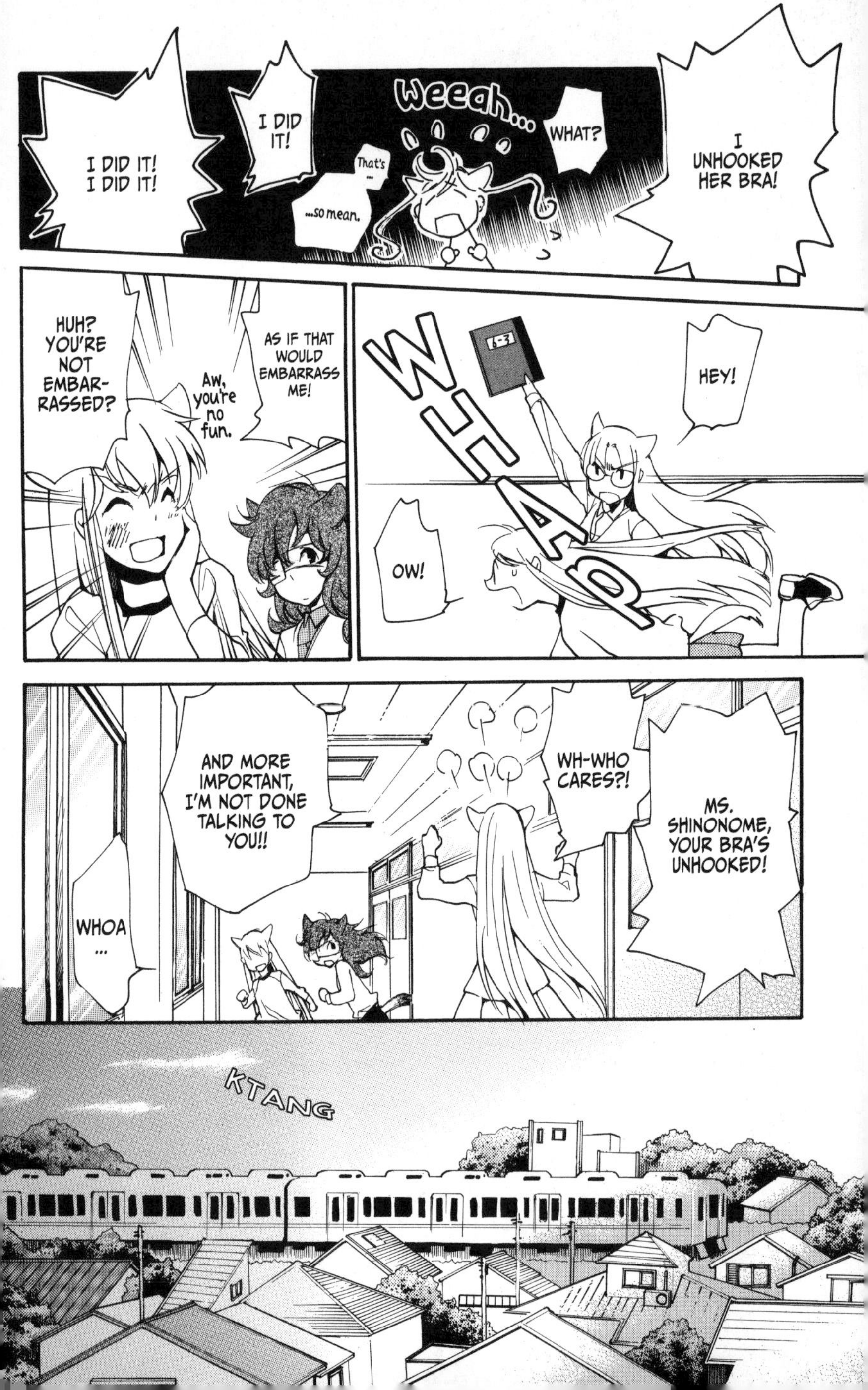
I UNHOOKED HER BRA!
WHAT?
Weeah...
That's ...
...so mean.
I DID IT!
I DID IT! I DID IT!
HEY!
WHAP
OW!
AS IF THAT WOULD EMBARRASS ME!
Aw, you're no fun.
HUH? YOU'RE NOT EMBAR-RASSED?
6-3
MS. SHINONOME, YOUR BRA'S UNHOOKED!
WH-WHO CARES?!
AND MORE IMPORTANT, I'M NOT DONE TALKING TO YOU!!
WHOA ...
KTANG

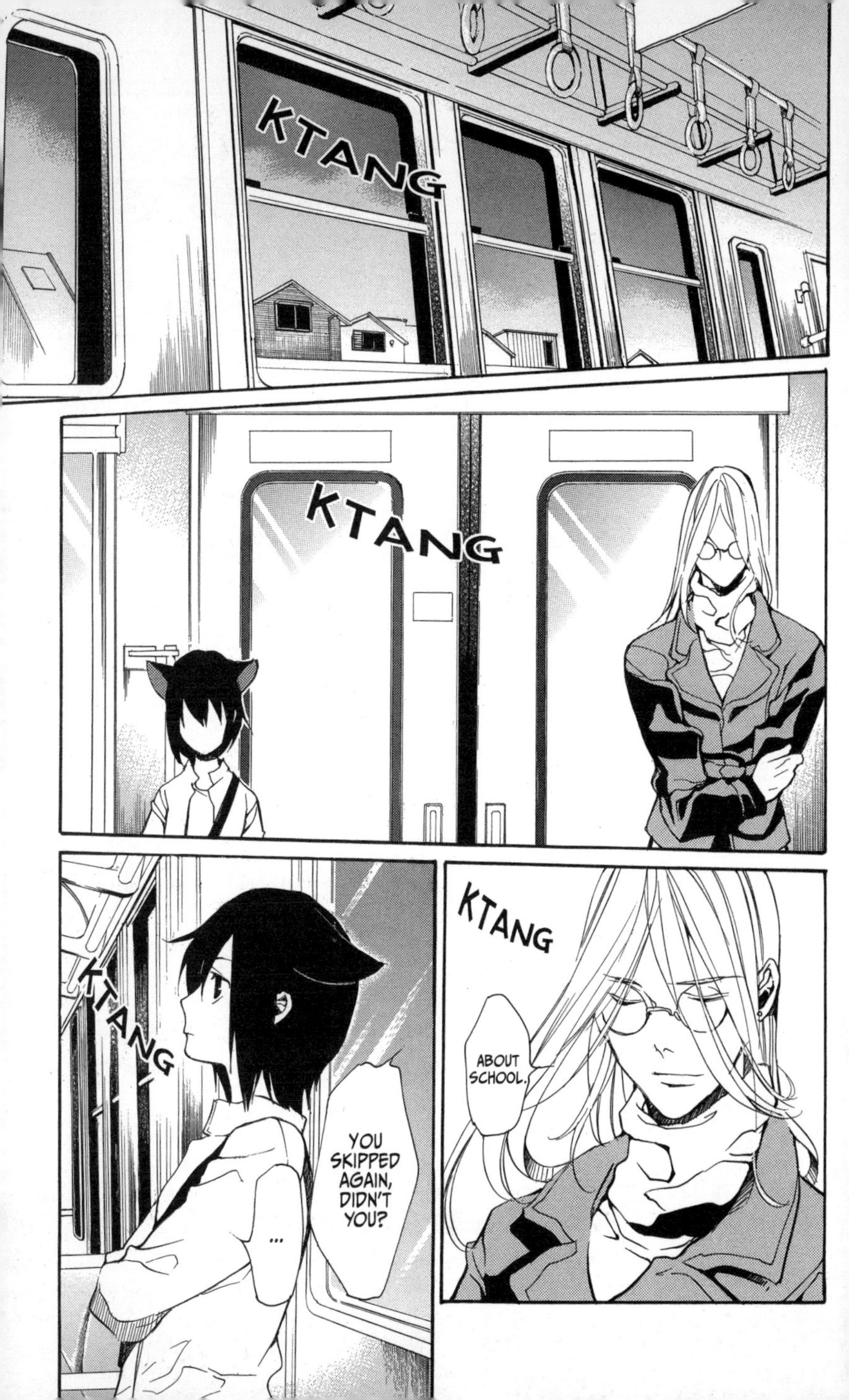
KTANG
KTANG
KTANG
ABOUT SCHOOL.
KTANG
YOU SKIPPED AGAIN, DIDN'T YOU?
...

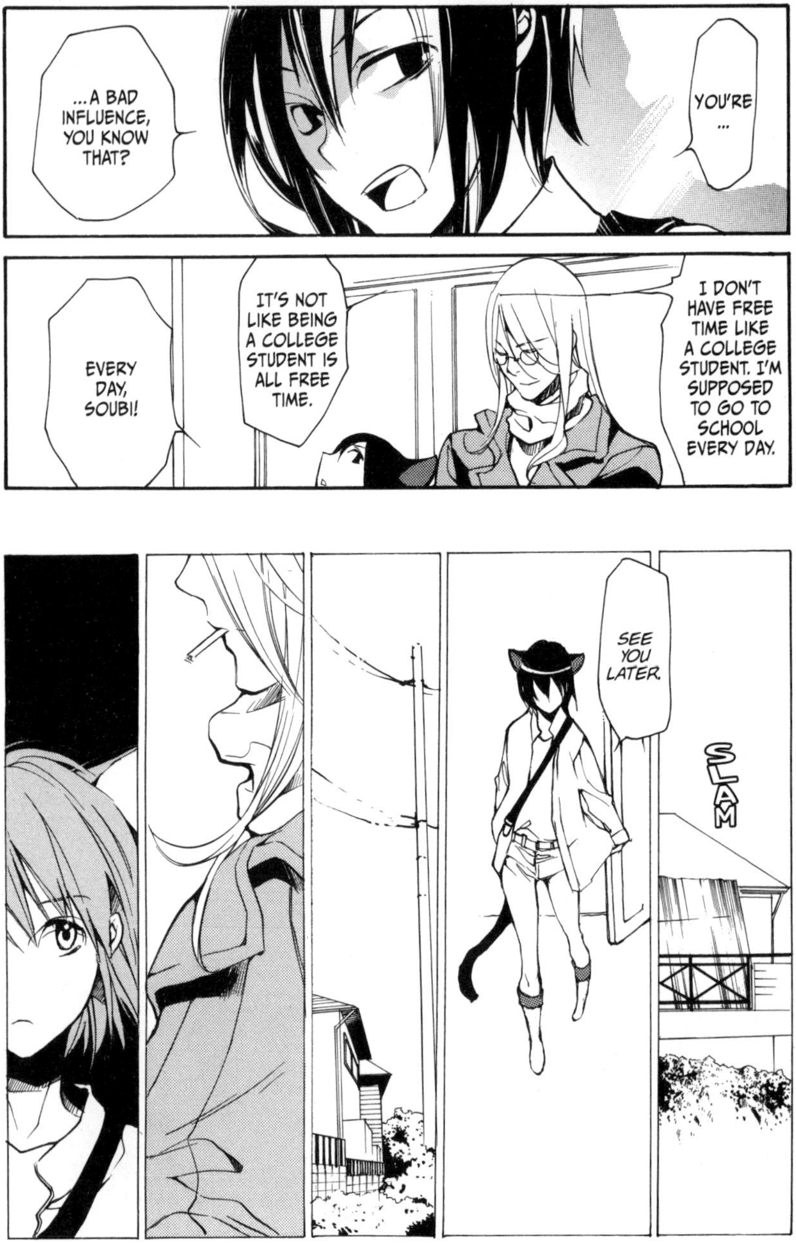
YOU'RE ...
...A BAD INFLUENCE, YOU KNOW THAT?
I DON'T HAVE FREE TIME LIKE A COLLEGE STUDENT. I'M SUPPOSED TO GO TO SCHOOL EVERY DAY.
IT'S NOT LIKE BEING A COLLEGE STUDENT IS ALL FREE TIME.
EVERY DAY, SOUBI!
SLAM
SEE YOU LATER.

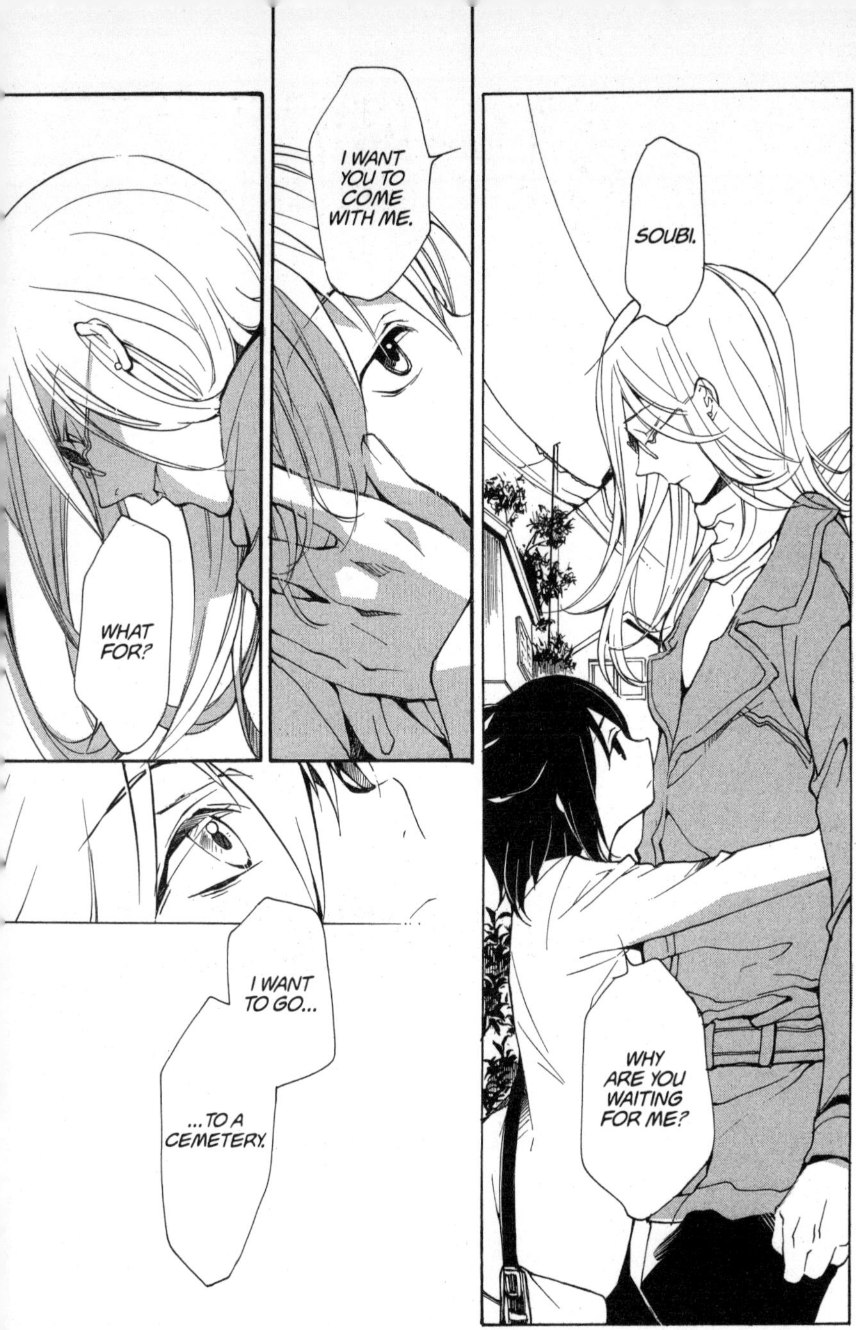
SOUBI.
WHY ARE YOU WAITING FOR ME?
I WANT YOU TO COME WITH ME.
WHAT FOR?
I WANT TO GO...
...TO A CEMETERY.

LOVELESS

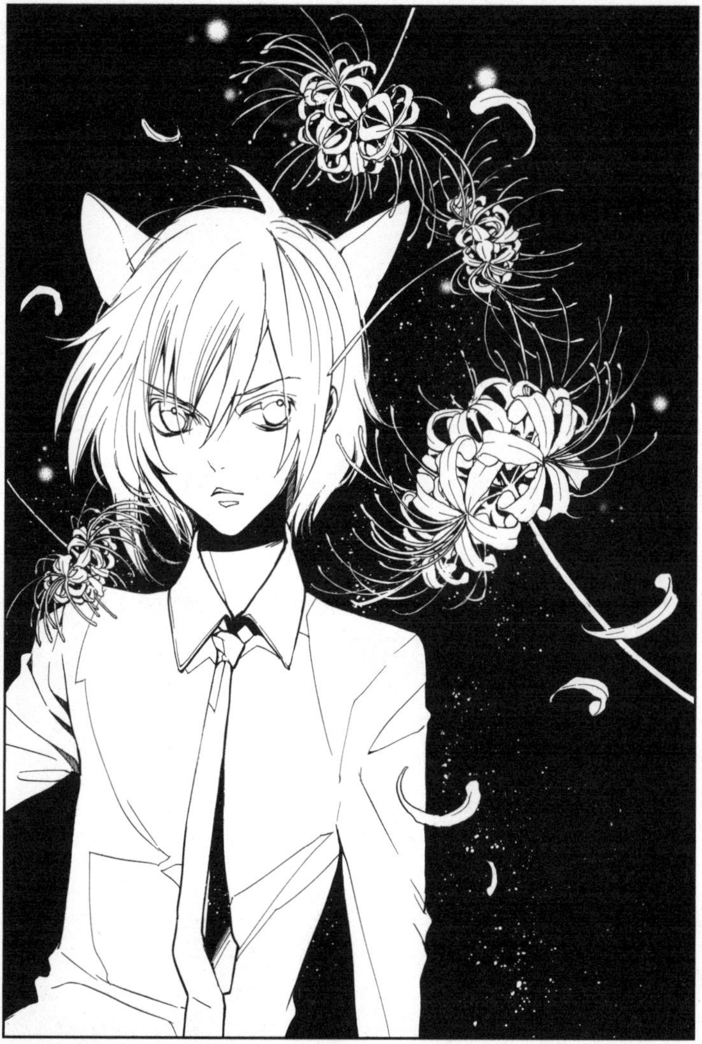

LOVELESS

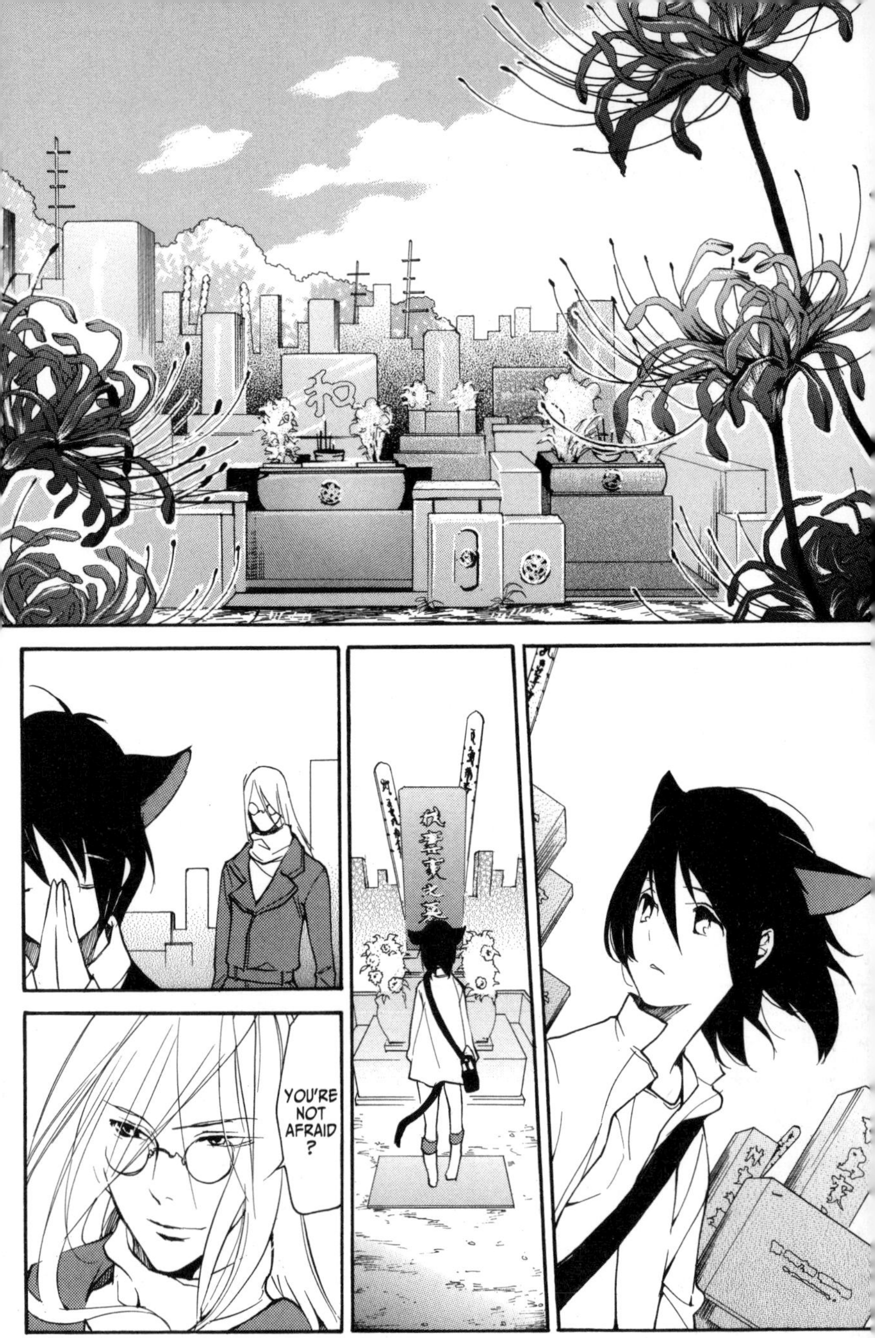
YOU'RE NOT AFRAID?

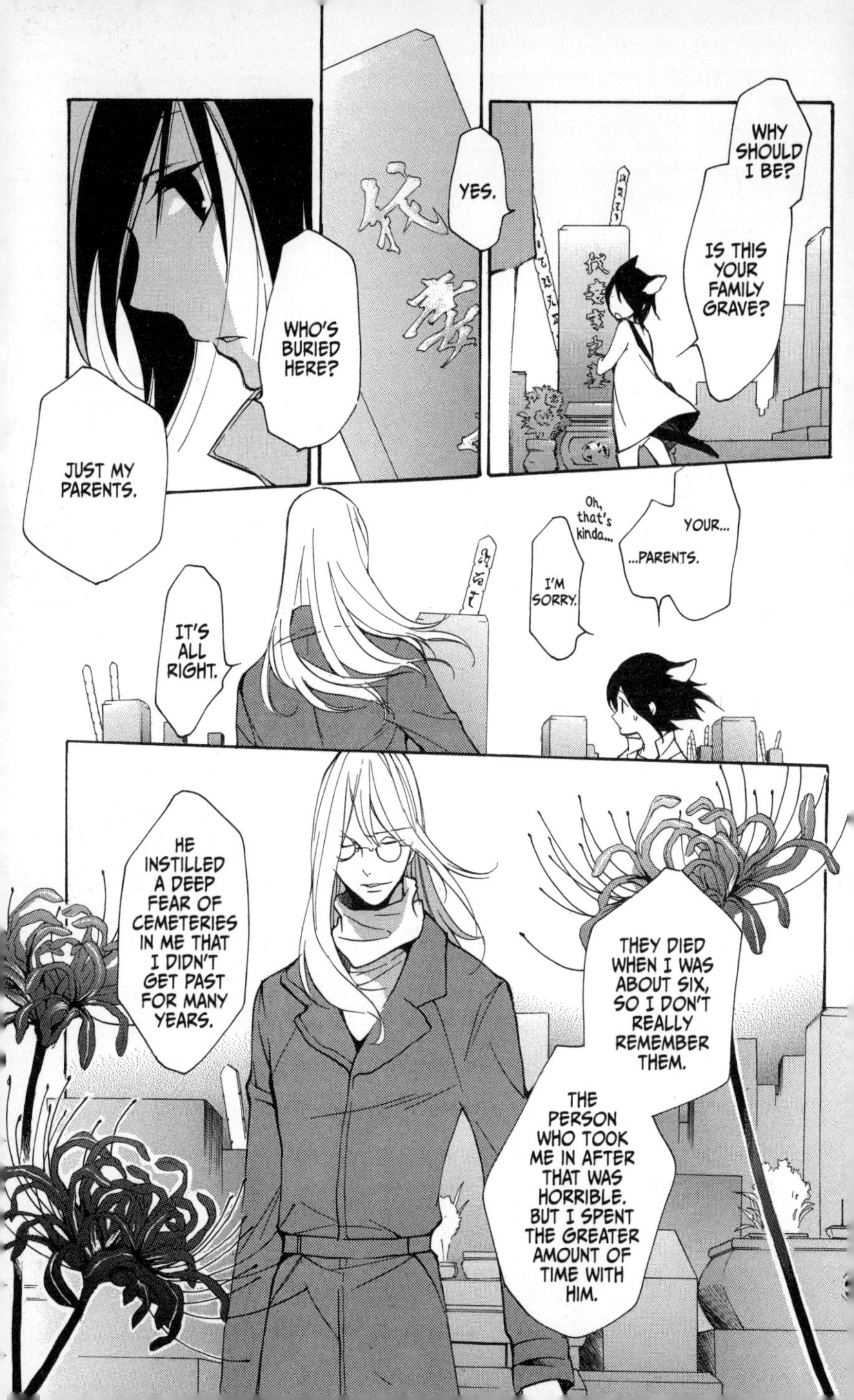

WHY SHOULD I BE?
IS THIS YOUR FAMILY GRAVE?
YES.
WHO'S BURIED HERE?
JUST MY PARENTS.
YOUR... ...PARENTS.
Oh, that's kinda...
I'M SORRY.
IT'S ALL RIGHT.
THEY DIED WHEN I WAS ABOUT SIX, SO I DON'T REALLY REMEMBER THEM.
THE PERSON WHO TOOK ME IN AFTER THAT WAS HORRIBLE. BUT I SPENT THE GREATER AMOUNT OF TIME WITH HIM.
HE INSTILLED A DEEP FEAR OF CEMETERIES IN ME THAT I DIDN'T GET PAST FOR MANY YEARS.

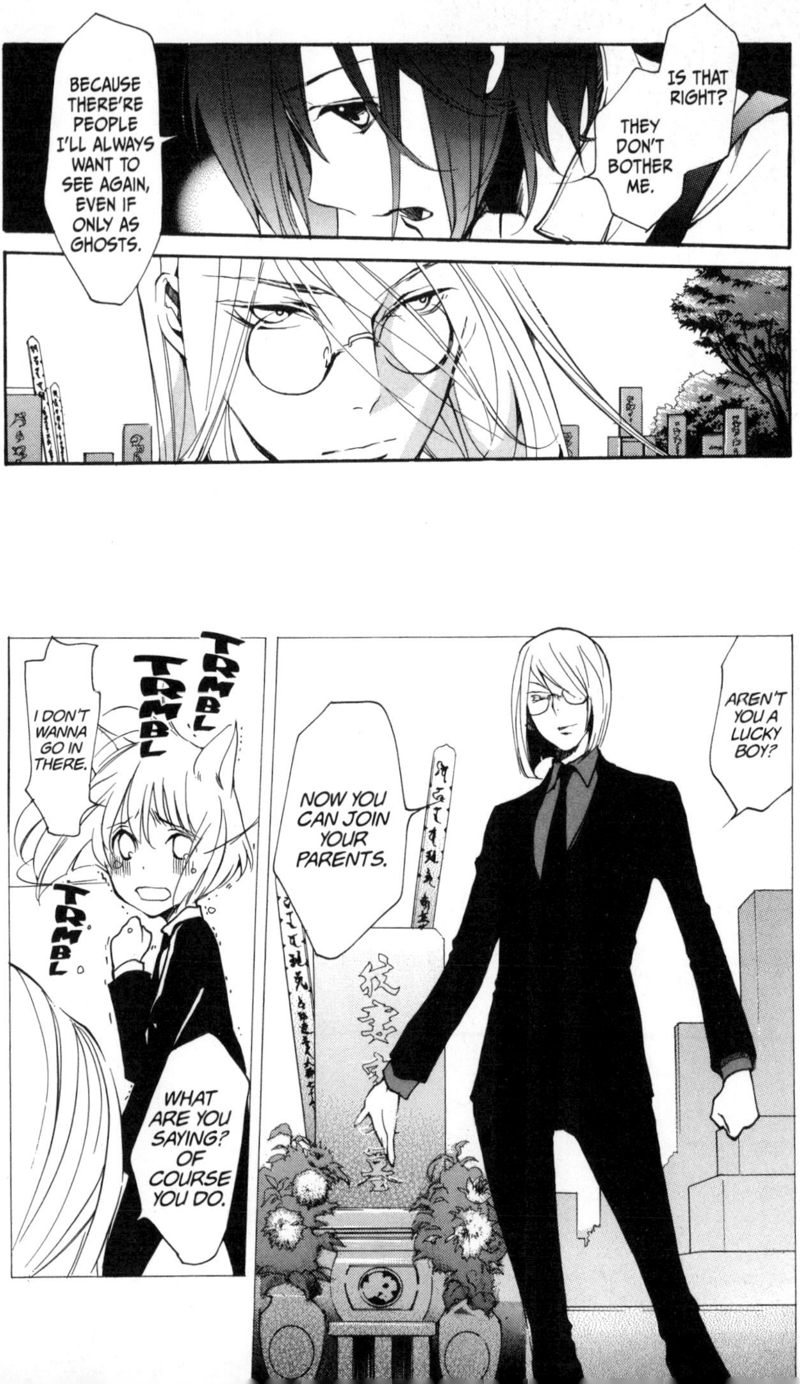
IS THAT RIGHT?
THEY DON'T BOTHER ME.
BECAUSE THERE'RE PEOPLE I'LL ALWAYS WANT TO SEE AGAIN, EVEN IF ONLY AS GHOSTS.
AREN'T YOU A LUCKY BOY?
NOW YOU CAN JOIN YOUR PARENTS.
TRMBL
TRMBL
I DON'T WANNA GO IN THERE.
TRMBL
WHAT ARE YOU SAYING? OF COURSE YOU DO.

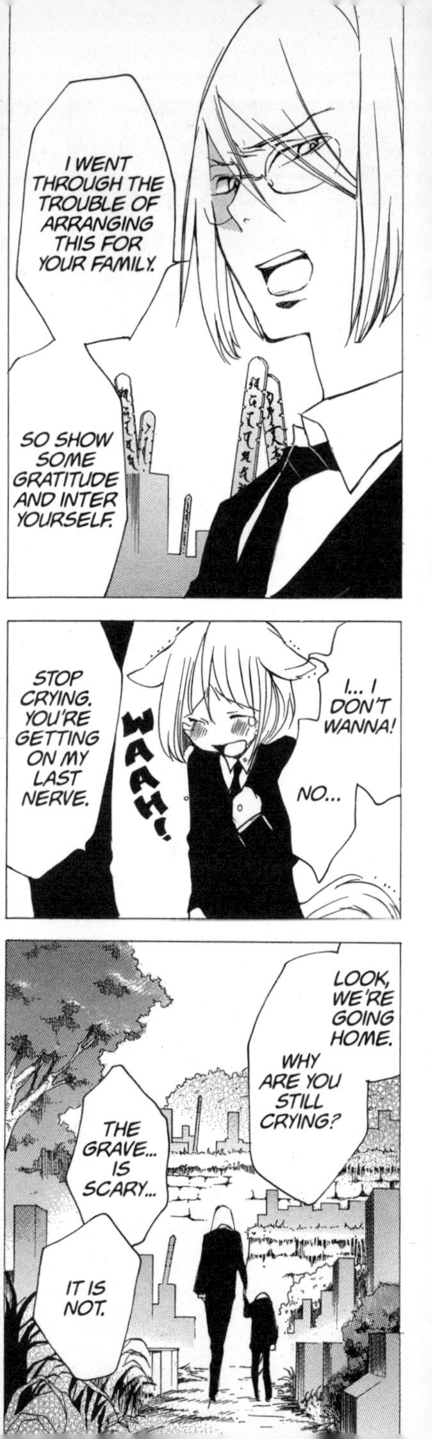
I WENT THROUGH THE TROUBLE OF ARRANGING THIS FOR YOUR FAMILY.
SO SHOW SOME GRATITUDE AND INTER YOURSELF.
I... I DON'T WANNA!
NO...
WAAH!
STOP CRYING. YOU'RE GETTING ON MY LAST NERVE.
LOOK, WE'RE GOING HOME.
WHY ARE YOU STILL CRYING?
THE GRAVE... IS SCARY...
IT IS NOT.
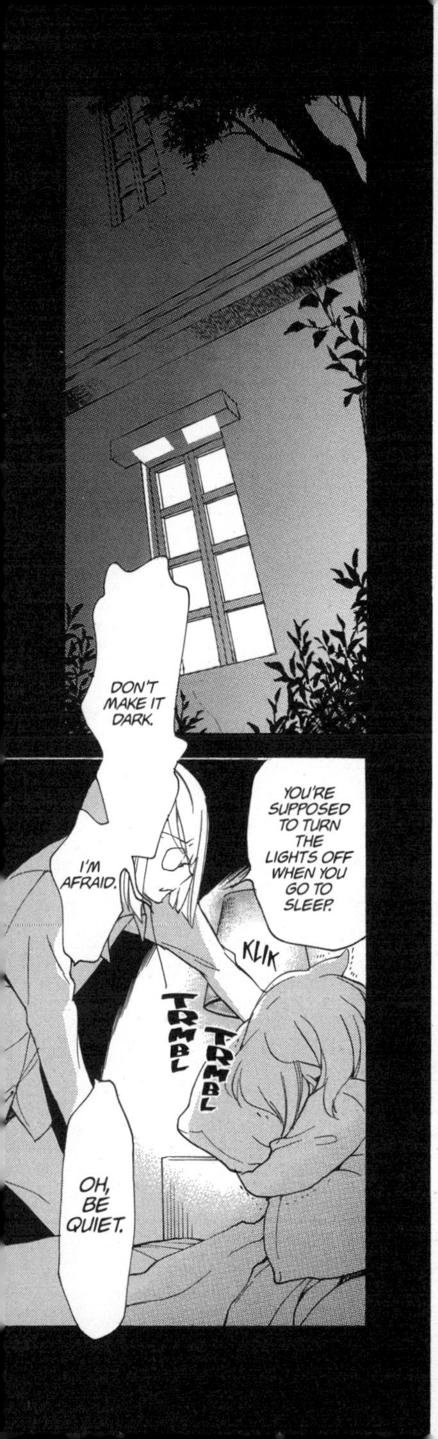
DON'T MAKE IT DARK.
YOU'RE SUPPOSED TO TURN THE LIGHTS OFF WHEN YOU GO TO SLEEP.
I'M AFRAID.
KLIK
TRMBL
TRMBL
OH, BE QUIET.

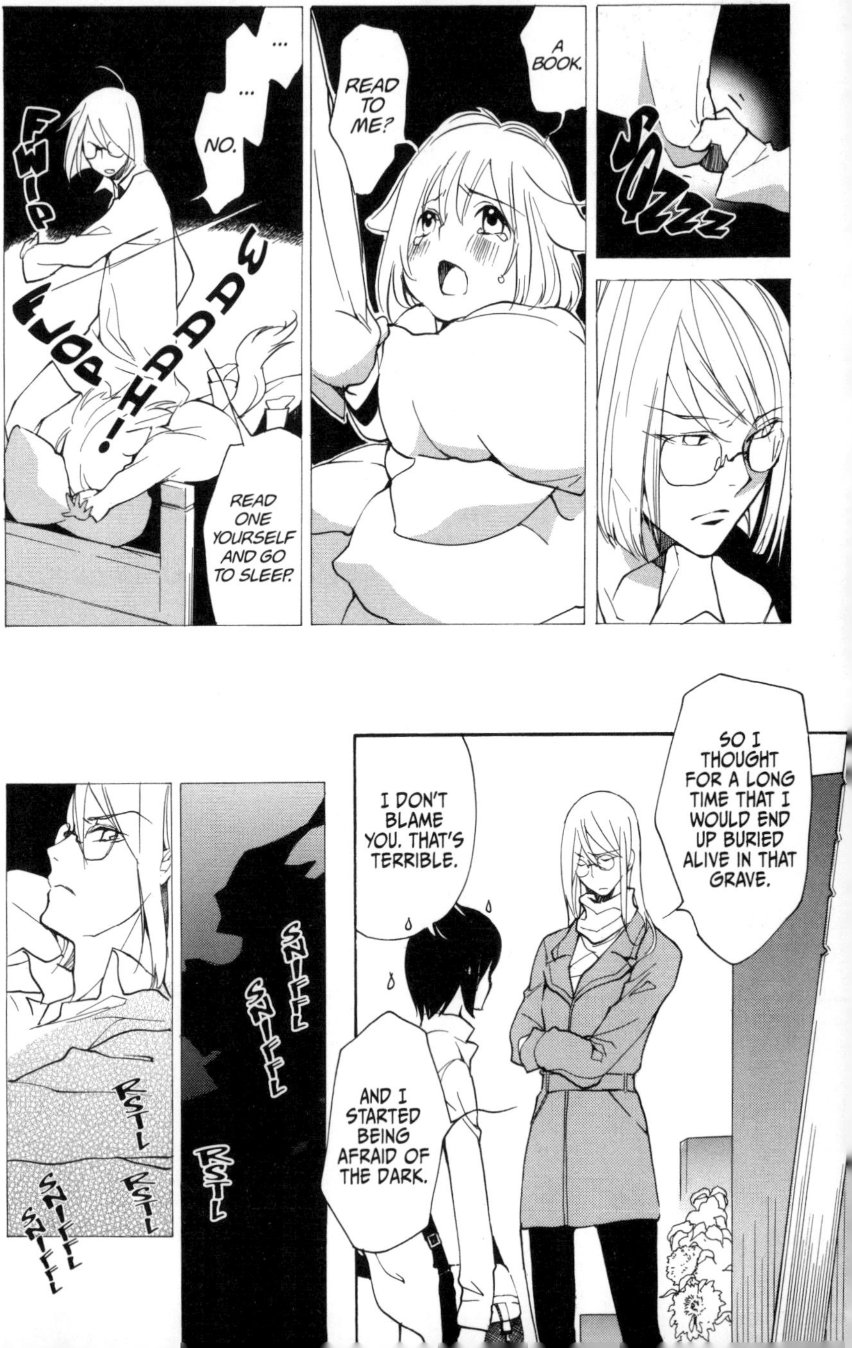
SQZZZ
A BOOK.
READ TO ME?
...
...
NO.
FWIP
WAAAAH!
FLOP
READ ONE YOURSELF AND GO TO SLEEP.
SO I THOUGHT FOR A LONG TIME THAT I WOULD END UP BURIED ALIVE IN THAT GRAVE.
I DON'T BLAME YOU. THAT'S TERRIBLE.
AND I STARTED BEING AFRAID OF THE DARK.
SNIFF
SNIFF
RSTL
RSTL
RSTL
SNIFF
SNIFF

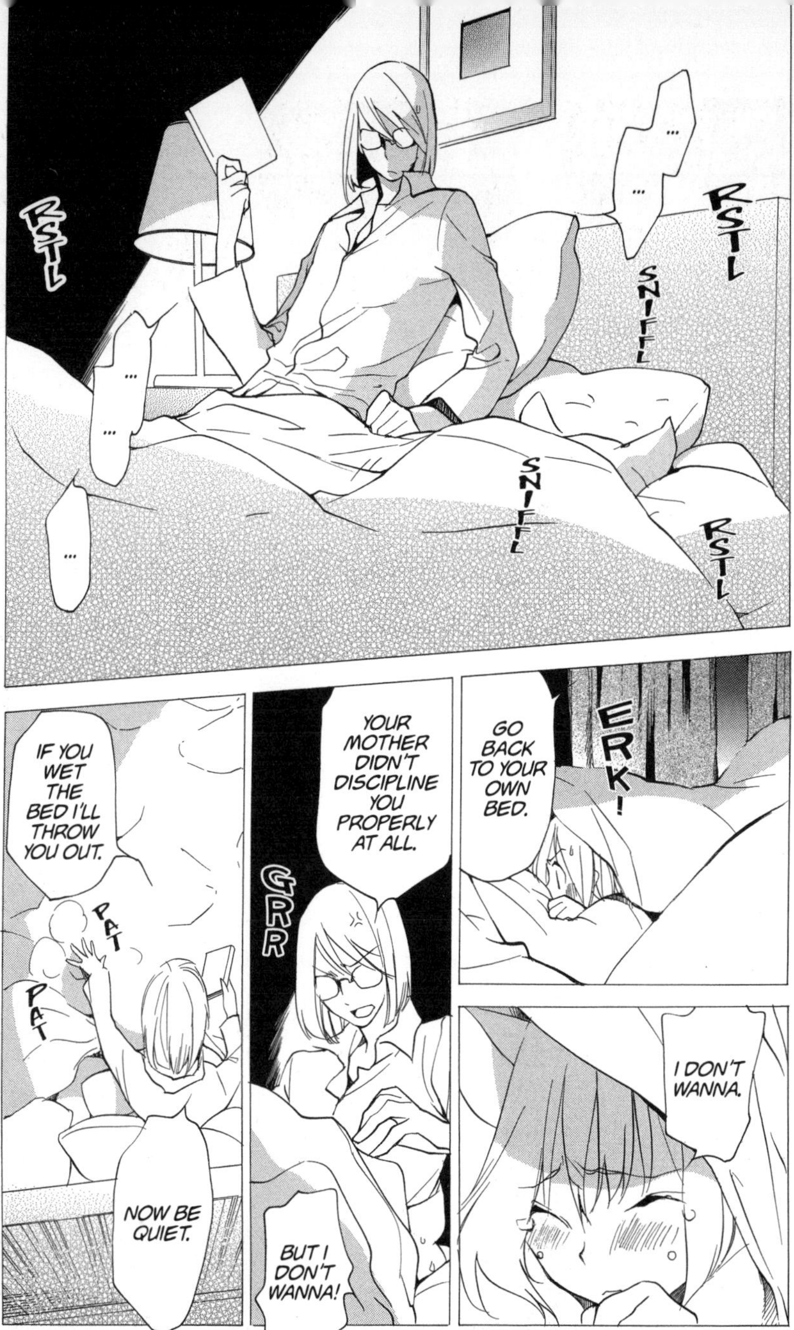
...
...
RSTL
SNIFFL
SNIFFL
RSTL
RSTL
...
...
...
ERK!
GO BACK TO YOUR OWN BED.
I DON'T WANNA.
YOUR MOTHER DIDN'T DISCIPLINE YOU PROPERLY AT ALL.
GRR
BUT I DON'T WANNA!
IF YOU WET THE BED I'LL THROW YOU OUT.
PAT
PAT
NOW BE QUIET.

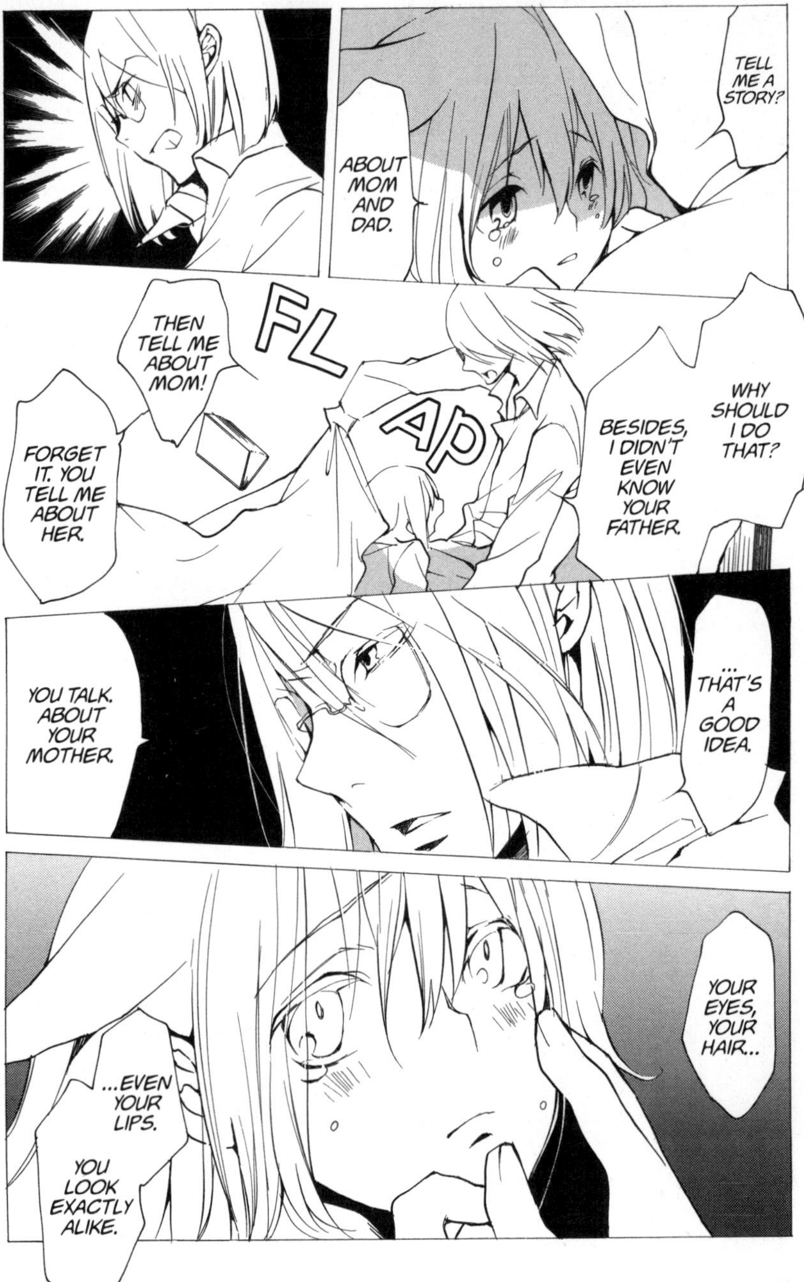
TELL ME A STORY?
ABOUT MOM AND DAD.
WHY SHOULD I DO THAT?
BESIDES, I DIDN'T EVEN KNOW YOUR FATHER.
FLAP
THEN TELL ME ABOUT MOM!
FORGET IT. YOU TELL ME ABOUT HER.
... THAT'S A GOOD IDEA.
YOU TALK. ABOUT YOUR MOTHER.
YOUR EYES, YOUR HAIR...
...EVEN YOUR LIPS.
YOU LOOK EXACTLY ALIKE.

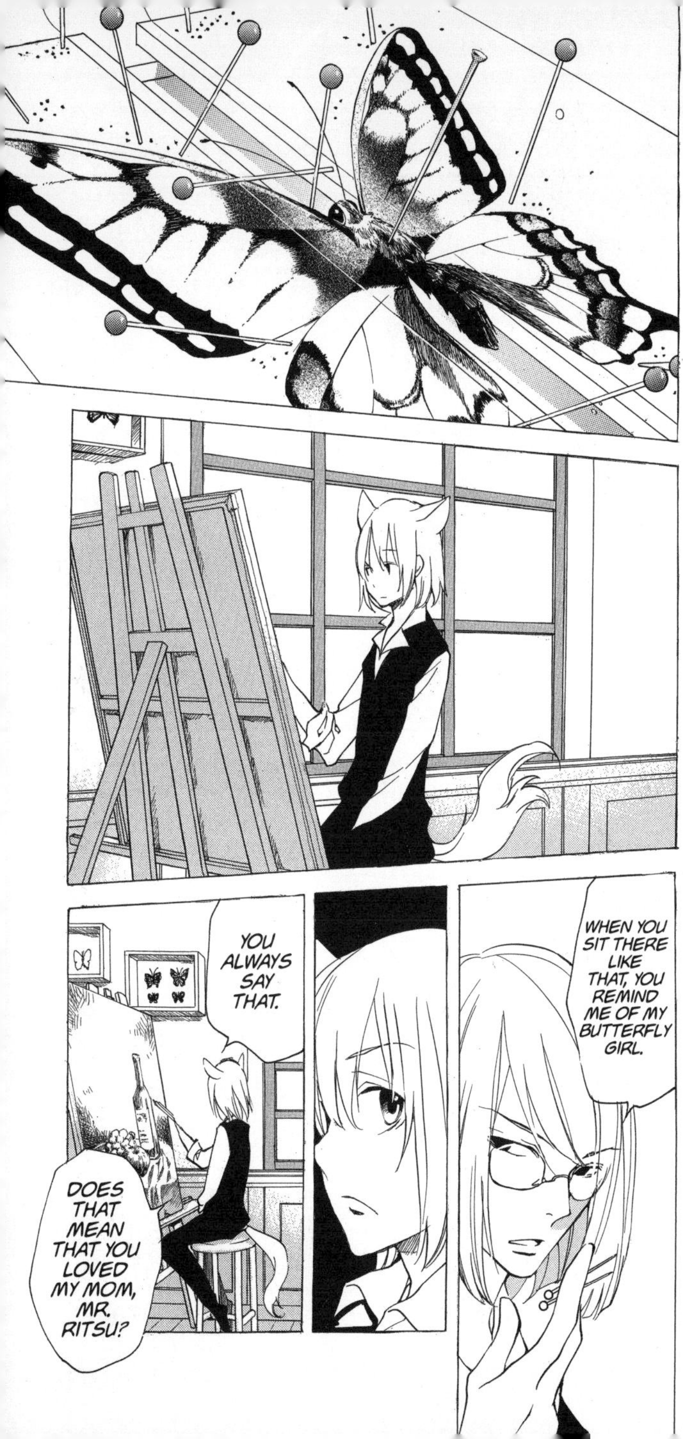
WHEN YOU SIT THERE LIKE THAT, YOU REMIND ME OF MY BUTTERFLY GIRL.
YOU ALWAYS SAY THAT.
DOES THAT MEAN THAT YOU LOVED MY MOM, MR. RITSU?

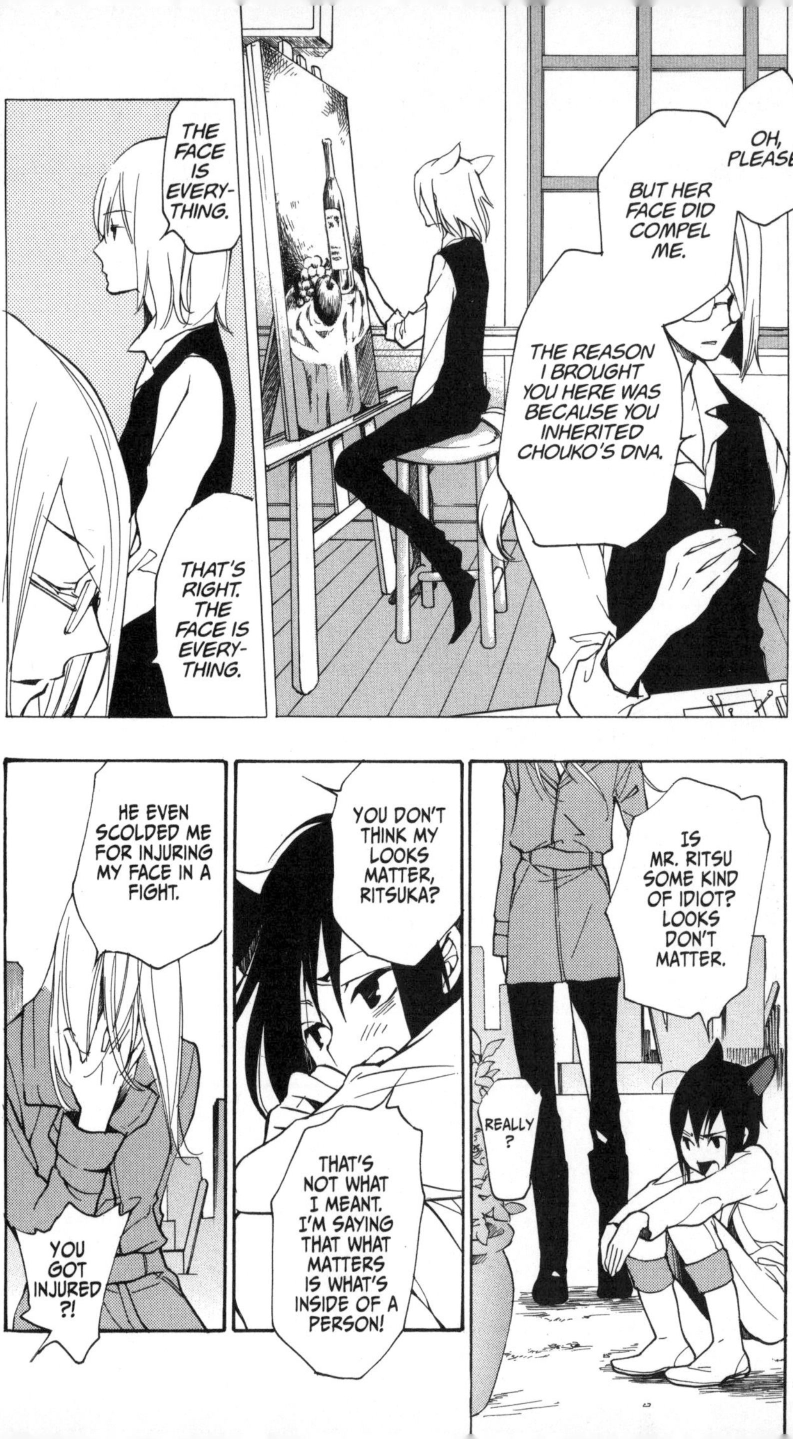
OH, PLEASE.
BUT HER FACE DID COMPEL ME.
THE REASON I BROUGHT YOU HERE WAS BECAUSE YOU INHERITED CHOUKO'S DNA.
THE FACE IS EVERYTHING.
THAT'S RIGHT. THE FACE IS EVERYTHING.
IS MR. RITSU SOME KIND OF IDIOT? LOOKS DON'T MATTER.
REALLY?
YOU DON'T THINK MY LOOKS MATTER, RITSUKA?
THAT'S NOT WHAT I MEANT. I'M SAYING THAT WHAT MATTERS IS WHAT'S INSIDE OF A PERSON!
HE EVEN SCOLDED ME FOR INJURING MY FACE IN A FIGHT.
YOU GOT INJURED?!

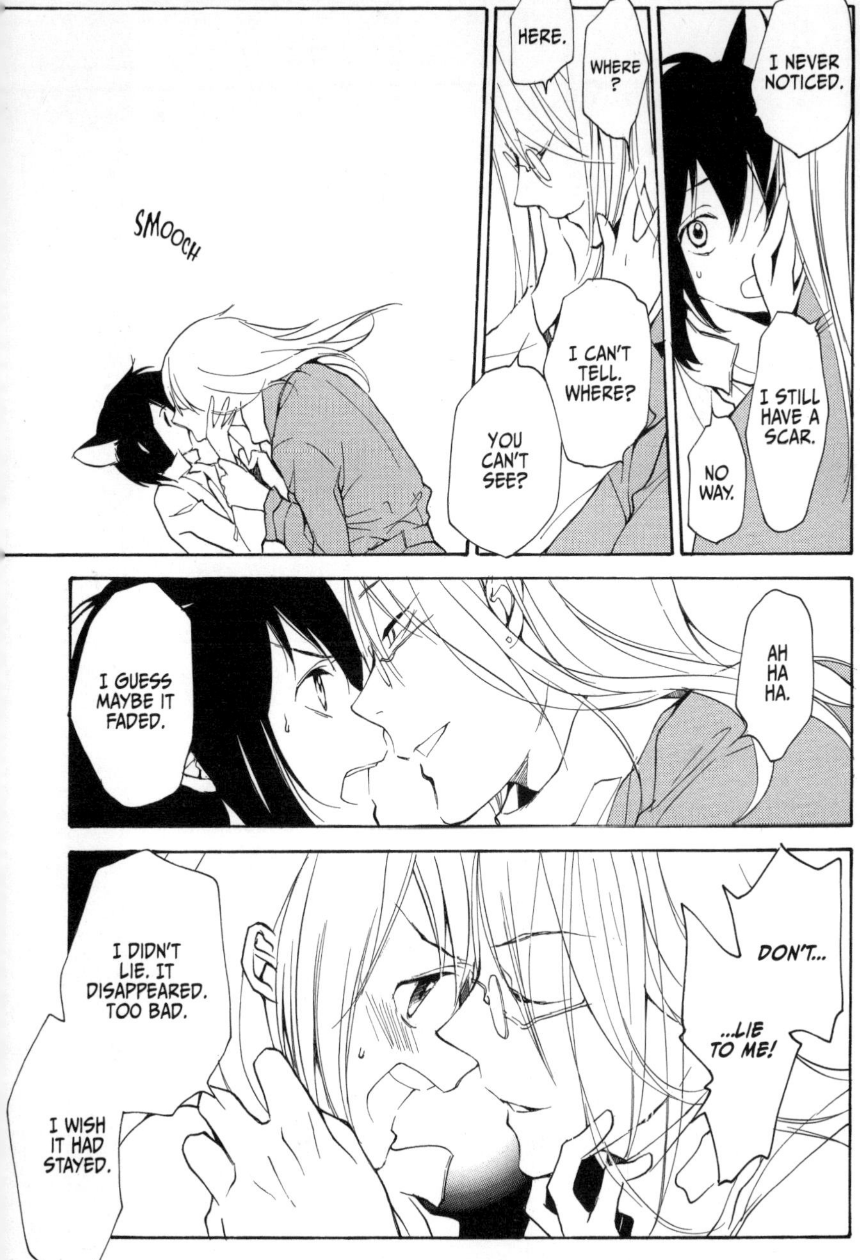
I NEVER NOTICED.
I STILL HAVE A SCAR.
NO WAY.
WHERE?
HERE.
I CAN'T TELL. WHERE?
YOU CAN'T SEE?
SMOOCH
AH HA HA.
I GUESS MAYBE IT FADED.
DON'T...
...LIE TO ME!
I DIDN'T LIE. IT DISAPPEARED. TOO BAD.
I WISH IT HAD STAYED.

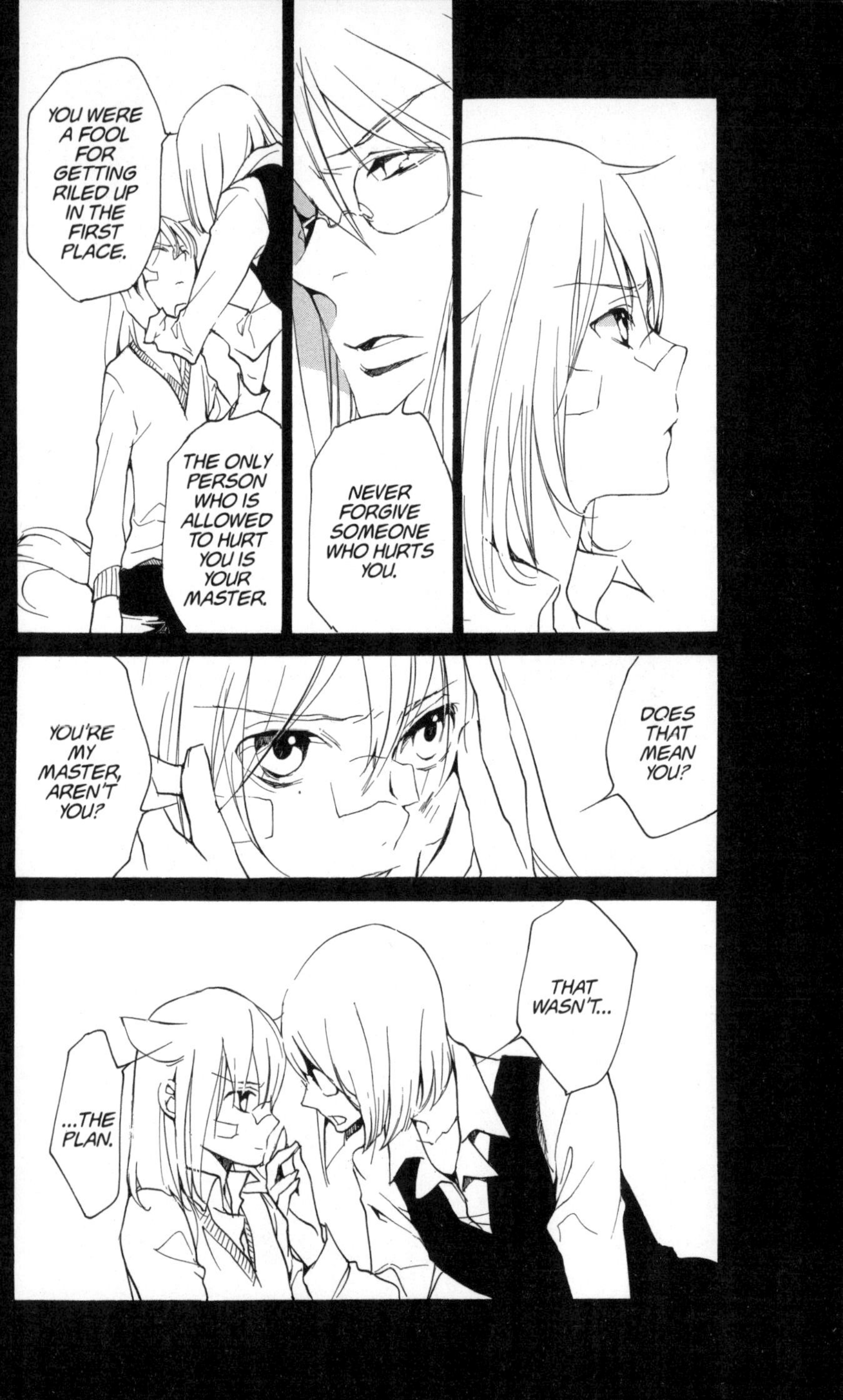
NEVER FORGIVE SOMEONE WHO HURTS YOU.
YOU WERE A FOOL FOR GETTING RILED UP IN THE FIRST PLACE.
THE ONLY PERSON WHO IS ALLOWED TO HURT YOU IS YOUR MASTER.
DOES THAT MEAN YOU?
YOU'RE MY MASTER, AREN'T YOU?
THAT WASN'T...
...THE PLAN.

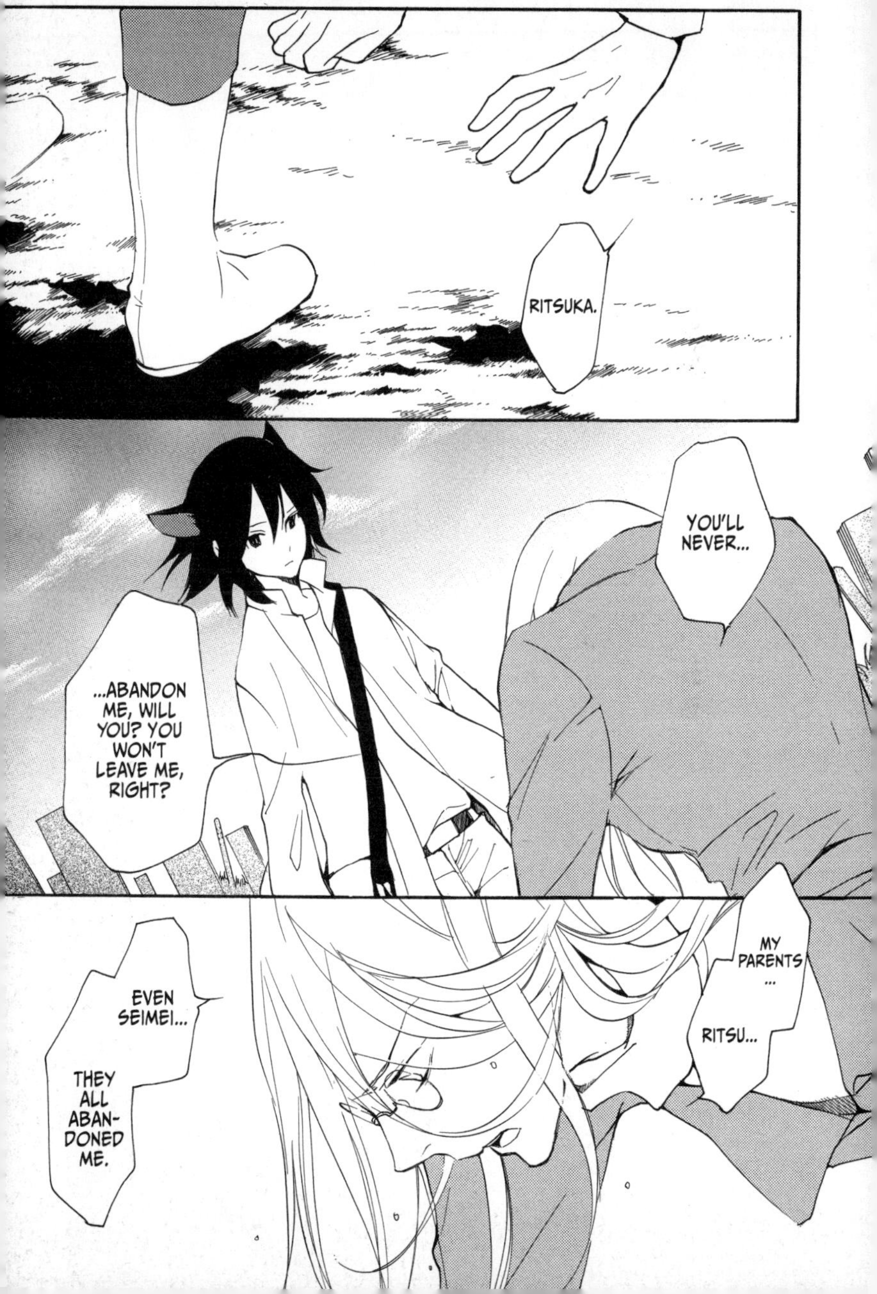
RITSUKA.
YOU'LL NEVER...
...ABANDON ME, WILL YOU? YOU WON'T LEAVE ME, RIGHT?
MY PARENTS...
RITSU...
EVEN SEIMEI...
THEY ALL ABAN-DONED ME.

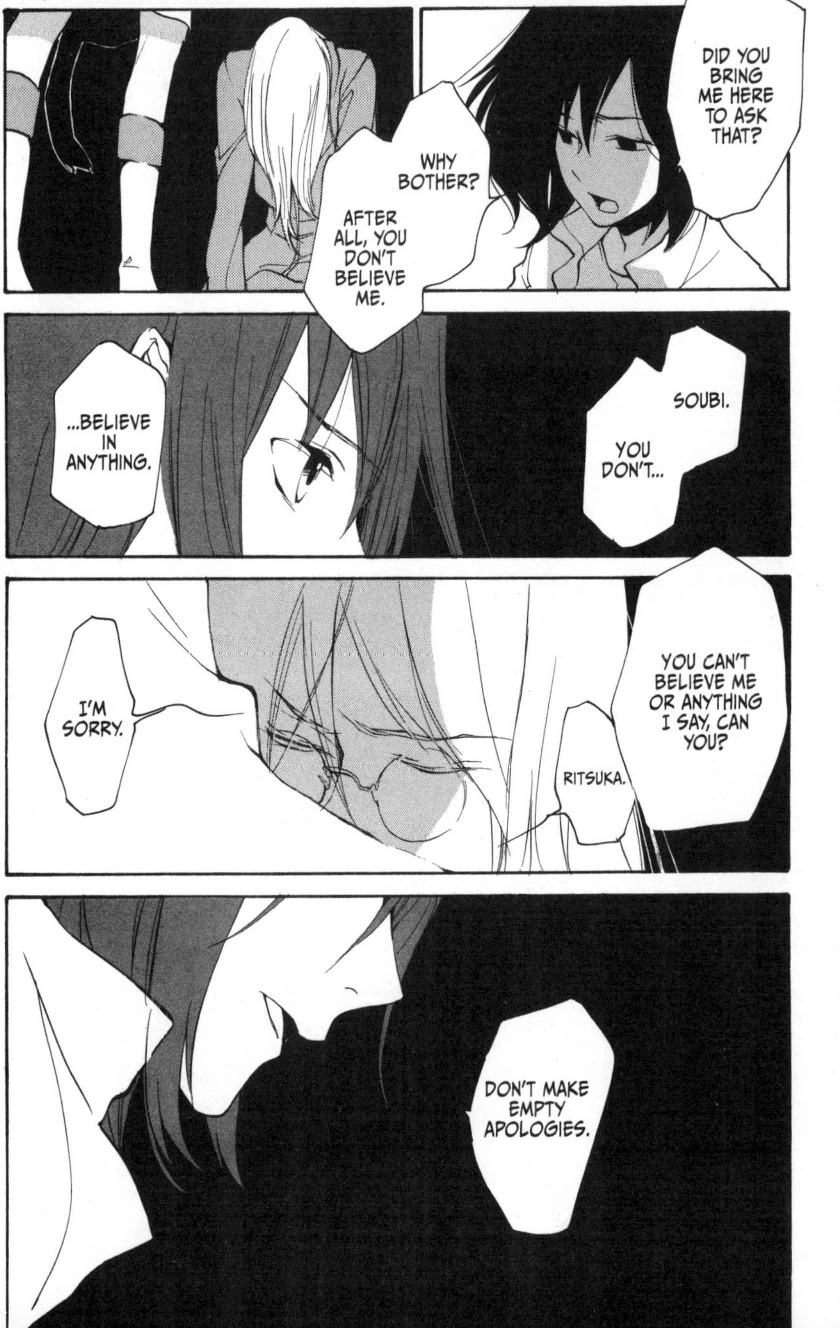
DID YOU BRING ME HERE TO ASK THAT?
WHY BOTHER?
AFTER ALL, YOU DON'T BELIEVE ME.
SOUBI.
YOU DON'T...
...BELIEVE IN ANYTHING.
YOU CAN'T BELIEVE ME OR ANYTHING I SAY, CAN YOU?
RITSUKA.
I'M SORRY.
DON'T MAKE EMPTY APOLOGIES.

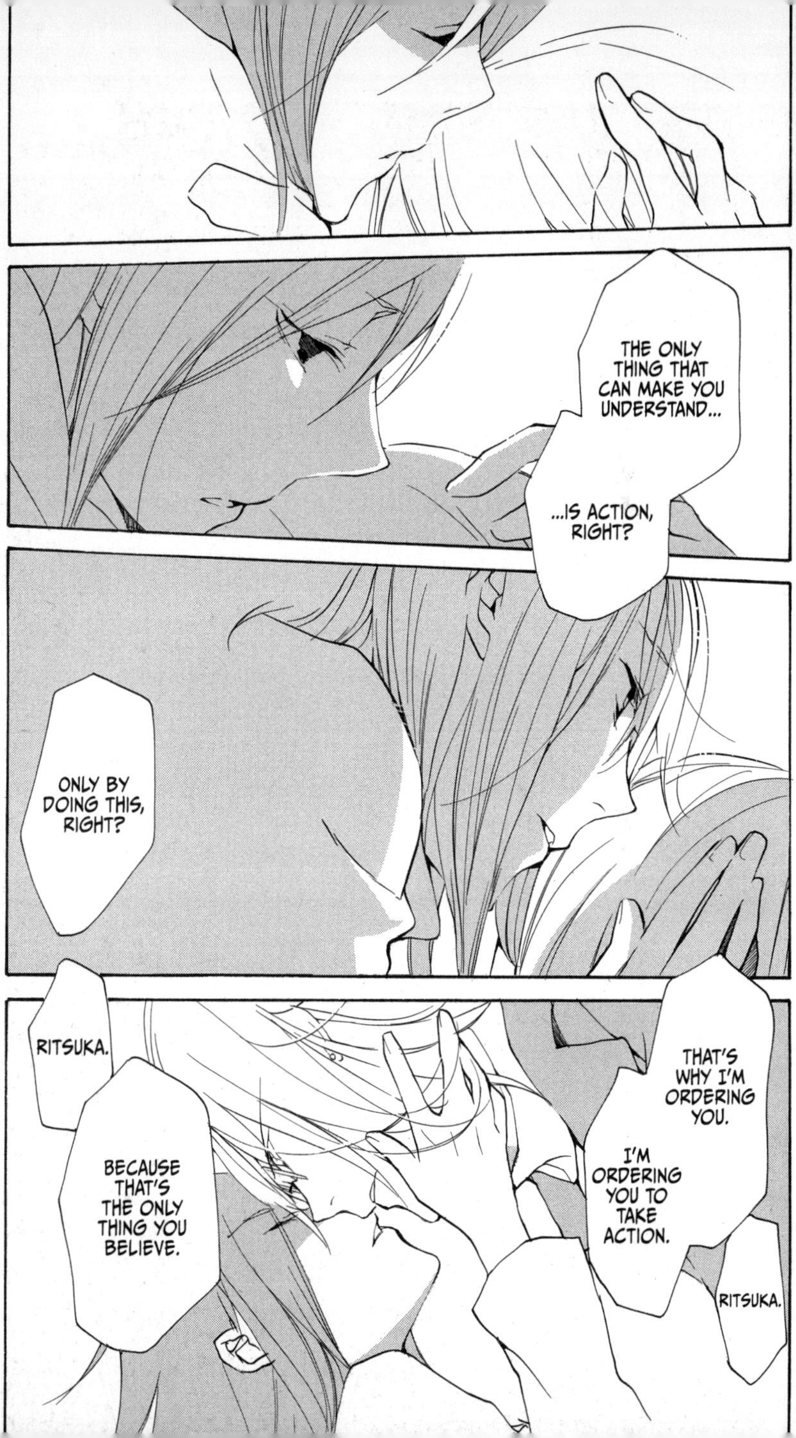
THE ONLY THING THAT CAN MAKE YOU UNDERSTAND...
...IS ACTION, RIGHT?
ONLY BY DOING THIS, RIGHT?
THAT'S WHY I'M ORDERING YOU.
I'M ORDERING YOU TO TAKE ACTION.
RITSUKA.
RITSUKA.
BECAUSE THAT'S THE ONLY THING YOU BELIEVE.

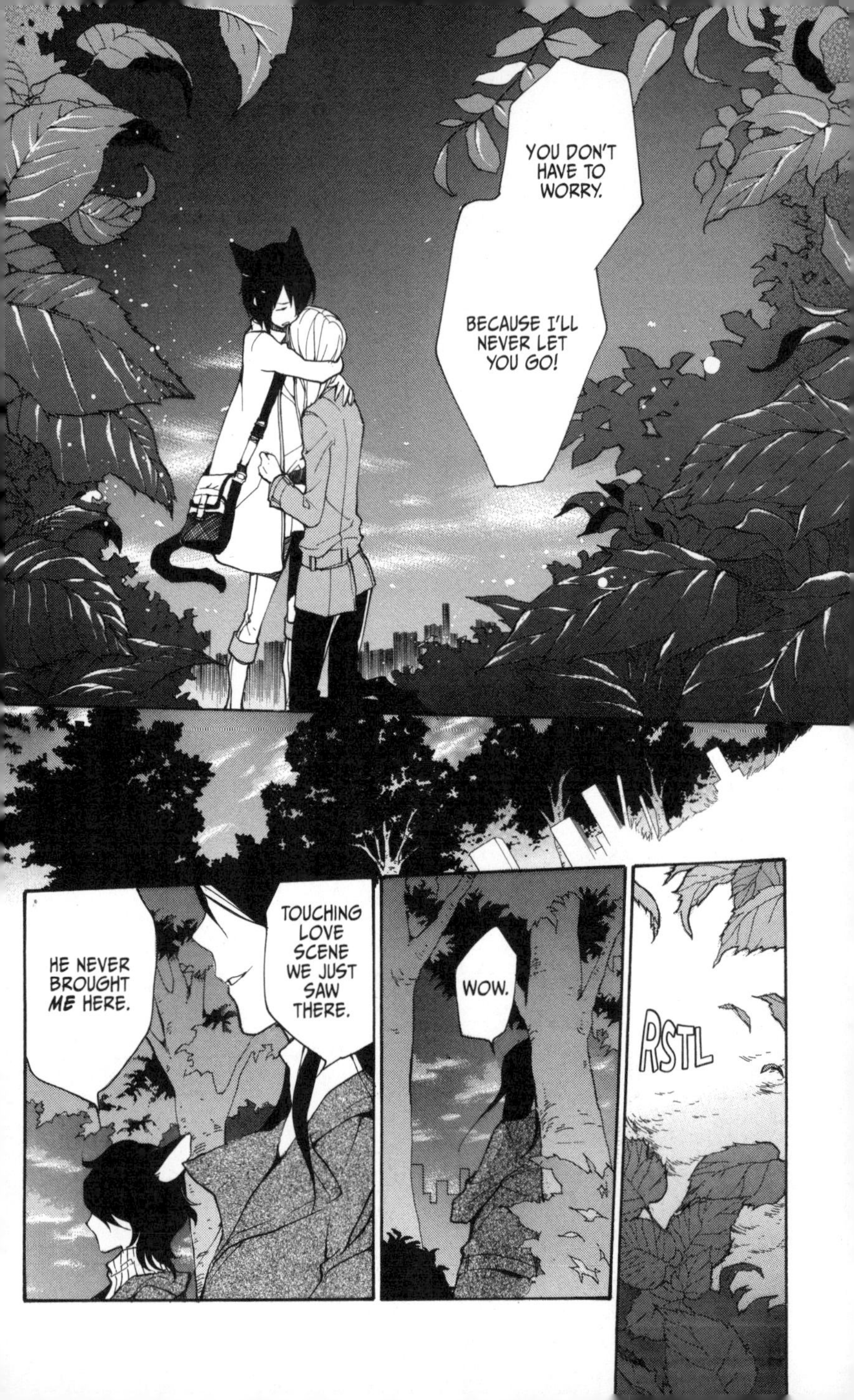
YOU DON'T HAVE TO WORRY.
BECAUSE I'LL NEVER LET YOU GO!
RSTL
WOW.
TOUCHING LOVE SCENE WE JUST SAW THERE.
HE NEVER BROUGHT ME HERE.

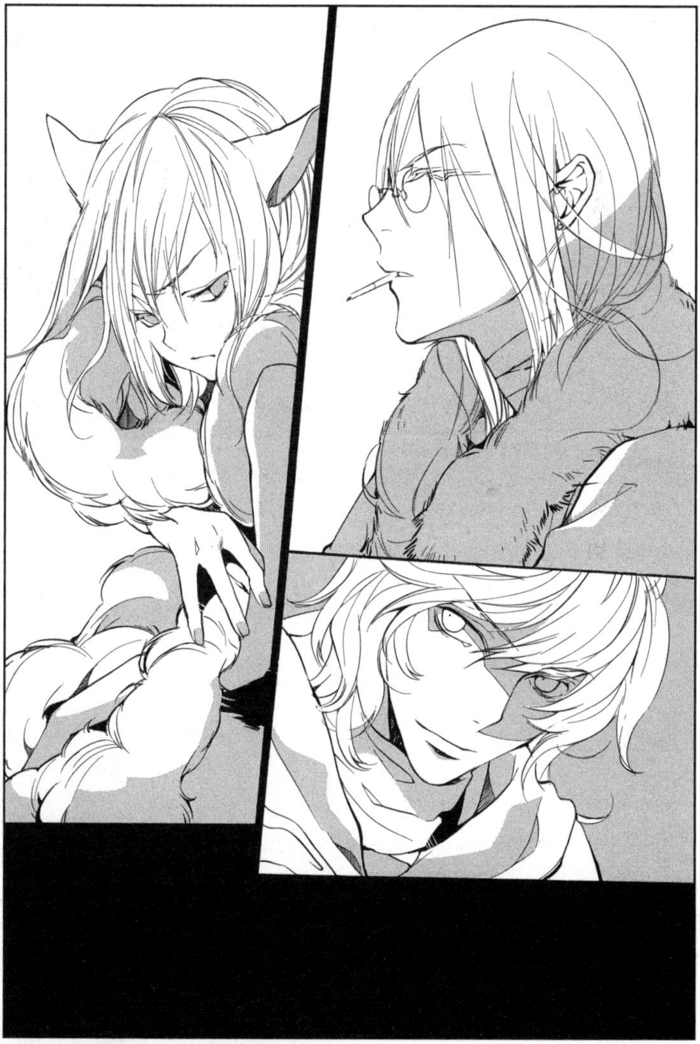

LOVELESS

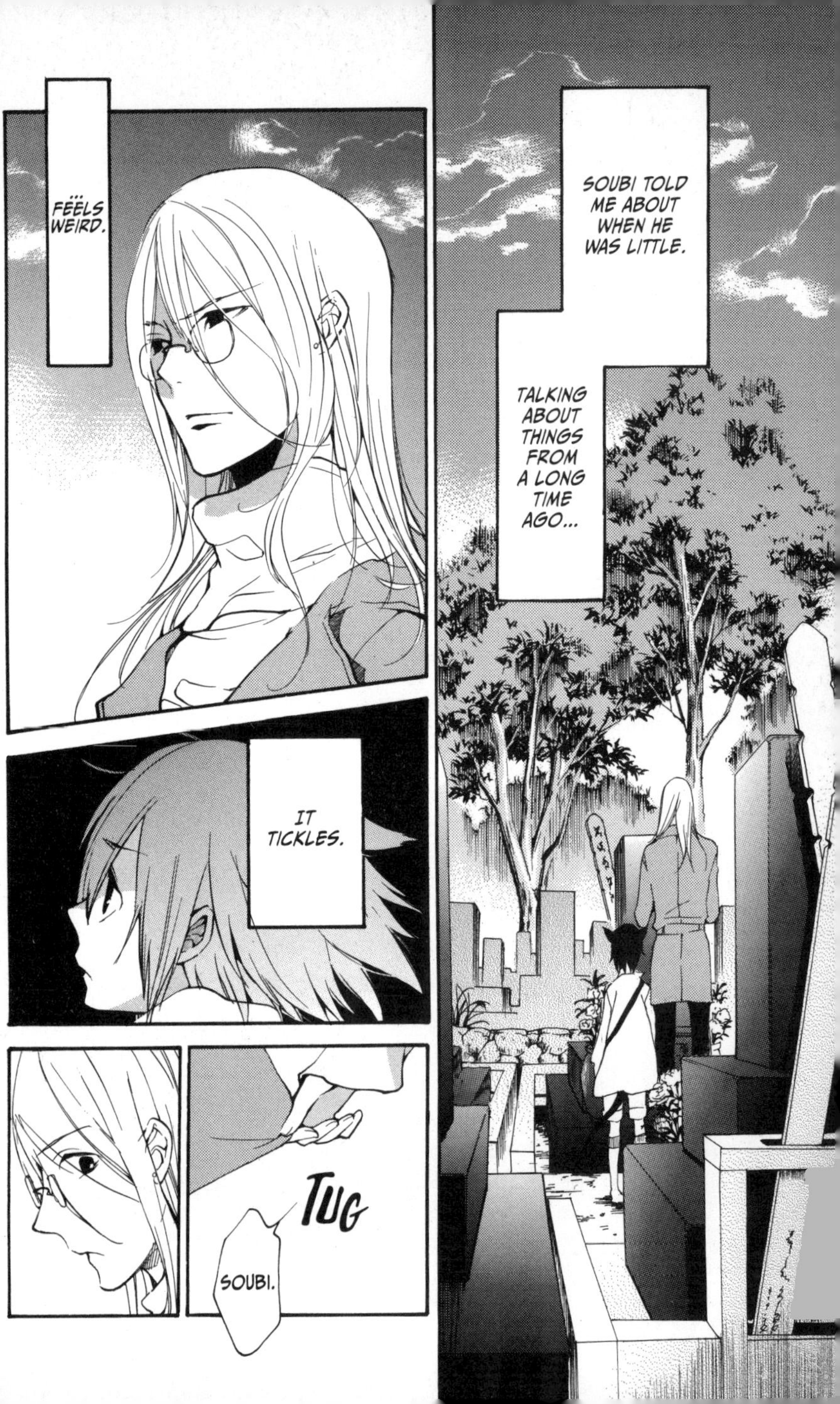
SOUBI TOLD ME ABOUT WHEN HE WAS LITTLE.
TALKING ABOUT THINGS FROM A LONG TIME AGO...
...FEELS WEIRD.
IT TICKLES.
TUG
SOUBI.

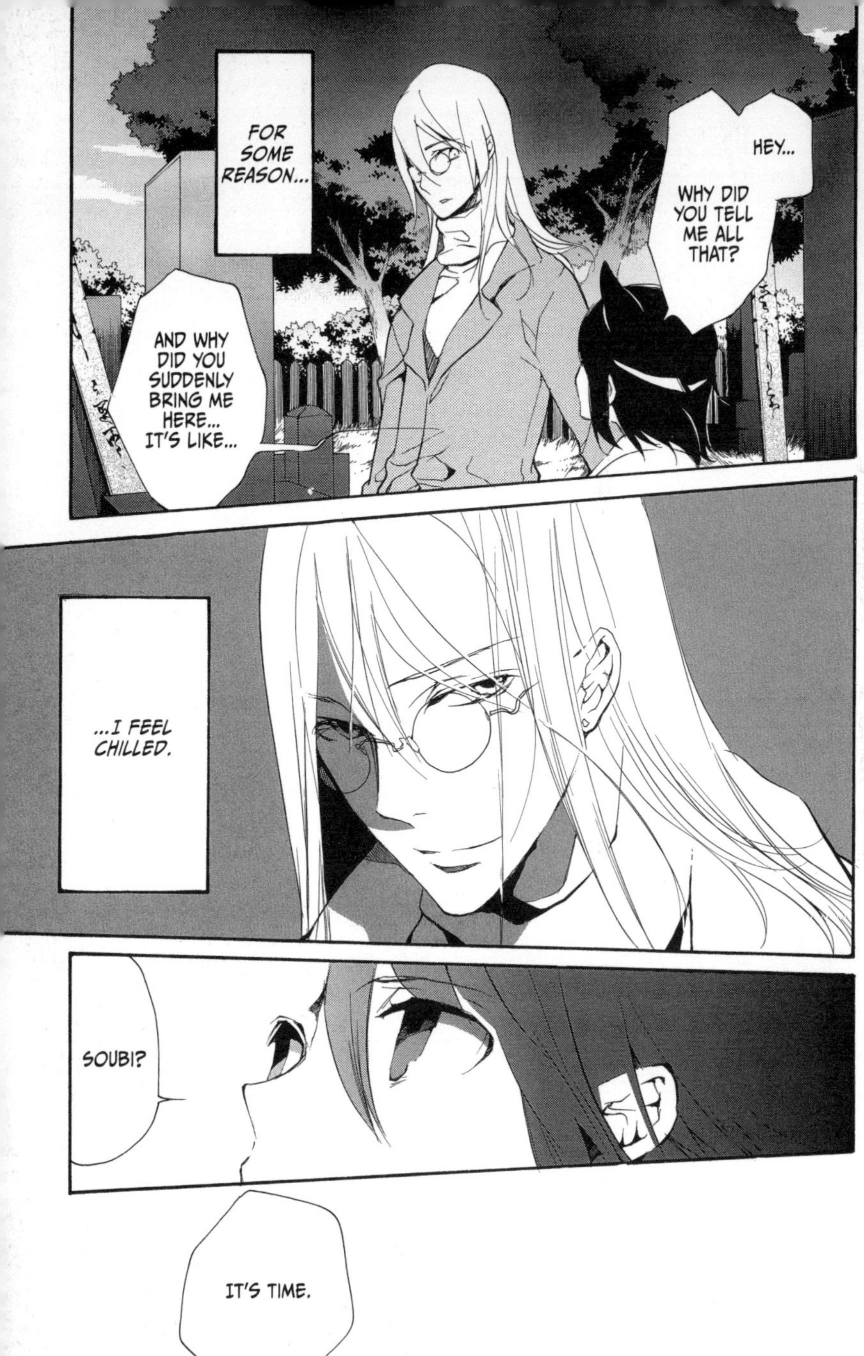
HEY...
WHY DID YOU TELL ME ALL THAT?
FOR SOME REASON...
AND WHY DID YOU SUDDENLY BRING ME HERE... IT'S LIKE...
...I FEEL CHILLED.
SOUBI?
IT'S TIME.

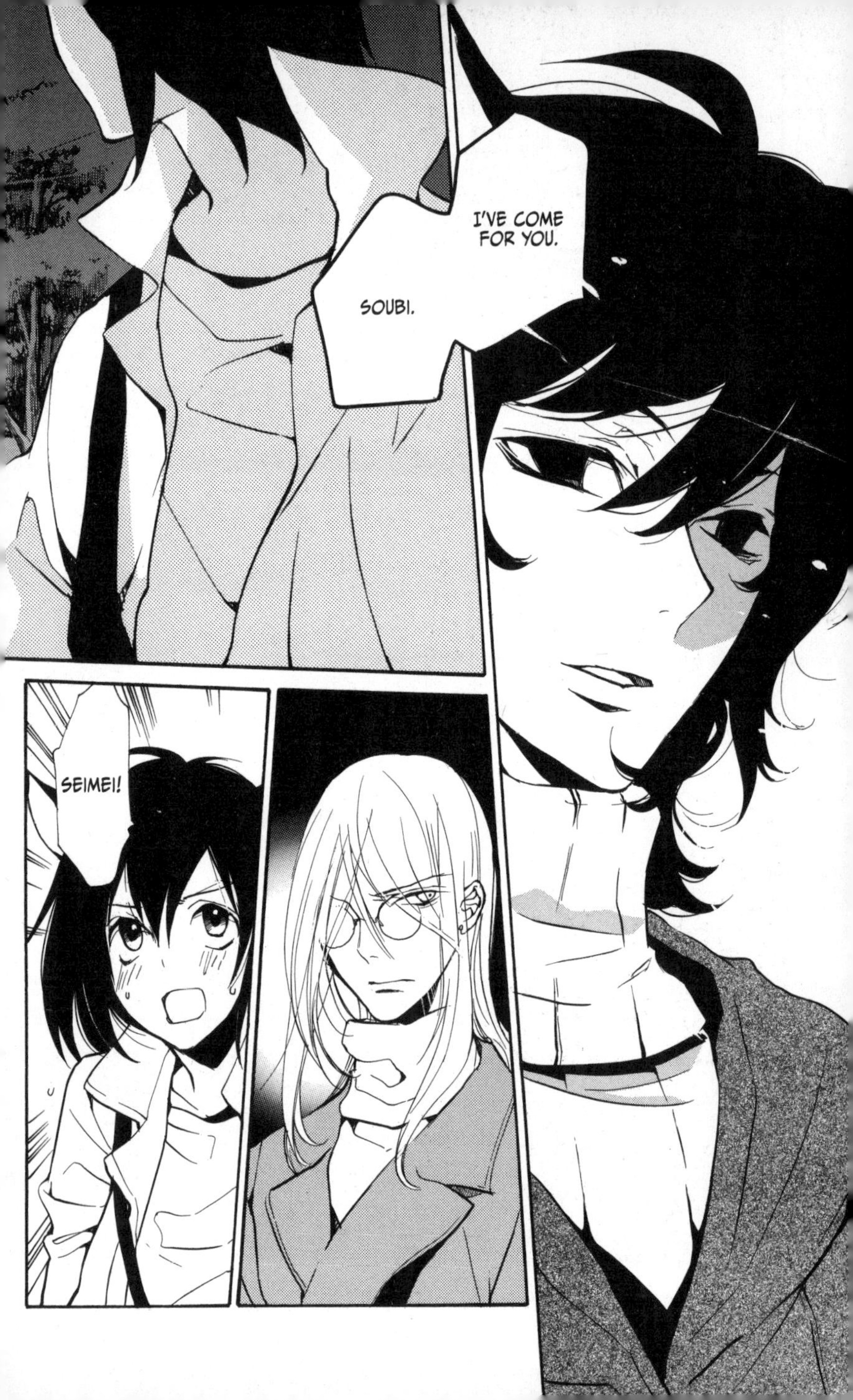
I'VE COME FOR YOU.
SOUBI.
SEIMEI!

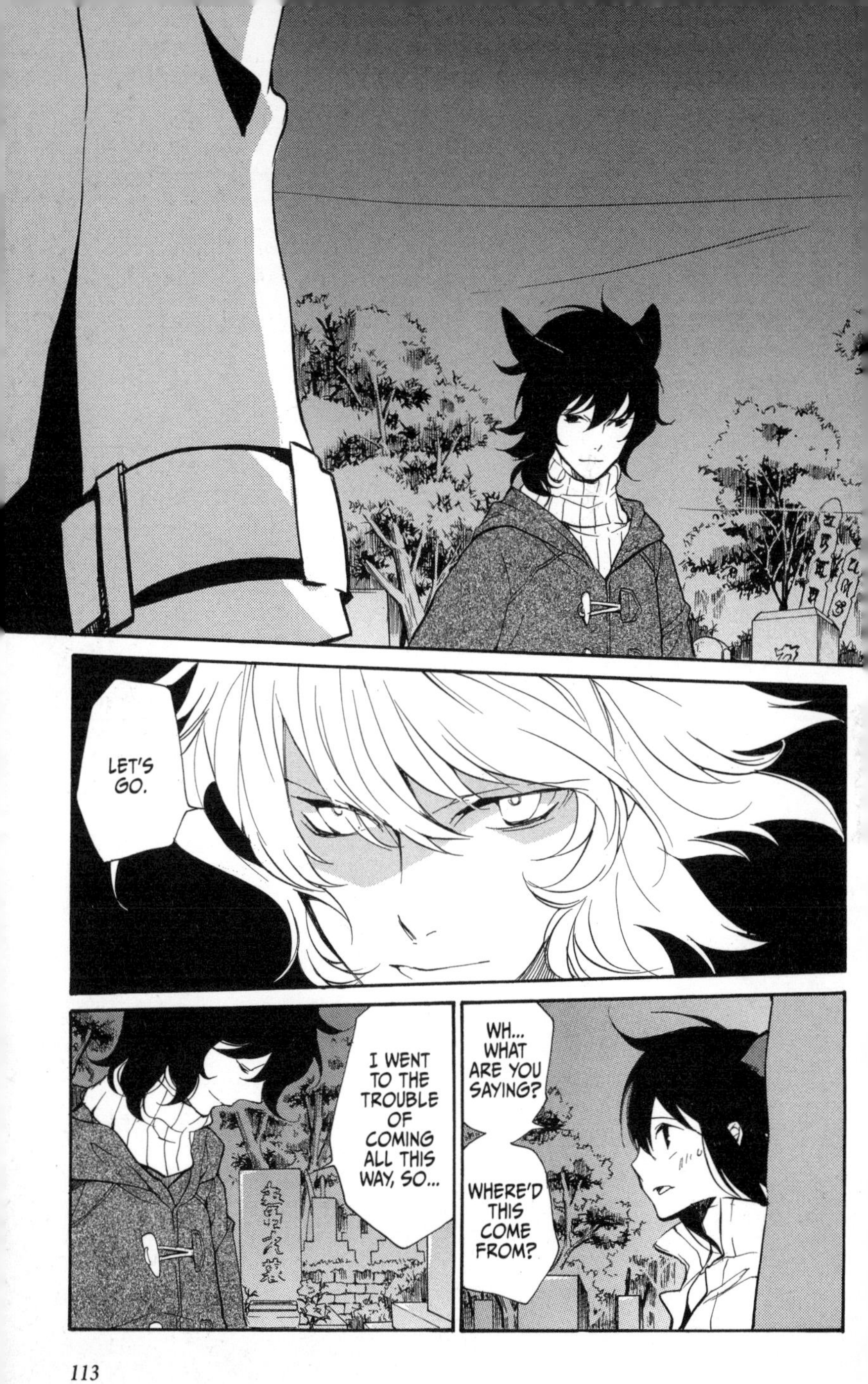
LET'S GO.
WH... WHAT ARE YOU SAYING?
WHERE'D THIS COME FROM?
I WENT TO THE TROUBLE OF COMING ALL THIS WAY, SO...

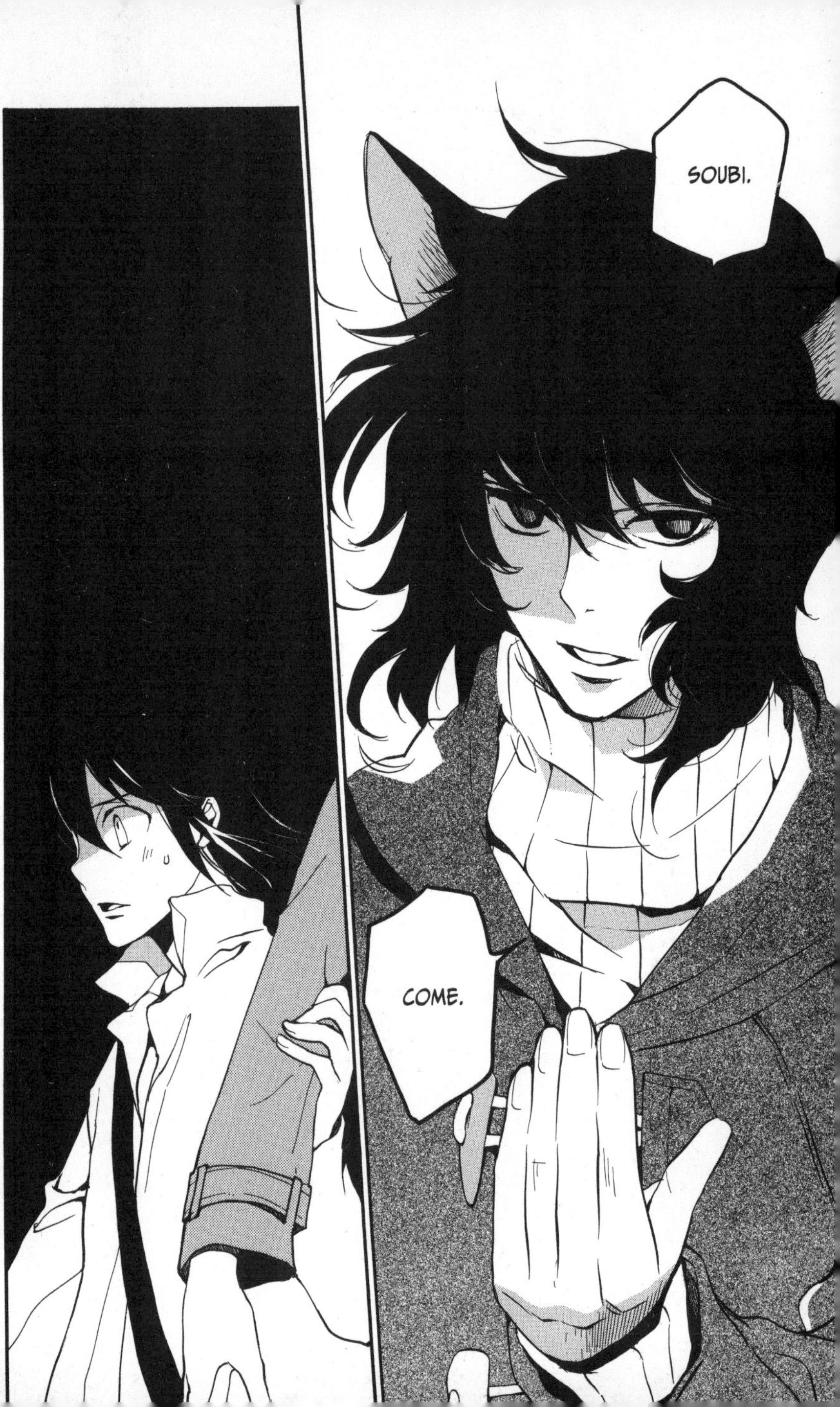
SOUBI.
COME.

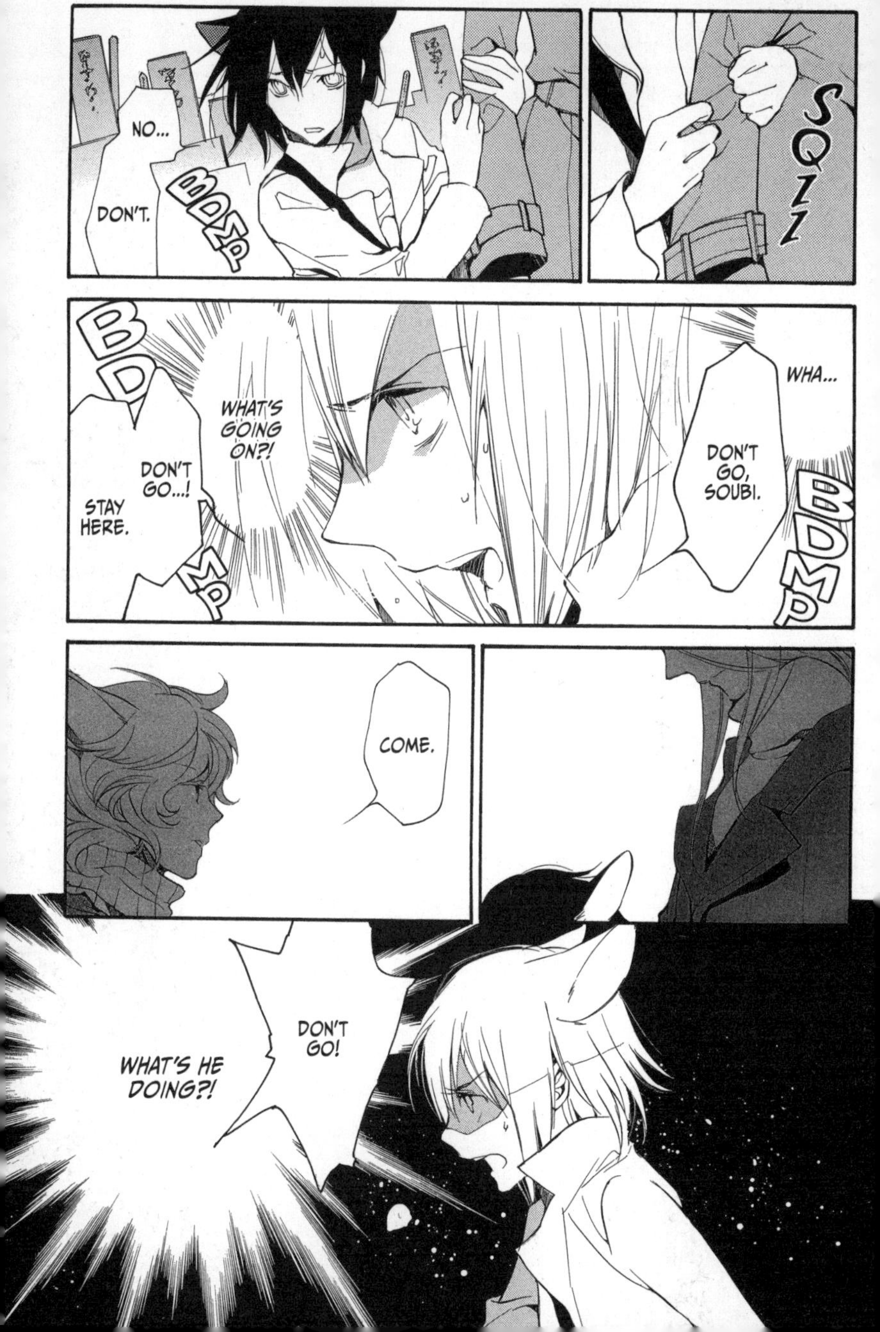
SQZZ
NO...
DON'T.
BDMP
WHA...
DON'T GO, SOUBI.
BDMP
WHAT'S GOING ON?!
DON'T GO...!
STAY HERE.
BDMP
COME.
DON'T GO!
WHAT'S HE DOING?!

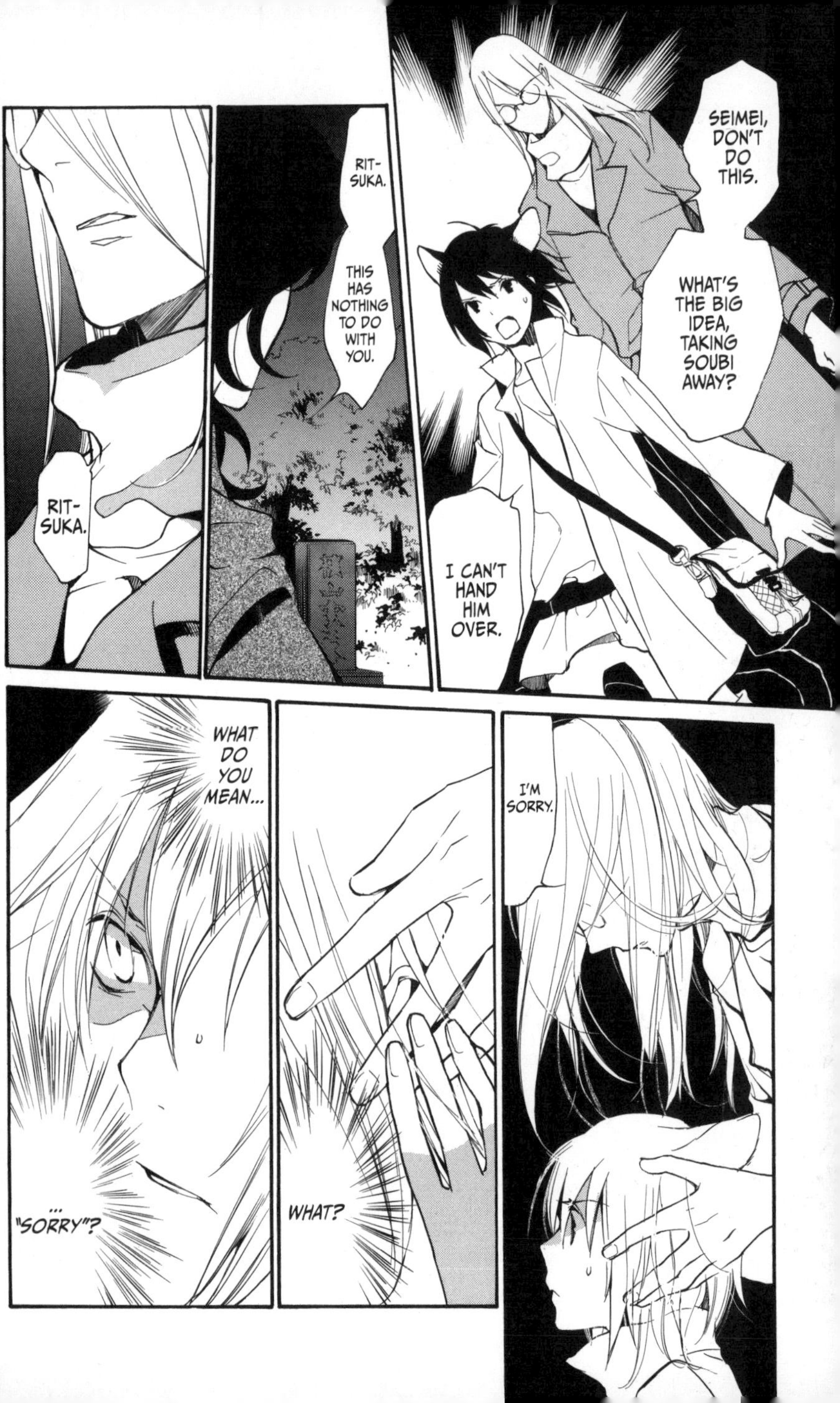
SEIMEI, DON'T DO THIS.
WHAT'S THE BIG IDEA, TAKING SOUBI AWAY?
I CAN'T HAND HIM OVER.
RIT-SUKA.
THIS HAS NOTHING TO DO WITH YOU.
RIT-SUKA.
I'M SORRY.
WHAT?
WHAT DO YOU MEAN...
... "SORRY"?

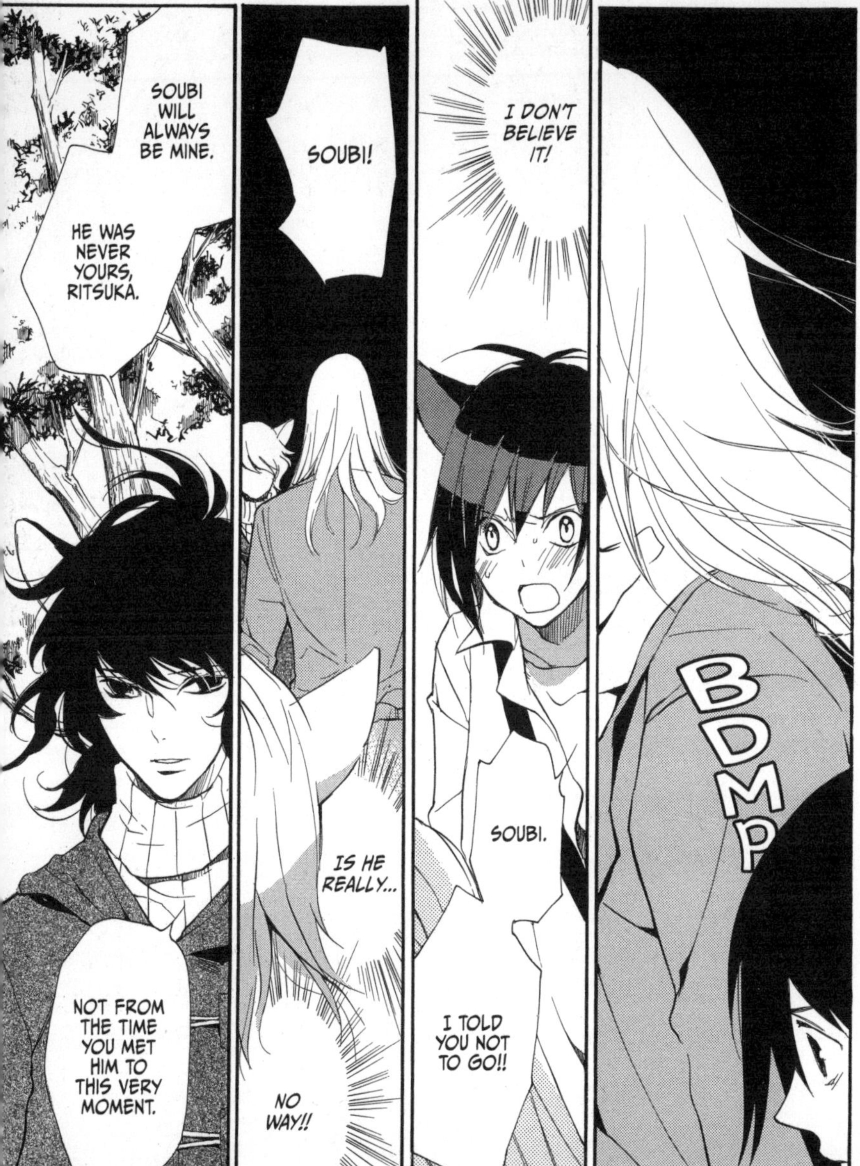
BDMP
I DON'T BELIEVE IT!
SOUBI.
I TOLD YOU NOT TO GO!!
SOUBI!
IS HE REALLY...
NO WAY!!
SOUBI WILL ALWAYS BE MINE.
HE WAS NEVER YOURS, RITSUKA.
NOT FROM THE TIME YOU MET HIM TO THIS VERY MOMENT.

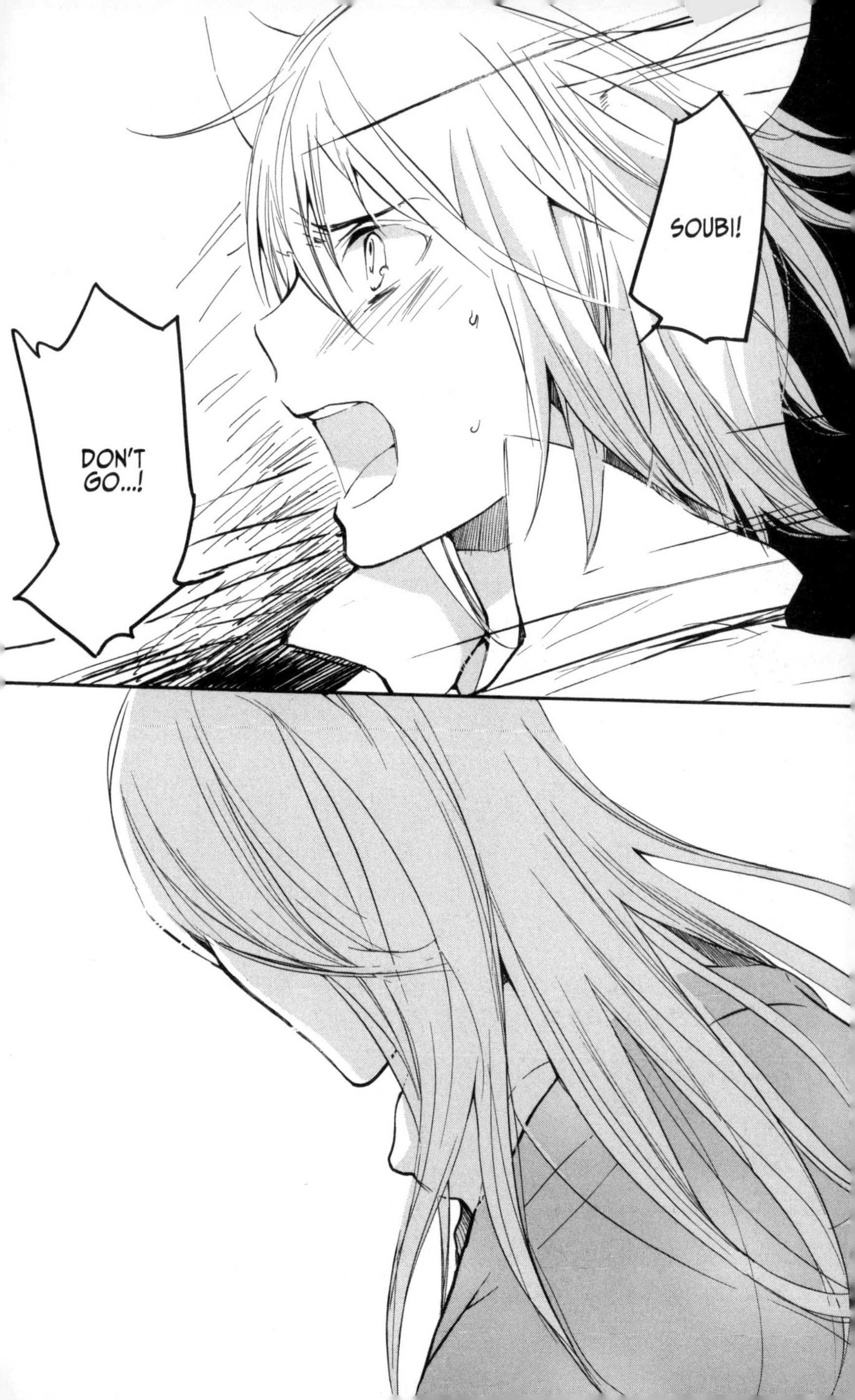
SOUBI!
DON'T GO...!

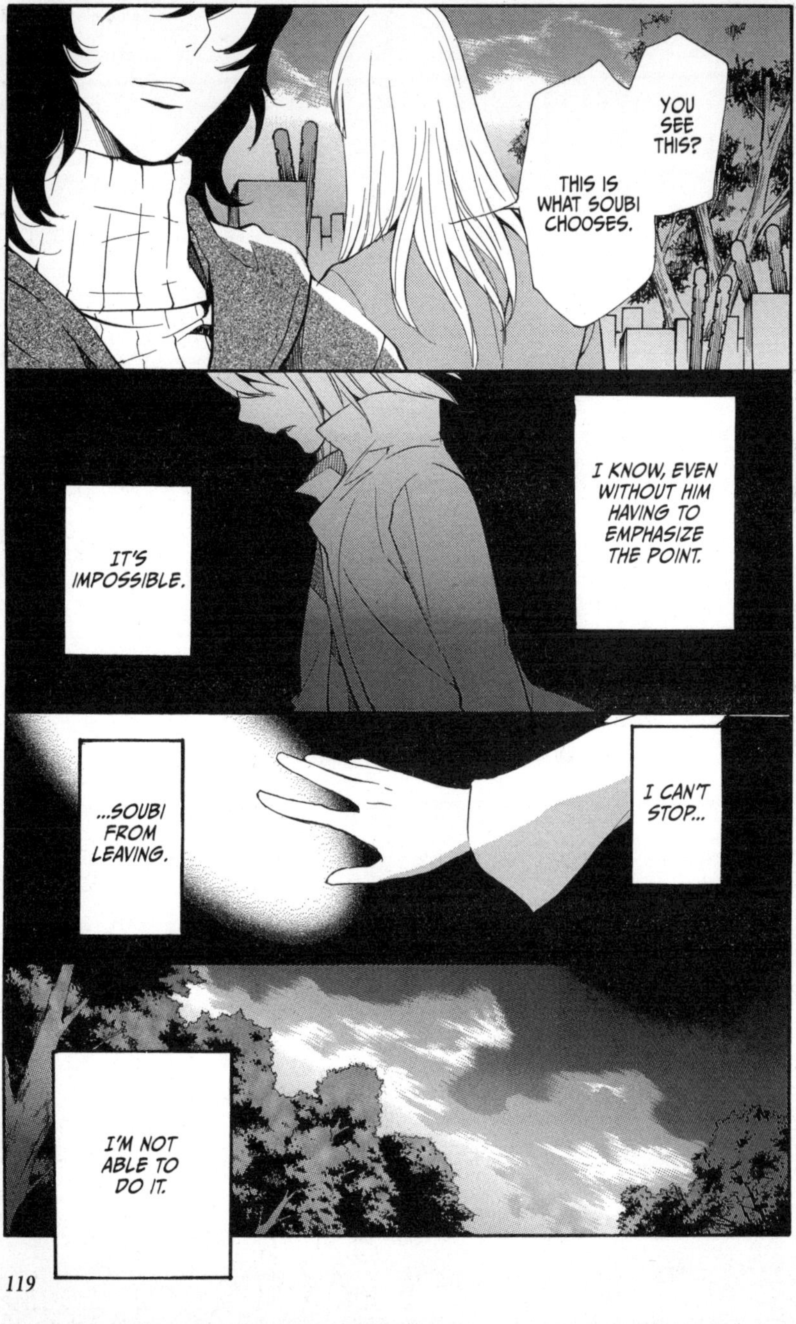
YOU SEE THIS?
THIS IS WHAT SOUBI CHOOSES.
I KNOW, EVEN WITHOUT HIM HAVING TO EMPHASIZE THE POINT.
IT'S IMPOSSIBLE.
I CAN'T STOP...
...SOUBI FROM LEAVING.
I'M NOT ABLE TO DO IT.

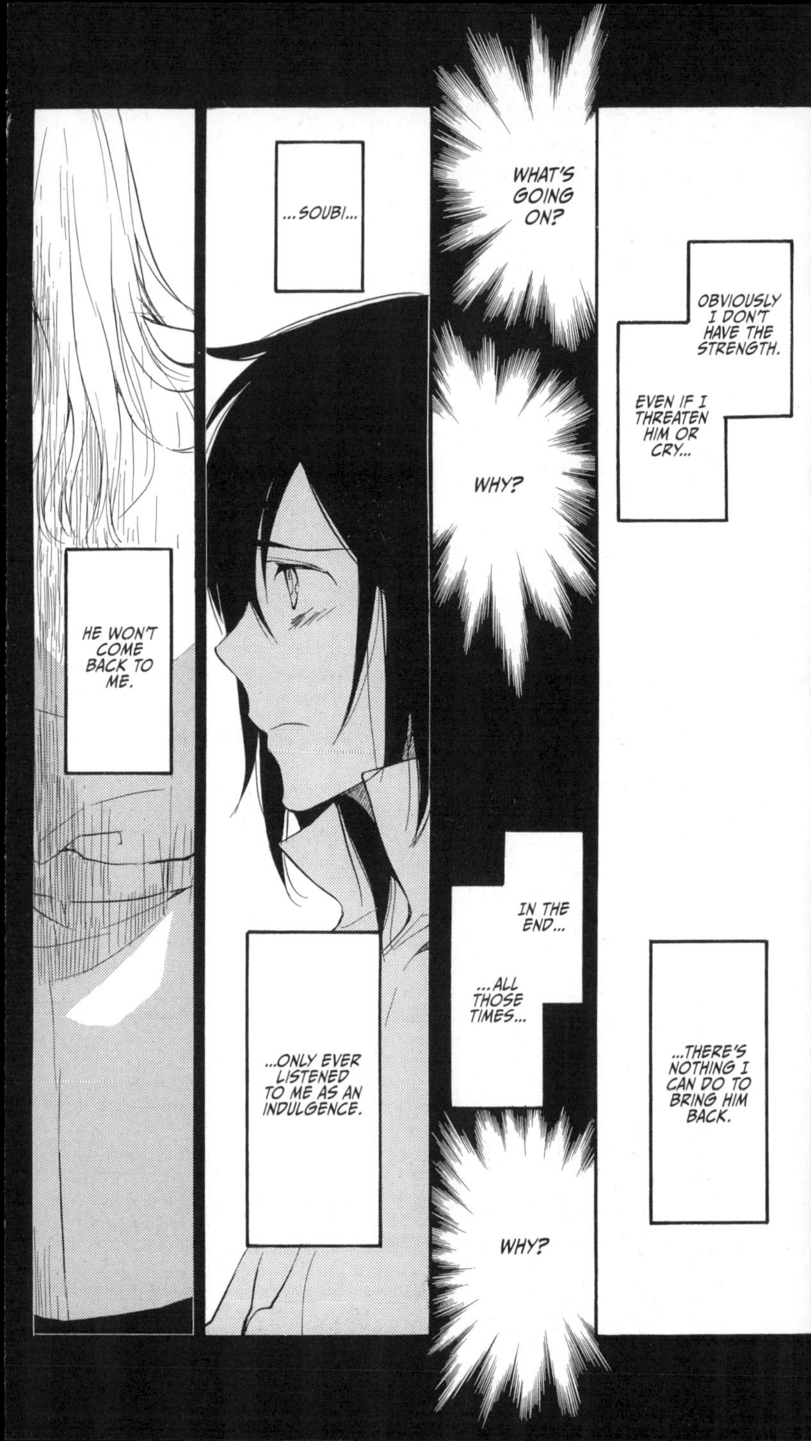
OBVIOUSLY I DON'T HAVE THE STRENGTH.
EVEN IF I THREATEN HIM OR CRY...
...THERE'S NOTHING I CAN DO TO BRING HIM BACK.
WHAT'S GOING ON?
WHY?
IN THE END...
...ALL THOSE TIMES...
WHY?
...SOUBI...
...ONLY EVER LISTENED TO ME AS AN INDULGENCE.
HE WON'T COME BACK TO ME.

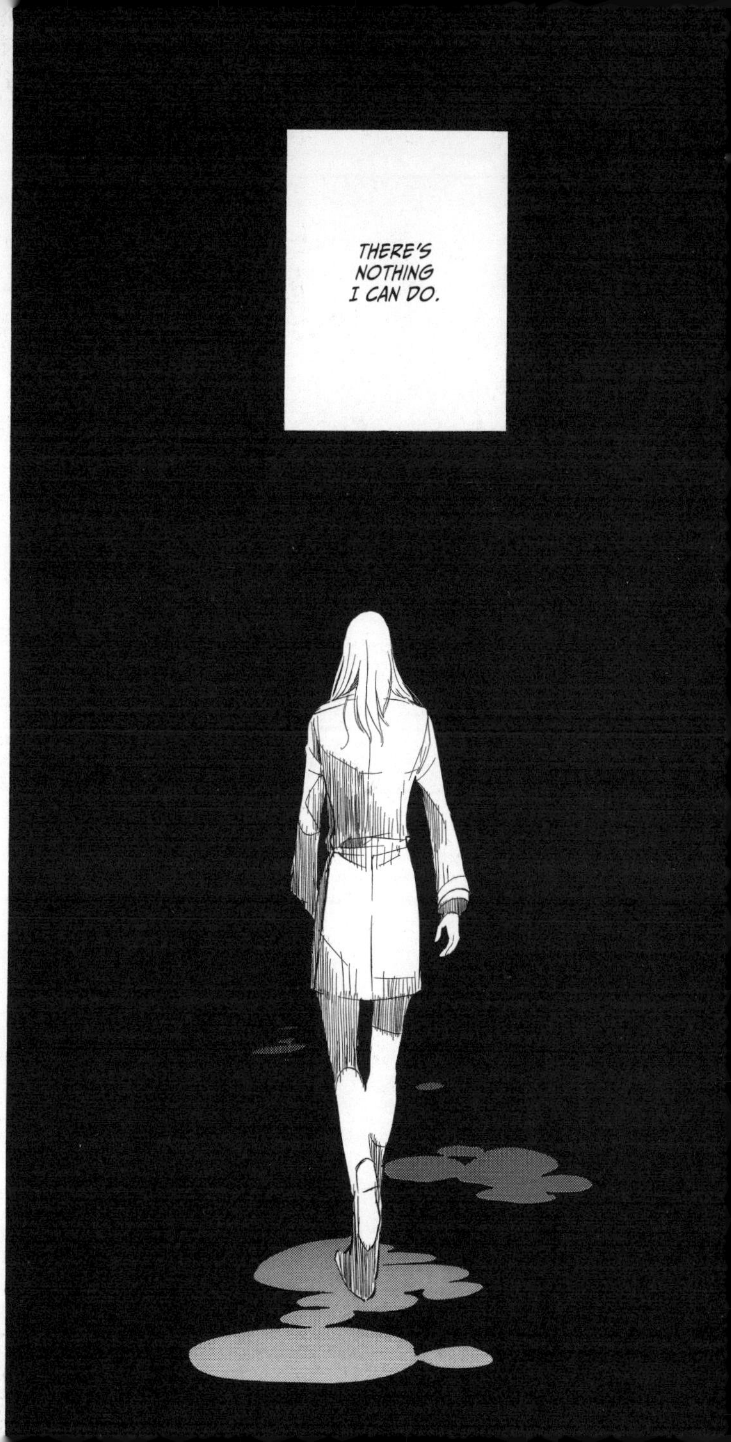
THERE'S NOTHING I CAN DO.

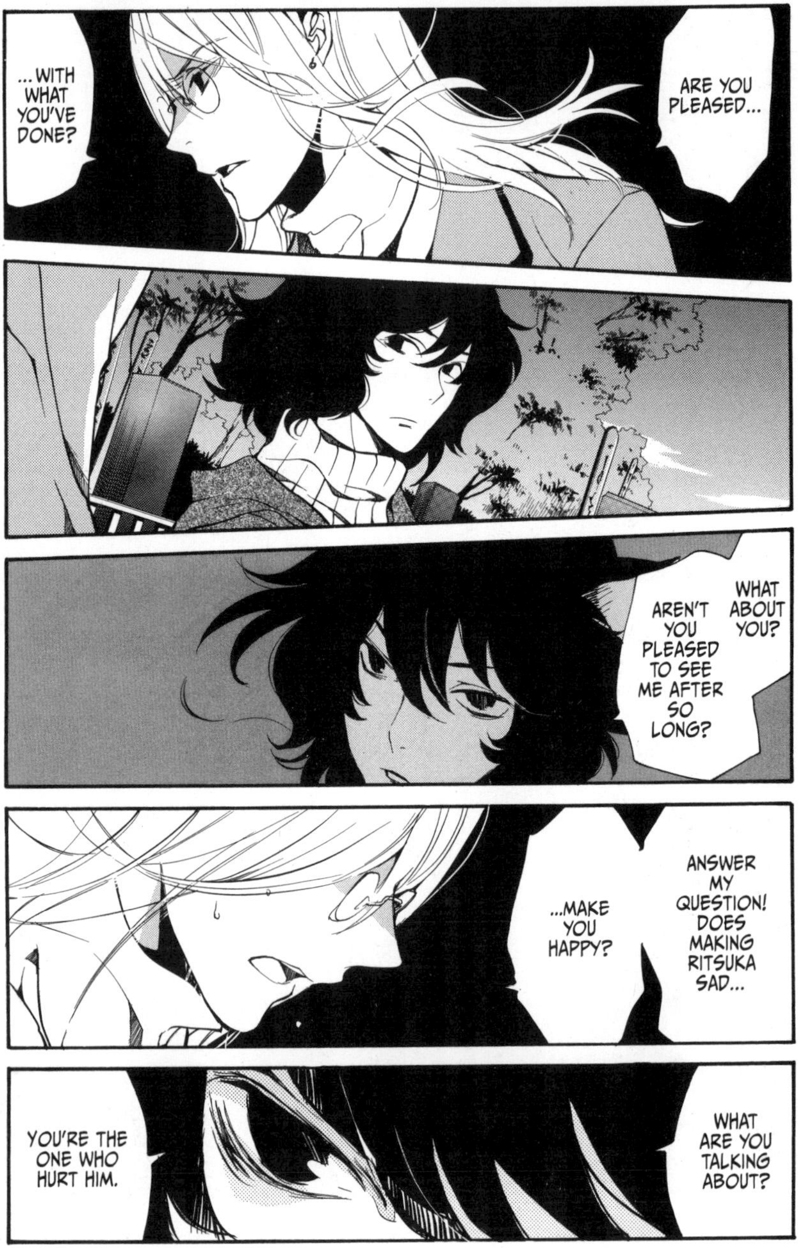
ARE YOU PLEASED...
...WITH WHAT YOU'VE DONE?
WHAT ABOUT YOU?
AREN'T YOU PLEASED TO SEE ME AFTER SO LONG?
ANSWER MY QUESTION! DOES MAKING RITSUKA SAD...
...MAKE YOU HAPPY?
WHAT ARE YOU TALKING ABOUT?
YOU'RE THE ONE WHO HURT HIM.

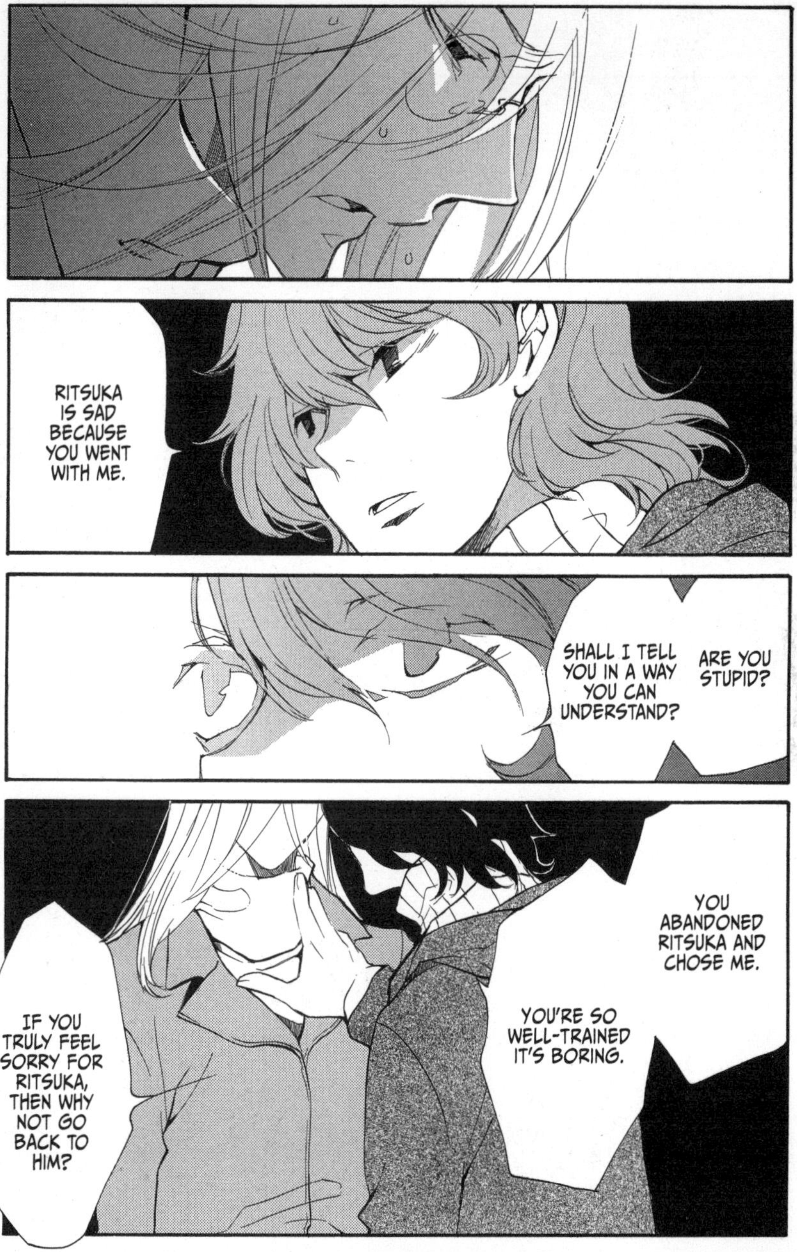
RITSUKA IS SAD BECAUSE YOU WENT WITH ME.
ARE YOU STUPID?
SHALL I TELL YOU IN A WAY YOU CAN UNDERSTAND?
YOU ABANDONED RITSUKA AND CHOSE ME.
YOU'RE SO WELL-TRAINED IT'S BORING.
IF YOU TRULY FEEL SORRY FOR RITSUKA, THEN WHY NOT GO BACK TO HIM?

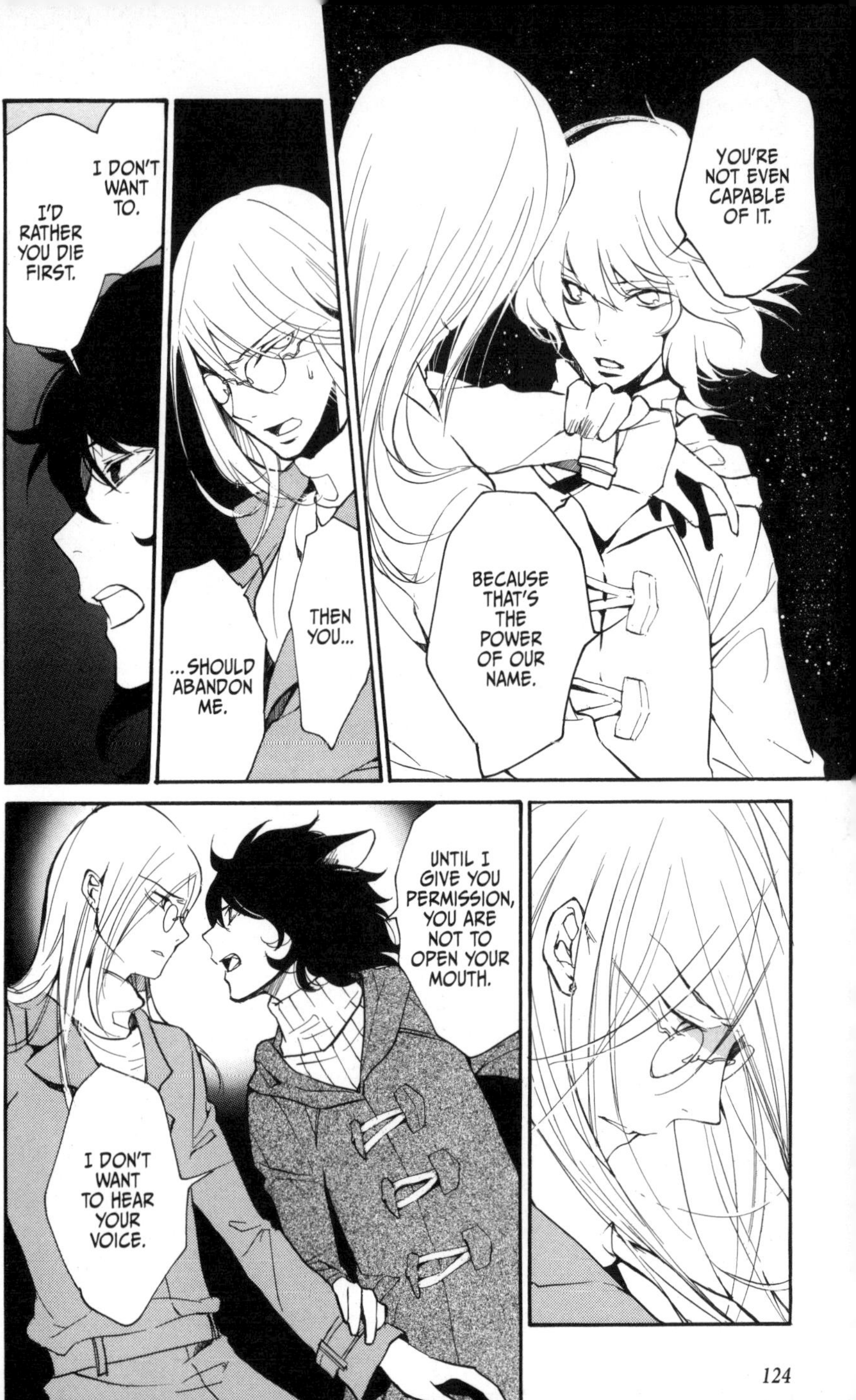
YOU'RE NOT EVEN CAPABLE OF IT.
BECAUSE THAT'S THE POWER OF OUR NAME.
THEN YOU...
...SHOULD ABANDON ME.
I DON'T WANT TO.
I'D RATHER YOU DIE FIRST.
UNTIL I GIVE YOU PERMISSION, YOU ARE NOT TO OPEN YOUR MOUTH.
I DON'T WANT TO HEAR YOUR VOICE.

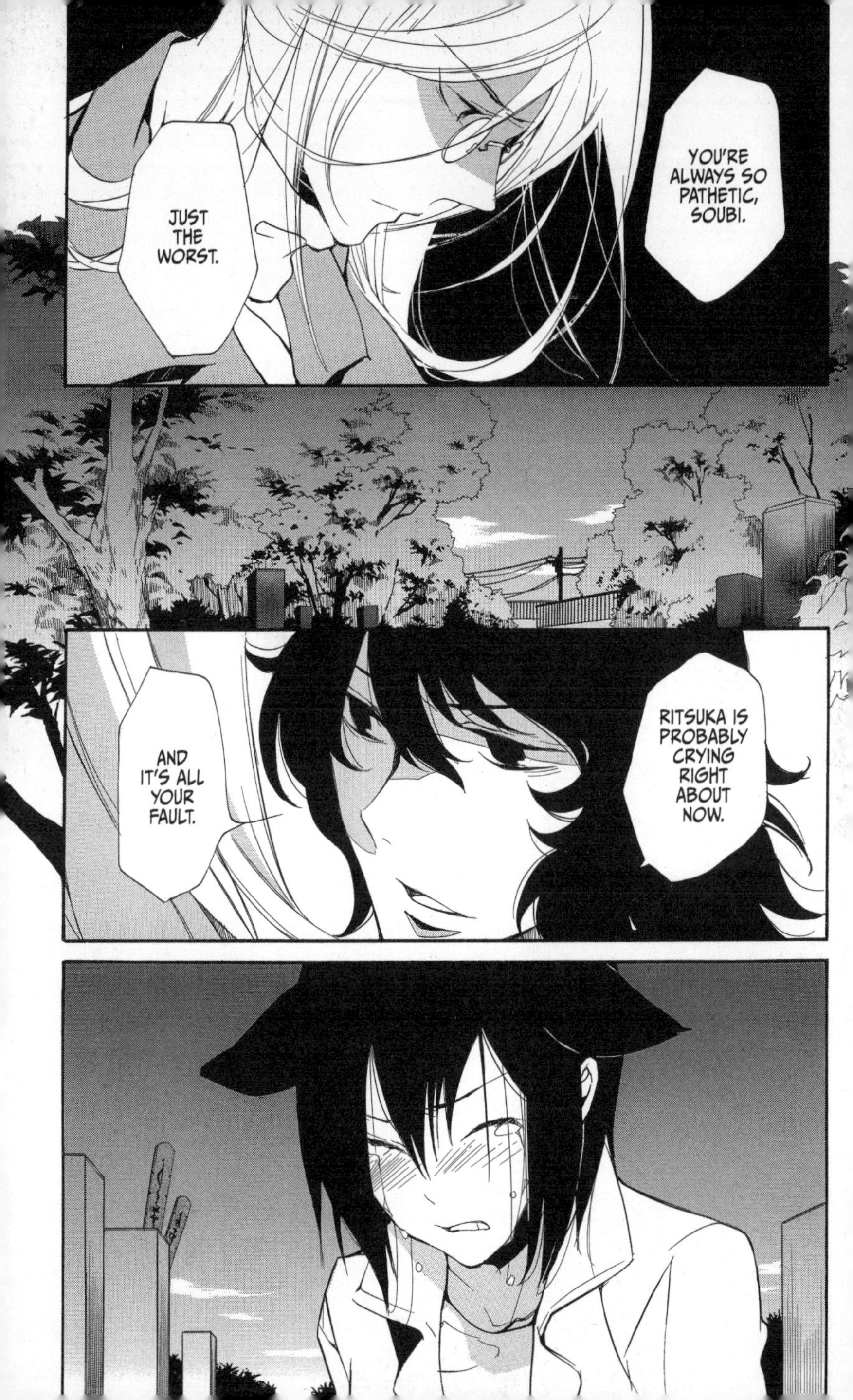
YOU'RE ALWAYS SO PATHETIC, SOUBI.
JUST THE WORST.
RITSUKA IS PROBABLY CRYING RIGHT ABOUT NOW.
AND IT'S ALL YOUR FAULT.

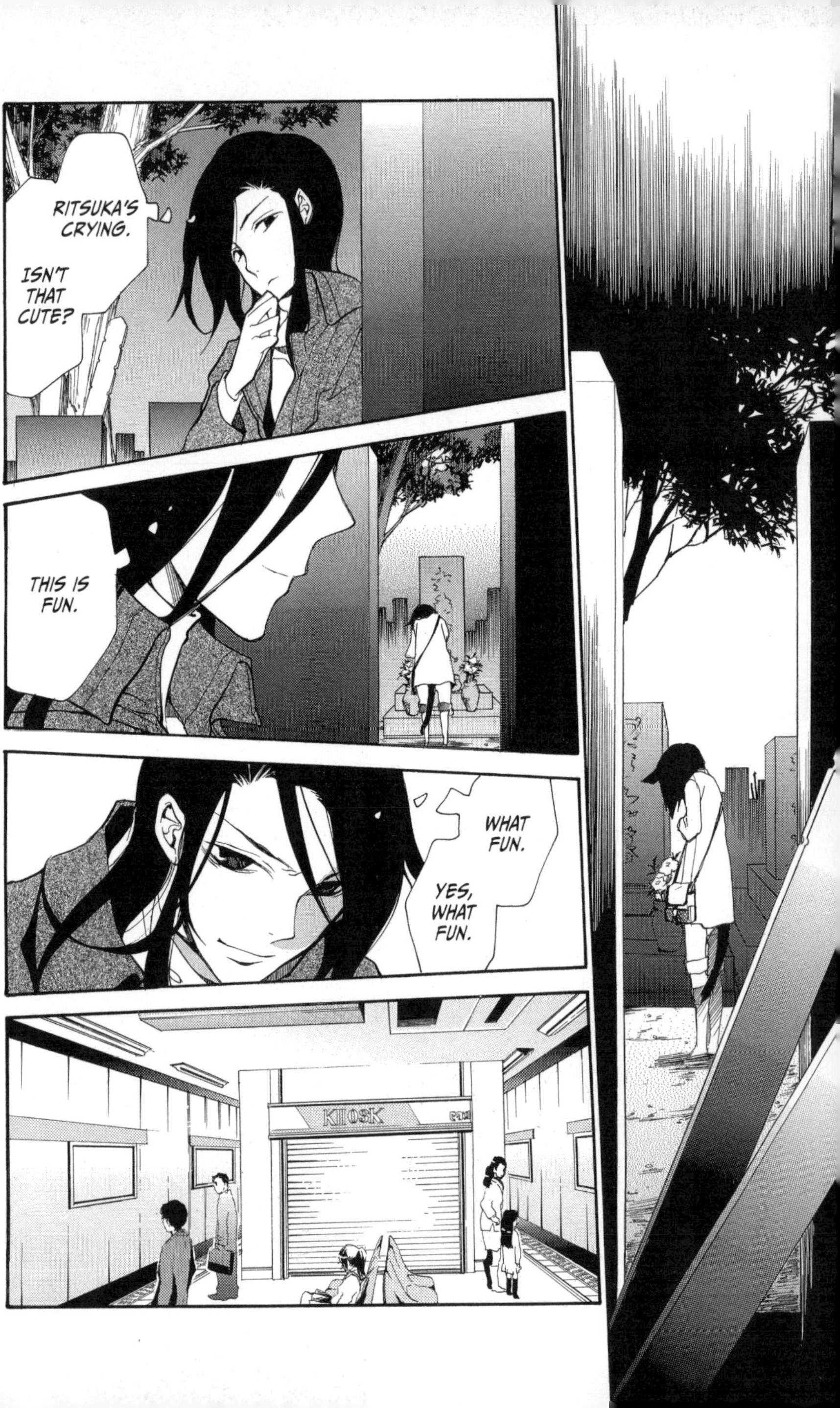

RITSUKA'S CRYING.
ISN'T THAT CUTE?
THIS IS FUN.
WHAT FUN.
YES, WHAT FUN.
KIOSK

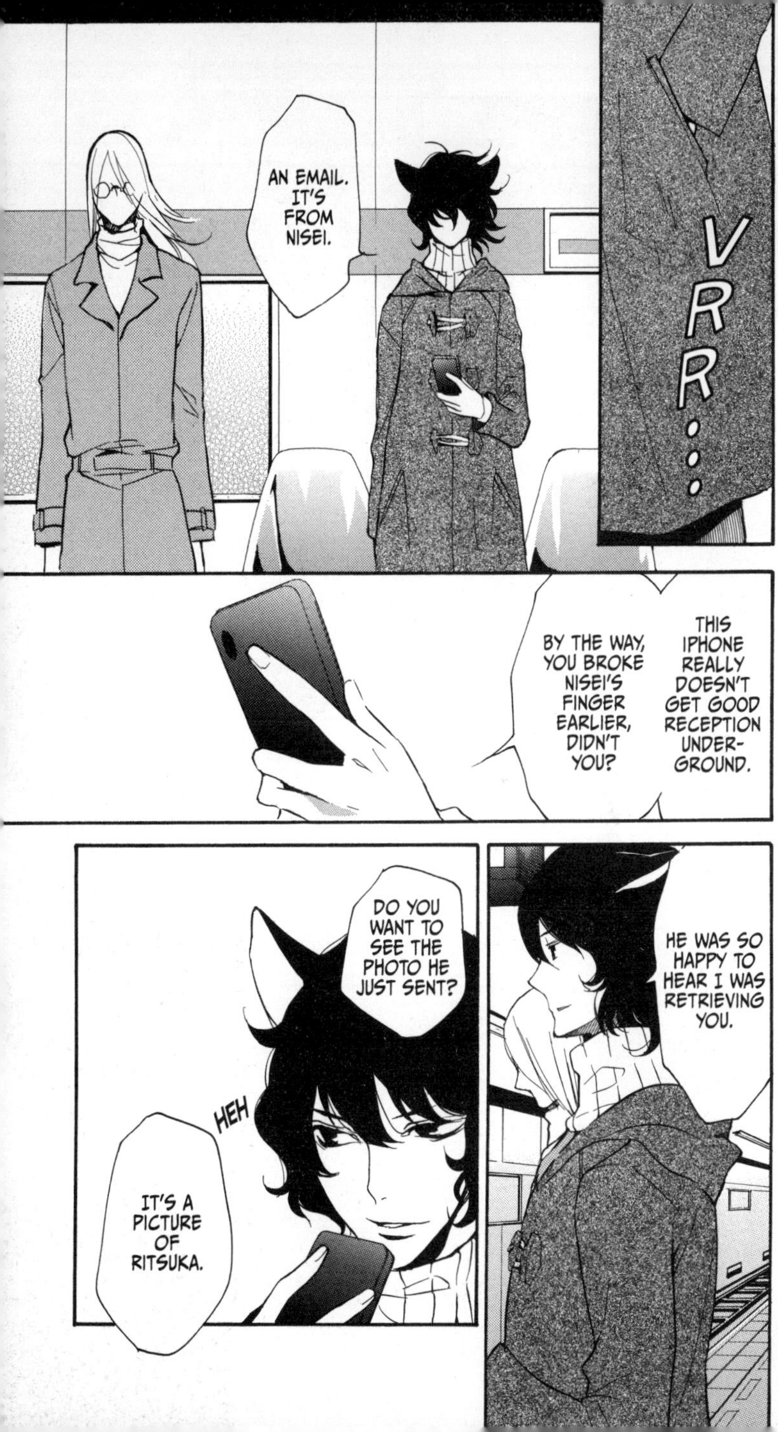
VRR...
AN EMAIL. IT'S FROM NISEI.
THIS IPHONE REALLY DOESN'T GET GOOD RECEPTION UNDER-GROUND.
BY THE WAY, YOU BROKE NISEI'S FINGER EARLIER, DIDN'T YOU?
HE WAS SO HAPPY TO HEAR I WAS RETRIEVING YOU.
DO YOU WANT TO SEE THE PHOTO HE JUST SENT?
HEH
IT'S A PICTURE OF RITSUKA.

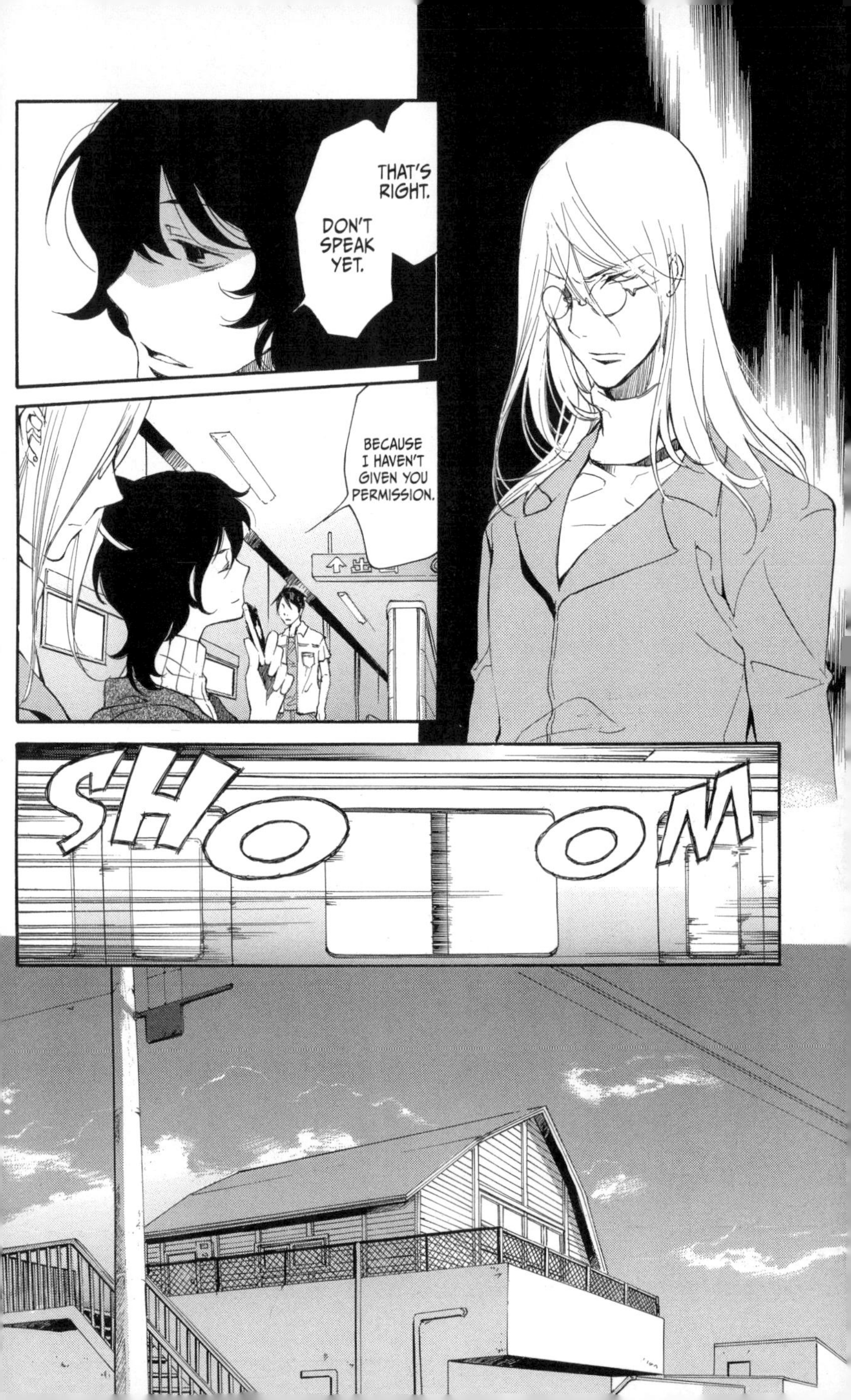
THAT'S RIGHT.
DON'T SPEAK YET.
BECAUSE I HAVEN'T GIVEN YOU PERMISSION.
SHO OM

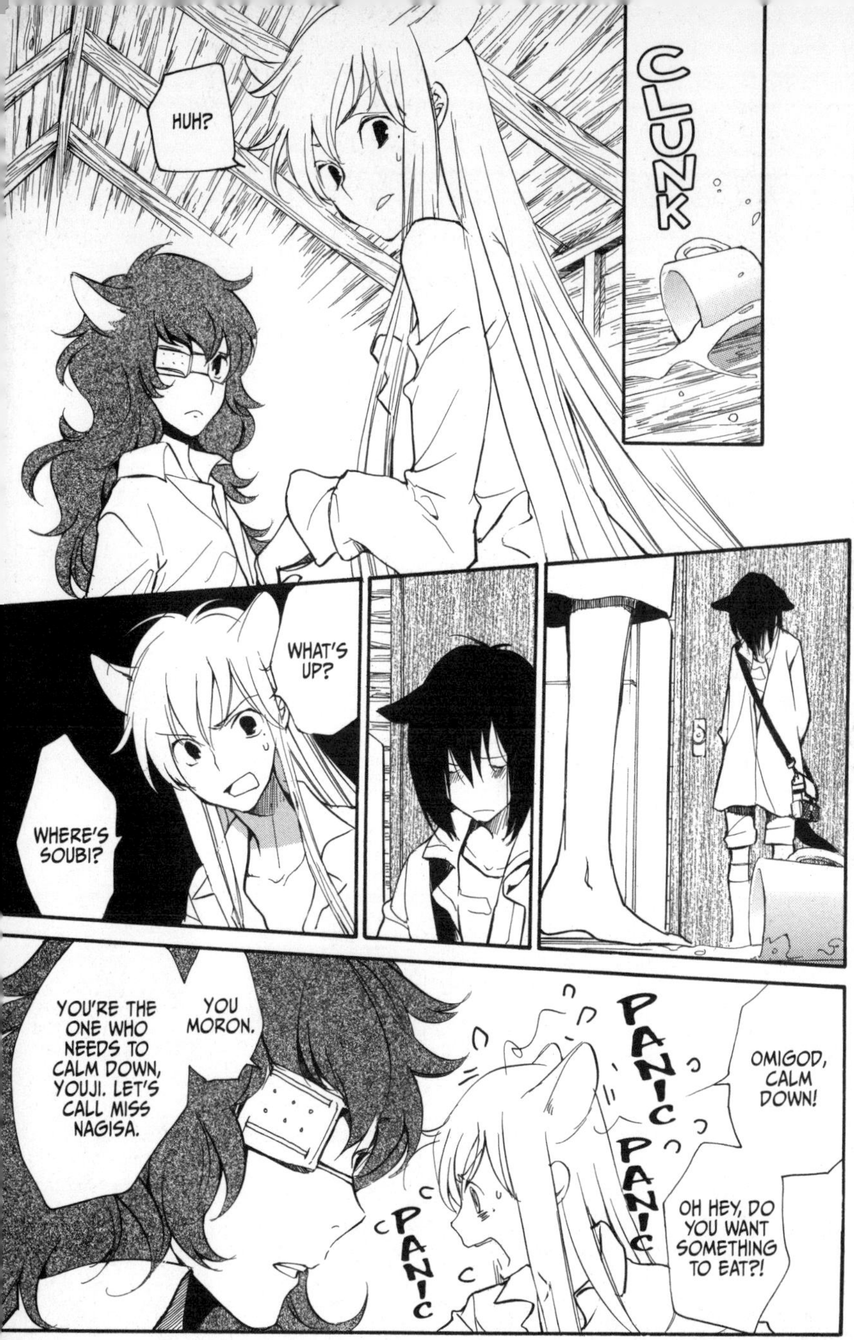
CLUNK
HUH?
WHAT'S UP?
WHERE'S SOUBI?
OMIGOD, CALM DOWN!
PANIC
PANIC
OH HEY, DO YOU WANT SOMETHING TO EAT?!
PANIC
YOU MORON.
YOU'RE THE ONE WHO NEEDS TO CALM DOWN, YOUJI. LET'S CALL MISS NAGISA.

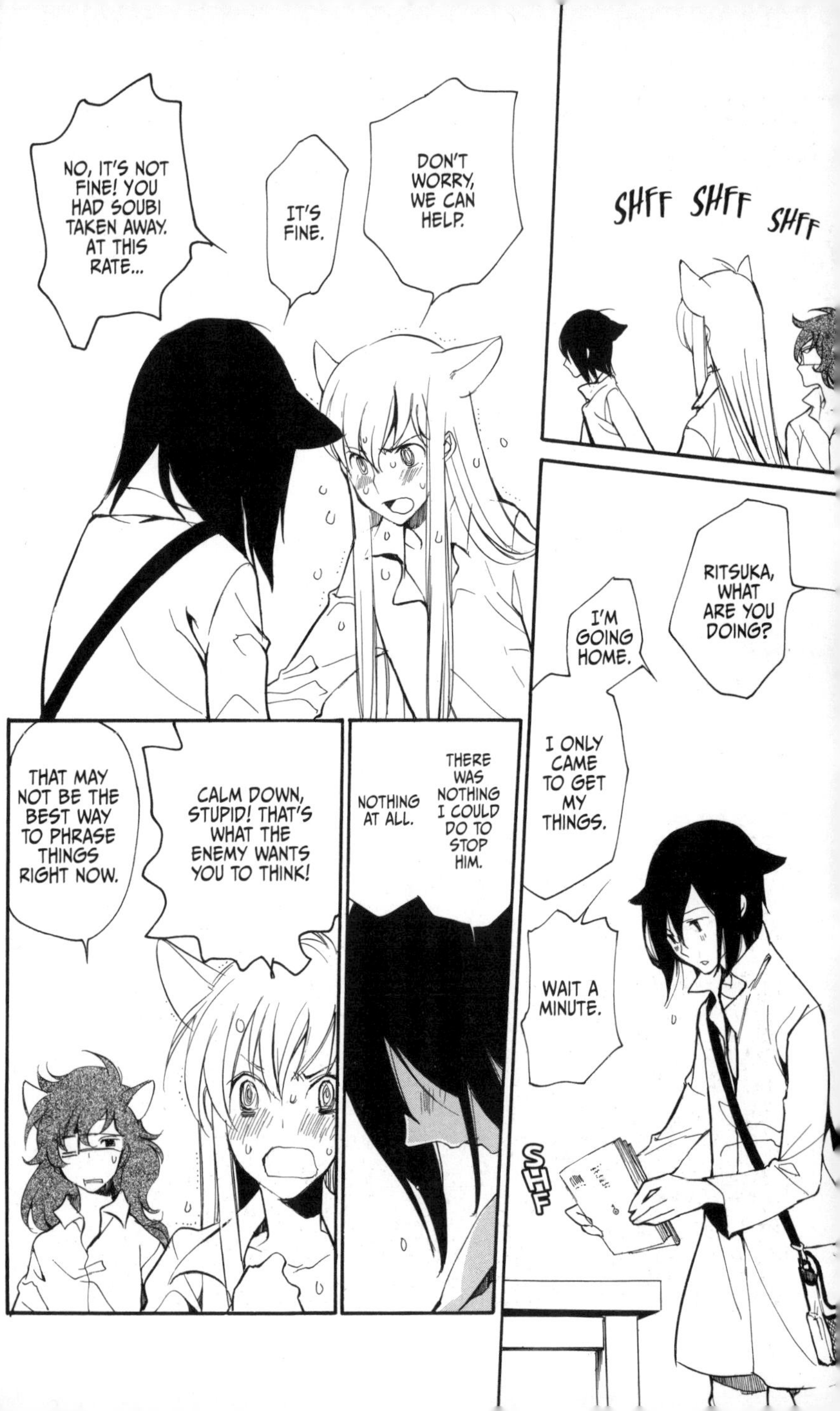
SHFF SHFF SHFF
RITSUKA, WHAT ARE YOU DOING?
I'M GOING HOME.
I ONLY CAME TO GET MY THINGS.
WAIT A MINUTE.
SHFF
DON'T WORRY, WE CAN HELP.
IT'S FINE.
NO, IT'S NOT FINE! YOU HAD SOUBI TAKEN AWAY. AT THIS RATE...
THERE WAS NOTHING I COULD DO TO STOP HIM.
NOTHING AT ALL.
CALM DOWN, STUPID! THAT'S WHAT THE ENEMY WANTS YOU TO THINK!
THAT MAY NOT BE THE BEST WAY TO PHRASE THINGS RIGHT NOW.

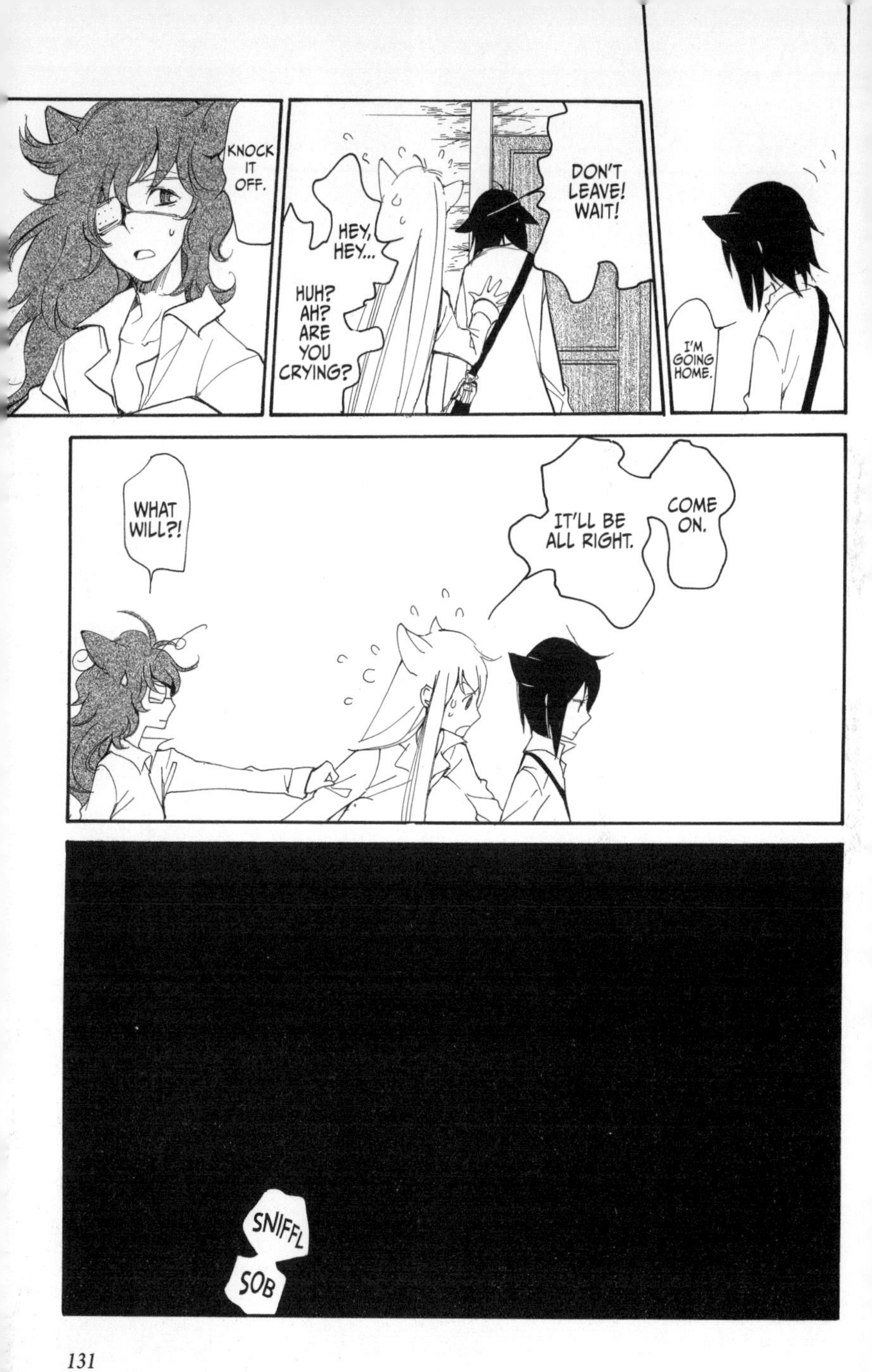
I'M GOING HOME.
DON'T LEAVE! WAIT!
HEY, HEY...
HUH? AH? ARE YOU CRYING?
KNOCK IT OFF.
COME ON.
IT'LL BE ALL RIGHT.
WHAT WILL?!
SNIFFL
SOB

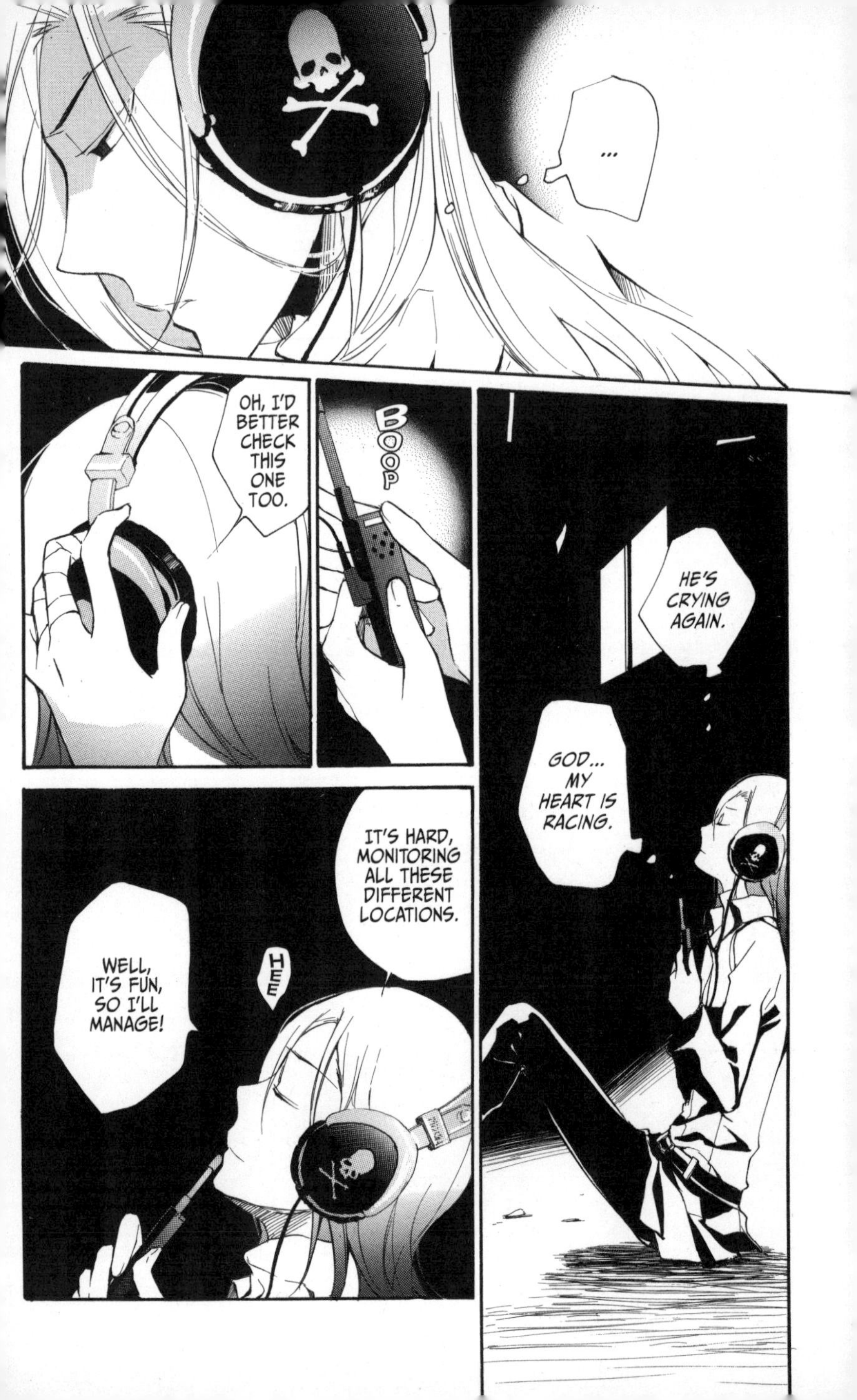
...
HE'S CRYING AGAIN.
GOD... MY HEART IS RACING.
BOOP
OH, I'D BETTER CHECK THIS ONE TOO.
IT'S HARD, MONITORING ALL THESE DIFFERENT LOCATIONS.
HEE
WELL, IT'S FUN, SO I'LL MANAGE!

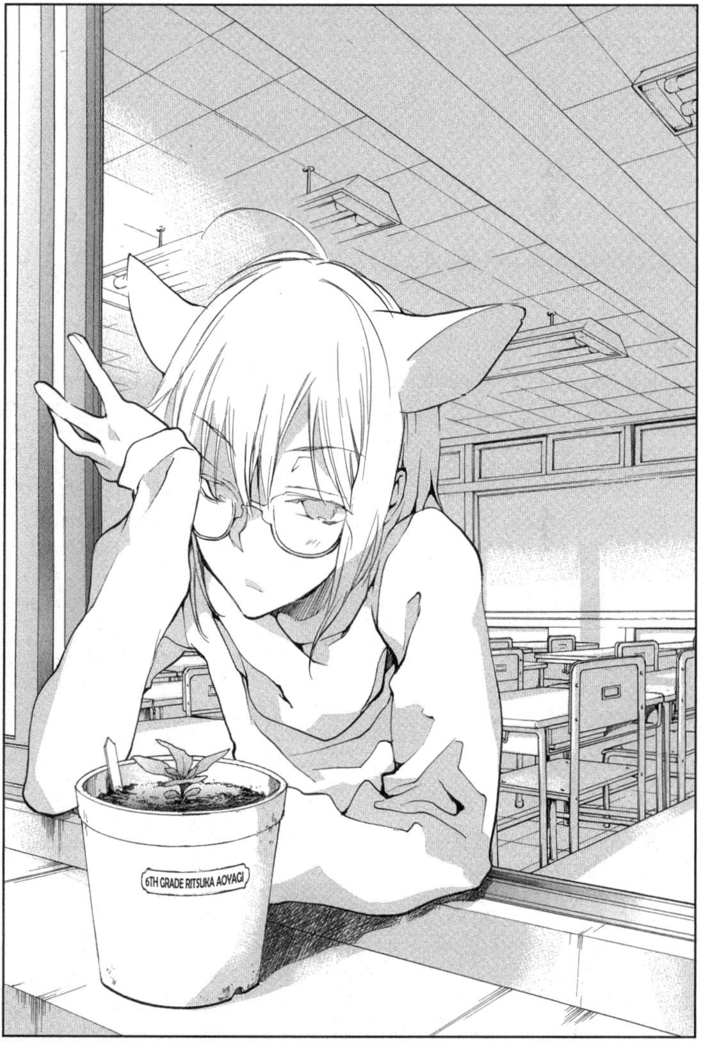
6TH GRADE RITSUKA AOYAGI

# LOVELESS

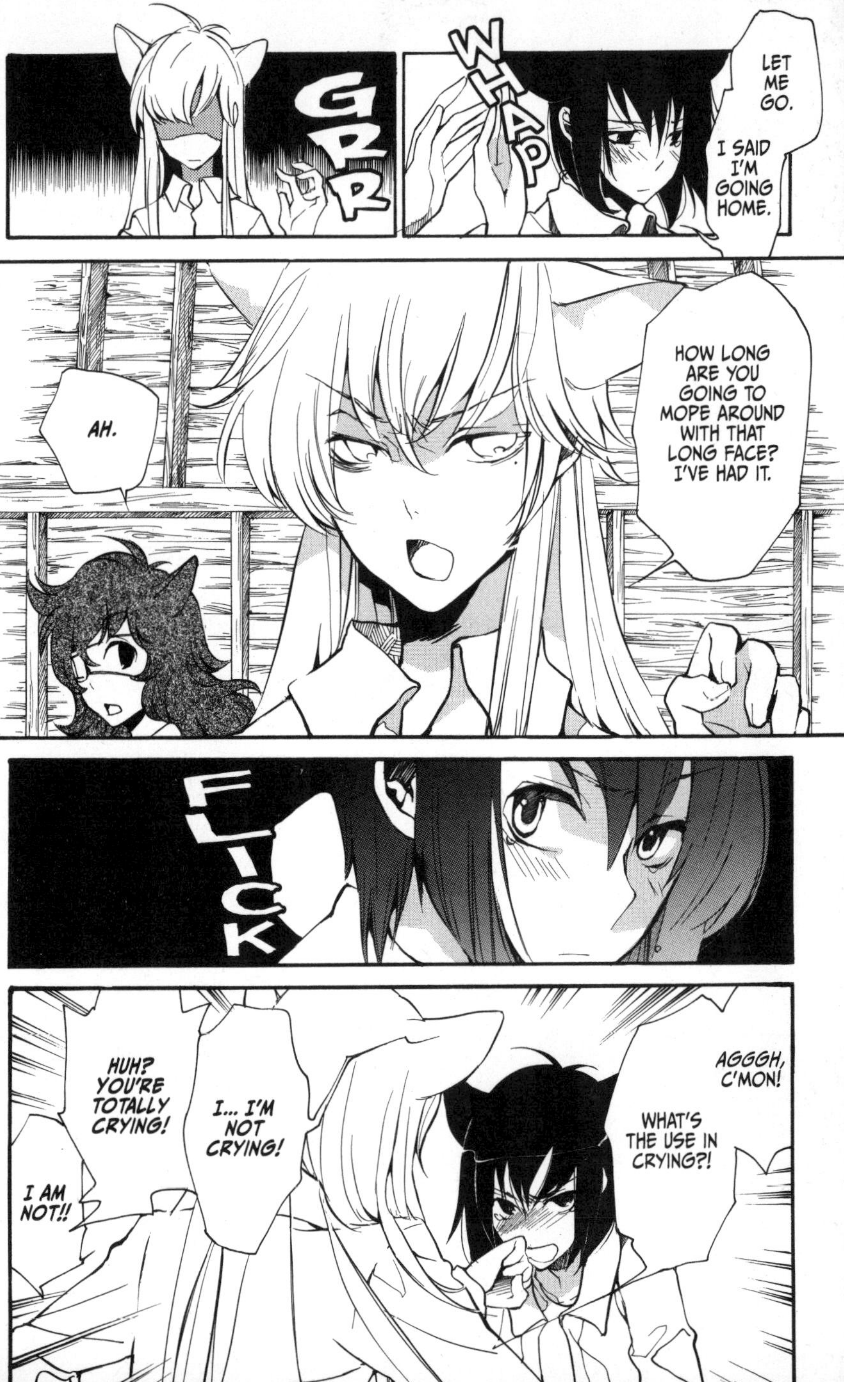
LET ME GO.
I SAID I'M GOING HOME.
WHAP
GRR
HOW LONG ARE YOU GOING TO MOPE AROUND WITH THAT LONG FACE? I'VE HAD IT.
AH.
FLICK
AGGGH, C'MON!
WHAT'S THE USE IN CRYING?!
I... I'M NOT CRYING!
HUH? YOU'RE TOTALLY CRYING!
I AM NOT!!

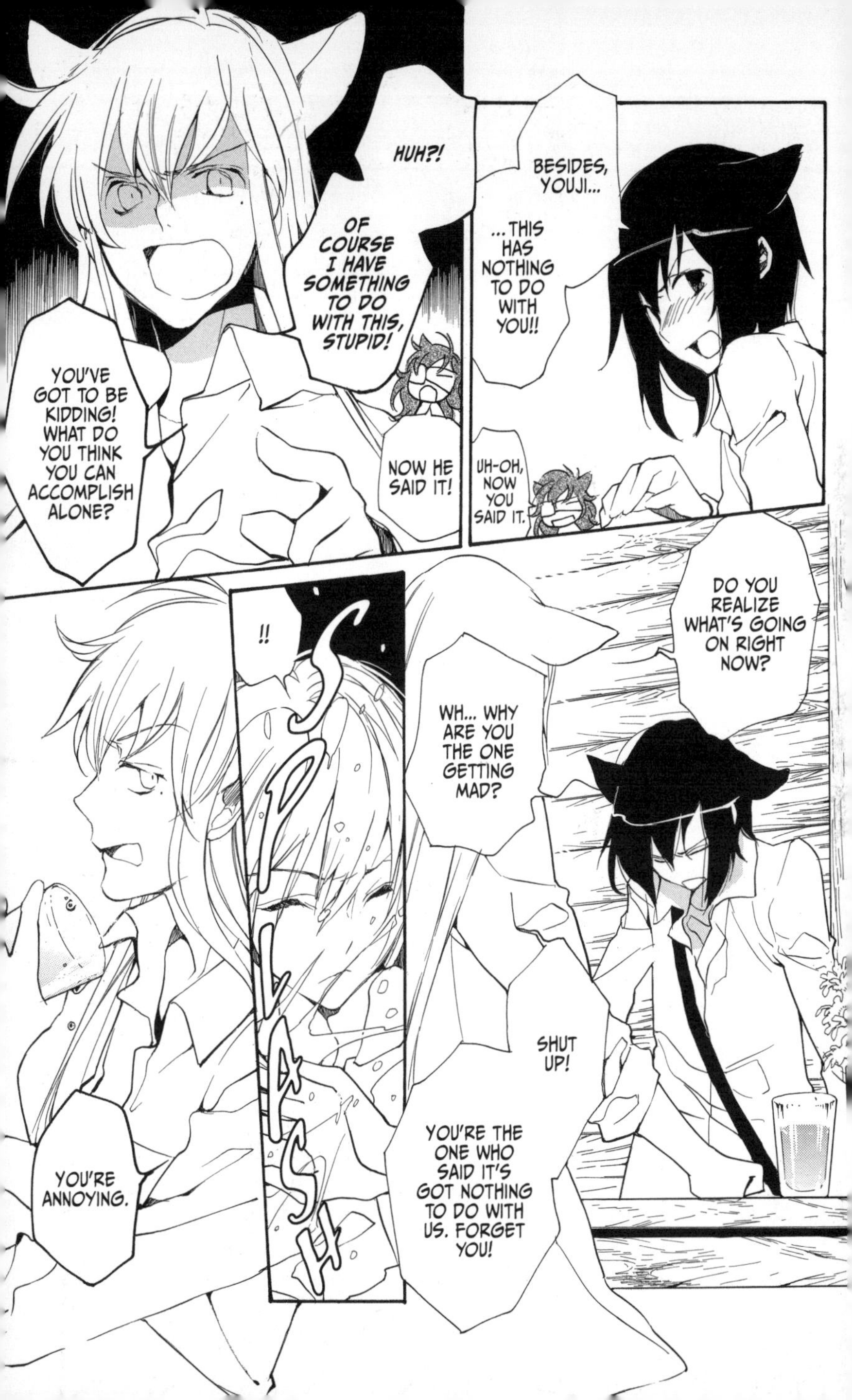
BESIDES, YOUJI...
...THIS HAS NOTHING TO DO WITH YOU!!
UH-OH, NOW YOU SAID IT.
HUH?!
OF COURSE I HAVE SOMETHING TO DO WITH THIS, STUPID!
YOU'VE GOT TO BE KIDDING! WHAT DO YOU THINK YOU CAN ACCOMPLISH ALONE?
NOW HE SAID IT!
DO YOU REALIZE WHAT'S GOING ON RIGHT NOW?
WH... WHY ARE YOU THE ONE GETTING MAD?
SHUT UP!
YOU'RE THE ONE WHO SAID IT'S GOT NOTHING TO DO WITH US. FORGET YOU!
!!
SPLASH
YOU'RE ANNOYING.

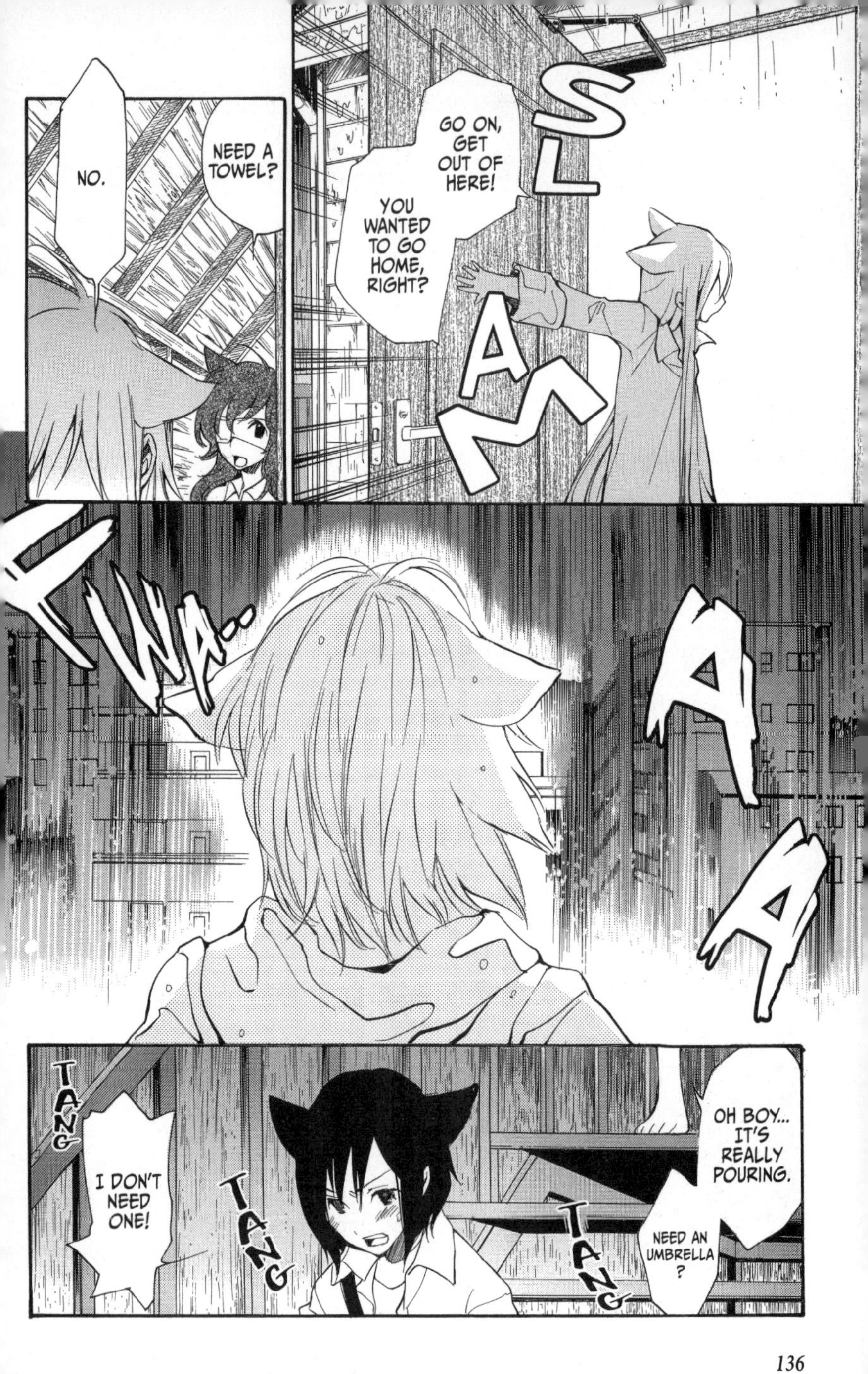
GO ON, GET OUT OF HERE!
YOU WANTED TO GO HOME, RIGHT?
SLAM
NEED A TOWEL?
NO.
FWA...
A
A
OH BOY... IT'S REALLY POURING.
NEED AN UMBRELLA?
TANG
TANG
TANG
I DON'T NEED ONE!

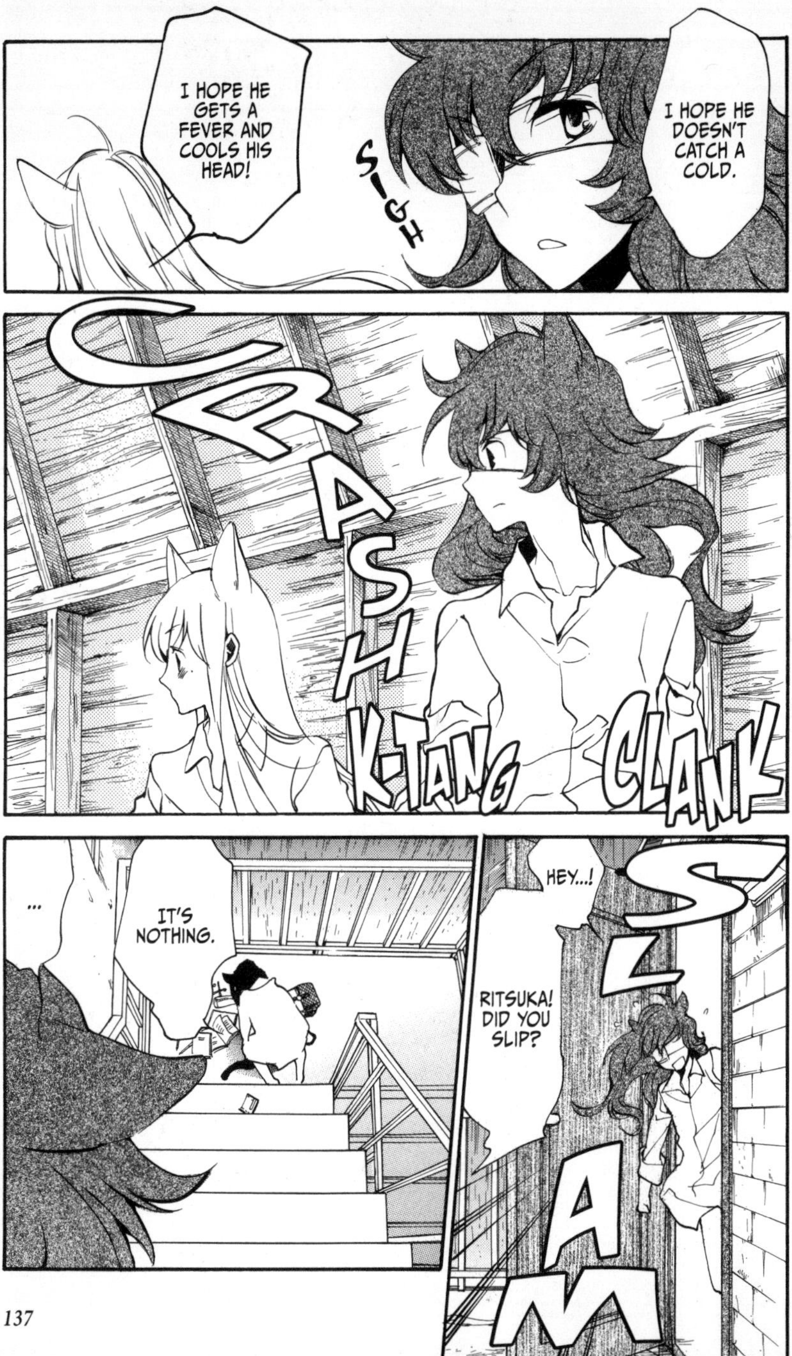

I HOPE HE DOESN'T CATCH A COLD.
SIGH
I HOPE HE GETS A FEVER AND COOLS HIS HEAD!
CRASH
CLANK
K-TANG
SLAM
HEY...!
RITSUKA! DID YOU SLIP?
IT'S NOTHING.
...

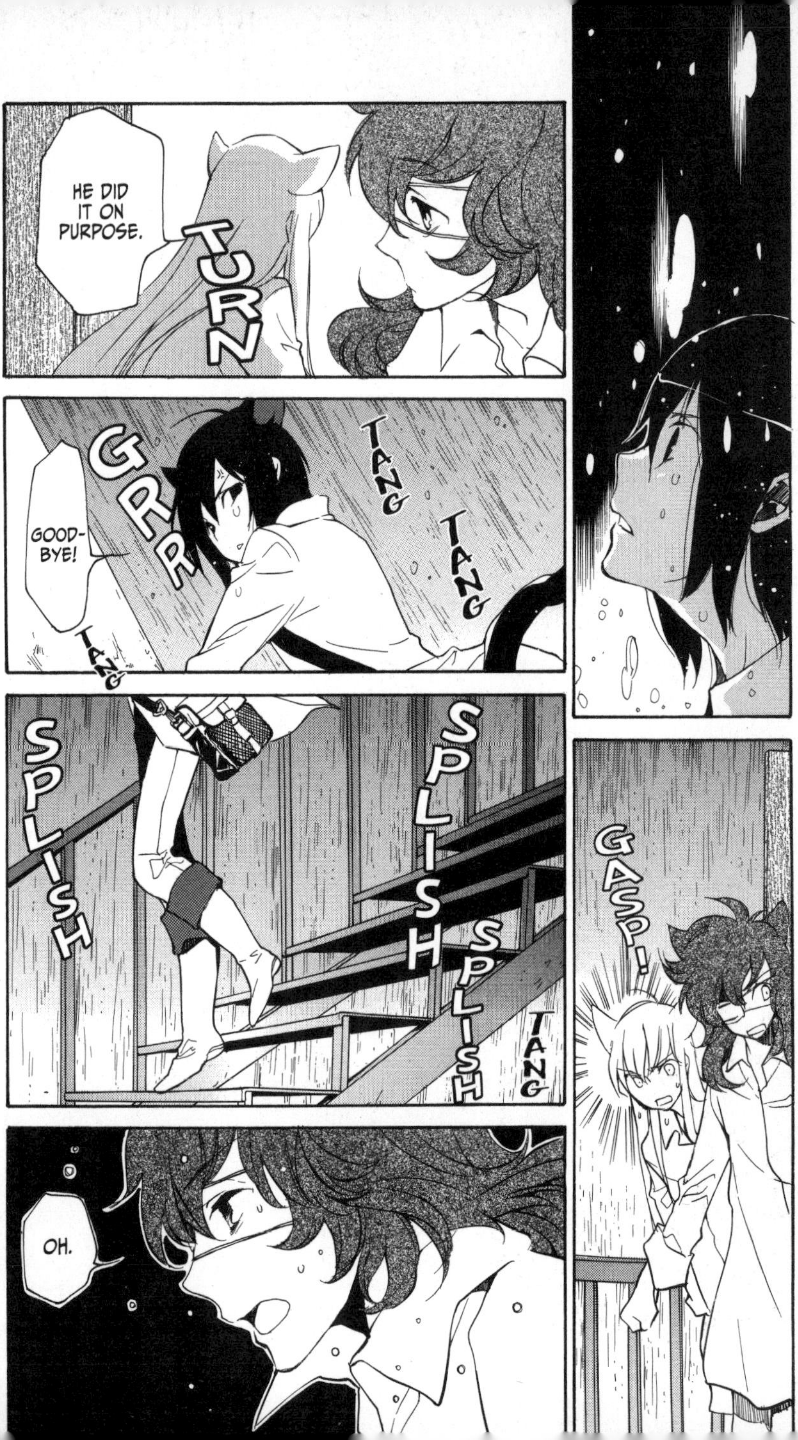
GASP!
HE DID IT ON PURPOSE.
TURN
GOOD-BYE!
GRRR
TANG
TANG
TANG
SPLISH
SPLISH
SPLISH
TANG
OH.

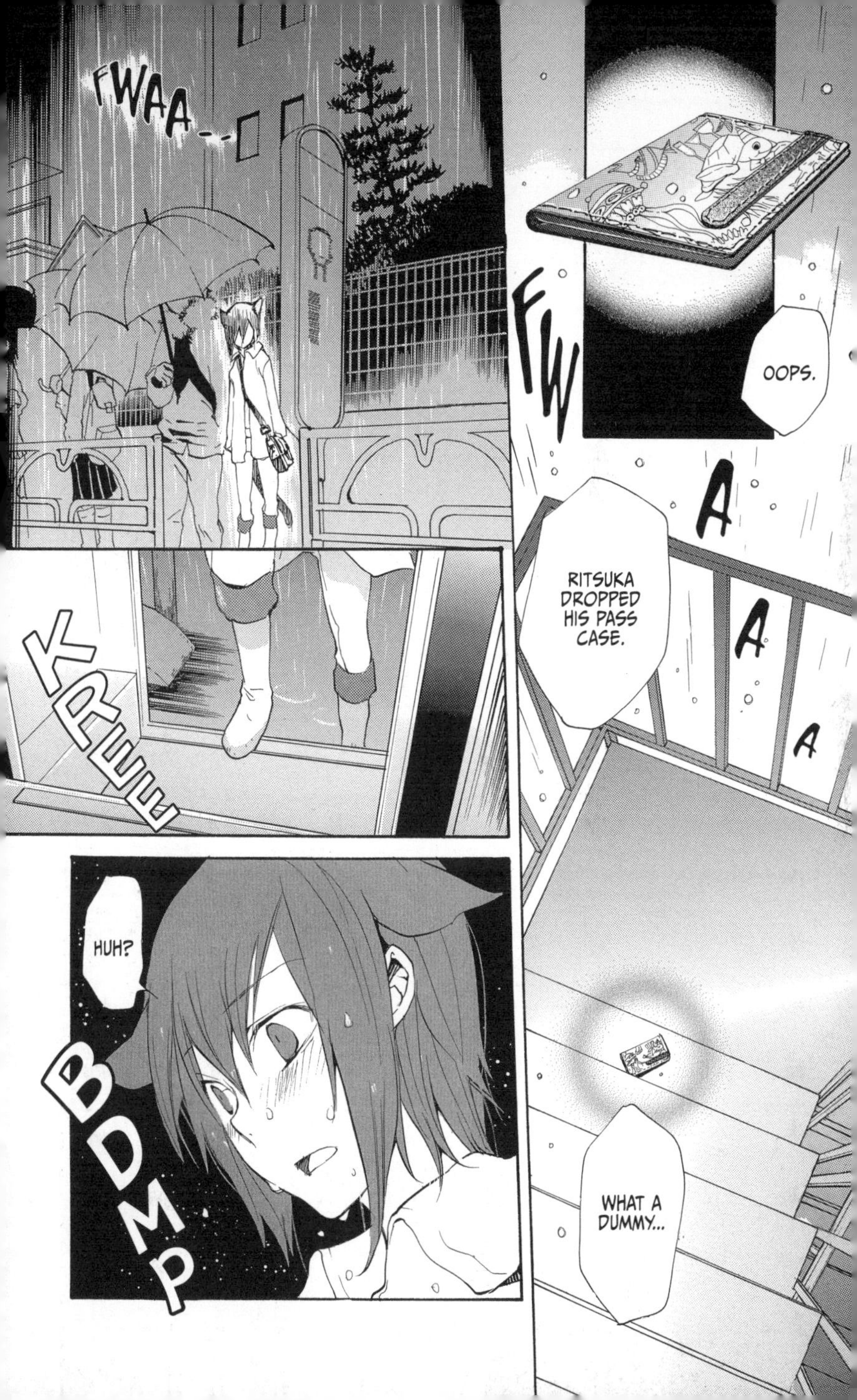
OOPS.
FWAAAA
RITSUKA DROPPED HIS PASS CASE.
WHAT A DUMMY...
FWAA...
KREEE
HUH?
BDMP

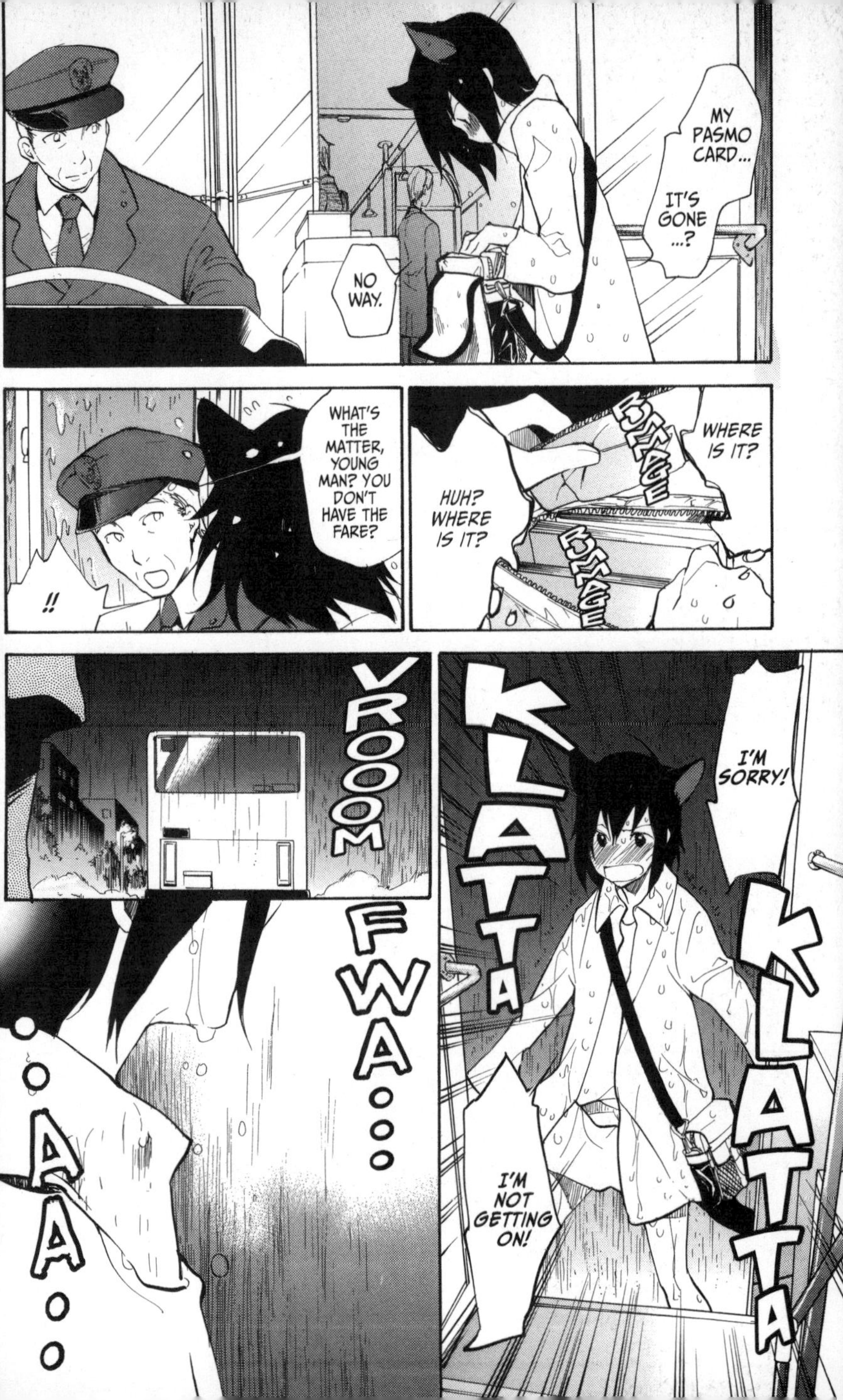
MY PASMO CARD...
IT'S GONE ...?
NO WAY.
WHERE IS IT?
HUH? WHERE IS IT?
WHAT'S THE MATTER, YOUNG MAN? YOU DON'T HAVE THE FARE?
!!
I'M SORRY!
KLATTA
KLATTA
I'M NOT GETTING ON!
VROOOM
FWAOOO
OOAAOO

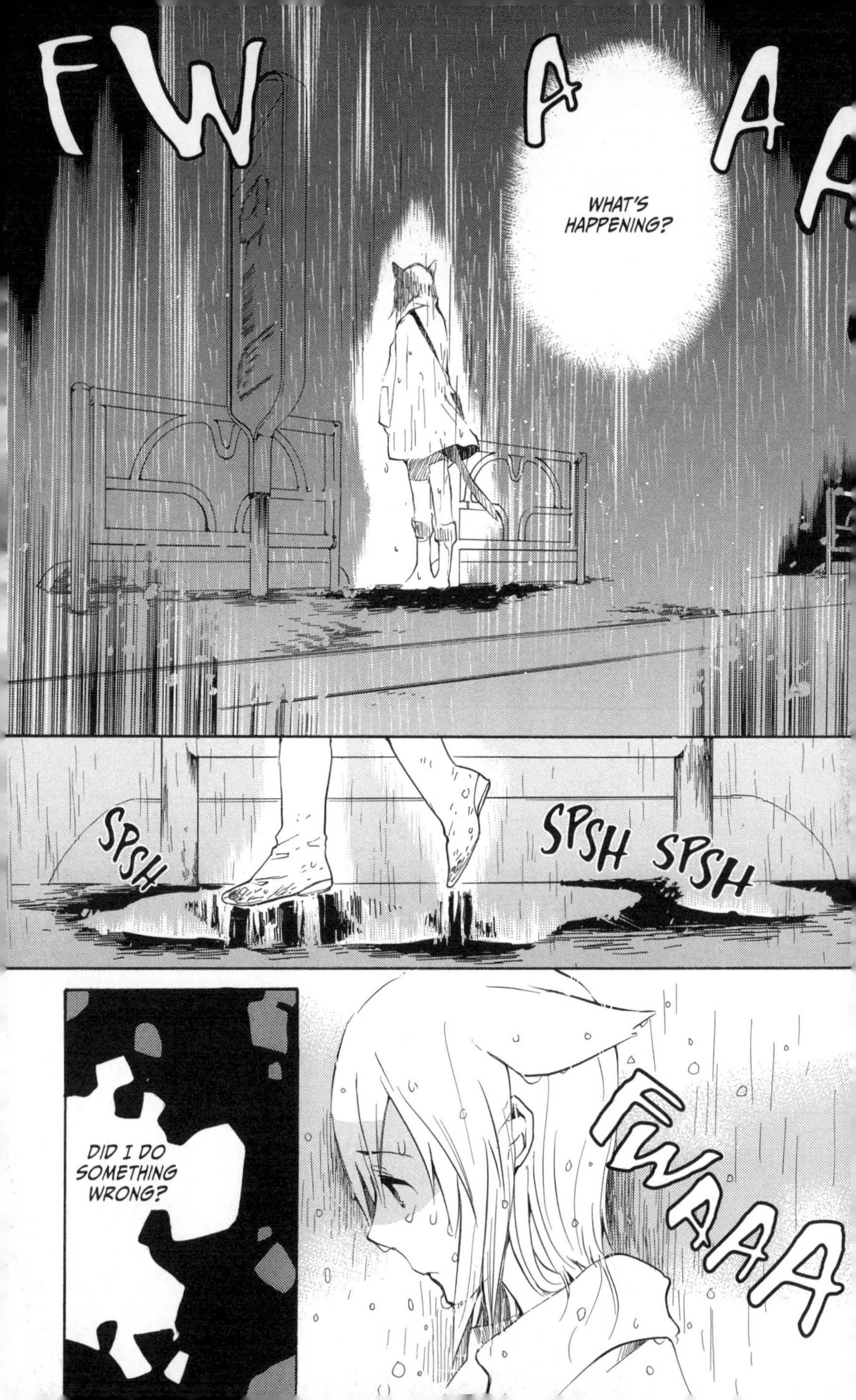
FWAA
WHAT'S HAPPENING?
SPSH SPSH
SPSH
FWAAA
DID I DO SOMETHING WRONG?

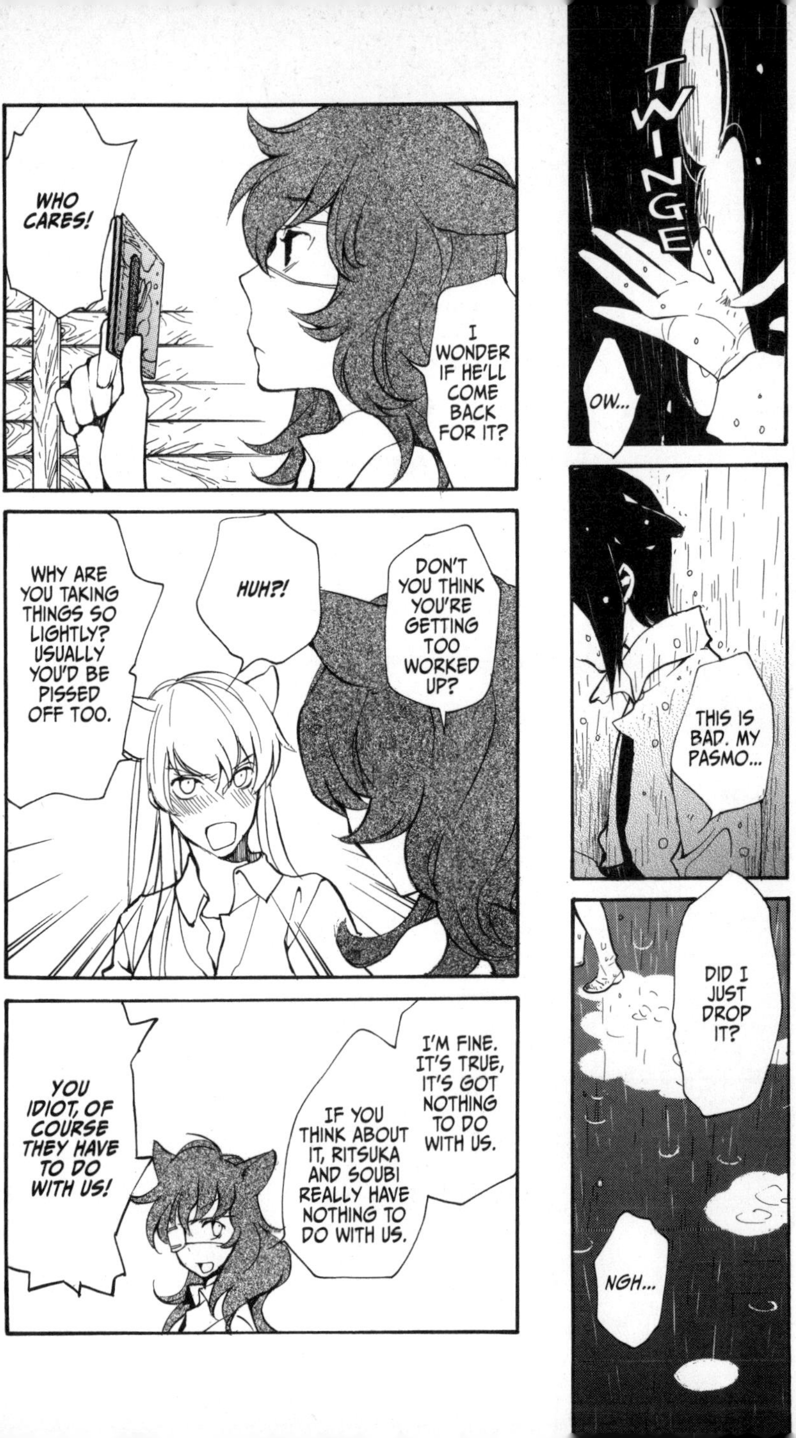
TWINGE
OW...
THIS IS BAD. MY PASMO...
DID I JUST DROP IT?
NGH...
I WONDER IF HE'LL COME BACK FOR IT?
WHO CARES!
DON'T YOU THINK YOU'RE GETTING TOO WORKED UP?
HUH?!
WHY ARE YOU TAKING THINGS SO LIGHTLY? USUALLY YOU'D BE PISSED OFF TOO.
I'M FINE. IT'S TRUE, IT'S GOT NOTHING TO DO WITH US.
IF YOU THINK ABOUT IT, RITSUKA AND SOUBI REALLY HAVE NOTHING TO DO WITH US.
YOU IDIOT, OF COURSE THEY HAVE TO DO WITH US!

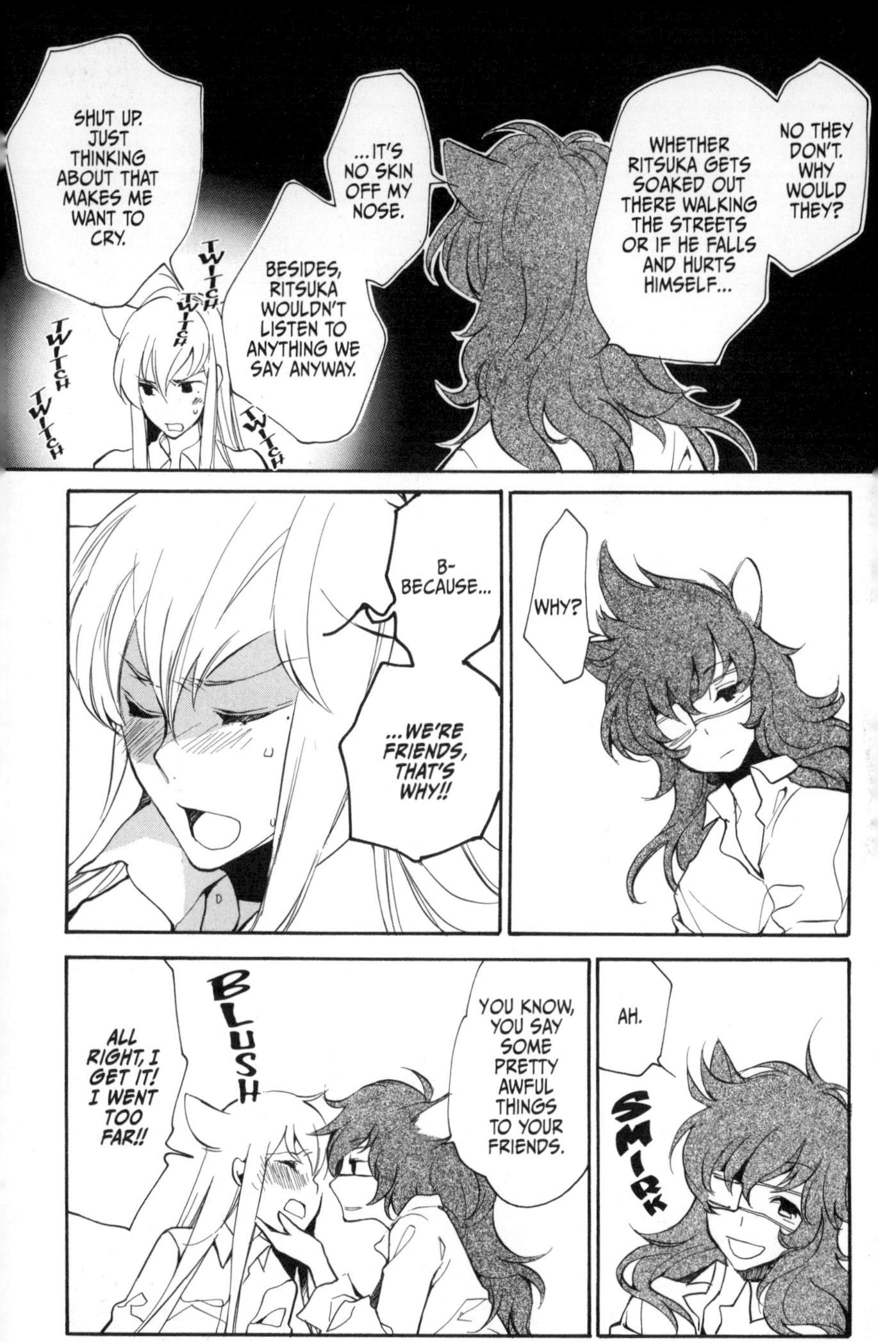

NO THEY DON'T. WHY WOULD THEY?
WHETHER RITSUKA GETS SOAKED OUT THERE WALKING THE STREETS OR IF HE FALLS AND HURTS HIMSELF...
...IT'S NO SKIN OFF MY NOSE.
BESIDES, RITSUKA WOULDN'T LISTEN TO ANYTHING WE SAY ANYWAY.
SHUT UP. JUST THINKING ABOUT THAT MAKES ME WANT TO CRY.
TWITCH
TWITCH
TWITCH
TWITCH
TWITCH
WHY?
B-BECAUSE...
...WE'RE FRIENDS, THAT'S WHY!!
AH.
SMIRK
YOU KNOW, YOU SAY SOME PRETTY AWFUL THINGS TO YOUR FRIENDS.
BLUSH
ALL RIGHT, I GET IT! I WENT TOO FAR!!

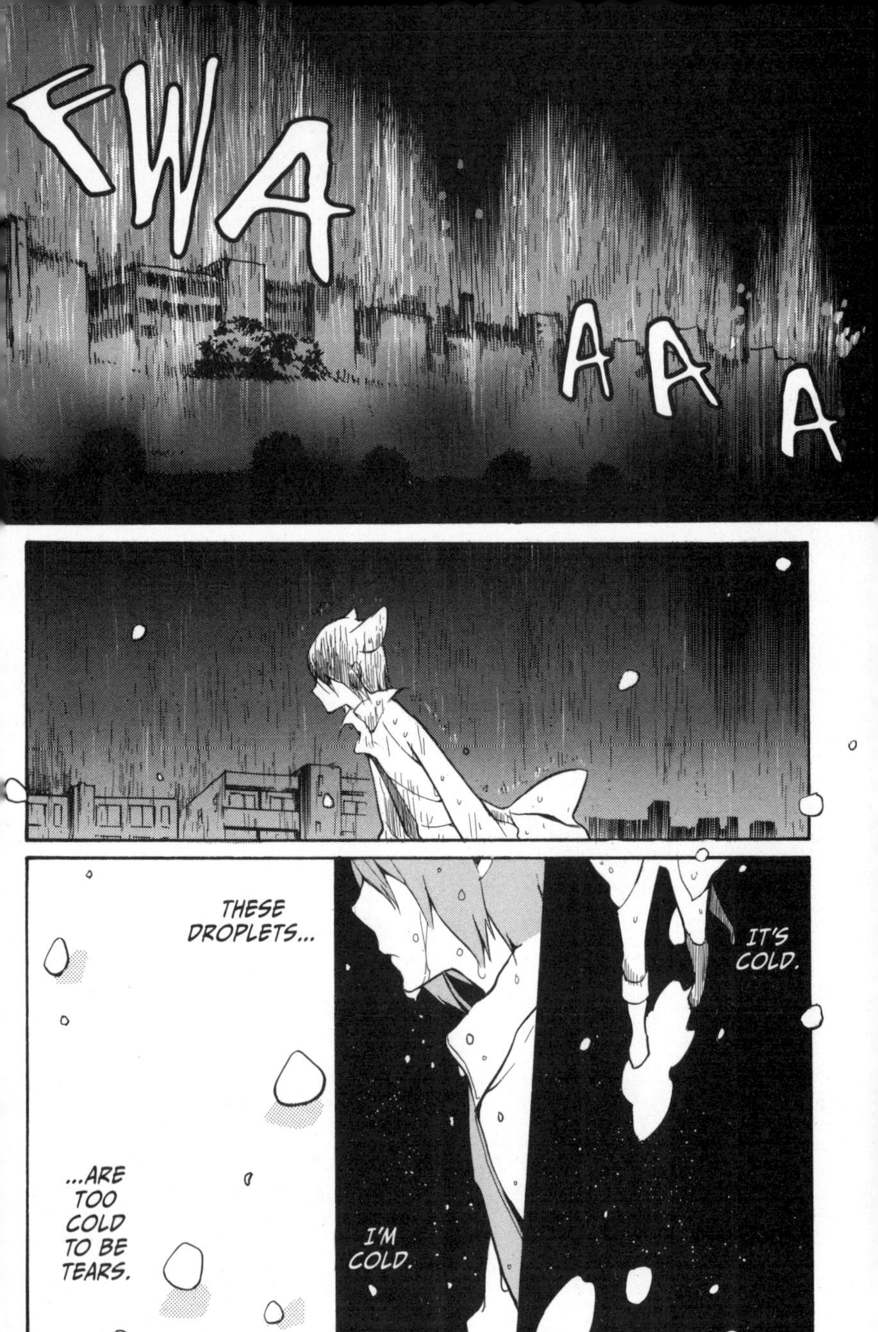
FWAAAA
IT'S COLD.
I'M COLD.
THESE DROPLETS...
...ARE TOO COLD TO BE TEARS.

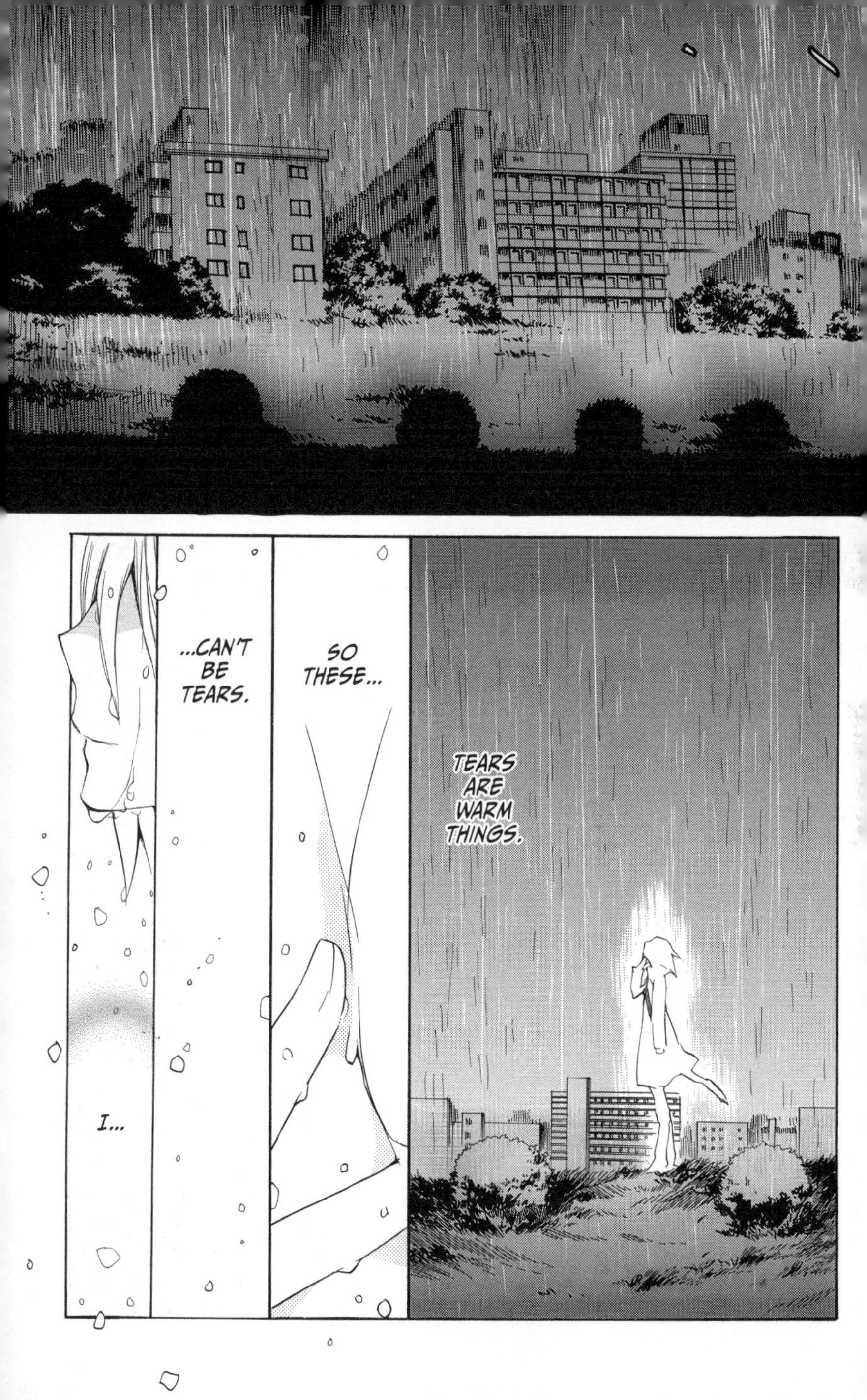

TEARS ARE WARM THINGS.
SO THESE...
...CAN'T BE TEARS.
I...

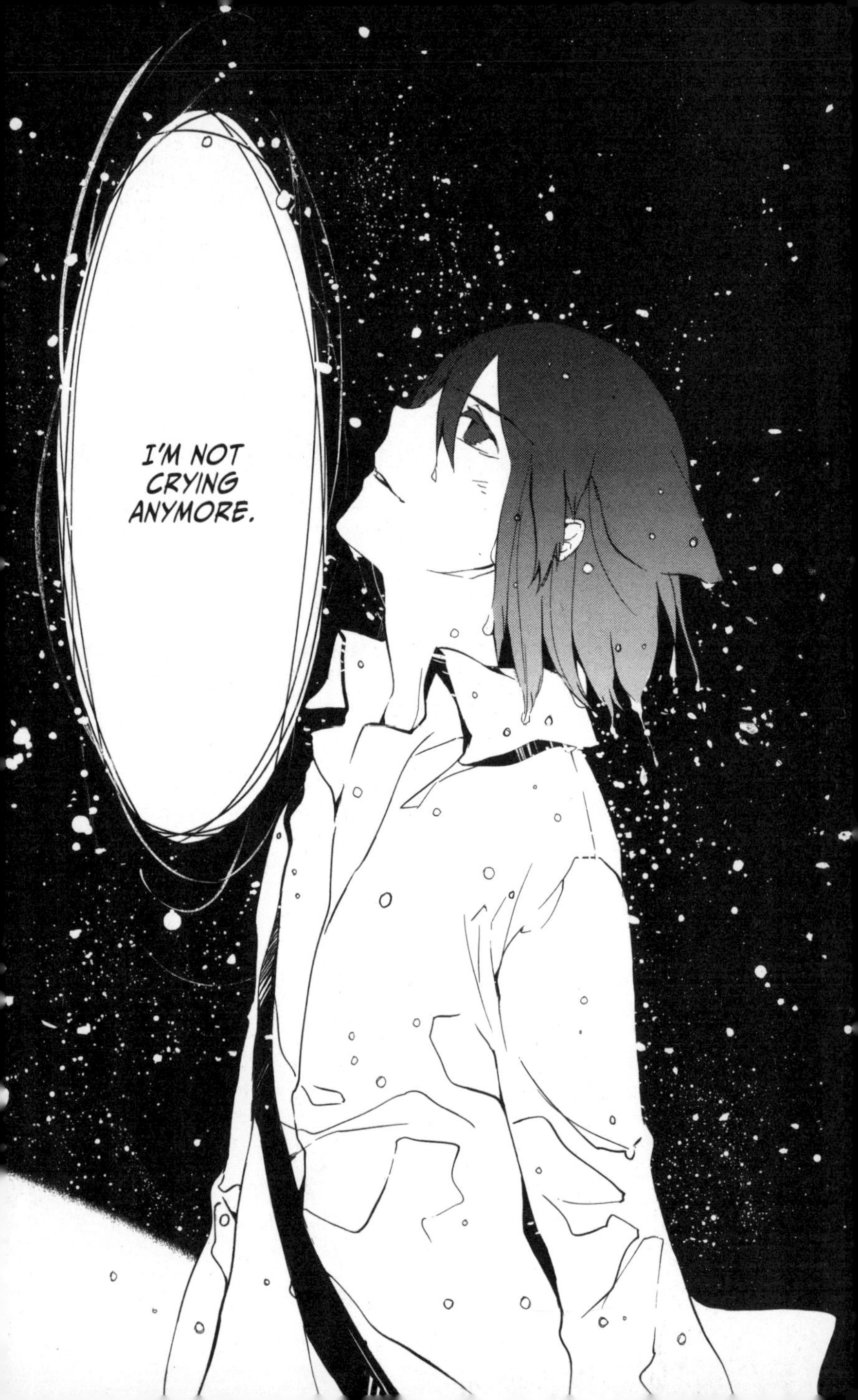
I'M NOT CRYING ANYMORE.

BAM!!
EEK!
I'M BACK!

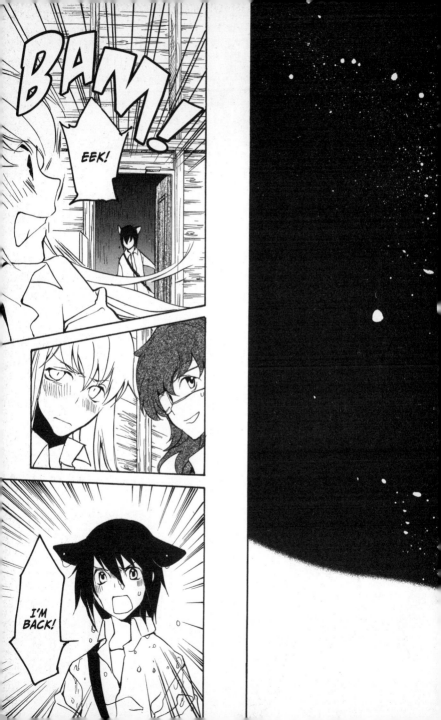

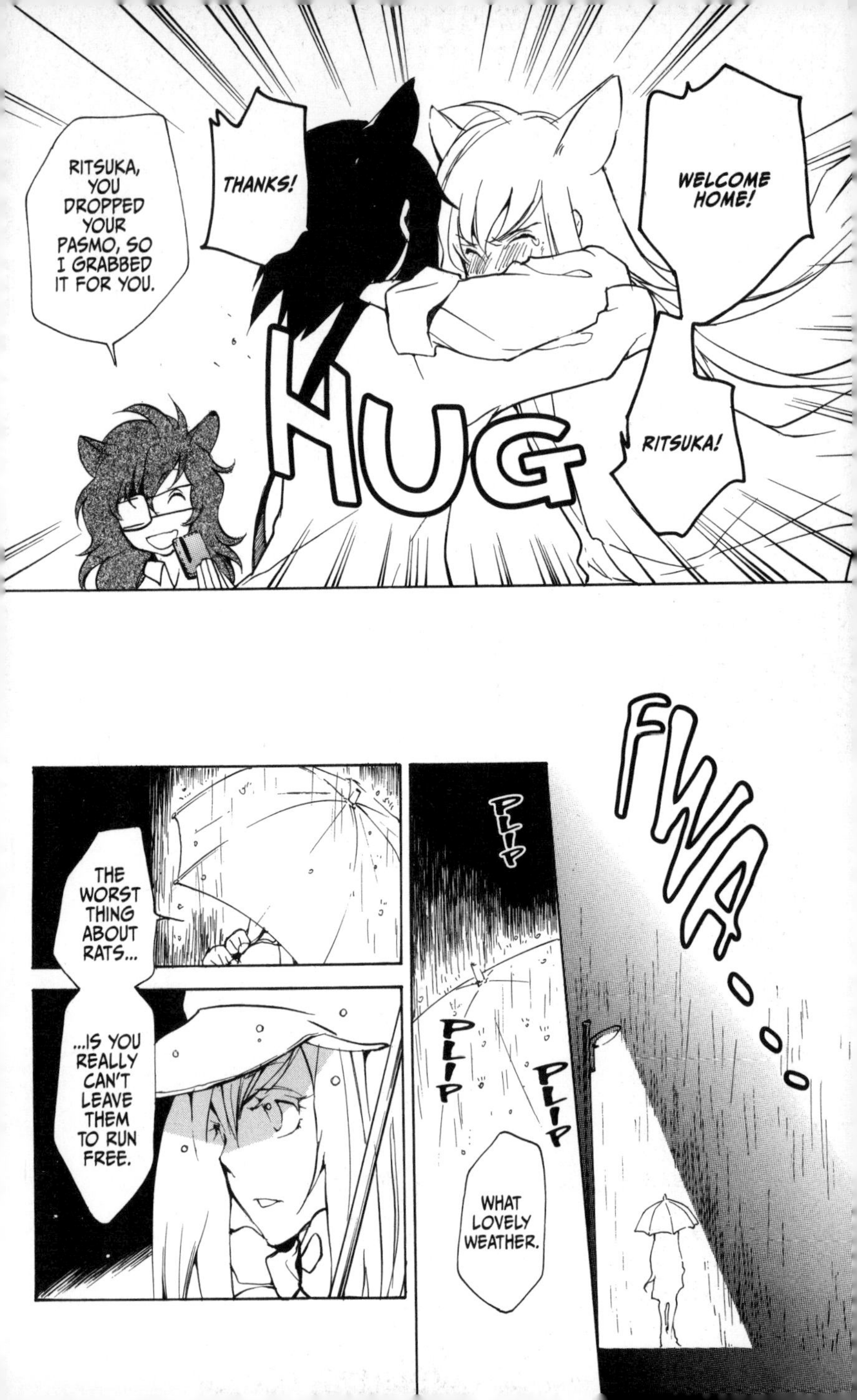
WELCOME HOME!
RITSUKA!
HUG
THANKS!
RITSUKA, YOU DROPPED YOUR PASMO, SO I GRABBED IT FOR YOU.
FWA...
PLIP
PLIP
PLIP
WHAT LOVELY WEATHER.
THE WORST THING ABOUT RATS...
...IS YOU REALLY CAN'T LEAVE THEM TO RUN FREE.

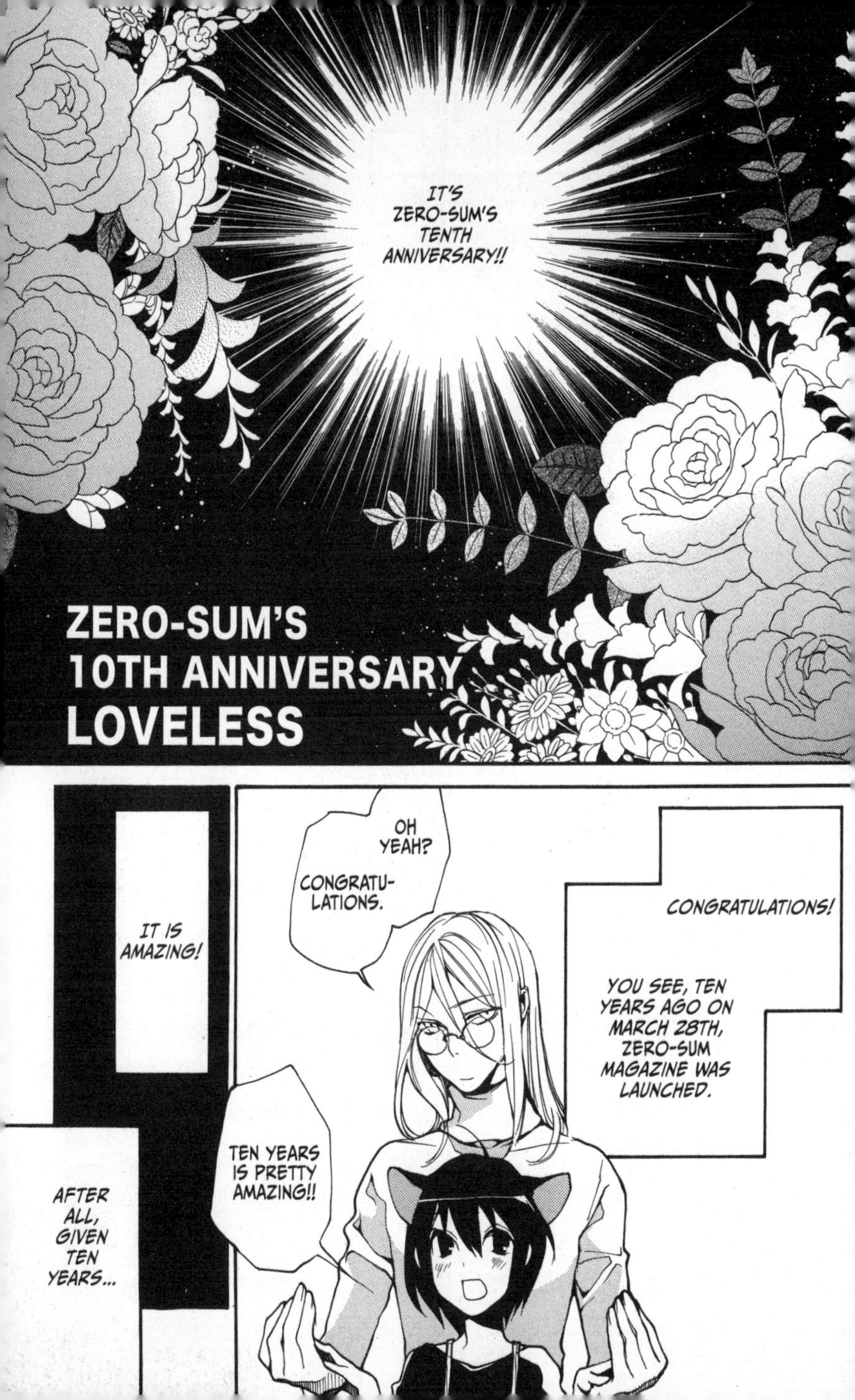
IT'S ZERO-SUM'S TENTH ANNIVERSARY!!
ZERO-SUM'S 10TH ANNIVERSARY LOVELESS
CONGRATULATIONS!
YOU SEE, TEN YEARS AGO ON MARCH 28TH, ZERO-SUM MAGAZINE WAS LAUNCHED.
OH YEAH?
CONGRATU-LATIONS.
TEN YEARS IS PRETTY AMAZING!!
IT IS AMAZING!
AFTER ALL, GIVEN TEN YEARS...

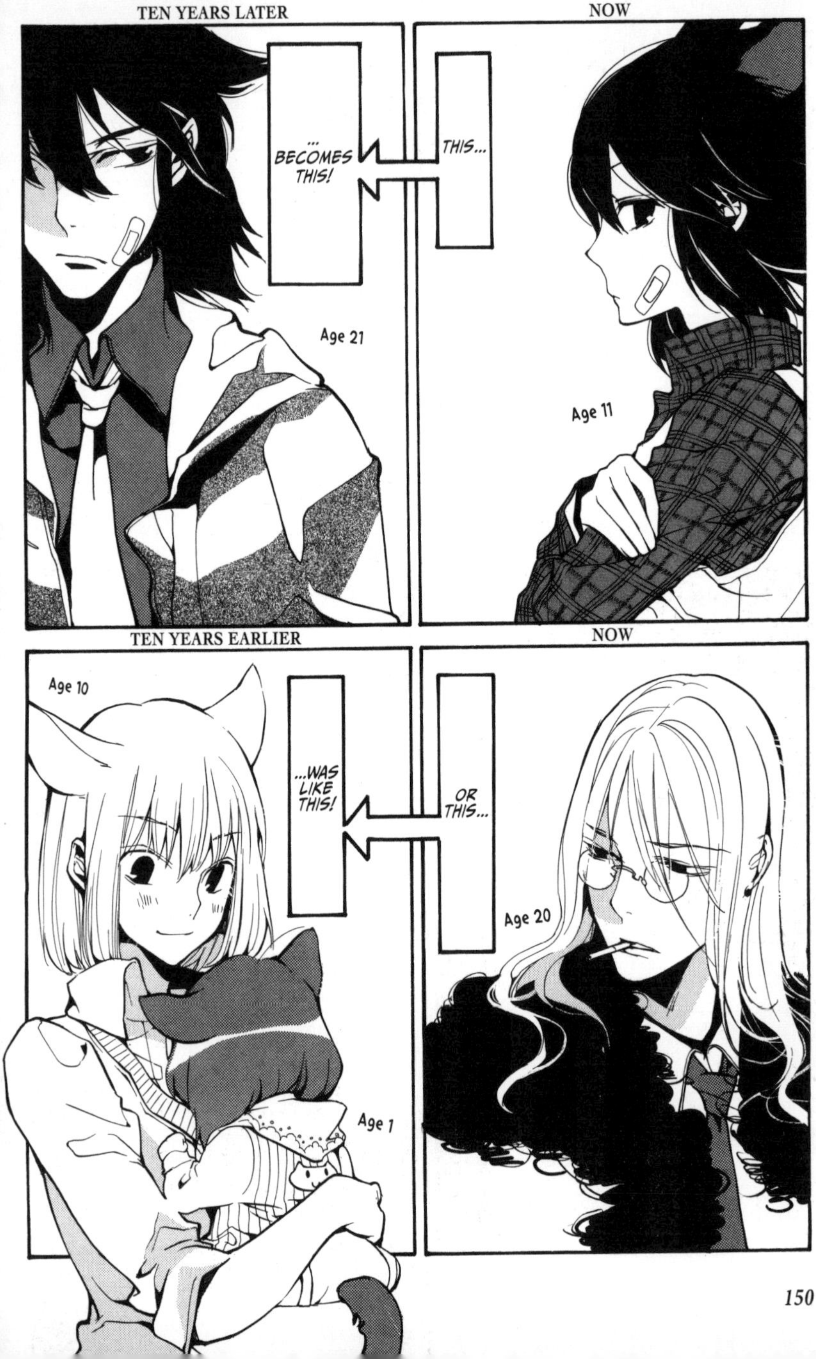
NOW
THIS...
Age 11
TEN YEARS LATER
...BECOMES THIS!
Age 21
NOW
OR THIS...
Age 20
TEN YEARS EARLIER
...WAS LIKE THIS!
Age 10
Age 1

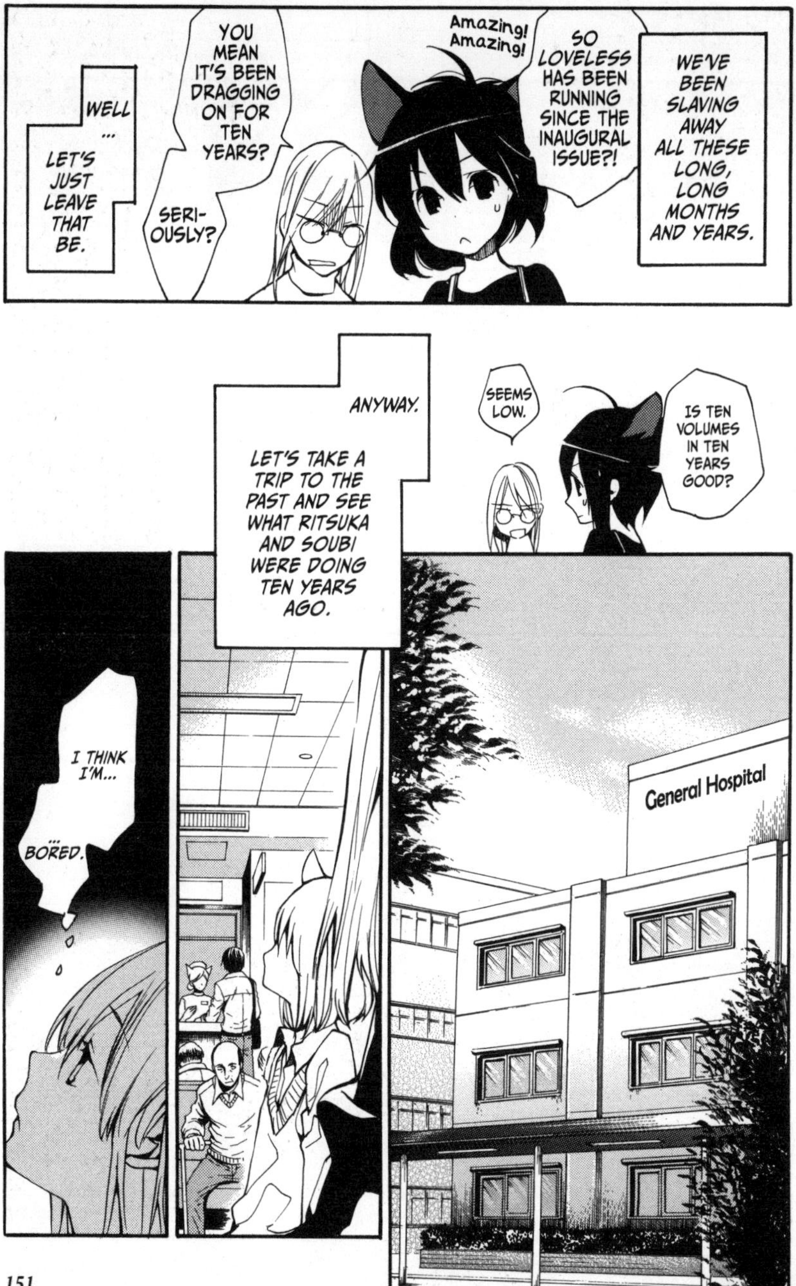
WE'VE BEEN SLAVING AWAY ALL THESE LONG, LONG MONTHS AND YEARS.
SO LOVELESS HAS BEEN RUNNING SINCE THE INAUGURAL ISSUE?!
Amazing! Amazing!
YOU MEAN IT'S BEEN DRAGGING ON FOR TEN YEARS?
SERI-OUSLY?
WELL ... LET'S JUST LEAVE THAT BE.
IS TEN VOLUMES IN TEN YEARS GOOD?
SEEMS LOW.
ANYWAY.
LET'S TAKE A TRIP TO THE PAST AND SEE WHAT RITSUKA AND SOUBI WERE DOING TEN YEARS AGO.
General Hospital
I THINK I'M...
...BORED.

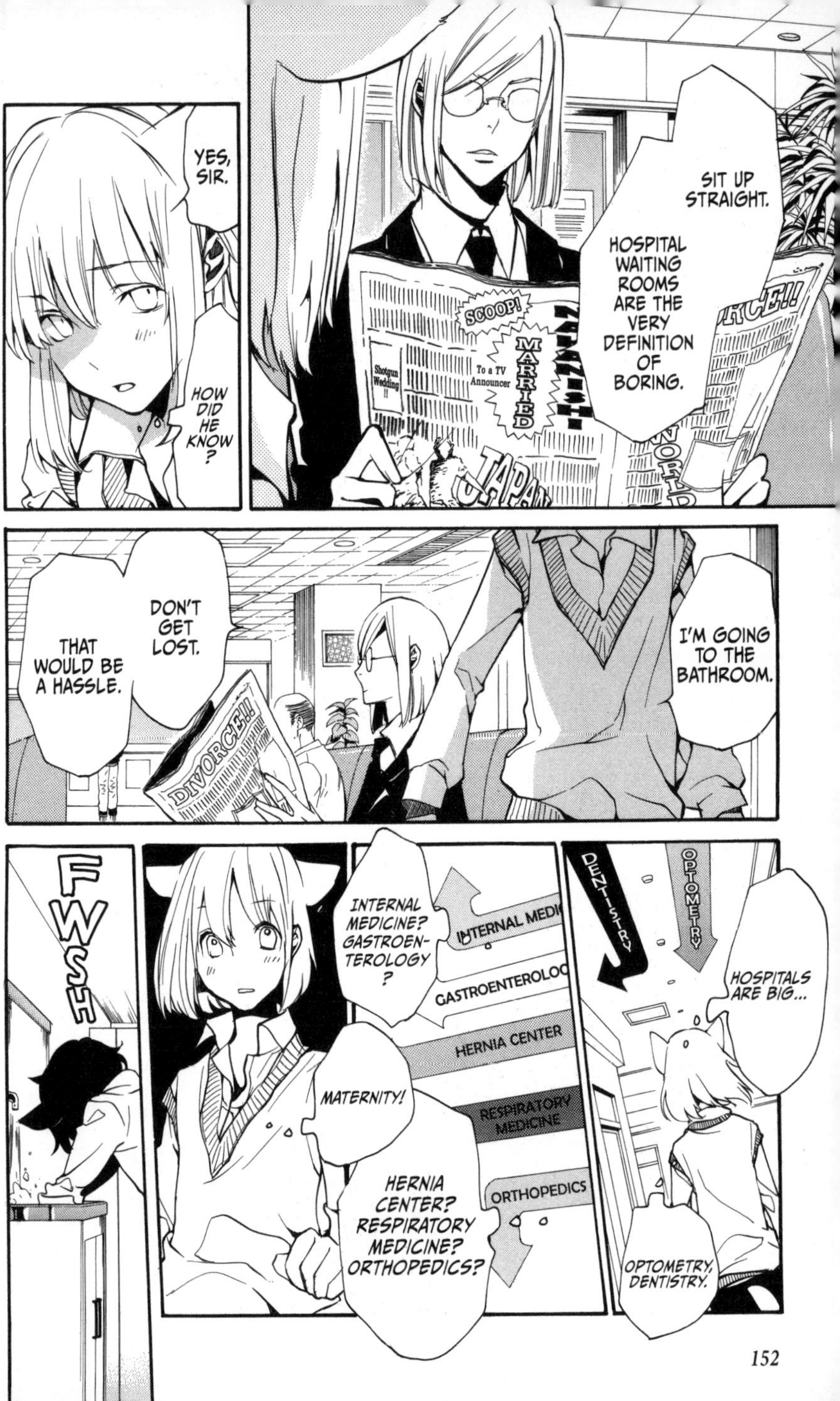
SIT UP STRAIGHT.
HOSPITAL WAITING ROOMS ARE THE VERY DEFINITION OF BORING.
SCOOP!
MARRIED
To a TV Announcer
Shotgun Wedding !!
YES, SIR.
HOW DID HE KNOW?
I'M GOING TO THE BATHROOM.
DON'T GET LOST.
THAT WOULD BE A HASSLE.
DIVORCE!!
DENTISTRY
OPTOMETRY
HOSPITALS ARE BIG...
OPTOMETRY, DENTISTRY.
INTERNAL MEDICINE? GASTROENTEROLOGY?
HERNIA CENTER
RESPIRATORY MEDICINE
ORTHOPEDICS
MATERNITY!
HERNIA CENTER? RESPIRATORY MEDICINE? ORTHOPEDICS?
FWSH

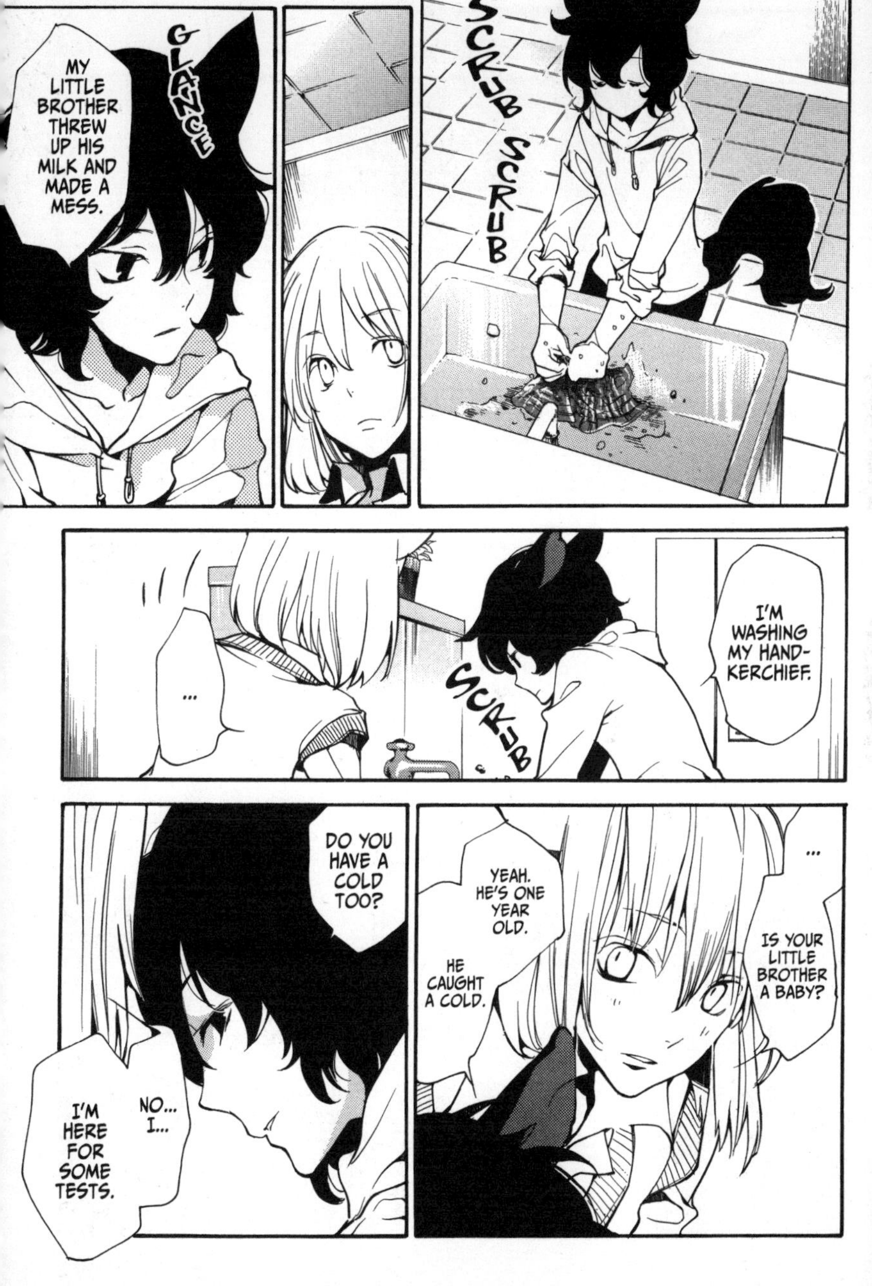
SCRUB SCRUB SCRUB
GLANCE
MY LITTLE BROTHER THREW UP HIS MILK AND MADE A MESS.
I'M WASHING MY HAND-KERCHIEF.
SCRUB
...
...
IS YOUR LITTLE BROTHER A BABY?
YEAH. HE'S ONE YEAR OLD.
HE CAUGHT A COLD.
DO YOU HAVE A COLD TOO?
NO... I...
I'M HERE FOR SOME TESTS.

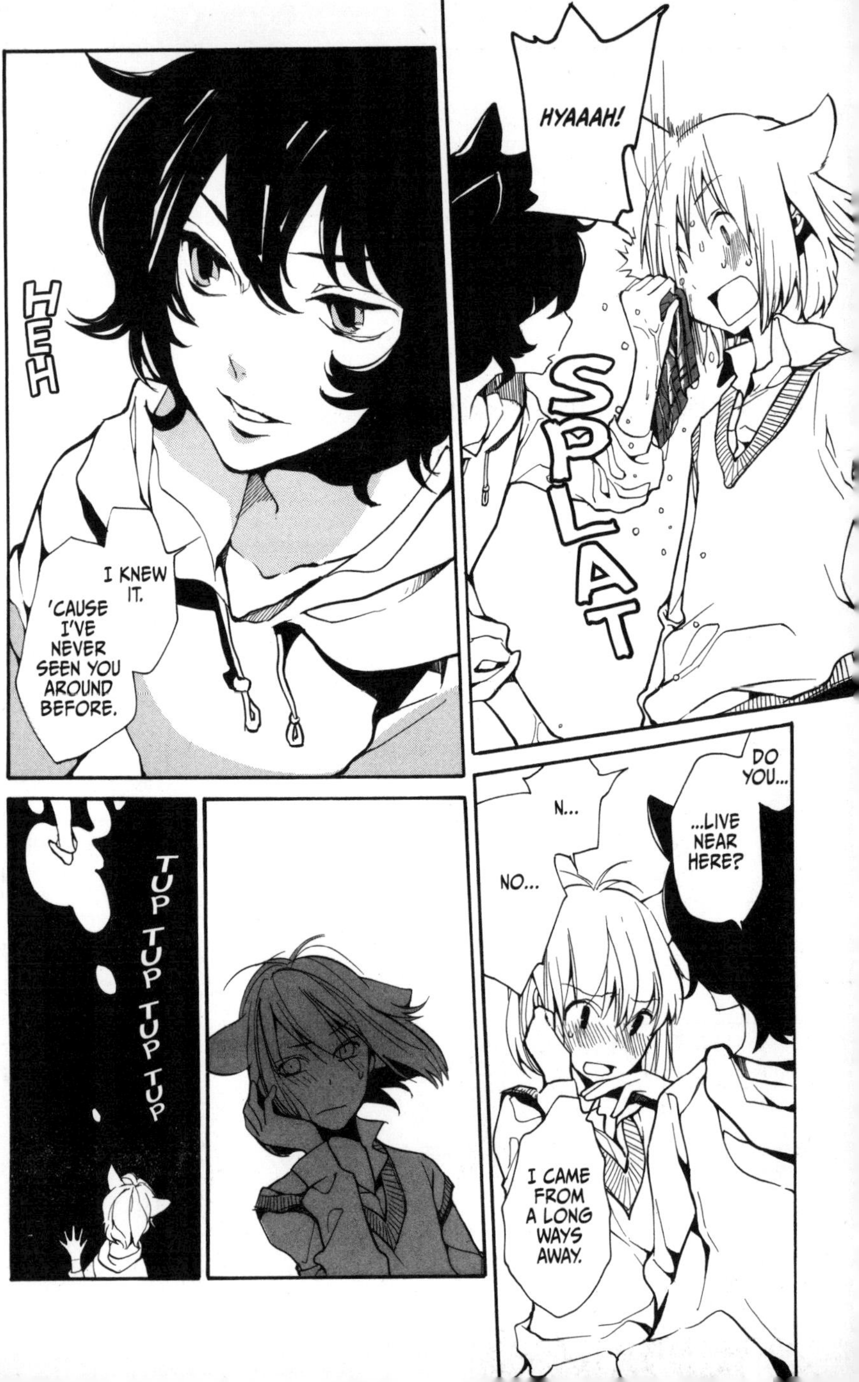
HYAAAH!
SPLAT
HEH
I KNEW IT.
'CAUSE I'VE NEVER SEEN YOU AROUND BEFORE.
DO YOU...
...LIVE NEAR HERE?
N...
NO...
I CAME FROM A LONG WAYS AWAY.
TUP TUP TUP TUP

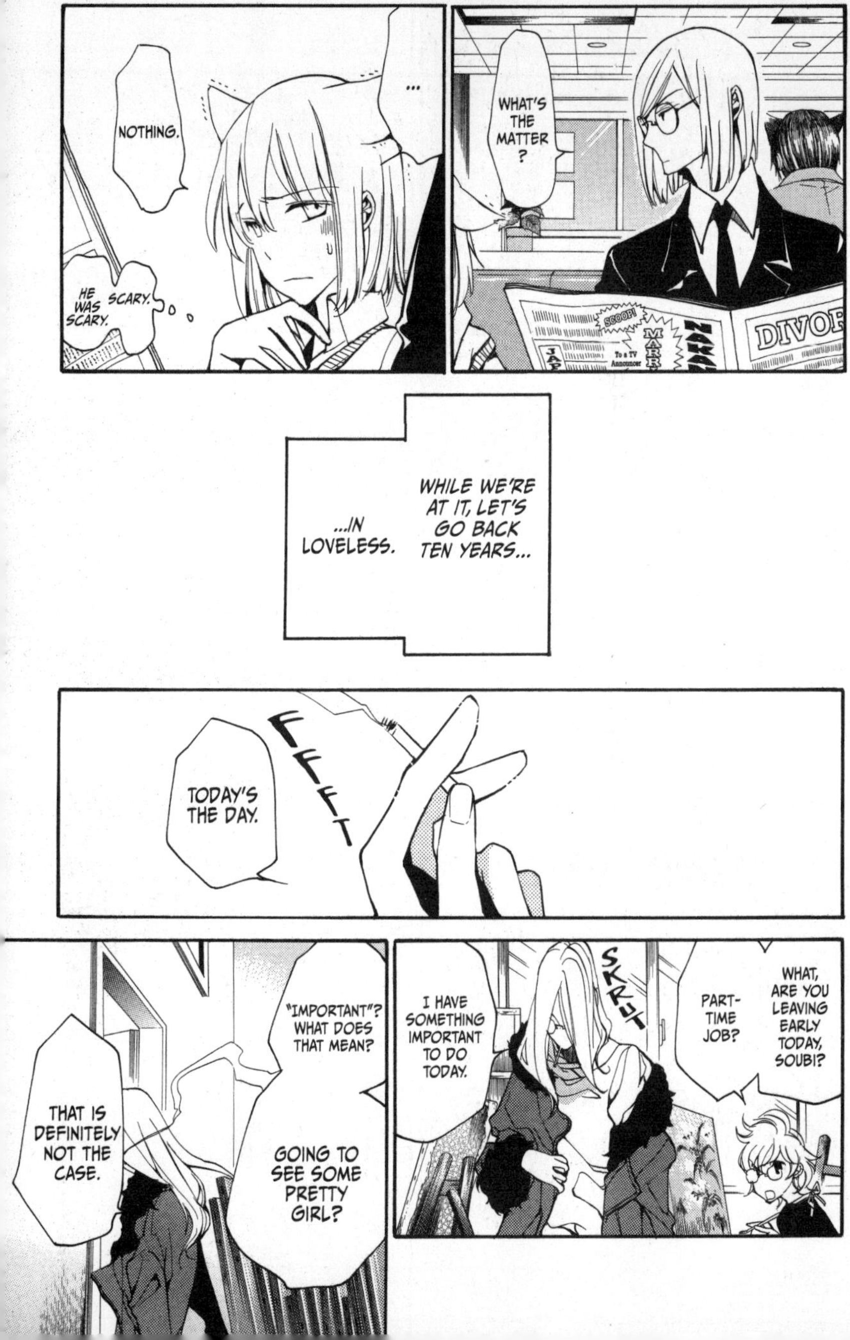
WHAT'S THE MATTER ?
SCOOP!
To a TV Announcer
...
NOTHING.
SCARY.
HE WAS SCARY.
WHILE WE'RE AT IT, LET'S GO BACK TEN YEARS...
...IN LOVELESS.
FFFT
TODAY'S THE DAY.
WHAT, ARE YOU LEAVING EARLY TODAY, SOUBI?
PART-TIME JOB?
SKRUT
I HAVE SOMETHING IMPORTANT TO DO TODAY.
"IMPORTANT"? WHAT DOES THAT MEAN?
GOING TO SEE SOME PRETTY GIRL?
THAT IS DEFINITELY NOT THE CASE.

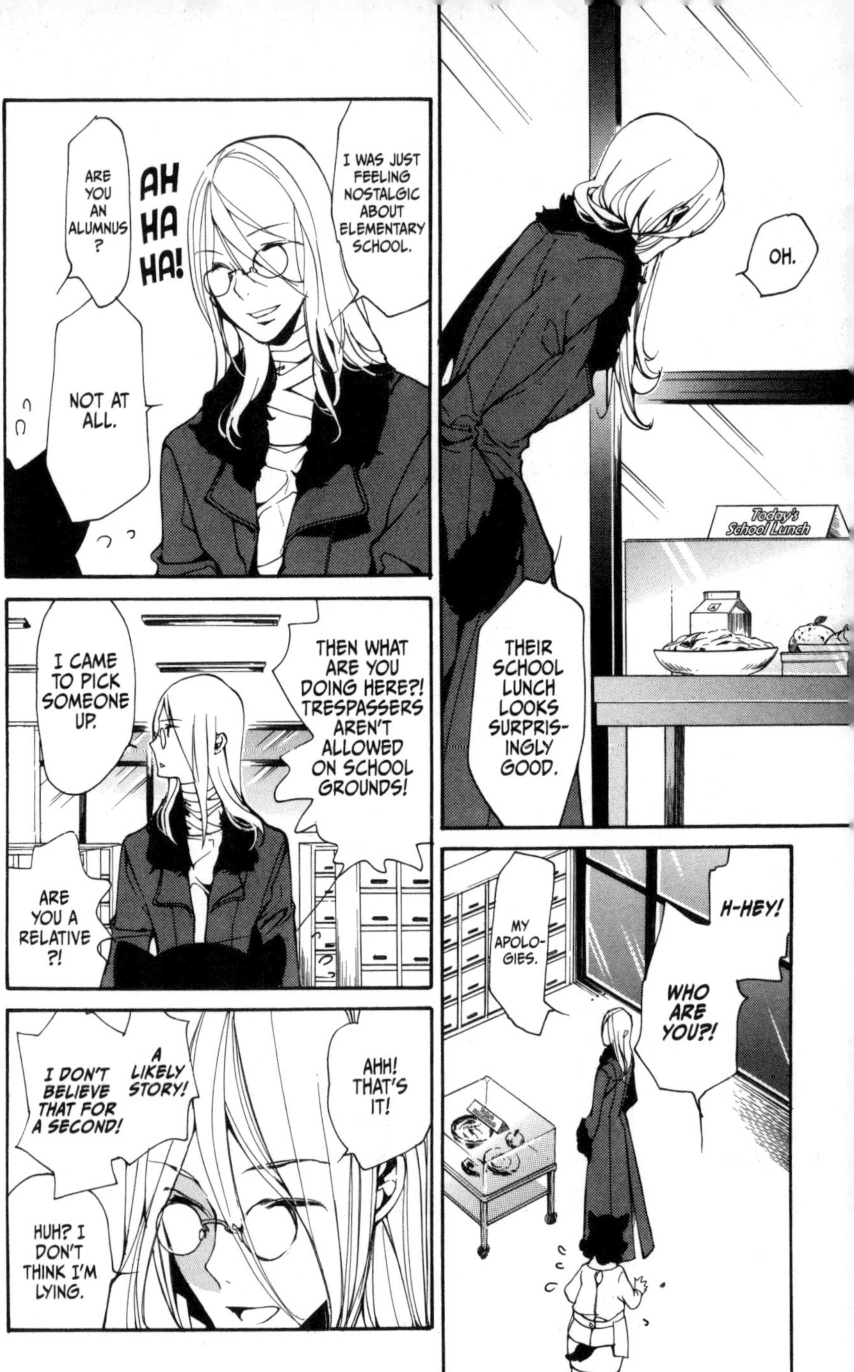
OH.
Today's School Lunch
THEIR SCHOOL LUNCH LOOKS SURPRISINGLY GOOD.
H-HEY!
WHO ARE YOU?!
MY APOLOGIES.
I WAS JUST FEELING NOSTALGIC ABOUT ELEMENTARY SCHOOL.
AH HA HA!
ARE YOU AN ALUMNUS?
NOT AT ALL.
THEN WHAT ARE YOU DOING HERE?! TRESPASSERS AREN'T ALLOWED ON SCHOOL GROUNDS!
I CAME TO PICK SOMEONE UP.
ARE YOU A RELATIVE?!
AHH! THAT'S IT!
A LIKELY STORY!
I DON'T BELIEVE THAT FOR A SECOND!
HUH? I DON'T THINK I'M LYING.

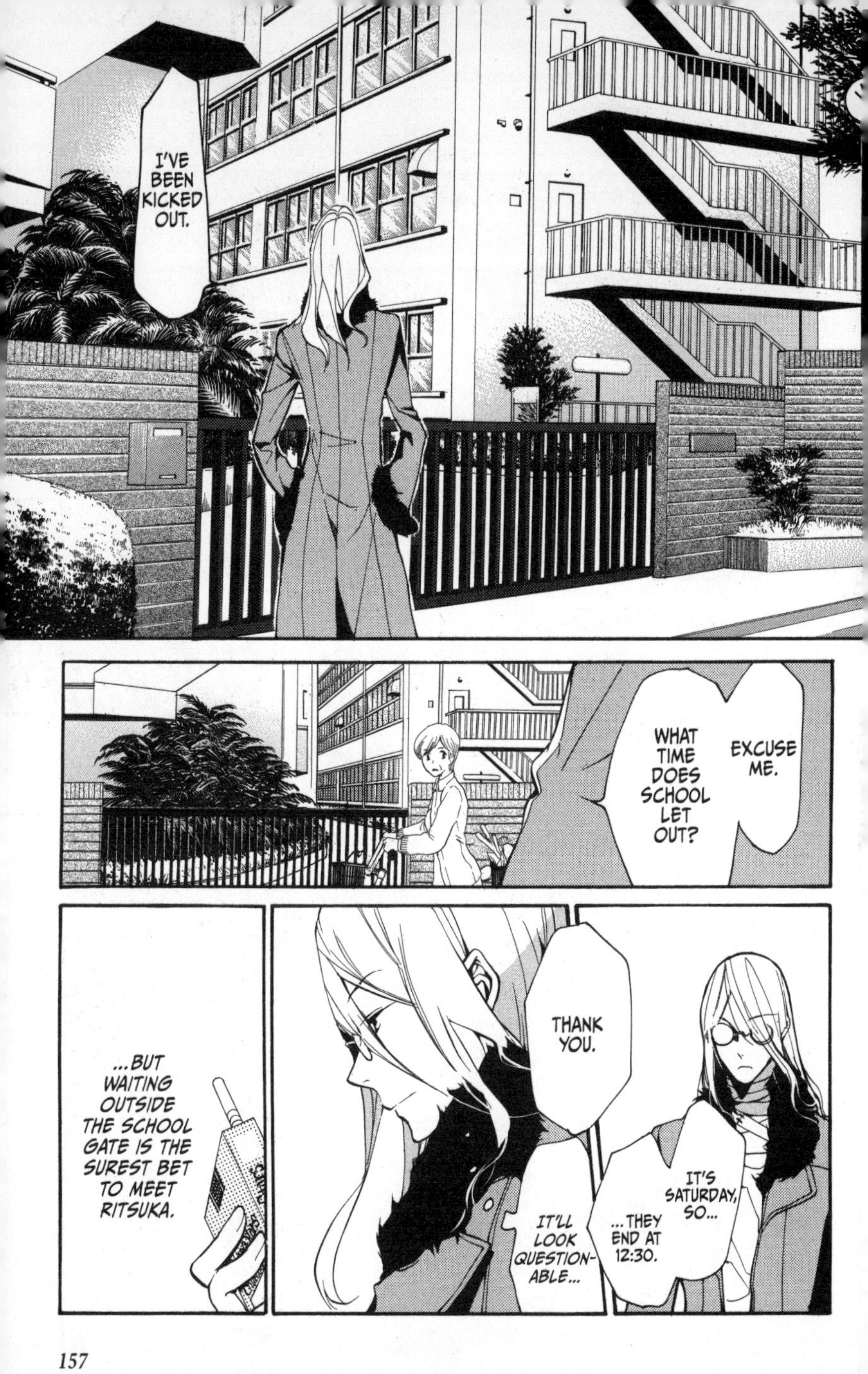
I'VE BEEN KICKED OUT.
EXCUSE ME.
WHAT TIME DOES SCHOOL LET OUT?
IT'S SATURDAY, SO...
...THEY END AT 12:30.
THANK YOU.
IT'LL LOOK QUESTIONABLE...
...BUT WAITING OUTSIDE THE SCHOOL GATE IS THE SUREST BET TO MEET RITSUKA.

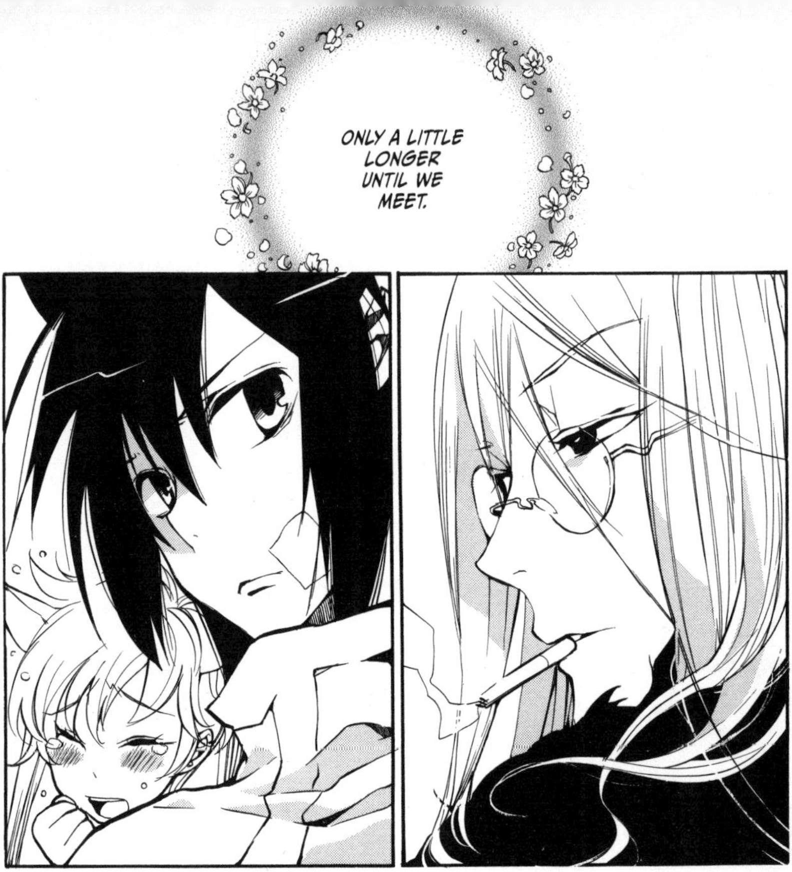
ONLY A LITTLE LONGER UNTIL WE MEET.

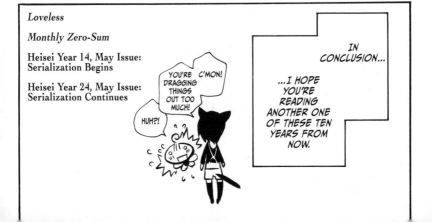

*Loveless*

*Monthly Zero-Sum*

Heisei Year 14, May Issue:
Serialization Begins

Heisei Year 24, May Issue:
Serialization Continues

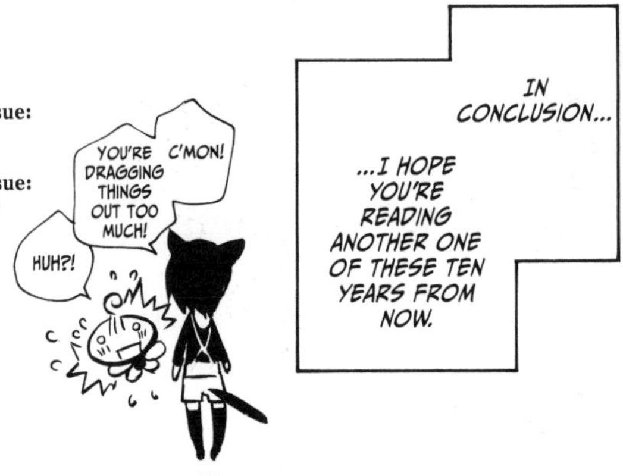
IN CONCLUSION...
...I HOPE YOU'RE READING ANOTHER ONE OF THESE TEN YEARS FROM NOW.
C'MON!
YOU'RE DRAGGING THINGS OUT TOO MUCH!
HUH?!

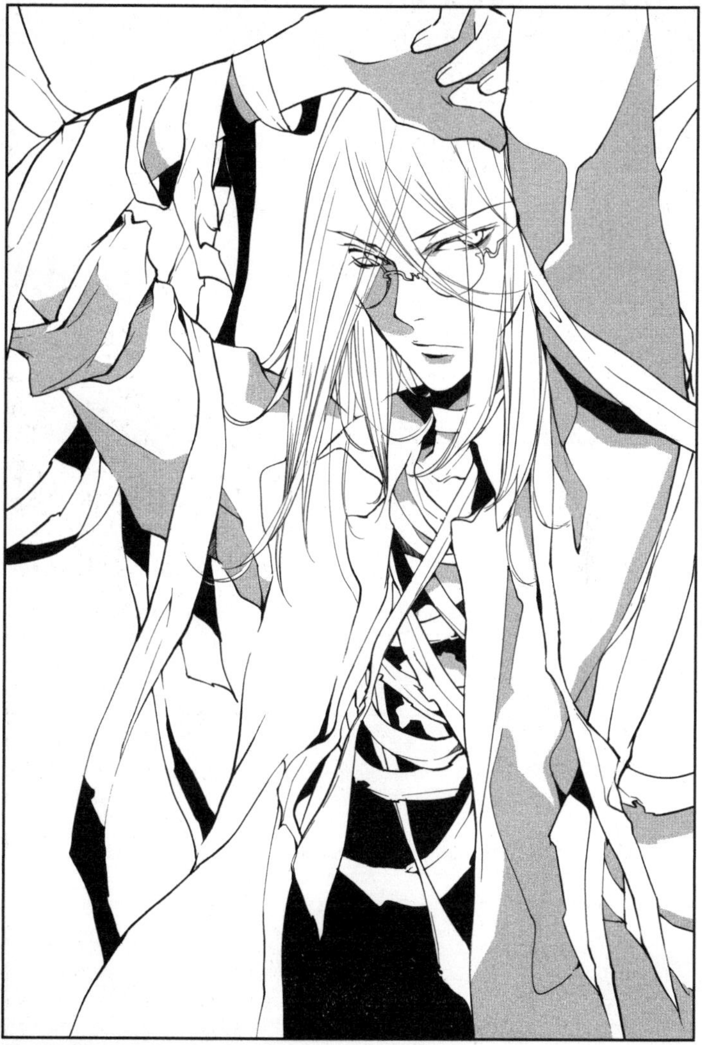

LOVELESS

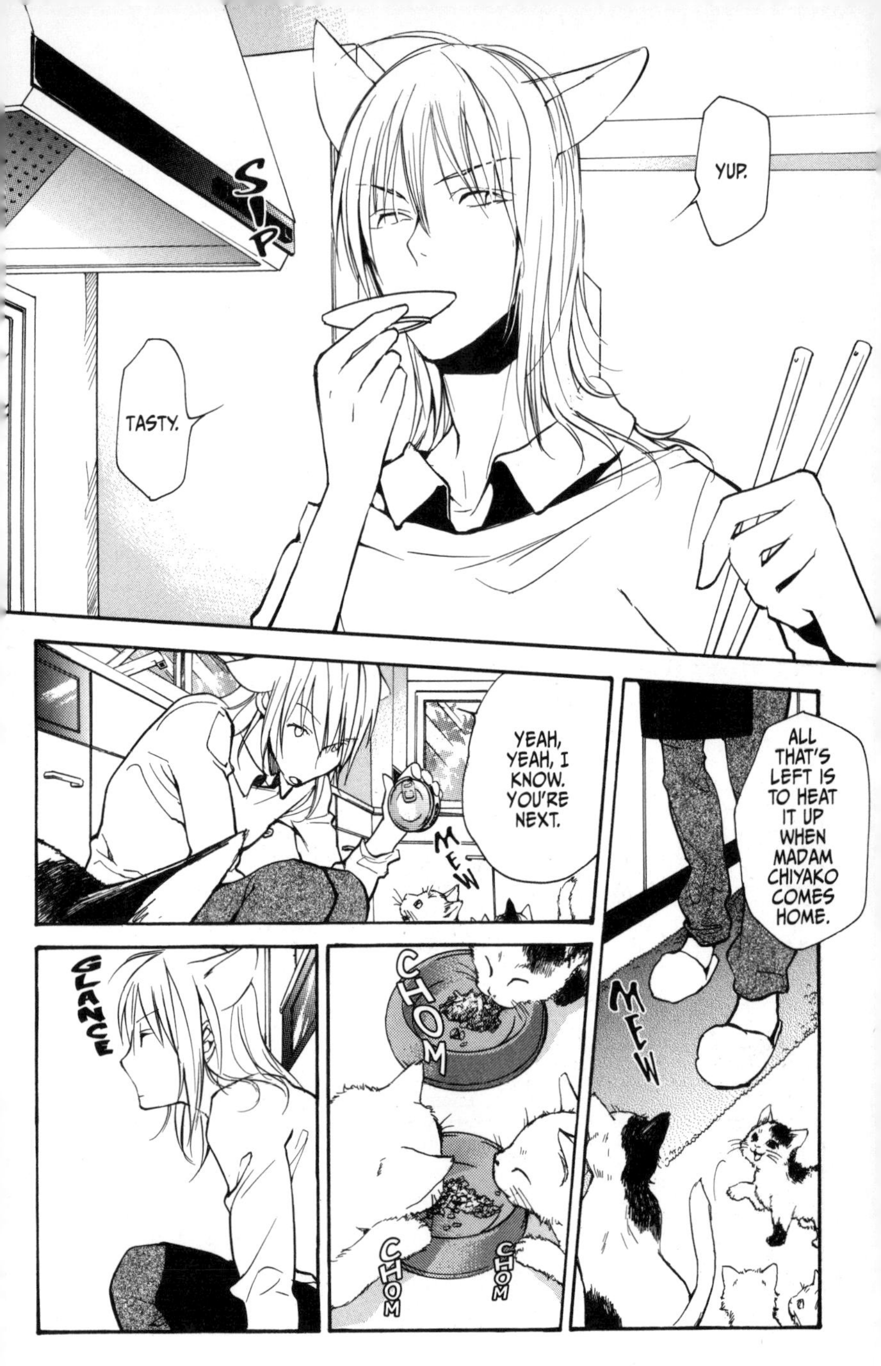
YUP.
SIP
TASTY.
ALL THAT'S LEFT IS TO HEAT IT UP WHEN MADAM CHIYAKO COMES HOME.
MEW
YEAH, YEAH, I KNOW. YOU'RE NEXT.
MEW
CHOM
CHOM
CHOM
GLANCE

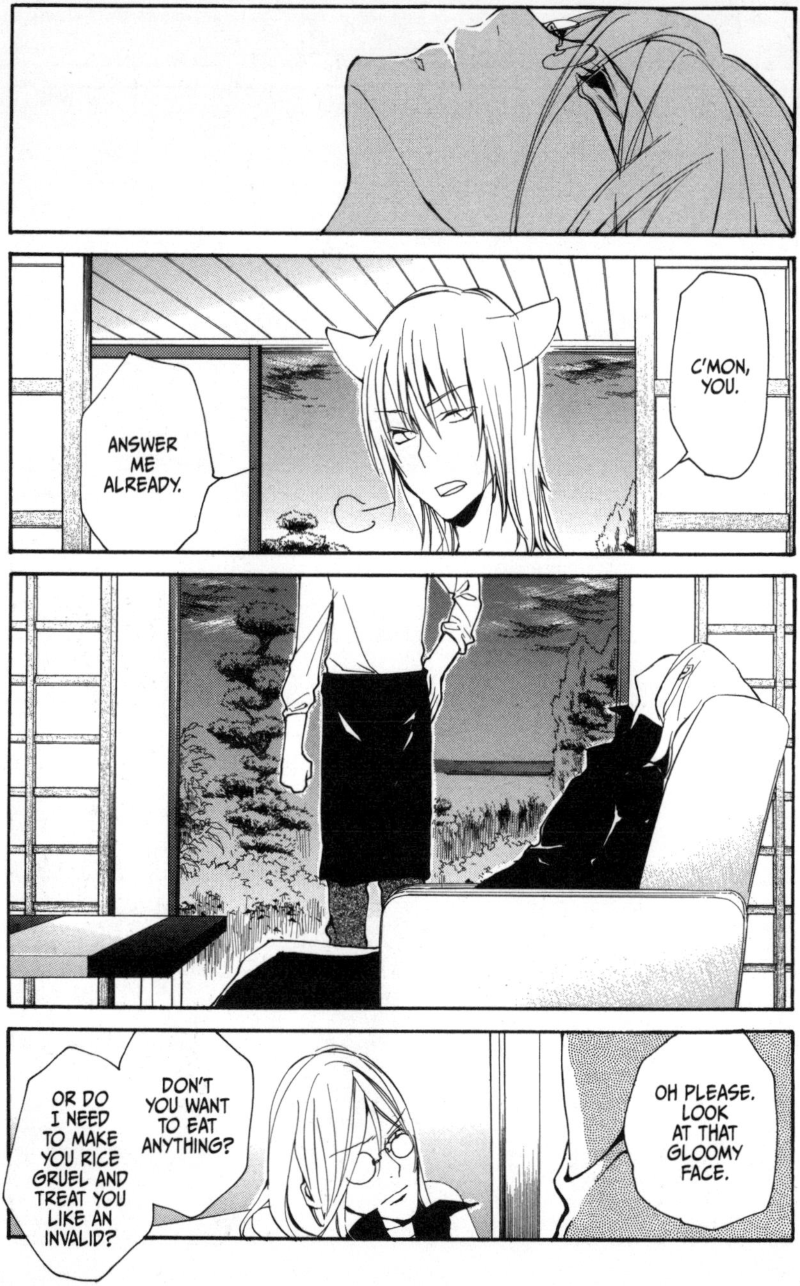
C'MON, YOU.
ANSWER ME ALREADY.
OH PLEASE. LOOK AT THAT GLOOMY FACE.
DON'T YOU WANT TO EAT ANYTHING?
OR DO I NEED TO MAKE YOU RICE GRUEL AND TREAT YOU LIKE AN INVALID?

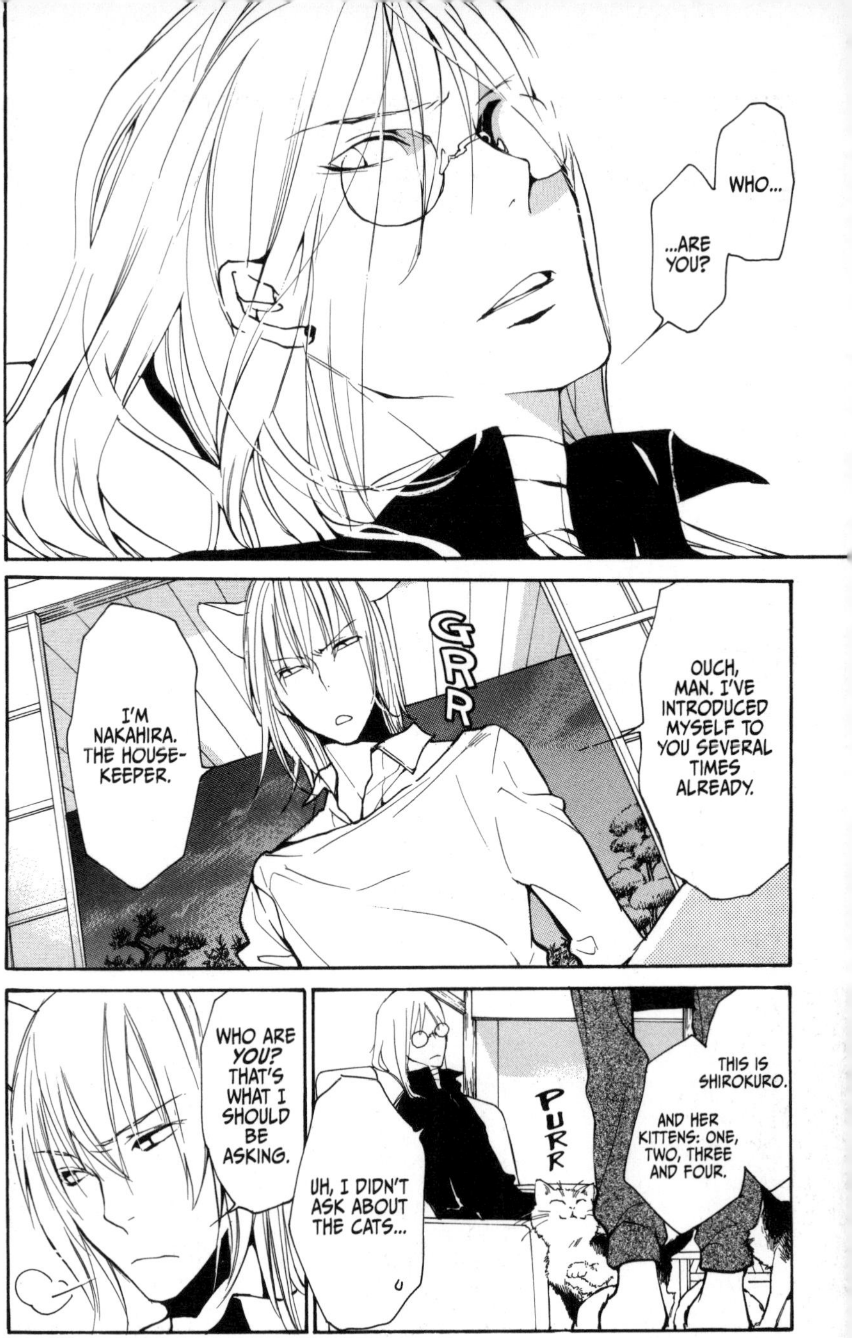
WHO...
...ARE YOU?
OUCH, MAN. I'VE INTRODUCED MYSELF TO YOU SEVERAL TIMES ALREADY.
GRR
I'M NAKAHIRA. THE HOUSE-KEEPER.
THIS IS SHIROKURO.
AND HER KITTENS: ONE, TWO, THREE AND FOUR.
PURR
UH, I DIDN'T ASK ABOUT THE CATS...
WHO ARE *YOU?* THAT'S WHAT I SHOULD BE ASKING.

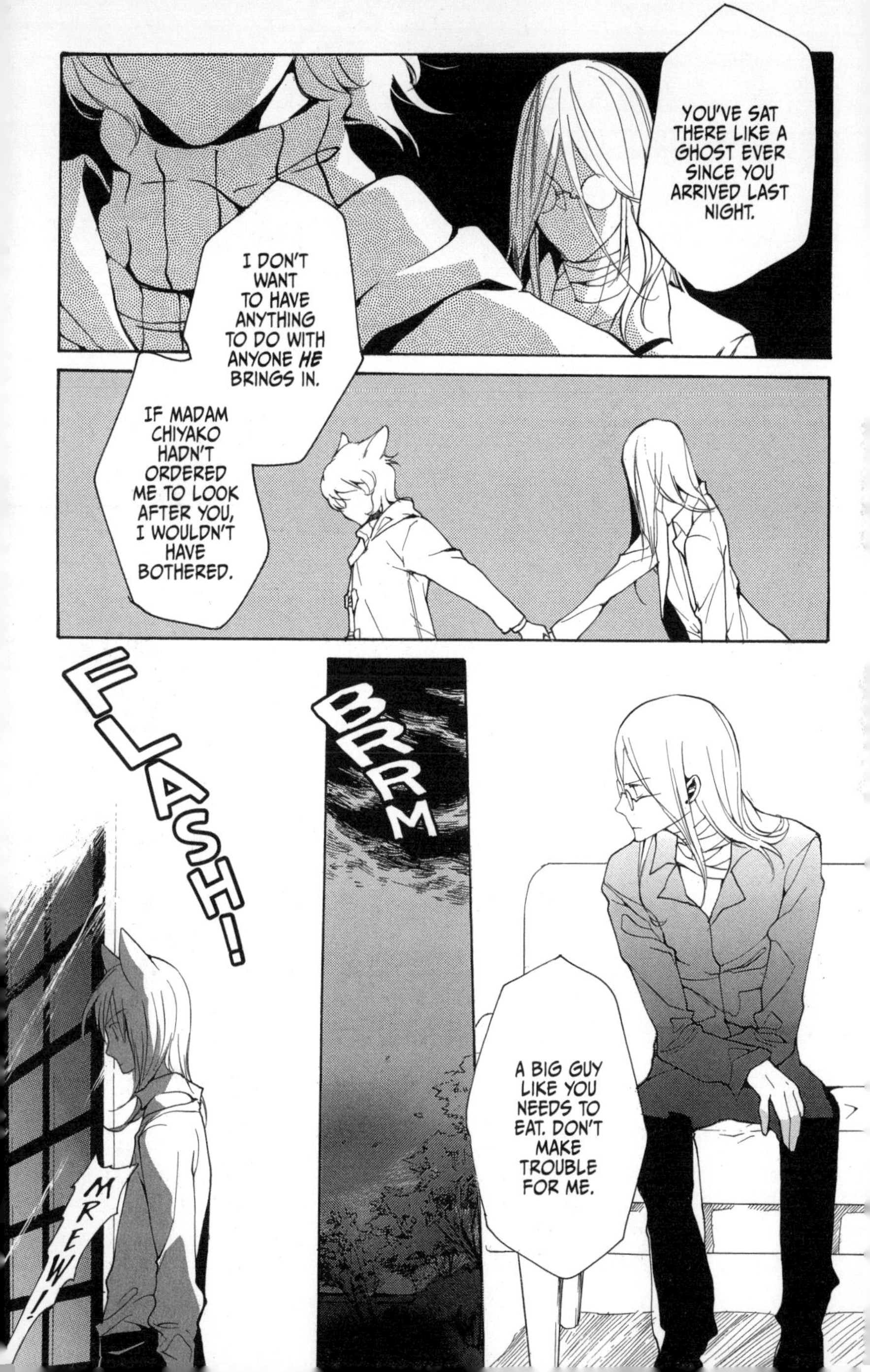
YOU'VE SAT THERE LIKE A GHOST EVER SINCE YOU ARRIVED LAST NIGHT.
I DON'T WANT TO HAVE ANYTHING TO DO WITH ANYONE *HE* BRINGS IN.
IF MADAM CHIYAKO HADN'T ORDERED ME TO LOOK AFTER YOU, I WOULDN'T HAVE BOTHERED.
A BIG GUY LIKE YOU NEEDS TO EAT. DON'T MAKE TROUBLE FOR ME.
BRRRM
FLASH!
MREW!

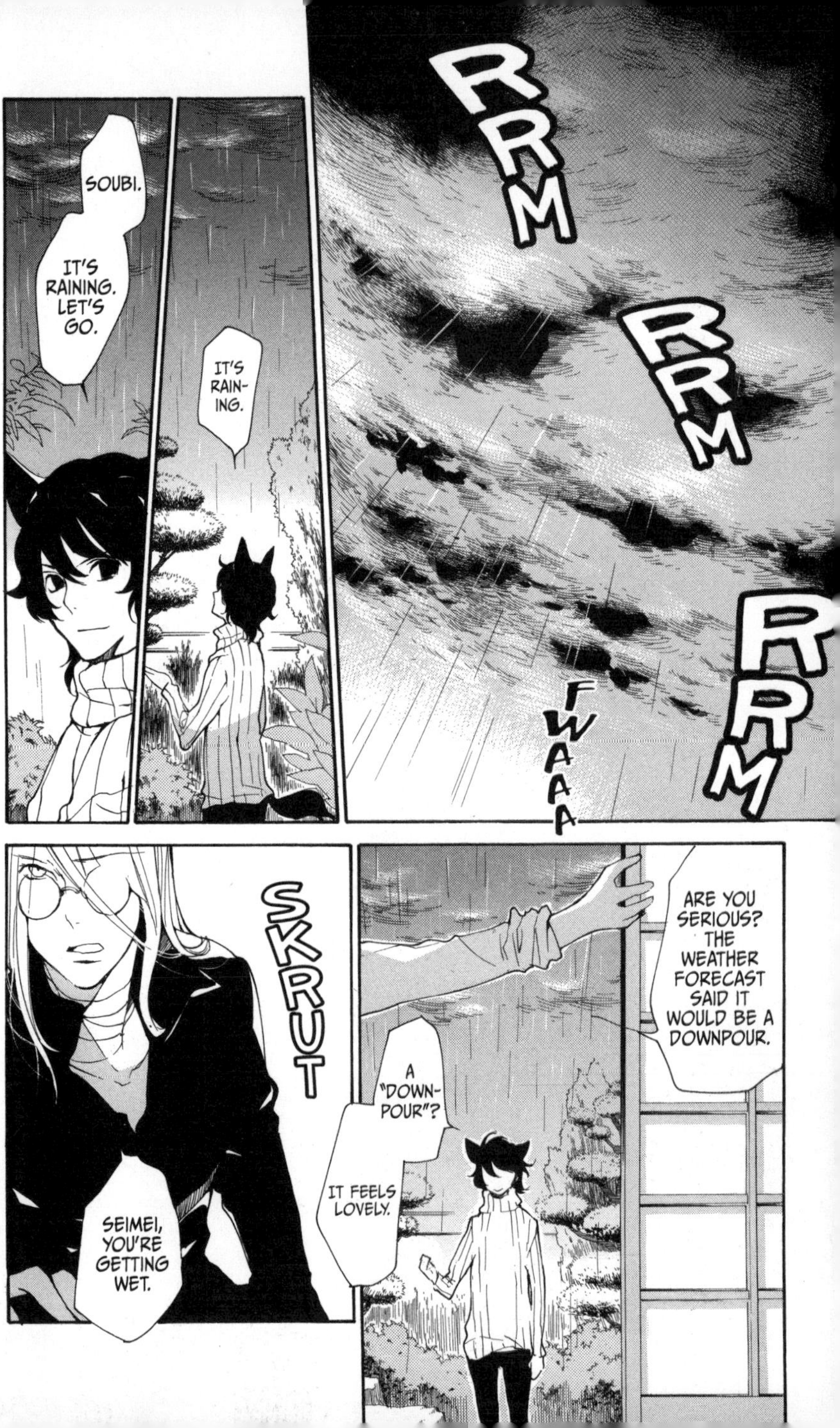
RRM
RRM
RRM
FWAAA
IT'S RAINING.
SOUBI.
IT'S RAINING. LET'S GO.
ARE YOU SERIOUS? THE WEATHER FORECAST SAID IT WOULD BE A DOWNPOUR.
A "DOWNPOUR"?
IT FEELS LOVELY.
SKRUT
SEIMEI, YOU'RE GETTING WET.

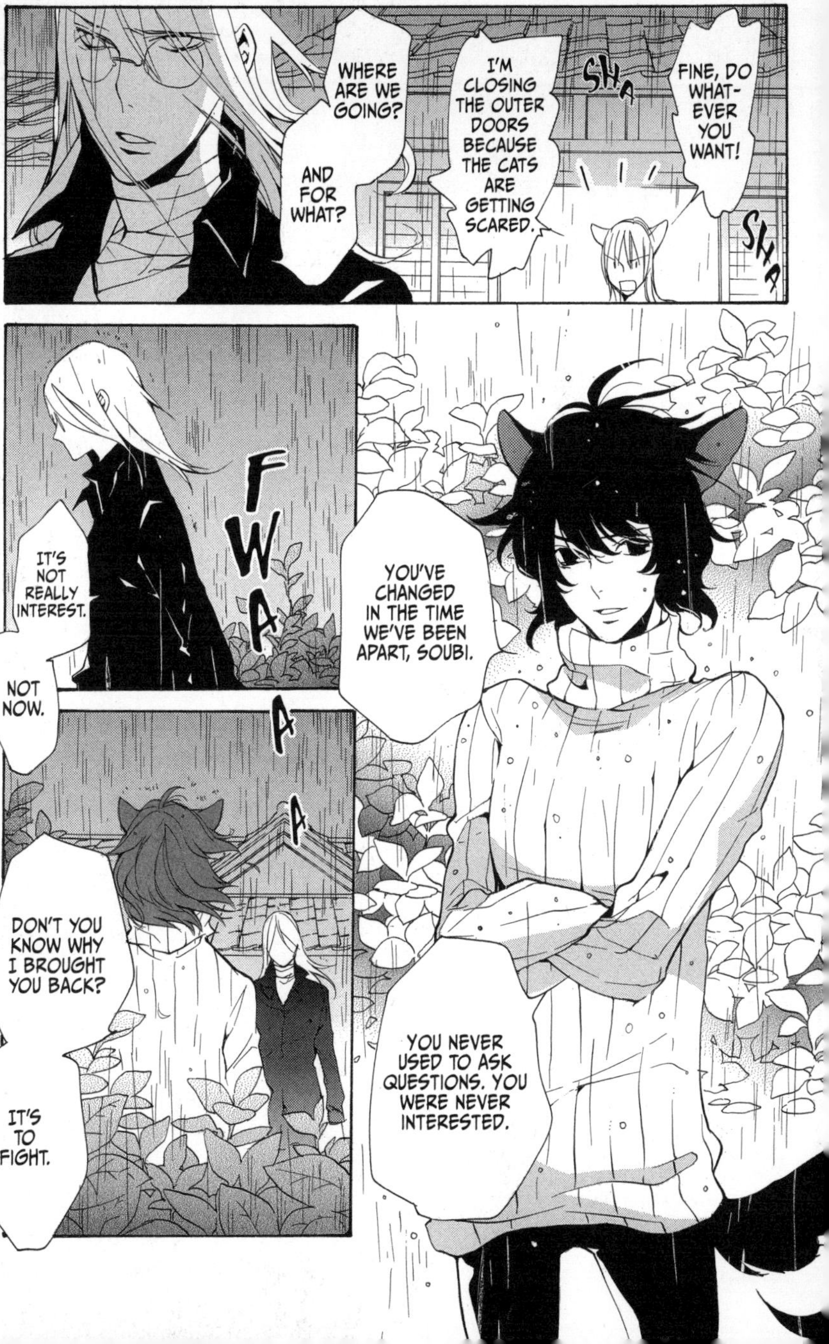
FINE, DO WHAT-EVER YOU WANT!
SHA
SHA
I'M CLOSING THE OUTER DOORS BECAUSE THE CATS ARE GETTING SCARED.
WHERE ARE WE GOING?
AND FOR WHAT?
YOU'VE CHANGED IN THE TIME WE'VE BEEN APART, SOUBI.
YOU NEVER USED TO ASK QUESTIONS. YOU WERE NEVER INTERESTED.
IT'S NOT REALLY INTEREST.
NOT NOW.
FWAAA
DON'T YOU KNOW WHY I BROUGHT YOU BACK?
IT'S TO FIGHT.

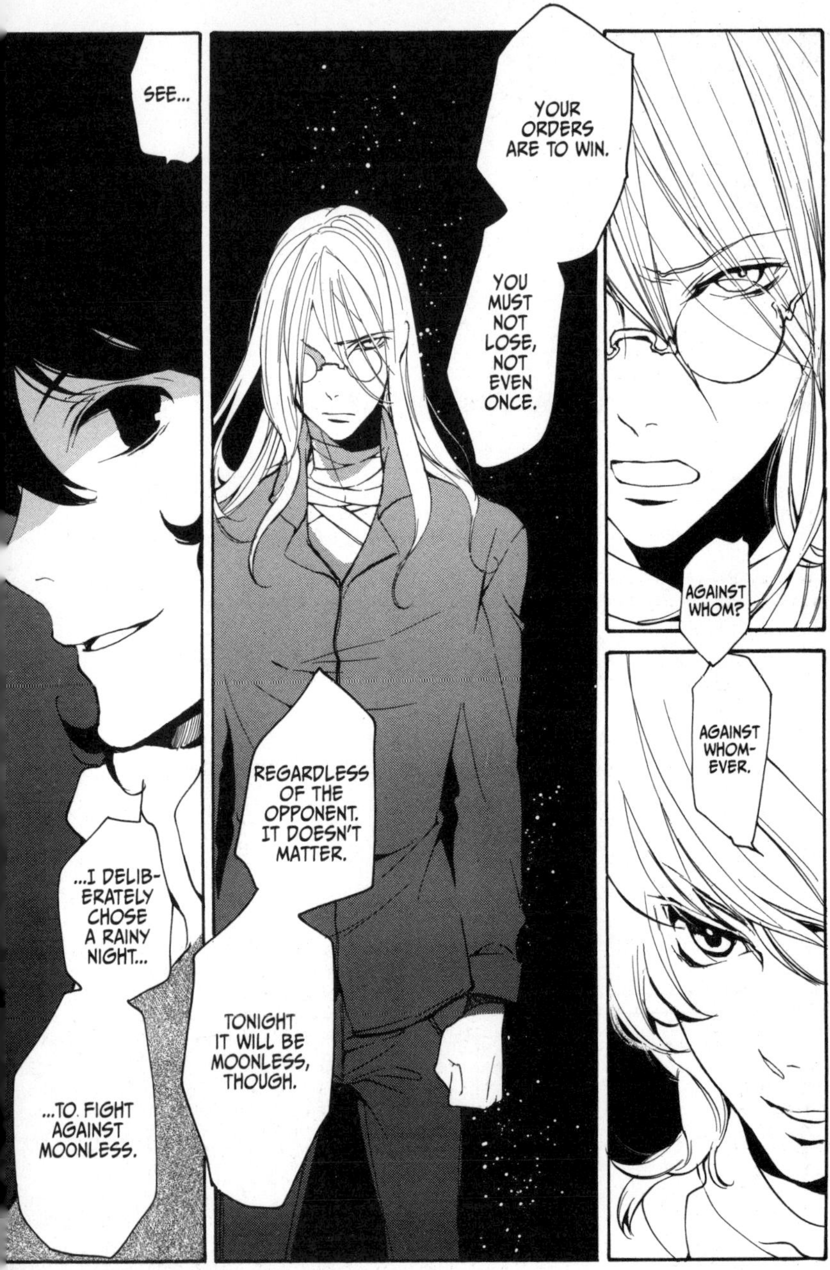
YOUR ORDERS ARE TO WIN.
YOU MUST NOT LOSE, NOT EVEN ONCE.
AGAINST WHOM?
AGAINST WHOM-EVER.
REGARDLESS OF THE OPPONENT. IT DOESN'T MATTER.
TONIGHT IT WILL BE MOONLESS, THOUGH.
SEE...
...I DELIB-ERATELY CHOSE A RAINY NIGHT...
...TO FIGHT AGAINST MOONLESS.

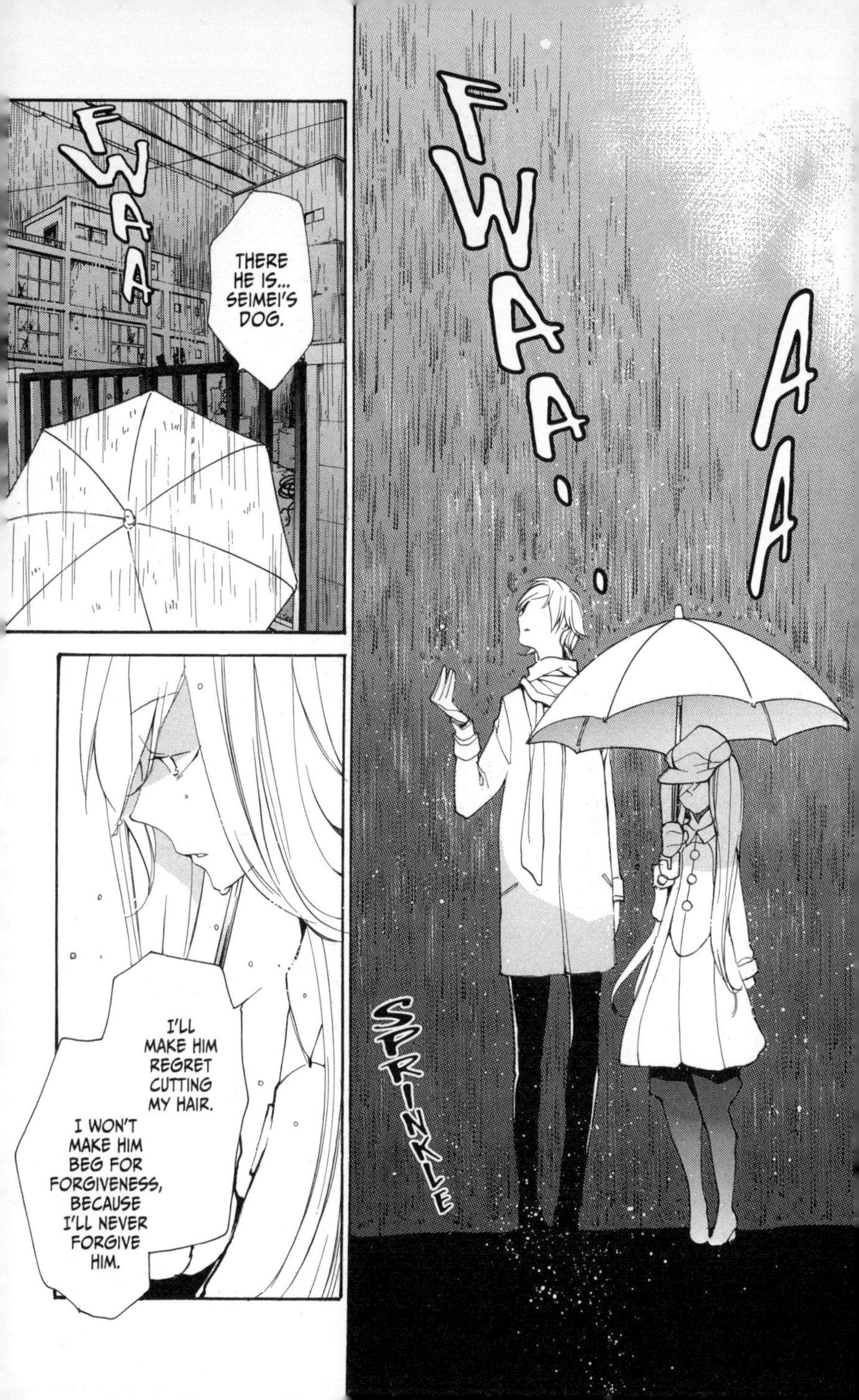
FWAA..
AA
SPRINKLE
FWAA
THERE HE IS... SEIMEI'S DOG.
I'LL MAKE HIM REGRET CUTTING MY HAIR.
I WON'T MAKE HIM BEG FOR FORGIVENESS, BECAUSE I'LL NEVER FORGIVE HIM.

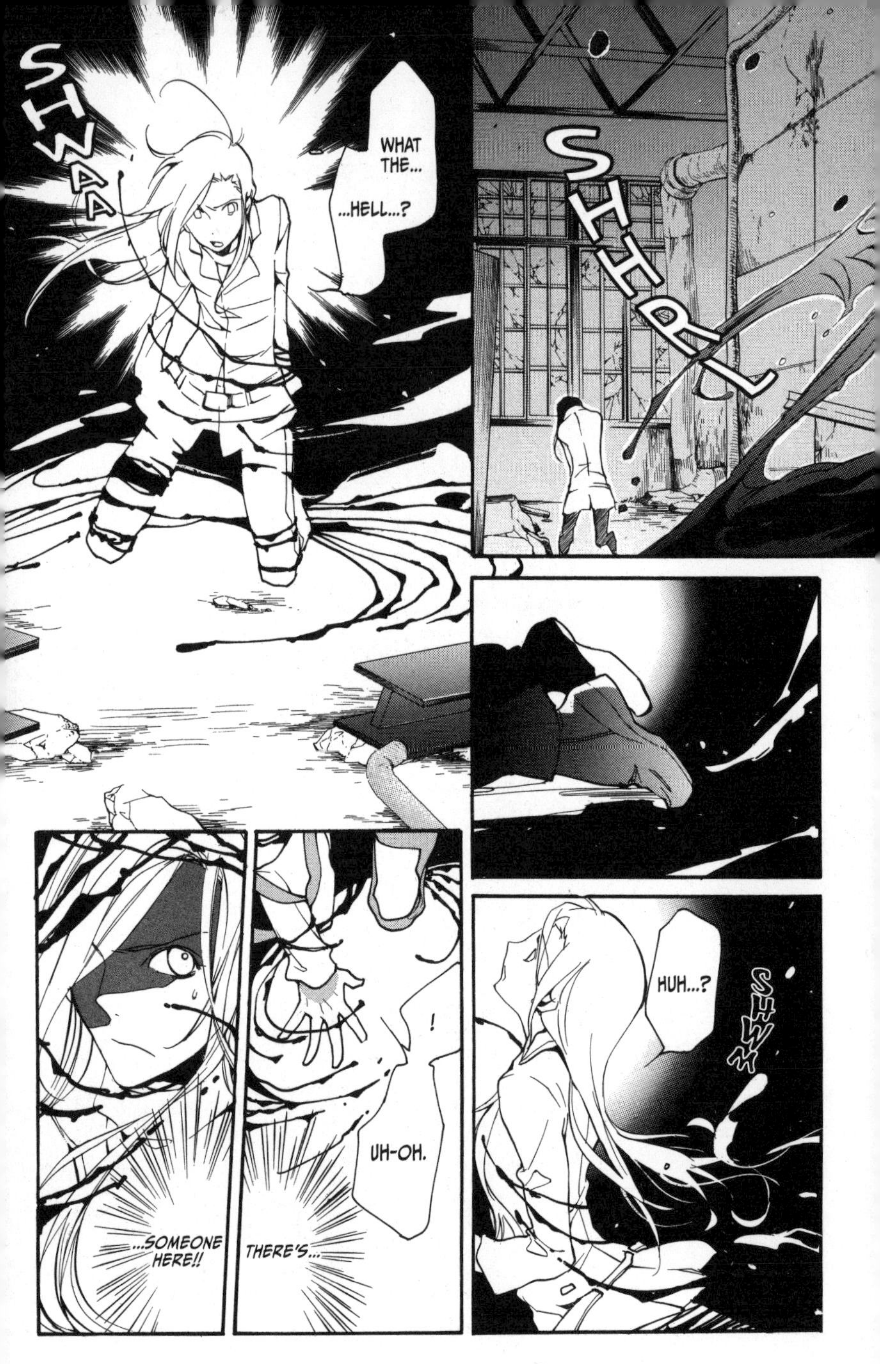
SHHRL
SHWAA
WHAT THE...
...HELL...?
HUH...?
SHWM
!
UH-OH.
THERE'S...
...SOMEONE HERE!!

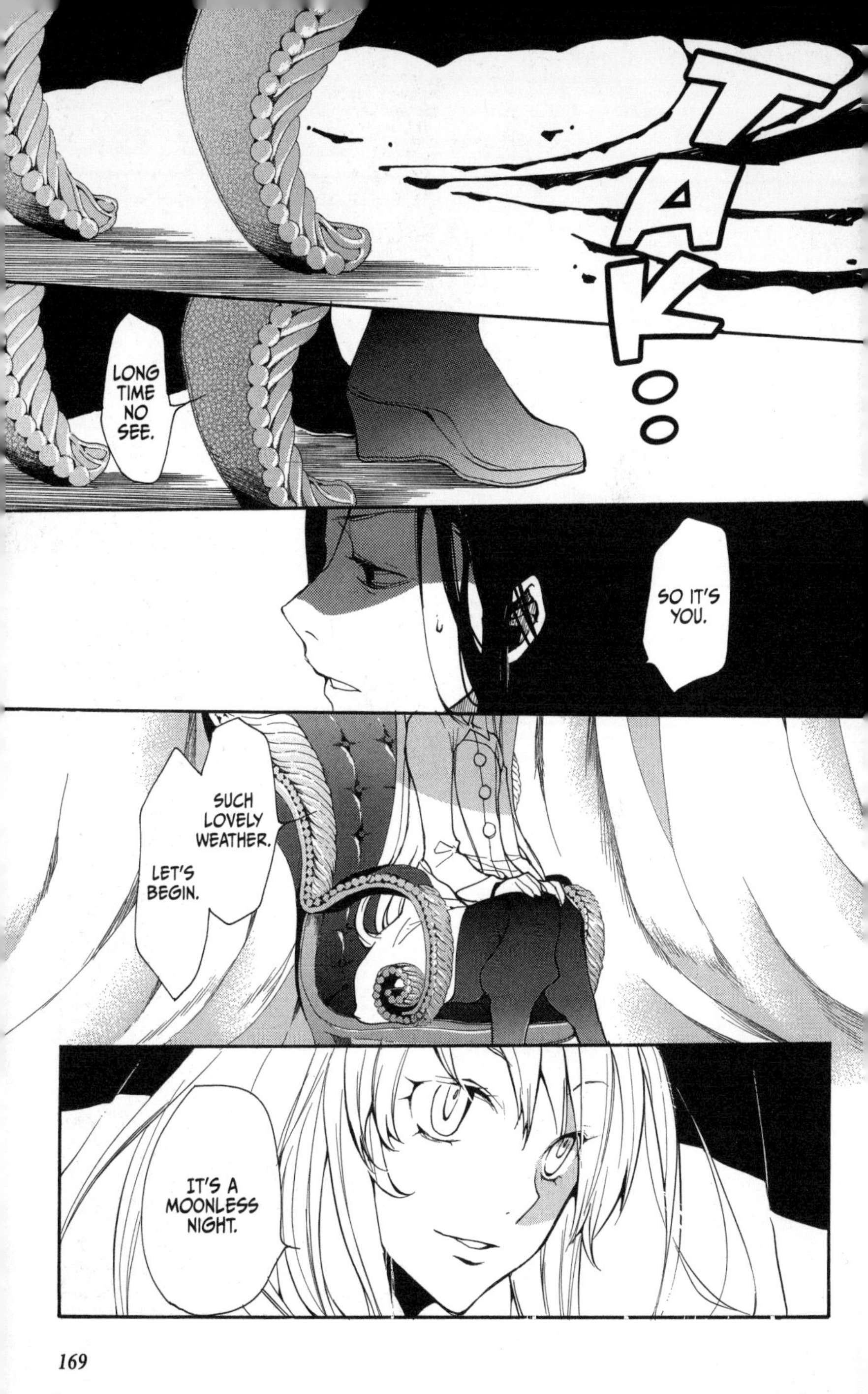
TAK
LONG TIME NO SEE.
SO IT'S YOU.
SUCH LOVELY WEATHER.
LET'S BEGIN.
IT'S A MOONLESS NIGHT.

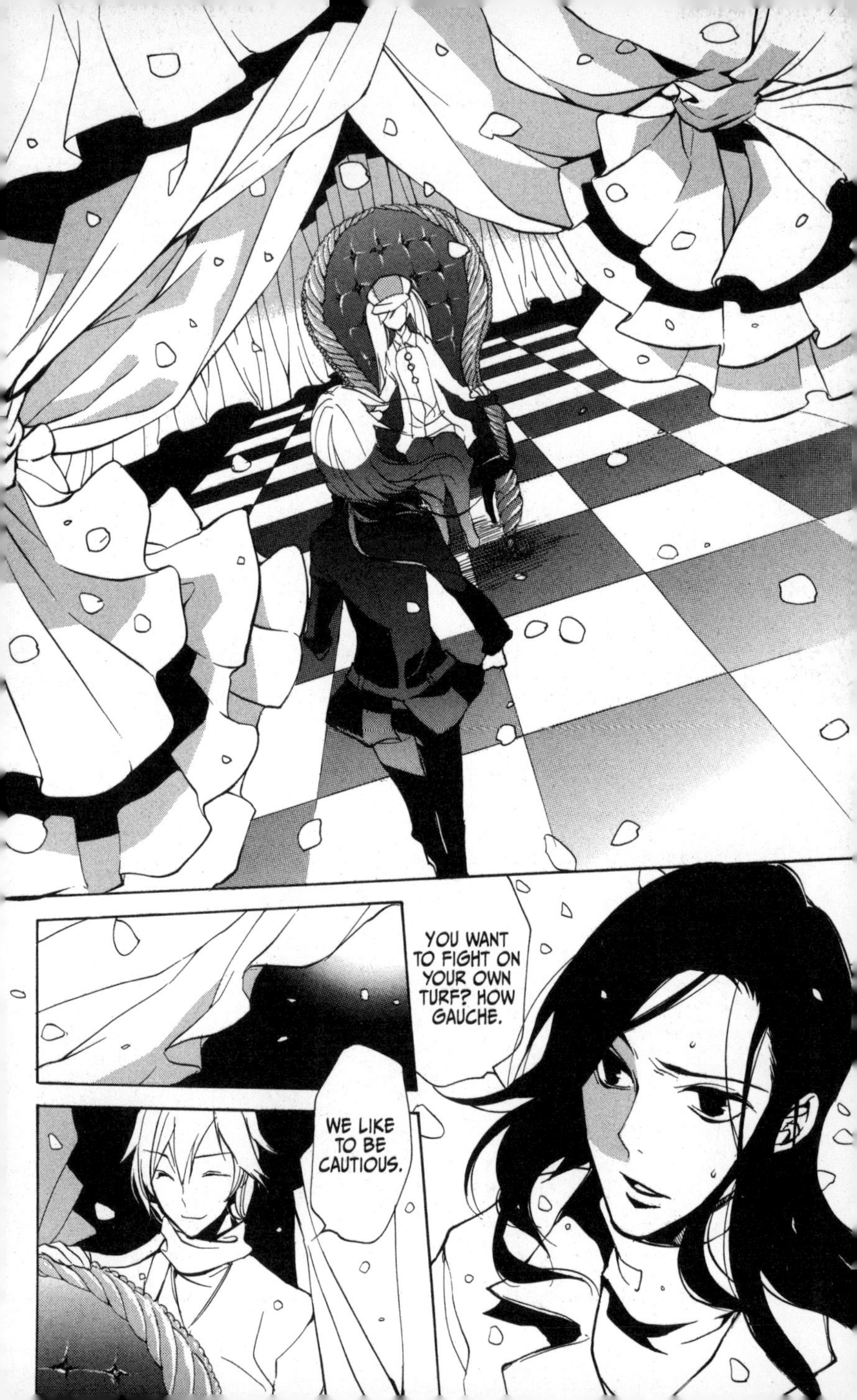
YOU WANT TO FIGHT ON YOUR OWN TURF? HOW GAUCHE.
WE LIKE TO BE CAUTIOUS.

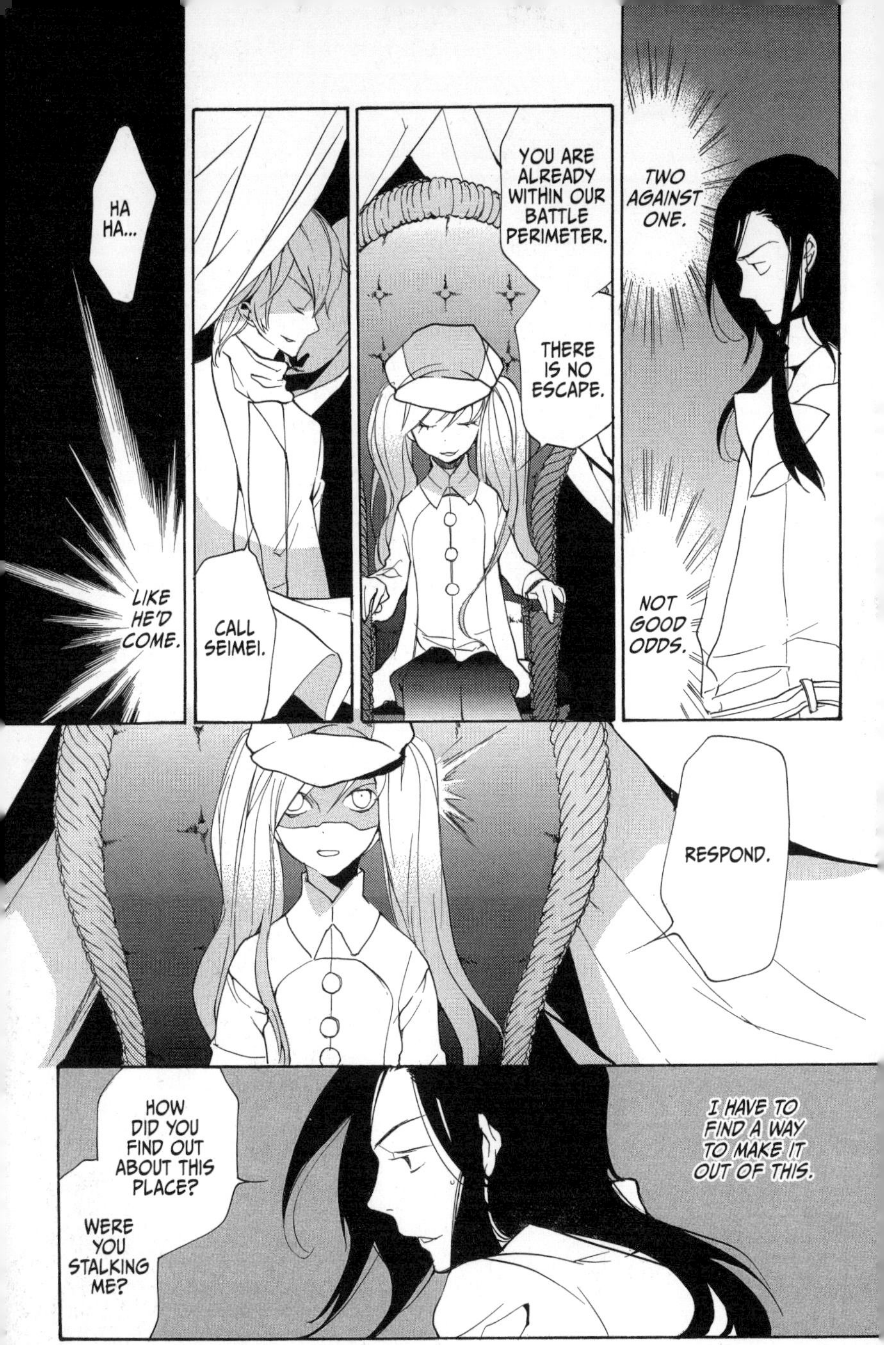
TWO AGAINST ONE.
NOT GOOD ODDS.
YOU ARE ALREADY WITHIN OUR BATTLE PERIMETER.
THERE IS NO ESCAPE.
CALL SEIMEI.
HA HA...
LIKE HE'D COME.
RESPOND.
I HAVE TO FIND A WAY TO MAKE IT OUT OF THIS.
HOW DID YOU FIND OUT ABOUT THIS PLACE?
WERE YOU STALKING ME?

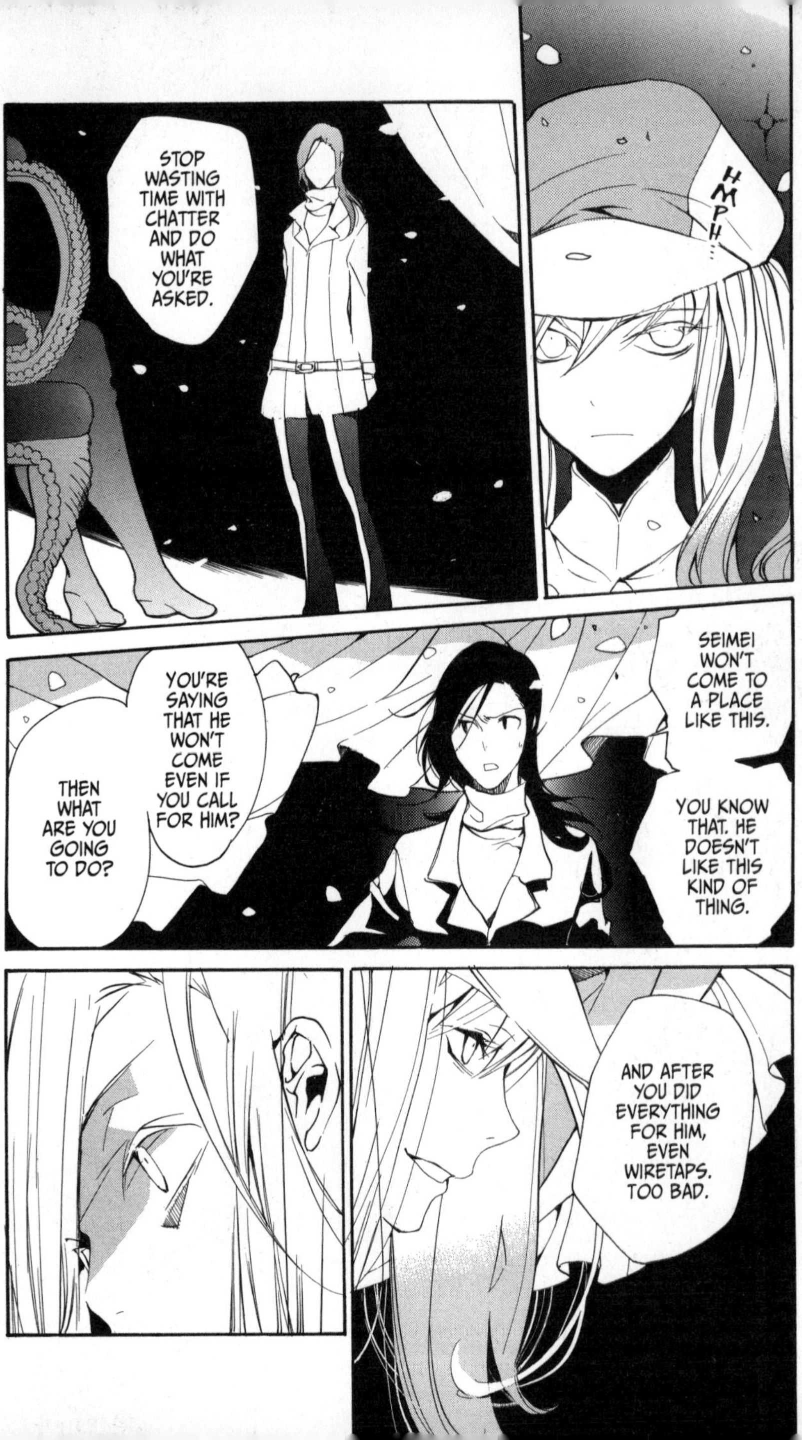
HMPH...
STOP WASTING TIME WITH CHATTER AND DO WHAT YOU'RE ASKED.
SEIMEI WON'T COME TO A PLACE LIKE THIS.
YOU KNOW THAT. HE DOESN'T LIKE THIS KIND OF THING.
YOU'RE SAYING THAT HE WON'T COME EVEN IF YOU CALL FOR HIM?
THEN WHAT ARE YOU GOING TO DO?
AND AFTER YOU DID EVERYTHING FOR HIM, EVEN WIRETAPS. TOO BAD.

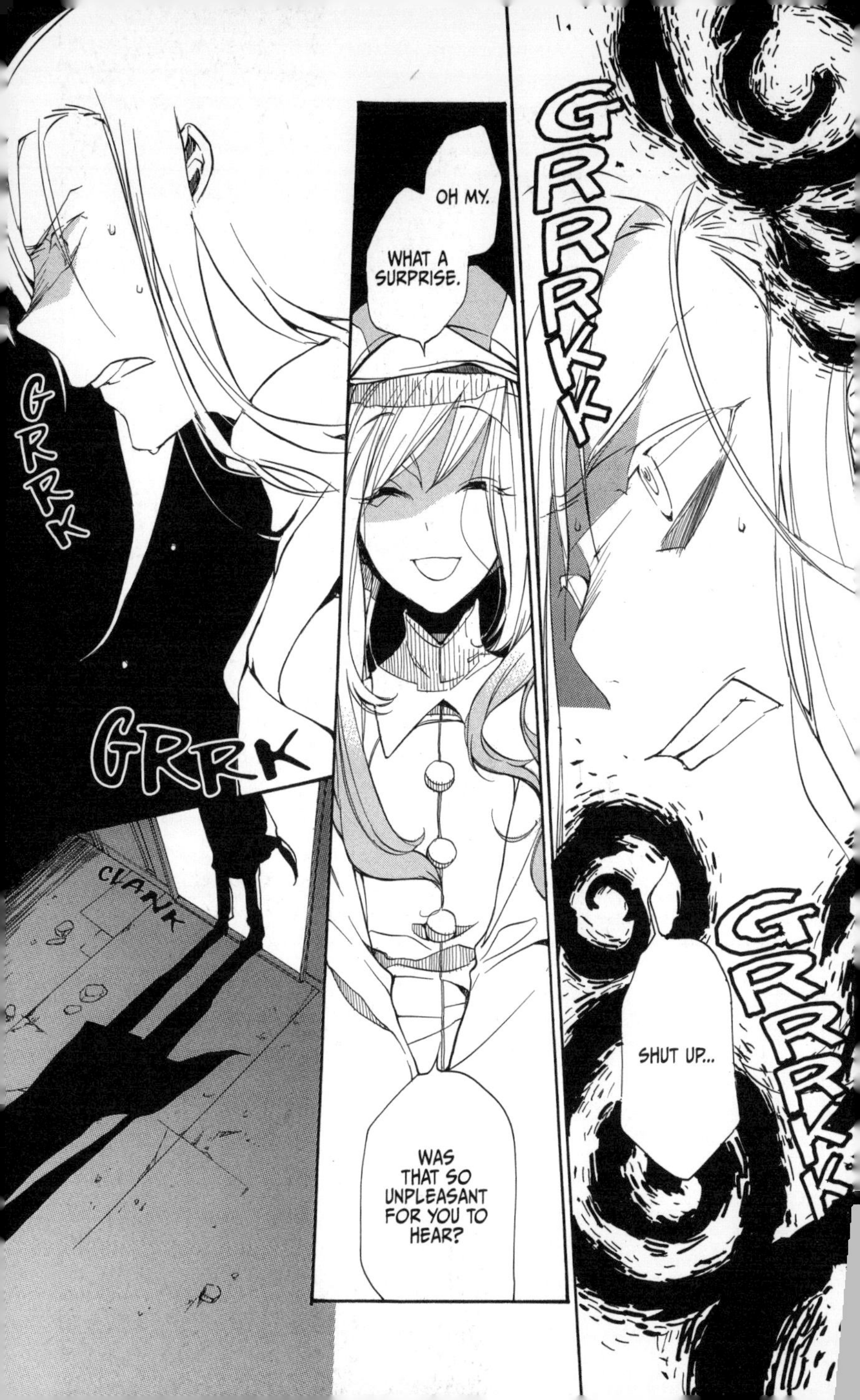
GRRRKK
GRRRKK
SHUT UP...
OH MY.
WHAT A SURPRISE.
WAS THAT SO UNPLEASANT FOR YOU TO HEAR?
GRRK
GRRK
CLANK

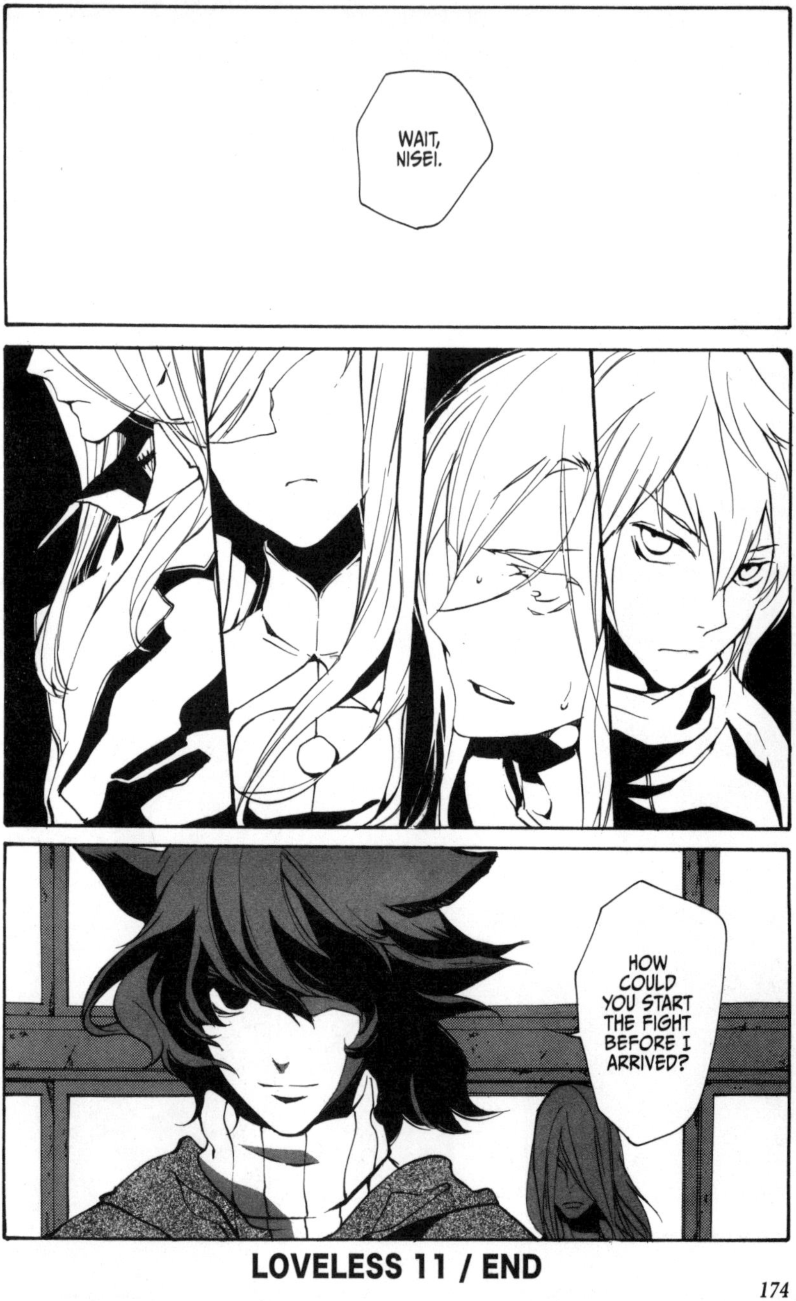
WAIT, NISEI.
HOW COULD YOU START THE FIGHT BEFORE I ARRIVED?

**LOVELESS 11 / END**

The other day I traveled to Ise. It was like...in these Shinto shrines, the gods reside! I enjoyed the blessed sight of a sunrise occurring between the Meoto-Iwa (Wedded Rocks) in Futamigaura. Japan really is a great country.

—*Yun Kouga, 2012*

YUN_KOUGA began her career as a doujinshi author and debuted in 1986 with the original manga *Metal Heart*, serialized in *Comic VAL*. She is the creator of the popular series *Loveless* and *Earthian*, along with many manga and anime projects, including character design for *Gundam oo*. Her works *Crown of Love* and *Gestalt* are also published by VIZ.

# Loveless
Volume 11
VIZ Media Edition

Story and Art by YUN KOUGA

Translation // RAY YOSHIMOTO
English Adaptation // LILLIAN DIAZ-PRZYBYL
Touch-Up Art + Lettering // ERIC ERBES
Design // FAWN LAU
Editor // HOPE DONOVAN

Loveless © 2012 by Yun Kouga
All rights reserved.
Original Japanese edition published by ICHIJINSHA, INC., Tokyo.
English translation rights arranged with ICHIJINSHA, INC.

Printed in the U.S.A.

Published by VIZ Media, LLC
P.O. Box 77010
San Francisco, CA 94107

10 9 8 7 6 5 4 3 2 1
First printing, June 2013

PARENTAL ADVISORY
LOVELESS is rated T for Teen and is
recommended for ages 13 and up.
This volume contains adult situations.
ratings.viz.com

www.viz.com

THIS IS THE END OF THE BOOK.

*Loveless* is printed from right to left in the original Japanese format
in order to present Yun Kouga's art as it was meant to be seen.